Norbert Schwarz   Seymour Sudman
Editors

Context Effects in Social and Psychological Research

With 10 Illustrations

Springer-Verlag
New York Berlin Heidelberg London Paris
Tokyo Hong Kong Barcelona Budapest

Norbert Schwarz
Program Director
ZUMA
6800 Mannheim
Germany

Seymour Sudman
Survey Research Laboratory
University of Illinois
Urbana, IL 61801
USA

Library of Congress Cataloging-in-Publication Data
Context effects in social and psychological research / Norbert
  Schwarz, Seymour Sudman, editors.
      p.   cm.
    Papers from a conference on Cognition and survey research, held
  September 28–October 1, 1989 in Kill Devil Hills, N.C., sponsored by
  the Zentrum für Umfragen, Methoden und Analysen, and by the Survey
  Research Laboratory and the Dept. of Business Administration,
  University of Illinois at Urbana-Champaign.
    Includes bibliographical references and index.
    ISBN 0-387-97705-8
    1. Social surveys—Psychological aspects—Congresses. 2. Context
  effects (Psychology)—Congresses. I. Schwarz, Norbert, Dr. phil.
  II. Sudman, Seymour. III. Zentrum für Umfragen, Methoden und
  Analysen (Germany) IV. University of Illinois at Urbana-Champaign.
  Survey Research Laboratory. V. University of Illinois at Urbana
  -Champaign. Dept. of Business Administration.
  HN29.C64 1991
  300′.72—dc20   91-31820

Printed on acid-free paper.

Camera-ready copy supplied by the authors.
Printed and bound by Braun-Brumfield, Inc., Ann Arbor, MI.
Printed in the United States of America.

9 8 7 6 5 4 3 2 1

ISBN 0-387-97705-8 Springer-Verlag New York Berlin Heidelberg
ISBN 3-540-97705-8 Springer-Verlag Berlin Heidelberg New York

Acknowledgments

The conference on which the present volume is based was supported by the Survey Research Laboratory and the Walter Stellner Memorial Fund of the Department of Business Administration, both of the University of Illinois at Urbana-Champaign, by the Zentrum für Umfragen, Methoden und Analysen, Mannheim, Germany, and by grant SWF 0044-6 from the Bundesminister für Forschung und Technologie of the Federal Republic of Germany to Norbert Schwarz.

Bibb Latané and Deborah Richardson hosted the conference at the Nags Head Conference Center in Kill Devil Hills, North Carolina. Their hospitality, the joys of southern cooking, and the outer banks of North Carolina greatly contributed to an enjoyable and productive meeting. Special thanks are due to Mary A. Spaeth, who edited all contributions to this volume and turned a pile of manuscripts into a readable book. Finally, we thank all conference participants for lively and controversial discussions from breakfast to midnight and for the fine chapters that they contributed.

Mannheim, Germany   Norbert Schwarz
Urbana, Illinois   Seymour Sudman
April 1991

Contents

Contributors

Chapter 1

Norbert Schwarz is Program Director at ZUMA, a social science methodology center in Mannheim, Germany, and "Privatdozent" of Psychology at the University of Heidelberg. He received degrees in Sociology (Dipl.-Soz., Dr. phil.) from the University of Mannheim and in Psychology (Dr. phil. habil.) from the University of Heidelberg. His research interests focus on human judgmental processes, in particular the interplay of affect and cognition, and the application of social cognition research to survey methodology. He serves on the editorial boards of several social science journals, including *Journal of Personality and Social Psychology* and *Public Opinion Quarterly.*

Seymour Sudman is Walter H. Stellner Distinguished Professor of Marketing, Professor of Business Administration and of Sociology, and Deputy Director and Research Professor at the Survey Research Laboratory, University of Illinois at Urbana-Champaign. He received his Ph.D. in Business from the University of Chicago. He is the author, co-author, or editor of 14 books and over 100 articles dealing primarily with survey methodology and response effects in surveys. His current research interests are related to cognitive aspects of proxy reporting in surveys.

Chapter 2

Howard Schuman is Program Director in the Institute for Social Research and Professor of Sociology, University of Michigan. He is also the current editor of *Public Opinion Quarterly.* His publications (with co-authors) include *Questions and Answers in Attitude Surveys: Experiments on Question Form, Wording, and Context* (1981), *Racial Attitudes in America: Trends and Interpretations* (1985), and "Generations and Collective Memories," *American Sociological Review* (1989).

Chapter 3

Fritz Strack is Senior Researcher at the Max-Planck-Institute for Psychological Research, Munich, Germany. His research is primarily in the area of social cognition and social judgment. Specifically, he is interested in the psychological processes underlying standardized situations.

Chapter 4

Roger Tourangeau is Senior Scientist in the Washington, DC, office of NORC. He has a Ph.D. in Psychology from Yale University and previously worked for 10 years in the Chicago office of NORC, where he served as a sampling statistician and conducted research on survey methods. He was one of the editors of the National Academy Press volume, *Cognitive Aspects of Survey Methodology: Building a Bridge between Disciplines* (1984). With Kenneth Rasinski, he co-authored a review of the literature on question-order effects that appeared in *Psychological Bulletin* (1988). Aside from his work on survey methodology, he has published a number of papers on issues in cognitive psychology, particularly the comprehension of figurative language.

Chapter 5

Jack M. Feldman is Professor of Psychology and Adjunct Professor of Management at the Georgia Institute of Technology. He received his Ph.D. from the University of Illinois, specializing in social and industrial/organizational psychology. His professional interests are in the application of theory in social cognition to problems of human judgment and behavior, especially in organizational contexts. Recent research concerns the role of constructive processes in judgment and behavior in many domains, including organizational and consumer decision making.

Chapter 6

Barbara A. Bickart is Assistant Professor of Marketing and Director of the Bureau of Economic and Business Research Survey Program, University of Florida in Gainesville. She received her Ph.D. in Business Administration at the University of Illinois at Urbana-Champaign. Her research examines the effects of knowledge structure, memory, and contextual factors on the survey response process.

Chapter 7

Leonard L. Martin is Associate Professor, Department of Psychology and Institute for Behavior Research, University of Georgia. He is currently finishing editing *Construction of Social Judgment* with Abraham Tesser.

Thomas F. Harlow is a graduate student in the Department of Psychology, University of Georgia.

Chapter 8

Dancker D. L. Daamen is Assistant Professor of Social Psychology at Leiden University, from which he received his degree (Drs.). His research interests and publications are in the areas of attitude formation, risk perception, and context effects in surveys.

Steven E. de Bie is Deputy Research Director of the Netherlands Court of Audit. He received is degree (Drs.) in Economics from the University of Amsterdam. He has worked as a researcher at the Department of Data Theory, as head of the data collection department at the Social Research Center (Leiden University), and as coordinator of data collection at the Association of Social Research Institutes (Amsterdam). He is the author of books and articles on survey research methodology.

Chapter 9

John Tarnai is Assistant Director of the Social and Economic Sciences Research Center, Washington State University, from which he received a Ph.D. in Experimental Psychology. His primary research interests are in computer-assisted telephone interviewing (CATI), survey measurement, and experimental designs.

Don A. Dillman is Director of the Social and Economic Sciences Research Center and Professor in the Departments of Sociology and Rural Sociology, Washington State University. He received his Ph.D. in Sociology from Iowa State University. He is the author of *Mail and Telephone Surveys: The Total Design Method* (1978) and approximately 100 other publications on telecommunications, rural society, and survey research methods.

Chapter 10

Jaak B. Billiet is Professor in Sociological Methodology and in Data Processing, Department of Sociology, Catholic University of Leuven, Belgium. He has a Ph.D. in Sociology. His current research deals with response effects in social surveys and with national surveys about xenophobia and political attitudes in Belgium.

Lina Waterplas was a former research assistant in the Department of Sociology, Catholic University of Leuven, and is currently employed in a division of the European Parliament, Luxembourg.

Geert Loosveldt is Assistant Professor in Social Statistics and Senior Research in the Department of Sociology, Catholic University of Leuven. He has a Ph.D. in Sociology. His current research deals with the analysis of interviewer-respondent interactions in social surveys.

Chapter 11

George F. Bishop is Professor of Political Science and Senior Research Associate in the Behavioral Sciences Laboratory, University of Cincinnati, where he directs The Greater Cincinnati Survey. He received his Ph.D. in Social Psychology from Michigan State University. He is an active participant in the American Association for Public Opinion Research, past president of the Midwest Association for Public Opinion Research, and has published a number of articles on question form and context effects in surveys in *Public Opinion Quarterly*, for which he presently serves as a member of the editorial board.

Chapter 12

Tom W. Smith is Director of the General Social Survey at NORC, University of Chicago. His chief research interests are social change and survey methodology. He is author of *Trends in Public Opinion* and editor of the Poll Report section of the *Public Opinion Quarterly*.

Chapter 13

Norbert Schwarz—see Chapter 1.

Hans-J. Hippler is Project Director at ZUMA, Mannheim, Germany. He received degrees in Sociology (Dipl.-Soz., Dr. phil.) from the University of Mannheim. His current research interests focus on cognitive aspects of survey methodology, the impact of mode of data collection on data quality, and communication and value research.

Elisabeth Noelle-Neumann is Director of the Institut für Demoskopie, Allensbach, Germany, which she founded in 1947. Since 1964 she has been Professor of Mass Communication Research at the University of Mainz. She has been a visiting professor in the Department of Political Science, University of Chicago, since 1978 and Georges Lurcy Visiting Professor since 1985. Having served as past president of World Association for Public Opinion Research, her numerous publications focus on survey research methodology, international comparisons of value systems, public opinion theory, and the effects of mass media. Since 1978 she has served as public opinion analyst of the German newspaper *Frankfurter Allgemeine Zeitung* and is currently co-editor of *International Journal of Public Opinion Research*.

Chapter 14

Jon A. Krosnick is Assistant Professor of Psychology and Political Science at The Ohio State University. He received his Ph.D. is Social Psychology from the University of Michigan. He is the author of two books and many journal articles and book chapters in psychology, sociology, and political science. He is a member of the editorial boards of *Public Opinion Quarter-*

ly, *Journal of Personality and Social Psychology,* and *Journal of Experimental Social Psychology* and recently served as invited guest editor for a special issue of *Social Cognition* that focused on political psychology. The primary foci of his research have been political cognition in the American public and cognitive aspects of survey questionnaire design for public opinion measurement.

Chapter 15

Eric S. Knowles is Professor of Psychology, Department of Psychology, University of Arkansas, Fayetteville, Arkansas. He received his Ph.D. from Boston University and has taught and chaired the psychology departments at the University of Wisconsin Green Bay and University of Arkansas. He has contributed research to social, environmental, and personality psychology, including a previous Springer-Verlag book by Ickes and Knowles, *Personality, Roles and Social Behavior* (1982). His current research includes programs in measurement reactivity, group identity, and forms of social awareness.

Michelle C. Coker is a Ph.D. graduate of the Clinical Psychology Program at the University of Arkansas, Fayetteville. She is currently working as a mental health practitioner in Kansas.

Deborah A. Cook is a graduate student in Social Psychology at the University of Arkansas. Her current research is in social cognition.

Steven R. Diercks is a former student in the Department of Psychology, University of Arkansas, who is currently working in the drug prevention field.

Mary E. Irwin and *John W. Neville* are graduate students in Clinical Psychology at the University of Arkansas.

Edward J. Lundeen is a Ph.D. graduate of the Clinical Psychology Program at the University of Arkansas. He is currently working as a mental health practitioner in Massachusetts.

Mark E. Sibicky is Assistant Professor of Psychology, Marietta College, Marietta, Ohio. He is a Ph.D. graduate of the Clinical Psychology Program at the University of Arkansas. His current research concerns social identity, empathy, and altruism.

Chapter 16

Gerald R. Salancik is David and Barbara Kirr Professor of Organization, Carnegie Mellon University, Pittsburgh, Pennsylvania. He received his Ph.D. in Social Psychology from Yale University, taught at the University of

Illinois at Urbana-Champaign, and studies information influences in attitude responses and organizational power and adaption.

Julianne F. Brand is Assistant Professor, DePaul University, Chicago. She is completing her Ph.D. in Organizational Behavior at the Department of Business Administration, University of Illinois at Urbana-Champaign, and studies cognitive biases in attitude judgments and organizing practices of entrepreneurs.

Chapter 17

Abigail T. Panter is Assistant Professor, Department of Psychology and the L. L. Thurstone Psychometric Laboratory, University of North Carolina at Chapel Hill. Her current research interests include psychometric models that identify person consistencies in the item response process and personality assessment.

Jeffrey S. Tanaka is Associate Professor, Departments of Educational Psychology and Psychology, University of Illinois at Urbana-Champaign. Among topics of current research interest are multivariate statistics with latent variables and the interface of personality and cognition.

Tracy R. Wellens received a Ph.D. in Social Psychology from New York University and is currently a postdoctoral fellow at ZUMA in Mannheim, Germany. Her research looks to socio-cognitive and linguistic factors applied to the item comprehension and interpretation process.

Chapter 18

Galen V. Bodenhausen is Assistant Professor of Psychology at Michigan State University. He received his Ph.D. from the University of Illinois at Urbana-Champaign. His research interests focus on social judgment processes, with particular emphasis on the role of stereotypes and prejudice on decision making and the interface of affective and cognitive systems in social perception and judgment.

Chapter 19

Linda M. Moxey is Lecturer in the Department of Psychology, University of Glasgow, Scotland, from which she received her Ph.D. in Psychology. She has been interested in the semantics of natural language quantifiers such as *few* and *a lot* and has also developed an interest in connectionism.

Anthony J. Sanford is Professor in the Department of Psychology, University of Glasgow. He received his Ph.D. in Psychology from Cantab. He has had a long-standing interest in cognitive science approaches to human understanding and in how knowledge is stored and accessed. His books include *Cognition and Cognitive Psychology* (1985), *The Mind of Man*

(1987), and, co-authored with S. G. Garrod, *Understanding Written Language* (1981).

Chapter 20

Thomas M. Ostrom is Professor of Psychology, Department of Psychology, The Ohio State University. He received his Ph.D. in Psychology from the University of North Carolina at Chapel Hill. He has published three books and served for seven years as the editor of *Journal of Experimental Social Psychology*. His research is in the area of social cognition, person perception, and attitudes.

Andrew L. Betz is graduate student in social psychology at The Ohio State University, from which he received his M.A. His research interests include the subliminal conditioning of attitudes and the effects of mental representation on social interference.

John J. Skowronski is Assistant Professor, Department of Psychology, The Ohio State University, teaching at the Newark Campus. He received his Ph.D. in Psychology from the University of Iowa. His primary research is on mental representations and use of social information; he has also published on the topics of autobiographical memory and the decision to become an organ donor.

Chapter 21

Norman M. Bradburn is the Tiffany and Margaret Blake Distinguished Service Professor at the University of Chicago. He is a member of the faculties of the Department of Psychology, Graduate School of Business, Graduate School of Public Policy Studies, and the College. Provost of the University of Chicago from 1984 to 1989, he has assumed the directorship of NORC, a social science research center affiliated with the University, a position that he has held twice before. At NORC he has been a Senior Study Director and Research Associate since 1961. As a social psychologist, he has been in the vanguard of the developing theory and practice in the field of sample survey research. His work has focused on the study of psychological well-being and assessments of the quality of life, nonsampling errors in sample surveys, and, recently, research on cognitive processes in responses to sample surveys. He has co-authored (with Seymour Sudman) two books on the methodology of questionnaire design and construction, and *Polls and Surveys: Understanding What They Tell Us* (1988).

Part I
Introduction and Historical Overview

1
Introduction

Norbert Schwarz and Seymour Sudman

This volume is the product of a conference on Cognition and Survey Research, which was held at the Nags Head Conference Center in Kill Devil Hills, North Carolina, on September 28–October 1, 1989. The conference and the preparation of this volume were jointly supported by ZUMA (Zentrum für Umfragen, Methoden und Analysen), Mannheim, Germany, and by the Survey Research Laboratory and Department of Business Administration, University of Illinois at Urbana-Champaign. The book is aimed at the same audiences as the earlier book in this series, *Social Information Processing and Survey Methodology* (Hippler, Schwarz, & Sudman, 1987), which was based on a 1984 conference held at ZUMA. We believe that both cognitive psychologists and survey researchers have benefited greatly from the dialog and research that have grown rapidly in the past decade between the two disciplines.

In our earlier book, several researchers, specifically, Strack and Martin (1987) and Tourangeau (1987), presented general theories of what respondents do to answer questions. These theories, building on earlier work, have now been widely accepted as a useful framework for studying cognitive processes related to survey methods, and each chapter in this book uses such a framework. There were also several interesting, but not highly related, methodological studies in that volume using cognitive insights. We are, of course, delighted that the earlier volume has been widely used and cited since it appeared.

In our introduction to that book, however, we indicated that we were troubled by the lack of more specific and useful cognitive theories and empirical tests of these theories. There was also some sense that the cognitive researchers and survey methodologists were not all speaking a common language. As we planned the Nags Head Conference, we decided to select a much narrower focus based on work that had been done since 1984. We had little difficulty in selecting "Context Effects in Social and Psychological Research" as the organizing theme for the conference and this book. The reasons were strong and obvious.

First, the issue of context effects has been an important and troublesome one in survey and social judgment research as well as in psychological testing.

Context effects have sometimes been observed and other times not observed, and predictions about when they would and would not occur have often been wrong. Even when context effects have been observed, the directions of those effects have often been unpredictable.

Second, but more importantly, since we were aware that significant theoretical conceptualization of context effects as well as empirical tests of these theories has been accomplished in the past five years, we felt that there was enough research already completed to make a conference worthwhile.

We think that the chapters in this volume demonstrate the correctness of our choice of topic. Much more than at earlier conferences with both survey researchers and cognitive psychologists present, the chapters in this book are interconnected and researchers are not talking past each other. The reader should come away with a reasonably coherent understanding of what we know today about context effects. Although there is still much more that we do not know, there is now at least a solid foundation of basic understanding on which to build.

In this Introduction, we shall not comment on the specific chapters and how they fit together; we leave that to Norman Bradburn in the concluding chapter. Here we simply outline the parts of this book. After this brief Introduction, a historical overview of context effects is given by Howard Schuman. The next and largest part of the volume relates to context effects caused by previous questions. The studies reported cannot really be separated into theoretical and applied papers. Instead, they all contain specific theoretical discussions of how context effects operate, and then they present empirical studies using surveys to test these theories.

This leads to a closely related part, the effects of order and context on the responses within a single question, still within the survey context. The next two parts relate to context effects in psychological testing and in making social judgments. Our sense, however, is that all of the parts use similar kinds of theoretical explanations and that the context of the empirical work does not seem to be of any great importance relative to the theory used to explain the results, much as one would expect on the basis of general theories of information processing.

In our view, this book is evidence that the blending of cognitive science and survey insights is proving fruitful and is indeed in a rapid growth phase. As this book goes to press, we have recently held a conference on "Autobiographical Memory and the Validity of Retrospective Reports," whose proceedings will be the next volume in this series.

2
Context Effects: State of the Past/State of the Art

Howard Schuman

In 1066, when William the Conqueror's fleet sailed from Normandy toward the English coast, only two of the 700 ships were lost at sea. However, one of those two contained the expedition's soothsayer. "It's no great loss," said William, "he couldn't even predict his own fate."

There is an unsettling analogy here to my lack of ability to foretell the importance of context effects in surveys, for in 1974 I noted as part of a larger discussion of response effects that the influence of question order on answers was essentially nonexistent:

> What strikes me most as a social psychologist is the extent to which respondents apparently consider each question in and of itself, without much attention to the earlier questions presented to them. The well-managed survey interview is more like a slide show than a motion picture, with each item viewed quite apart from what preceded or is to succeed it. (Schuman, 1974)

Had this 1974 statement been correct, the conference that led to the present volume would presumably never have been held.

How could I have been so clearly wrong in 1974, particularly when it seems intuitively obvious that context shapes all of our behavior? It is perhaps worthwhile for readers to try to place themselves back in the mid-1970s in order to see how such a conclusion might have been reached.

Some History, Personal and Otherwise

One major reason for the conclusion was that only a small number of apparent context effects were clearly noted in the survey methodological literature (e.g., Cantril, 1944, pp. 28–29), which itself was fairly thin at that point, and those few were isolated examples of uncertain reliability.[1] Some accounts were entirely

---

[1] In earlier writing, I and most others have often used "context effects" and "question-order effects" more or less interchangeably. However, Bishop, Hippler, Schwarz, and Strack (1988) have pointed up one important difference by showing that context

anecdotal, and the few quantitative reports came mainly from the dark ages of quota sampling, of inattention to significance testing (which, whatever its limitations, introduces a certain amount of self-discipline into our endless search for positive findings), and often of inadequate reporting of basic data as well.[2] When one looked for serious attempts to test for context effects in a systematic way, only a single such study could be found, and that one by Bradburn and Mason (1964) reported essentially no effects at all from a number of manipulations of question order. Moreover, Sudman and Bradburn (1974), in their review of past response effects of all kinds, concluded that "there do not appear to be any sizable response effects associated with placement of questions after related questions" (p. 33), although they noted that more research was desirable.

In addition to the then-available published literature, Otis Dudley Duncan and I had recently carried out well over 100 split-ballot experiments that varied question order in the 1971 Detroit Area Study, some intentionally and some as a byproduct of wording and other changes. The great majority of these did not produce reliable differences between questionnaire forms (Schuman & Presser, 1981, pp. 25–27, 34–35, 44, 47–48, 53–54).[3] Thus, despite the intuitive sense that the generic problem of context should be important in questionnaires, as it is in the rest of life, I arrived at the radical conclusion that such effects were either trivial or too rare and idiosyncratic to be of much interest in survey research.

The three or four years after my 1974 conclusion merely solidified my own view, since two more deliberately constructed context experiments that Stanley Presser and I carried out for our later book also were quite negative (Schuman & Presser, 1981, pp. 33–34). In addition, my attempt to replicate one of the most theoretically plausible and important published examples of a context effect by Willick and Ashley (1971) produced no sign at all of the original finding (Schuman & Presser, 1981, pp. 41–42), confirming my skepticism about the reliability of such isolated reports. The well-known fallacy of positive results is as strong in this area as in other parts of social science: Only "significant differences" tend to reach publication, making it essential to subject such reports to independent replication.

---

effects can occur in self-administered questionnaires where question order is not controlled by the investigator. In addition, some order effects (e.g., due to "fatigue") may not be a matter of context in the sense of "transfers of meaning" (Schuman & Presser, 1981, p. 23). These are important theoretical distinctions to keep in mind, although in this chapter I shall not attempt to be so precise in language at every point.

[2]Several reports presented no numbers at all, which gave them about the same scientific status as accounts of individual sightings of a monster in Loch Ness. Other reports (e.g., Duverger, 1964) gave percentages supposedly due to context but provided neither Ns nor significance tests that allowed evaluation of the null hypothesis.

[3]T. W. Smith (1988a) later carried out a somewhat similar analysis for the General Social Survey and drew the same conclusion.

Yet, by the end of the 1970s, it began to be clear that context can produce effects of both practical importance and theoretical interest in standard surveys, and my and Presser's 1981 volume on survey questions and answers recognized the importance of the issue by making it the focus of the first substantive chapter in the book. Since then it has become ever more evident that context is a challenging problem for survey investigators—and for social and cognitive psychologists—even though it also remains true that such effects are not common and are only occasionally large in size and import in actual surveys.

What initially altered my own views were two somewhat accidental findings—it would be nice to claim that they were theoretically driven, but they were not—plus several new published reports by others. The first of the two findings occurred in March 1979 when, for an entirely different purpose, we "borrowed" one item on abortion attitudes from the General Social Survey (GSS) but noted that the new distribution that we obtained was quite different from the one reported in the 1978 GSS codebook (see Table 2.1). At first we assumed that this was due to any number of uninteresting differences between our telephone survey and the GSS face-to-face survey, and we tried various statistical adjustments to make the effect disappear. However, the adjustments were not very successful, and since we also noted that the abortion item that we had used in isolation had appeared second in a series of abortion questions in the GSS, we carried out a split-ballot experiment in June 1979 to test for a context effect. Contrary to our expectation, the experiment replicated quite well the difference that had appeared nonexperimentally. Subsequent experiments by Bishop, Oldendick, and Tuchfarber (1985) and a large number of further experiments by myself and colleagues, which are summarized in Table 2.2 and discussed below, make it clear that what has come to be known as the "abortion context effect" is basically a robust finding, although one that has proved exceedingly difficult to interpret with assurance.[4] The effect takes on added interest because it changes results on a widely used survey indicator of attitudes toward a major social issue and also because it involves contrast rather than the more usual consistency between two survey questions.[5]

The other accidental finding grew out of our review of the early response-

---

[4]Confidence intervals can be calculated based on the pooled data from the nine experiments: 6.2% to 15.2% for the difference between two means, based on the assumption of simple random sampling. Four of the differences in Table 2.2 fall outside this interval, but only in one case (July 1983) is the deviation very large.

[5]In addition to the nine replications on national samples shown in Table 2.2, I repeated the experiment as part of a 1990 face-to-face survey with University of Michigan undergraduates. The right to an abortion was supported for the married woman by 79% of those receiving the question first ($N = 251$) but by only 62% of those receiving the same question after answering the question about the defective fetus ($N = 243$); chi-square = 16.8, $df = 1$, $p < .001$. Thus the effect is, if anything, even stronger in a population of sophisticated young adults whose overall level of support for legalized abortion is higher than is the case for the general population.

TABLE 2.1. Discrepancy between NORC and SRC Results on General Abortion Question (%)

Do you think it should be possible for a pregnant woman to obtain a legal abortion if she is married and does not want any more children?	NORC GSS-78[a]	SRC 79-March[b]	Adjusted SRC[c]
Yes	40.3	58.4	54.9
No	59.7	41.6	45.1
Total	100.0	100.0	100.0
N	(1,483)	(490)	

$\chi^2 = 48.34$, $df = 1$, $p < .001$

Source: This table is adapted from Schuman and Presser (1981, Table 2.5).

[a] Appeared second in a series of items about abortion. The preceding item read: "Do you think it should be possible for a pregnant women to obtain a legal abortion if there is a strong chance of serious defect in the baby?"

[b] No preceding items dealt with the issue of abortion.

[c] SRC results standardized on NORC educational distribution.

effects literature. A rather obscurely located and nonmethodological article by Hyman and Sheatsley (1950) contained a brief allusion to a large context effect obtained when studying post–World War II American attitudes toward Soviet and American journalists. The effect was not well documented in the article, and since the items did not seem to us especially vulnerable and we were still convinced that most such reports were due to sampling or other chance error, we decided to invest scarce research money in order to demonstrate that it could *not* be replicated. In other words, as with the abortion item, I really believed strongly in the null hypothesis.[6]

To our considerable surprise, however, the basic context effect—referred to below as a "reciprocity effect"—did replicate, as shown in Figure 2.1. To the questionnaire form where a question on allowing Communist reporters into this country appeared first, 55% of the respondents in 1980 agreed, but to the form where that item followed a question on allowing American reporters into Russia, the percentage rose to 75% ($p < .001$). The obvious interpretation is that agreement to the American reporters question makes salient the norm of reciprocity to respondents when they confront the subsequent Communist reporters question.[7]

[6] Statisticians like to point out that with large enough samples the null hypothesis will almost always be rejected. However, with the size samples typically used in survey research, this is definitely not the case, and furthermore any practical increase (e.g., doubling) of sample size is much more likely in my experience to eliminate a "borderline" effect taken too seriously than it is to discover a trivial real effect.

[7] To keep the present discussion brief, only the effect on the Communist reporters item is shown and discussed here, but the American reporters item also shows the effect of the reciprocity norm, although in the reverse direction (responses to the

TABLE 2.2. Nine Replications of Abortion Context Effect Experiments (RDD Telephone Sample Surveys of U.S. Population)

		% Favoring Abortion for Married Women				
Year	Month	Marr/Def[a]	Def/Marr[b]	Diff.	χ^2 (1 df)	p
1979	June	60.2 (309)	48.0 (302)	12.2	9.13	.0025
1979	August	66.6 (326)	49.2 (305)	17.4	19.57	.0000
1981	February	54.6 (163)	45.5 (178)	9.1	2.82	.0933
1981	May	55.8 (113)	51.8 (112)	4.0	0.036	.55
1981	July	52.5 (120)	47.5 (120)	5.0	0.6	.44
1981	October	63.1 (187)	54.1 (185)	9.0	3.14	.0765
1983	July	62.0 (158)	39.8 (196)	22.2	17.29	.0000
1986	July/August	63.2 (337)	54.7 (327)	8.5	4.92	.0266
1989	March/April	56.3 (245)	47.4 (247)	8.9	3.96	.047
Pooled data		60.2 (1,958)	49.2 (1,972)	11.0	47.35	.0000

Note: Base *N*s are shown in parentheses.
[a]Married woman item appeared first, before defective-fetus item.
[b]Married woman item appeared second, after defective-fetus item.

However, the results of the replication were more startling than simply the confirmation of a large context effect, for the 1980 data replicated the earlier (1948) result, so that they produced what remains one of the most important of all such findings: a quite meaningful interaction of context itself with time. The questionnaire form that makes the reciprocity norm salient shows *no* change between 1948 and 1980, whereas the other form shows a large change (increased acceptance of Communist reporters). In other words, fear of Communists as such had decreased over the 32-year interval, but the effect on responses of the norm of

American reporters item decrease following the Communist reporters item). Moreover, both effects are located primarily among respondents who agree with the American reporters item when it comes first, or disagree with the Communist reporters item when it comes first—producing what T. W. Smith (1982) calls "conditional order effects." See Schuman and Presser (1981, pp. 28–31) for the full results with the two items, including the interaction with time discussed below.

COMMUNIST REPORTERS ITEM:

> Do you think the United States should let
> Communist reporters from other countries
> come in here and send back to their papers
> the news as they see it?

AMERICAN REPORTERS ITEM:

> Do you think a Communist country like
> Russia should let American newspaper
> reporters come in and send back to their
> papers the news as they see it?

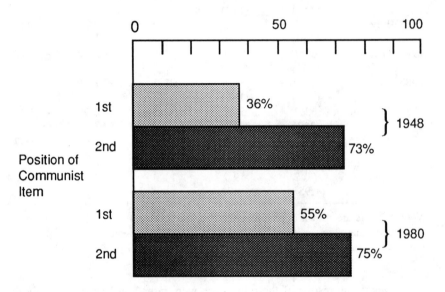

FIGURE 2.1. Context Effects on Reporters Questions

reciprocity had not altered over the same period. As a result, radically different conclusions about social trends emerge from the two contexts—no change over time in one context, substantial change in the other—with *neither* being an artifact in the invidious sense of the term. (I should add that the initial three-way relation with time replicated two months later, which is not something that always happens with unexpected and complex interactions.) Thus, the results show how thoroughly inherent the effects of context are in the measurement process itself and how completely entwined they can be with substantive conclusions.

By this point—mid-1980—I was certainly beginning to change my own mind about context effects, but the process was greatly aided by several articles that had recently appeared or were about to appear. The one that attracted most attention, by Turner and Krauss (1978) in *The American Psychologist,* drew on possible context differences to explain discrepancies between NORC and Harris data on trends in confidence in national institutions; yet it was possible to regard the interpretation as uncertain because there was no experimental demonstration and Harris data have often been out of line with other surveys. T. W. Smith (1979) also suggested a quite plausible context explanation for an interesting discrepancy with a general happiness item, although again at that point without experimental validation that compelled acceptance. (Both of these sets of problems, I should note, have turned out to be at least partly contextual but also more complex than was initially thought; see T. W. Smith, 1981a, 1986b; Schuman & Presser, 1981, pp. 42–43, 46; Schwarz, Strack, & Mai, 1991). Perhaps the most convincing report for a skeptic was a paper by McFarland (later published in 1981) that used experimentation to demonstrate context effects on self-reports of political and religious interest. The effects were intuitively meaningful because they involved vague summary items, and they showed considerable potential for both generalization and discriminant validity:[8] generalization because there are a lot of other broad summary items in surveys that may be similarly affected, and discriminant validity because McFarland was able to point to plausible conceptual differences between two of his items that showed context effects and two others that did not, although his interpretation of why this happened probably needs some amendment. In any case, by the end of the 1970s, for whatever reason, studies began to accumulate suggesting that context hypotheses might have a real role to play in solving puzzling findings that appeared in survey data.

Convinced now of the potential importance of context effects, Presser and I returned with more open minds to earlier reports previously treated too lightly and also made a more thorough search for reports possibly missed in our previous literature review. This yielded some additional evidence; and by late 1980, when our chapter on context effects was completed, it was possible to cite about two dozen studies, in addition to our own, showing that context produces reliable differences, although we also cite in that chapter more than a dozen studies reporting equally clear negative evidence. Probably the two dozen positive reports would now be at least two or three times that number, and more are being discovered all the time. We have all reached a point where the simple demonstration of a context effect in a survey has little interest unless there is some further important theoretical or practical point to be made.

Context Effects as Challenges for Survey Research

Once we acknowledge that substantial context effects do occasionally occur in surveys, it is worth reflecting further on why they are important to discover and

---

[8] Valuable further work on the basic effect involving self-reports of political interest is summarized by Bishop (1987).

understand. Let us consider the question first from the standpoint of the survey researcher with a substantive interest in the study of attitudes.

One reason, but perhaps the least important, is that such effects ordinarily change univariate or marginal results; and when surveys are treated as referenda, this has practical implications. Thus, the abortion item that was affected in the experiment reported earlier has a distribution that crosses the 50% or majority point depending on its context (see Table 2.1), and this has some symbolic importance. A more telling example occurred when conflicts between two surveys that were carried out to predict voter choices in a Connecticut election led to the discovery and subsequent experimental demonstration of a context effect based on the order of questions about candidates for different offices (Crespi & Morris, 1984). Indeed, it is worth noting in this connection that political party labels, whether in surveys or on ballots, are simply officially sanctioned contexts designed to influence voter choices between candidates.

Much more important to serious survey researchers is the effect of context on analytic uses of survey data and particularly the risk that it creates for one of the most important contributions that surveys make: the study of trends over time by replication of the same questions at regular intervals. This difficulty comes about in at least three different ways, which are increasingly difficult to guard against.

First is the problem of maintaining context constant over time. The abortion question shown in Table 2.2 can apparently be used to track change in either context, as long as the context is held constant. That is, both contexts lead to the conclusion of no change on the item, and if one is willing to count on this identity of trends occurring in the future, then the main safeguard is to keep the context constant. This is not easy, since it is rarely practical to repeat an entire questionnaire unaltered at each point that change is to be measured; but the difficulty is reduced somewhat by the fact that context effects nearly always seem to involve items that are clearly related in subject matter. Anyone attempting to use survey questions to measure changes in social attitudes should pay special attention to repeating all of the preceding questions that concern the same subject.[9] (For self-administered questionnaires, as noted earlier, subsequent as well as preceding items can produce context effects.)

A second and more serious problem for studies of change is the fact that different contexts, *even* if maintained religiously, do not necessarily lead to the same conclusions about trends. This is shown decisively by the reporters experiments in Figure 2.1. Such results tell us that change itself is complex and that unless we study it in more than one context, we may be seriously misled.

---

[9]One safeguard that cannot be counted on is the traditional assumption of survey researchers that an item is not likely to be affected by an earlier item if the two are in separate parts of the questionnaire. See Bishop (1987) and Schuman, Kalton, and Ludwig (1983) for evidence against this assumption. See also Ottati, Riggle, Schwarz, and Kuklinski (1989) and Schwarz et al. (1991) for further complexities regarding number and spacing of items.

Thus, for some purposes it may be necessary to replicate more than one context over time.

A third type of context effect can apparently appear where there is no variation at all in question order but where the meaning of the context-producing question itself changes. Such an instance seems to have occurred in a recent study of trends in white racial attitudes toward integration in America (Schuman, Steeh, & Bobo, 1985). We identified 11 relevant questions, each of which had been repeated several times between the 1940s and the 1980s. Ten of these questions showed a monotonic increase in white support for equal treatment, as shown in Figure 2.2. However, the eleventh, which is a completely general question about whether the respondent favors "desegregation, strict segregation, or something in between," showed a marked curvilinear relation, with an upward trend until about 1970 and then an equally strong downward trend over the next several years. The curvilinearity was particularly strong among college-educated Northern respondents, as shown in Figure 2.3. There was some reason to be concerned that this single exception might be the best indicator of the "true" trend, but there was also a possibility that its meaning had been distorted because of the position that it regularly occupied in National Election Study questionnaires. In fact, a hypothesized preceding context-producing item dealt with attitudes toward school desegregation, and our other information indicated that such attitudes had changed sharply among higher educated northern whites at exactly the same point in time as the inflection in Figure 2.3, primarily because of the introduction of court-ordered busing in the North.

We therefore carried out a formal context experiment, and it turned out that the question shown in Figure 2.3 proved extremely sensitive to context in exactly the way hypothesized, leading to the conclusion that the item was a poor indicator rather than an especially good indicator of trends over time. (See Schuman et al., 1985, pp. 93–96, for further details and additional evidence.) Thus, in this case there was no change in question order at all: Only a discrepancy in results alerted the investigators to a possibly hidden effect due to context.

The three types of effects just described show how complex the contextual problem can be. No simple "fix" is available, not even complete maintenance of constant context, and instead the problem must be handled by careful analysis that looks at all of the evidence and remains aware of the potential problems. (Particularly important is avoidance wherever possible of conclusions based on changes in a *single* item for inferences about trends.) Given the importance of surveys for studying social change—and, one might add, the importance of studying social change as a prime reason for doing surveys—the possibility of misinterpreting a trend due to context effects presents a major threat.

In addition to trends over time, context effects can interact with other important analytic variables, education being the one examined most often thus far. Investigators are sometimes tempted to interpret such interactions as the result of the susceptibility of less sophisticated or less informed people to response effects of all kinds, on the assumption that they lack stable attitudes and are easily influenced by the questioning process itself. However, this approach is probably

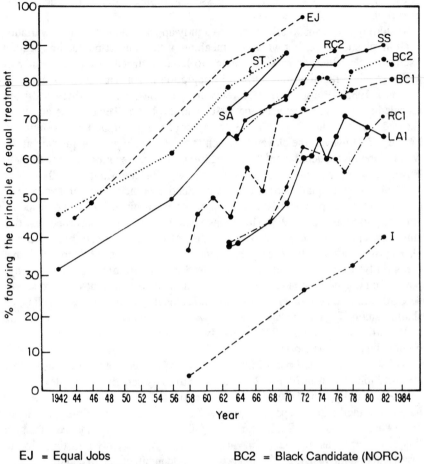

EJ = Equal Jobs
ST = Segregated Transportation
SA = Same Accommodations
RC2 = Residential Choice. 2 alter-
      natives (ISR)
SS = Same School

BC2 = Black Candidate (NORC)
BC1 = Black Candidate (Gallup)
RC1 = Residential Choice. 1 alter-
      native (NORC)
LAI = Laws against Intermarriage
I   = Intermarriage

FIGURE 2.2. Attitudes toward Principles of Equal Treatment: National Trend Lines

not correct for at least some context effects, where interactions of response, context, and education require a more substantive interpretation. In these cases, less educated respondents are especially prone on a particular question to express an attitude that is likely to constrain, by means of the norm of reciprocity, their response to a subsequent question (see Schuman & Presser, 1981, pp. 30–31; Schuman & Ludwig, 1983, pp. 118–119).

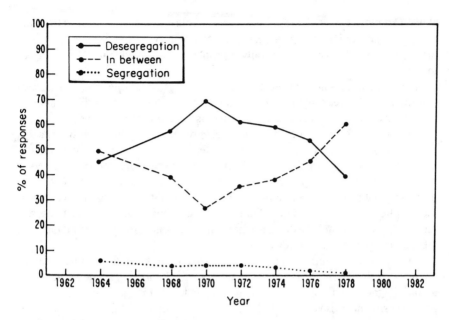

General Segregation (ISR): "Are you in favor of *desegregation*, strict *segregation*, or something in between?
1. Desegregation   2. Something in between   3. Strict segregation

FIGURE 2.3. Attitudes toward Segregation as a Principle, among Northern, College-Educated Whites

Context Effects as Challenges for Cognitive Psychology

The increasing interest of cognitive psychologists in survey response effects generally, and in survey context effects specifically, is a very promising development. I assume that it is occurring because, on the one hand, surveys provide a comparatively natural set of phenomena that offer scientific stimulation and challenge and, on the other hand, the psychologist's theories and laboratory findings can demonstrate their fruitfulness when applied in a survey setting. Effects that have turned up in surveys can be thought of as posing natural puzzles, much as did the variety of finches on the Galapagos Islands, the Basque language in Spain, or marsupials in Australia: They are oddities that, looked at rightly, raise serious scientific questions that might not be noted otherwise. Both of these benefits will be maximized, I believe, if psychologists take quite seriously past survey findings on context and attempt to show how they can be understood and generalized. This means, however, that it is not enough to point to laboratory analogues of survey context effects, to provide new theoretical labels to what is already known, or even to create in surveys effects on items far removed from the kind typically included in real surveys. The cognitive–survey connection will prove meaningful to both parties only if problems are solved that are meaningful to both parties.

It is sometimes said that there is so much "noise," complexity, and lack of control in real surveys that problems such as the ones described earlier cannot be solved successfully. However, such problems have yielded to survey-based experiments (see, for example, the experiments reported by Bishop, 1987, clarifying the way that respondents interpret "interest in politics"), and it is far too early—and too easy—to claim that psychological hypotheses cannot be tested in standard surveys. The expense of doing so is a more serious obstacle, but there is no reason that solutions cannot be developed in laboratory or classroom settings, then applied at a final stage in ordinary surveys. In any case, whatever the population, it is important that the same items and the same analysis be included in the laboratory or classroom research.

Moreover, the solutions may require a social emphasis as well as a purely cognitive one. The reporters experiment described earlier provides a good example. Together with three earlier experiments located in past literature and one new experiment carried out in 1983 (Schuman & Ludwig, 1983), an explanation in terms of a norm of reciprocity seems quite compelling. It is not enough to say that respondents feel a need to be consistent in their answers, since consistency is a vague term that does not allow prediction to which situations will be seen to demand consistency and which will not. It is only when consistency is operationalized in terms of the norm of reciprocity, as formulated by anthropologists and sociologists (Mauss, Levi-Strauss, Gouldner), that an explanation for this particular effect is reached that is satisfactory and has some predictive power. There is still a need for further understanding of the conditions under which the norm operates symmetrically rather than asymmetrically, but here again social as well as cognitive psychology is probably going to be needed.

The abortion context effect, replicated many times as shown in Table 2.2, provides a much more difficult challenge, for attempts by survey researchers to explain it have thus far proved unsuccessful. Our own initial explanation was in terms of ambivalence combined with a "subtraction effect." Agreement to legalizing abortions in the case of a possible defect in the unborn child is widely accepted (by about 85% of the population), but agreement in the much more general case of a woman who prefers not to have any more children is viewed as more problematic (agreement by around 50% of the population). Given a high degree of ambivalence about the issue of abortion, many conflicted people indicate agreement when only the more general item is asked because the item is seen to "include" justifications (such as a possibly defective fetus) of which they approve; but when the item about the defective fetus is asked first, some of those who agree to it feel that they have already shown some positive support for abortion under extreme circumstances, and they now indicate their ambivalence by disagreeing with the item about the women who does not want more children. Although the "subtraction hypothesis" has some theoretical appeal, especially since it is, as Strack, Martin, & Schwarz (1988) note, simply another label for one of Grice's (1975) conversational rules, it did not fit the original experimental data very well (Schuman & Presser, 1981, p. 38), and subsequent attempts to find evidence for it in respondent explanations of their answers have provided little support.

Another hypothesis noted originally (Schuman & Presser, 1981, p. 38) and favored by others (Bishop et al., 1985) focuses on the contrast that is emphasized or deemphasized by context. When the more general married woman item appears alone (or first, which is the same thing), it is regarded more seriously as a reason; but when it occurs after the defective-fetus item, the explanation about not wanting any more children is regarded as relatively trivial, which leads to greater rejection of it. Compelling as this explanation seems, attempts to confirm it have met with failure. If the explanation is correct, then it should be possible to substitute other serious reasons for the item about the defective unborn baby. However, one attempt to do this by substituting an item justifying abortion because of rape and another attempt to substitute an item on the mother's health have not led to clearcut context effects (see Table 2.3).[10] Perhaps these failures are due to sampling error, since some specific results in Table 2.2 were also not significant at conventional levels, and further replications would certainly be desirable. But there has also been little evidence of awareness of contrast in respondent open-ended explanations, and for the time being such a theoretical interpretation remains unproven.

Even a partial explanation of the abortion context effect in terms of ambivalence has proved elusive. In an early experiment, respondents who indicated to a later question on ambivalence that they found it hard to reach a decision on the abortion issue showed a larger context effect than those who said that they were quite certain of their views (Schuman & Presser, 1981, pp. 39–40). However, two later attempts to replicate this result failed. In addition, the ambivalence item itself shows evidence of being influenced by the previous abortion items, making a clear test difficult to carry out.[11]

I have gone into some detail on the abortion context-effect findings—although by no means including all of our or others' efforts—in order to show that what seem like very plausible cognitive hypotheses have thus far been tested unsuccessfully. Of course, it is possible that we have not operationalized the

---

[10]The percentage of the population agreeing with abortion in the case of rape is almost exactly the same as in the case of a possible defect in the baby, and the percentage agreeing in the case of the health of the mother is even higher. In addition, although it has been possible to substitute for the married woman item another GSS item on a woman wanting an abortion because she is poor (which yields about the same agreement) and obtain a significant effect in combination with the defect item, the rape/low-income combination also failed to produce a significant context effect ($p > .10$).

[11]A more complete account through 1988 of our experiments on the abortion context effect can be found in Scott (1988).

TABLE 2.3. Failures To Obtain Clearcut Context Effects on Abortion Items

Item	% Favoring Abortion for Married Women		Diff.	χ^2 (1 df)	p
	Married/Health	Health/Married			
1. Health of mother[a] (Jan. 1981)	52.5 (497)	47.0 (449)	5.5	2.88	.09
	Married/Rape	Rape/Married			
2. Rape[b] (Jun. and Jul. 1989)	54.1	56.4	2.3	0.28	NS

[a]"Do you think it should be possible for a pregnant women to obtain a legal abortion if the woman's health is seriously endangered by the pregnancy?"
[b]"Do you think it should be possible for a pregnant women to obtain a legal abortion if she becomes pregnant as a result of rape?"

measures well, that some important factor has not been controlled, or that an entirely different theoretical explanation is needed. Given the amount of relevant data gathered both by my research program and by others, the abortion context effect seems like a problem where more focused work of a cognitive–social nature would be useful.

There are other unexplained context effects that can be the subject of research by cognitive psychologists. What is important is that the effects themselves become at some point the focus of theorizing and experimentation rather than, as noted earlier, merely theoretical analogues. The latter may or may not provide explanations, and the only way to find out is to test the theory—or if necessary, theories—on the *original* problem. Unless all of the important results from the original context effect can be explained by the theoretical models, we may be fooling ourselves into thinking that we have an adequate explanation when we do not.

There is an even broader aspect to the context problem that requires sophisticated theoretical treatment. Context includes more than just the influence of one question on another. It also includes the effects of the interviewer, the interview setting, and indeed the historical setting. Without attempting to deal with all such complexity, it is worth calling attention to one past finding that brings together questions and interviewers. It involves a survey question that shows a quite large effect due to race of interviewer, yet none at all due to what seemed an equally relevant manipulation of question order (Schuman & Presser, 1981, p. 47). Apparently, both questions and respondents can be extremely sensitive to one type of contextual influence, yet completely insensitive to another type. Thus, at present we do not have a good grasp of how questionnaire context effects relate to other response effects in surveys. Bringing together two or more different types of contexts and showing how they interact to influence responses represents a larger challenge for the future, one that if met would enrich both our understanding of surveys and our understanding of social cognition.

Context Effects as Challenges for Philosophers, Linguists, and Others

Context effects also pose challenges for larger issues involving the nature of validity and error. This is clearest in the case of the several experiments that show the importance of the norm of reciprocity. What attitude a respondent expresses toward a person or group is influenced by whether or not the norm of reciprocity is evoked. However, *both* the attitude that ignores the norm and the attitude that takes it into account are equally valid, as are the trends over time that each pair of attitude questions produces. Moreover, in these cases it cannot really be argued that the questions are poorly framed or vague or that the attitudes are particularly unstable. The reciprocity norm simply changes the way in which the object is perceived, as it does in many real-life settings. Just such a norm holds sway with dinner invitations and with arms control negotiations. Why not then with survey responses as well?[12]

To the extent that validity can be defined at all in the reciprocity case, it has to do with the relation of the attitude responses to the investigator's goal in asking the question rather than with the question considered alone. Thus, validity is not a property or attribute of a survey question, and it is misleading to think of questions in such terms. The same question (or set of questions) can be valid for one purpose and invalid for another purpose.

Can we say that *any* of the effects produced by context involve invalidity, error, or artifact? This is a difficult issue. The item on "desegregation, segregation, or something in between" discussed earlier was in fact treated in this way, since our interpretation was that respondents heard the question to refer to school desegregation when in fact it was intended to be much more general. The distinction proposed here, although not with great confidence, concerns whether or not a context effect simulates what goes on in ordinary life. The reciprocity effects do that in a quite realistic way, whereas the desegregation item involves a "misunderstanding" by respondents that is probably limited to the questionnaire and could in any case be cleared up with further explanation.

The experiments on self-reported interest in politics seem to occupy a middle ground, since the amount of interest that a respondent presents can be seen as being influenced by preceding items in somewhat the same way as in ordinary life. When survey questions—or natural events—stimulate personal interest, then indeed the respondent does report, and presumably does feel, greater interest in politics; but when the difficulty of the preceding questions (which involve tests of knowledge)—or the complexity of events—inform respondents of their

---

[12]When a question on limiting Japanese products from entering the United States was asked alone and those respondents who opposed such limitations were probed, most of them cited a concern over reciprocity as their reason. The use of context to make the norm salient to all simply increases the proportion answering on that basis (see Schuman & Ludwig, 1983, p. 117).

ignorance, then interest in politics is disclaimed. The issue becomes to what extent the survey simulates real life, and the interest-in-politics questions seem to me to fall in a gray area. In this sense, there is a context continuum, with those effects that should be treated as valid at one end and those effects that should be treated as artifactual at the other end. It also seems likely that the valid end involves specific questions that change sharply in meaning and that the artifactual end involves quite general questions that vary across a wide range of meanings. I believe that this issue deserves closer examination, perhaps by philosophers interested in such linguistic problems.

The Future

It seems unlikely that a single theory of context effects will emerge from the effects discovered thus far or to be discovered in the future. Instead, we are likely to identify types of effects, each with its own theoretical explanation. For this reason, we continue to need to report new types of effects, and we also need to continue to generalize where several effects are discovered or can be created that have the same theoretical explanation. Thus, "context" may end up being an umbrella term covering several theoretically unrelated types of ideas. This should not trouble us greatly—even physicists still have to live with several fundamental forces that may or may not turn out to be unifiable.

Experimental work, whether in surveys or in laboratories, is clearly essential to this task, since only by such randomized comparisons can effects be discovered and studied. From one standpoint, we are fortunate because there is good reason to think that contextual forces in surveys are in no important ways different from what occurs in the rest of life, whether artifactually or not. In this sense, all context effects should be seen as substantive findings, since survey responses, as we are so often reminded, are not merely self-reports of preexisting states and behaviors; they are behaviors themselves.

Acknowledgments. My thanks for advice and help to Jacqueline Scott, Cheryl Rieger, and the editors of this book.

Part II
Question-Order Effects
in Surveys

3
"Order Effects" in Survey Research: Activation and Information Functions of Preceding Questions

Fritz Strack

The expression "order effect" refers to the well-documented phenomenon that different orders in which the questions (or response alternatives) are presented may influence respondents' answers in a more or less systematic fashion (cf. Schuman & Presser, 1981). Thus, Question A may be answered differently if it is asked before Question B compared with a situation in which the order of the two questions is reversed. This, of course, implies that the survey researcher controls the *sequence* in which the questions are presented. If this is not the case, the relative position of a question is less important in determining its influence (cf. Schwarz, Strack, Hippler, & Bishop, in press). To avoid unnecessary complications, however, the scope of this chapter will be confined to situations in which the questions have to be answered in the sequence in which they are presented.

In this chapter, I shall first argue that "order effects" can be conceptualized as influences of preceding questions that differ in the degrees to which the question content determines the response. I shall further contend that, as a consequence, different methodological strategies are necessary to test for such influences. Then I want to show that preceding questions may exert their influence in three psychologically different ways that depend on (a) respondents' awareness of the preceding question at the time of answering a subsequent one and (b) the perception that the questions in sequence are meant to be episodically related. If respondents are unaware of the previous influences, preceding questions may trigger automatic activation processes. If, however, respondents are aware of such determinants, they may deliberately act on them. The type of deliberate action, in turn, depends on the perception of an intended episodic relationship between the questions. If no such relationship is perceived, respondents may suppress the potential influence of a preceding question. Otherwise, respondents may draw inferences about the intended meaning on the basis of Grice's (1975) rules of conversation.

"Order Effects" as Question Effects: Methodological Considerations

A survey researcher studying order effects on Question A may employ the basic experimental design described in Figure 3.1. This design consists of two conditions that differ with respect to the relative position of the two questions. The investigator typically wants to find out if Question A is answered differently if it is asked prior to or subsequent to Question B. However, if one applies the logic of causal influence to this research problem, then it is, of course, not the order that affects the answer but the *preceding* question that may have an effect on the subsequent one and not vice versa. In terms of the logic of the psychological experiment (cf. Aronson, Ellsworth, Carlsmith, & Gonzales, 1990), the design consists of a treatment condition and a no-treatment control condition. The research problem, then, is whether Question B has an effect on Question A. Therefore, the *question-order effect* is actually a *question effect,* an effect of a question that is previously asked versus not asked. As a consequence, we are dealing with the effects of preceding questions.

Question effects can be classified on the basis of the direction of their influence. If a preceding question influences the answer to a subsequent question in the same direction, one may label the effect "assimilation." If the influence goes in the opposite direction, one may term it a "contrast effect." It should be noted that this terminology is merely descriptive and does not imply any assumptions about possible underlying processes (cf. Hovland, Harvey, & Sherif, 1957).

However, there are two aspects of the preceding question that must be differentiated. This distinction refers to whether the response is under the control of the content of the preceding question or not. That is, if the content of a question elicits predominantly positive or negative responses, the valence of the dominant response may be used as a criterion for assimilation or contrast, and the means of the relevant experimental conditions must be compared in a *between-subjects* design. An example is a study by Ottati, Riggle, Wyer, Schwarz, and Kuklinski (1989) in which respondents expressed a more positive attitude toward the general issue of free speech if a preceding question referred to a positively evaluated target (e.g., the American Civil Liberties Union) than if it referred to a target with negative valence (e.g., the American Nazi Party). However, this content assimilation effect was only found in their study if the related questions were separated in the questionnaire. If, however, the specific question immediately preceded the general question, a contrast effect was obtained such that the positive content led to a more negative general attitude and vice versa.

Alternatively, responses to a preceding question may not be under the control of the content but may be distributed along the response scale. In this case, there is no predominant response, and the individual reaction must be used as a criterion for assimilation and contrast. Schuman, Presser, and Ludwig (1981), for example, found that respondents who had expressed a favorable attitude toward a specific aspect of the legalization of abortion (i.e., the case of a possibly defective baby) before they expressed their opinion about legalization in general

FIGURE 3.1. Experimental Conditions to Test Order Effects

answered less favorably than did respondents who gave favorable answers to the specific question afterward. Testing for contrast (or assimilation) effects under such conditions requires a *repeated measures* design and a classification according to the preceding response. These effects may be tested by comparing the means of the target answers for the classification conditions as in Schuman et al. (1981) or by calculating correlation coefficients (cf. Strack, Martin, & Schwarz, 1988). In survey research, there have been several approaches toward investigating the determinants of assimilation and contrast. A strategy pursued by Schuman and Presser (1981) consisted of a classification of the questions according to the relation in which they stood to each other and an examination of the resulting direction of influence that the preceding question had on the subsequent one. Schuman and Presser categorized two questions according to whether or not their contents stood in a part–whole relationship and provided examples for part–whole contrast effects, part–whole consistency (i.e., assimilation) effects, part–part contrast effects, and part–part consistency effects.

Relevant Psychological Processes

An alternative possibility consists of identification of the different psychological tasks that a respondent has to solve in order to reach the goal of answering a question and explanation of the influence of preceding questions on the basis of these processes. In Strack and Martin (1987; cf. also Tourangeau, 1984; Tourangeau & Rasinski, 1988), we proposed a model that differentiates between three types of processes: the interpretation of the question, the generation of an opinion, and the transformation of the generated opinion into the appropriate response format that is provided.

The model suggests that answering a preceding question may influence the answer to a subsequent one in ways that depend on the particular process. In this chapter, I would like to concentrate on the first of these tasks, the interpretation of a question and the influence that comes from questions that have been previously answered. What are the psychological consequences of answering a question? In a very basic sense, it is the activation of information, what social psychologists call a "priming effect" (cf. Higgins, Rholes, & Jones, 1977). This information is either contained in the previous question or activated by the respondent in order to generate an answer to the previous question. Merely by having been activated before, the information subsequently becomes more accessible. Moreover, this process can occur without the respondent's awareness (for a more recent summary on accessibility effects, see Higgins, 1989).

Thus, respondents may not even remember the episode of having answered a particular question, but the fact that they did may exert its influence. It is similar to the following familiar experience: An author writes a manuscript and, on re-reading it, notices that she has used a rather unusual expression several times in close succession. Very likely, this repetition was caused by the higher accessibility of the particular word as a consequence of its prior use. However, such repetitions are stylistically undesired, and therefore the author typically replaces this word while editing the manuscript. But if the author had remembered the *episode* of having used this word before, she would have prevented its repeated use at the time that she was writing it.

This anecdotal evidence is consistent with experimental results suggesting that the influence of a stimulus event may only be counteracted if subjects are conscious of the source of the influence at the time that they engage in the task. This was demonstrated by Kubovy (1977), who had subjects report "the first digit that came to their mind." For part of the subjects, Kubovy activated the digit "1" by subtly mentioning it in the instruction ("Give the first *one* digit that comes to mind"). Under this condition, more subjects uttered "one" than under a control condition in which the number was not mentioned. However, if the influence attempt was more blatant such that subjects became aware of the source of influence at the time that they generated their digit ("Give the first *one* digit that comes to mind, like one"), the number of times "one" was mentioned dropped to baseline. Thus, the effect of exposing the subjects to the particular stimulus was strongest if the awareness of the episode itself was attenuated.

These different processes of influences as a consequence of the awareness of the source have recently been conceptualized by Jacoby and his collaborators (e.g., Jacoby, 1984; Jacoby & Kelley, 1987) in a bifunctional model of memory that assumes that dependent on the task, human memory may operate both as an object and as a tool. In tasks that require recall, for example, memory functions as an object. While their attention is directed toward their past experiences, subjects may inspect their memory and describe its content to others. However, other cognitive tasks such as perception or interpretation do not necessarily require subjects to engage in a search of memory while their attention is directed toward the present, that is, the target of perception or interpretation. However, the contents of memory nevertheless exert their influence even if the focus of attention is directed toward the task (cf. Tulving, Schacter, & Stark, 1982). If the subject is unaware of the influence, memory functions as a tool.

What, then, are the consequences of shifting the attentional focus of a perceiver or interpreter toward that past experience that is responsible for the unconscious influence? Jacoby and Kelley (1987) assume that subjects try to *correct* for the influence from memory. Such a correction, however, is not possible by simply "filtering out" the extraneous influence from one's experience. Rather, such a correction requires people to invoke general knowledge about the nature and the size of the effect.

Jacoby and his colleagues report findings about judgments of fame that support their reasoning. On the basis of the observation that assessments of a person's fame are often based on the subjective familiarity of the name, previous exposure to the name should affect both feelings of familiarity and fame ratings. However, if judges are aware of the extraneous influence, the influence of previous exposures should be attenuated. This prediction was supported by a study conducted by Jacoby, Woloshyn, and Kelley (1989). They found that under conditions of divided attention, previous reading of nonfamous words increased judgments of fame more than under conditions of full attention. Conversely, words were judged to be less famous if subjects had to recognize the word before they made the fame judgment (Jacoby, Kelley, Brown, & Jasechko, 1989). This pattern of results is also consistent with findings by Schwarz and Clore (1983), who found that subjects used their present mood as a basis for judgments of subjective well-being only if they were not aware of the source of their mood at the time of the judgment. That is, if bad weather put people in a dejected mood, they only reported being "unhappy with life in general" if their attention was not directed to the irrelevant meteorological source of their mood.

This prediction is also consistent with evidence from studies by Martin (1985, 1986), who found that prior exposure to categories influenced subsequent interpretations of ambiguous behaviors in a semantically consistent fashion (assimilation effect) if the exposure task was unexpectedly interrupted. If subjects completed the preceding exposure task, the ambiguous behaviors were interpreted in a semantically inconsistent fashion (contrast effect), since individuals try to suppress extraneous influences if the priming episode is blatant rather than subtle. If we assume that blatantness causes subjects to direct their attention toward the priming task itself as a source of influence, Martin's results support Jacoby's model. Additional evidence comes from a study by Lombardi, Higgins, and Bargh (1987), who found that subjects who recalled the priming sentences were likely to show contrast in a subsequent interpretation task, whereas subjects who were unable to recall these sentences were likely to show an assimilation effect.

Taken together, these findings suggest that a previous question may exert two types of influence: one that operates automatically, outside of the awareness of the respondent, and another that operates on the awareness of the episode of influence. More precisely, the latter operates on the awareness of the fact that this particular question has been asked.

So far, however, the evidence for the effect of the awareness of the activation episode has been either indirect or merely correlational. To manipulate this variable more directly, we (Strack, Schwarz, Bless, Kübler, & Wänke, 1990) conducted an experiment in which subjects were reminded of the activation episode. The experimental paradigm was one that has been frequently used in priming studies in the social-cognition context by Higgins, Bargh, Wyer, Srull, and others. Subjects received the description of a behavioral episode that was ambiguous with respect to its valence. In our example, the protagonist, Thomas, a teaching assistant, provided his friend who had already failed the exam in the past with the new exam questions. Thomas' behavior could be interpreted to be either friendly and helpful or dishonest, and we were interested to learn if the prior activation of one or the other set of concepts would influence this interpretation.

To activate these concepts, subjects did a completely unrelated task in which they had to judge how high certain notes were that were presented to them. More importantly, there were filler words between the notes that were either synonyms of "helpful/friendly" or of "dishonest." The idea was that the activation of those concepts would subsequently influence the interpretation of the ambiguous behavior by virtue of their increased accessibility.

The results in Figure 3.2 show that the target person was rated much more favorably when subjects had been previously exposed to the positive "friendly/helpful" concepts than when they had heard the negative "dishonest" descriptions. We think that subjects were not necessarily aware of this influence. The conclusion is based on the fact that when we reminded them of the episode of activating the information, the results were quite different. The reminding consisted of directing subjects' attention toward the episode by letting them indicate on a rating scale how well they remembered some of the features of this task that were unrelated to the primed content itself.

As can be seen from Figure 3.2, the ratings were reversed under the reminding condition. Subjects' ratings of the target were influenced in the evaluatively opposite direction. Thus, the result was not assimilation but contrast. This suggests that if subjects are aware of the episode and its potential influence on their responses, they can decide whether and how to use the activated information. In this case, it seems that our subjects did not want to be influenced by this irrelevant task and therefore overcorrected.

Application to the Survey Situation

It appears that a typical survey situation contains both the automatic and the controlled aspect. A question is asked and concepts are activated. At the same time, respondents may or may not be aware of the influence of the question. If they are, then they can decide *if* they want to use the information and *how* they want to use it.

As an illustration, consider the phenomenon of ambiguity and its manifestation in the survey context in the form of fictitious issues (cf. Bishop, Oldendick, Tuchfarber, & Bennett, 1980; Bishop, Tuchfarber, & Oldendick, 1986) such as the "agricultural trade act" or the "monetary control bill." In previous research, opinions about such fictitious topics were seen as "non-attitudes" (Converse, 1970), whose expression was presumably motivated by the desire to appear knowledgeable.

In the present perspective, however, a fictitious issue is ambiguous information that needs to be interpreted before an opinion is generated. Once respondents engage in determining the meaning of the question, the psychological principles that guide the interpretation are similar to the ones in the previously described experiment (Strack et al., 1990).

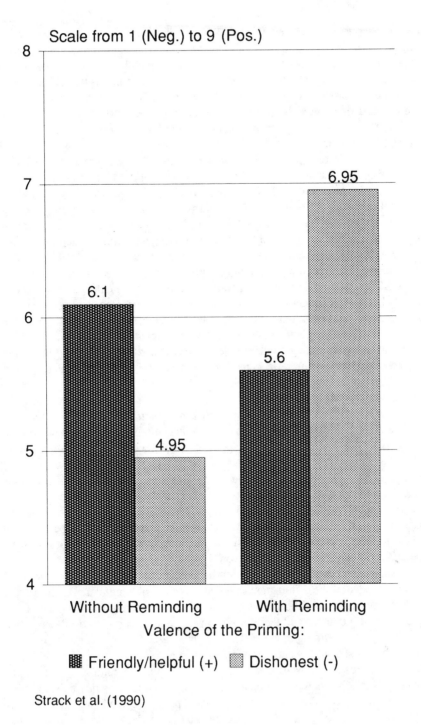

FIGURE 3.2. Priming and Ratings of Likability

We (Strack, Schwarz, & Wänke, 1990, experiment 1) studied the interpretation of fictitious issues by asking students whether they were in favor of or opposed to an "educational contribution for students" that was supposedly considered by the administration. We did that under two conditions that differed with respect to the preceding question. Half of the respondents were asked to estimate the amount of money that a typical Swedish student would obtain from the government, and the other respondents were asked to estimate the average tuition in the United States.

The results were straightforward: Respondents expressed a much more favorable opinion when the previous question was about students *receiving* money than when it was about students *paying* money. Although we did not study this possibility further, it is likely that the influence of the preceding question can operate on both the automatic and the controlled level. The mere accessibility of the concept would affect the interpretation of the question in the same direction as the awareness of the influencing event, since in this case, unlike the previous experiment, the preceding question (the priming event) is *not* irrelevant but reflects the intention of the survey researcher. In other words, the respondents can infer what the questioner must have meant when they become aware of the question episode, that is, when they remember it at the time that they generate the answer to the subsequent question. In this case, respondents can infer that the fact that this particular knowledge question is asked immediately prior to the general attitude question reflects the survey researcher's intention with respect to the referent of the subsequent question.

Thus, a preceding question may have two functions for the interpretation of a subsequent question. First, it has an *activation function* in that it activates information in a rather automatic fashion such that certain concepts can be brought to mind with greater ease at a later point in time. Second, a preceding question may have an *information function* in that it provides an informational basis to infer the *intended* meaning of the question. This, however, is only possible if the respondents are aware of the priming episode, that is, of the fact that a *semantically related* question has been asked previously. This is, however, not enough. Over and above the awareness of this episode, the respondents must perceive the two questions as being *episodically related;* that is, the two questions must be perceived as "meant to belong together."

It should be noted that this was not the case in the first study when subjects were reminded of the priming episode that was ostensibly unrelated to the second task. Under such conditions, we assume that respondents want to generate an independent judgment and therefore try to suppress the presumed influence that comes from the priming episode. The results obtained under the reminding conditions suggest that this suppression results in a contrast effect. These findings parallel the results by Martin (1986), who explained the contrast effect that he obtained for subjects who completed the priming task in his study by suggesting that they remembered the semantically related priming episode but did not see an episodic relation to the response that they had to provide. As a consequence, they tried to suppress the previous influence (cf. Levinson, 1983).

If respondents remember the priming episode/preceding question and, in addition, perceive the questions as meant to belong together and not as a random and unrelated presentation, they may infer the questioner's intention and identify the intended referent in the particular situation, which constitutes the pragmatic aspect of the interpretation.

In our previous example in which a knowledge question preceded an ambiguous question about people's attitudes toward an educational contribution, respondents may have (a) remembered the knowledge question and (b) inferred that the two items were meant to be related. If these conditions are fulfilled, respondents may infer the intended meaning on the basis of the conversational rules that were developed by the linguist Paul Grice (1975). These principles are implicit to any verbal interaction or cooperative conversational exchange, and they allow the listener, or the comprehender, in a natural situation to apply these rules to infer the intended meaning of an utterance.

We have previously discussed the general importance of the Gricean principles for the survey situation (e.g., Schwarz, Strack, & Mai, 1991; Strack & Martin, 1987; Strack et al., 1988) because it shares many properties of a natural conversation. Therefore, I do not want to discuss them in more detail again. I only want to mention two of those rules that apply to our examples and that have the opposite consequences for the answer. One is the Maxim of Relevance; the other is the Maxim of Quantity.

The Maxim of Relevance requires that the content of a subsequent contribution in a conversation refers to the content of the preceding one. This was possibly the case in our fictitious-issue study. Respondents inferred that the fictitious "educational contribution" referred to the previous examples; the result is an assimilation effect in the sense that target judgment is influenced in the direction of the implications of the context stimulus, in this case, the previous question. In this sense, the content of the ambiguous question is assimilated toward the nonambiguous preceding knowledge question.

On the other hand, the Gricean principles may also prevent a respondent from using the content of a previous question to interpret a subsequent one, and this should result in a contrast effect. This is the case if the Maxim of Quantity applies. The Maxim of Quantity requires the speaker or a respondent to be informative and to avoid redundancy. By the same token, it allows the respondent to infer that the referent of the target question is not the same as the referent of the previous context question. This is illustrated by the following fictitious conversation (cf. Strack et al., 1988):

Questioner: How is your wife?
Respondent: (answer)
Questioner: And how is your family?
Respondent: (answer)

What can the respondent in this conversation infer about what the questioner means by "family"? More specifically, is the question about the "family" meant to include the respondent's wife or not? Grice's Maxim of Quantity would imply "no," since the respondent can assume that questioners do not want information that they already have. Please note that the Gricean rule only applies if the two questions are perceived as belonging together, that is, as belonging to the same conversational context. Had the first question been asked by an unrelated third person, the rule would not be applicable.

Within this Gricean perspective, we studied the general–specific issue (Strack et al., 1988) and replicated the original "subtraction effect" (cf. Schuman et al., 1981). However, the effect was only obtained if the respondents were induced to perceive the two questions as belonging to the same conversational context. Specifically, respondents had to indicate their happiness with life in general either before or after they had reported how happy they were with a specific domain of their life, namely, their dating. The correlation between the two measures was low ($r = .16$) if the questions were asked in the general–specific order. The correlation increased dramatically if the order was reversed and the two questions were placed on two separate pages of the questionnaire ($r = .55$). However, if the two questions were preceded by a lead-in that made it explicit that they belonged together, the correlation dropped again ($r = .26$). This pattern of results was recently replicated and extended, using a German sample, by Schwarz et al. (1991). Together, these findings clearly suggest that the perceived episodic relation between two questions is a necessary precondition for the Gricean principles to operate and for the subtraction effect to occur.

However, subtraction effects as a function of Gricean principles may not only be observed for part–whole influences; they may also operate if two questions stand in a part–part relation. This should be true if there is a great overlap in the content. That is, if two questions are very similar in what they refer to and if they are perceived as sharing the same conversational content, then the Gricean Maxim of Quantity should be applicable and require respondents to be informative by differentiating between their answers.

In a recent study (Strack et al., 1990, experiment 2), we used "happiness" and "satisfaction" as two concepts that are very similar although not identical. Therefore, we expected the answers to be highly correlated (cf. Diener, 1984). However, if the two questions are perceived as belonging together, the correlation should be attenuated. This hypothesis was tested in an experimental survey in which respondents were asked to rate both their happiness and their satisfaction with life in general on an 11-point scale. Under the No Conversational Context condition, the two items were presented in two different questionnaires with different letterheads, different colors of the paper, different typefaces, etc. The question about happiness with life in general was always placed last in the first questionnaire, and the satisfaction question was the first item on the second questionnaire. To generate a "conversational context," we simply put a frame around the two questions with a lead-in that said, "Here are two questions about your life."

The results were as expected. Happiness and satisfaction correlated almost perfectly ($r = .96$) when the questions were asked in different questionnaires. The correlation, however, was substantially reduced ($r = .75$) when they were placed together in a box. Also, the average ratings of "happiness" and "satisfaction" differed under the context condition but not when the questions were asked in two questionnaires. Taken together, these findings show that Grice's conversational rules are not only useful in accounting for influences of specific questions on answers to more general ones but also helpful in explaining mutual influences between questions that are semantically very similar. The results suggest that if the conditions for the Gricean rules are fulfilled, respondents will try to be optimally informative and differentiate their answers. Thus, if the questions are perceived as related, respondents will identify the intended referents of the questions as being more different than when the two questions are unrelated, that is, when they belong to two different questionnaires.

General Discussion

The present analysis of question-order effects suggests that preceding questions may influence answers to subsequent questions through both their content and the responses that they elicit. Depending on its direction, the influence may produce an assimilation or a contrast effect.

To *predict* the direction of the influence, however, it is necessary to understand the underlying psychological processes. Figure 3.3 summarizes the interpretative processes as they have been postulated in this chapter. Most fundamentally, the present model implies that influences of previous questions in survey-type situations can be understood as a priming event that has two functions: an activation function and an information function. The activation influence increases the subsequent accessibility of the activated information, it occurs quite automatically, and it does not require the respondent to be aware of the priming episode. The result is an assimilation effect in the judgment.

The information function, however, requires that the respondent be aware of the priming episode. Moreover, it demands that there be a perceived episodic relation between the two questions, in the sense that they are perceived as sharing the same conversational context. If these conditions are met, respondents utilize the Gricean Maxims to infer the questioner's intention. The result, assimilation or contrast, should depend on the maxim that is applicable in the situation. In the reported experimental examples, this was either the Maxim of Relevance, which led to assimilation, or the Maxim of Quantity, which led to contrast.

Finally, there is the possibility that subjects are aware of the priming influence but do not perceive the episode to be related to the judgment task. Under those circumstances, the Gricean rules do not apply; and subjects may try to suppress this extraneous, biasing influence or, to be more precise, they may correct for it (cf. Jacoby & Kelley, 1987).

Admittedly, even a comprehensive analysis of order effects that restricts its scope to the task of interpreting a question becomes complicated if the relevant psychological processes are taken into account. However, as the accumulating findings from the application of social-cognition research to standardized question

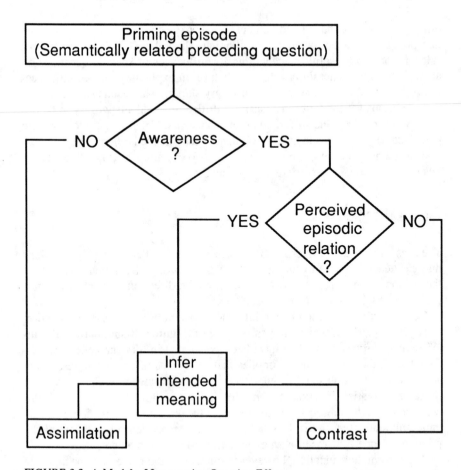

FIGURE 3.3. A Model of Interpretive Question Effects

situations clearly demonstrate, in order to understand and predict response effects (cf. Schuman & Presser, 1981), it is not sufficient to classify the stimuli of influence and the elicited responses by using surface characteristics. It is necessary to understand the generating cognitive and affective mechanisms that underlie the effects.

Acknowledgments. This research was supported by a grant from the Deutsche Forschungsgemeinschaft (Str 264/2) to Fritz Strack and Norbert Schwarz. The author gratefully acknowledges helpful comments from Norbert Schwarz and Seymour Sudman.

4
Context Effects on Responses to Attitude Questions: Attitudes as Memory Structures

Roger Tourangeau

Introduction

If attitudes are enduring structures, then it is reasonable to assume that they are stored in long-term memory and are organized according to the same principles as other material in memory. Innocuous though it may seem, the conception of attitudes as structures in long-term memory has wide-ranging implications concerning the organization of attitudes and the process through which respondents answer attitude questions.

Attitude Organization

The traditional view of attitudes, which serves as the rationale for such attitude measurement procedures as Thurstone and Guttman scaling, assumes that attitudes are essentially unidimensional, varying along a single underlying continuum of favorability (see, e.g., Dawes & Smith, 1985). Although this conception has proven tremendously fruitful, it does have a number of limitations. It is clear, for example, that a single evaluative dimension cannot capture the substantive differences that separate those who hold opposing views on controversial social issues. For instance, Luker's (1984) study of abortion activists demonstrates that positions on the abortion issue are rooted in beliefs about such topics as sex roles and religious authority. A position on abortion entails more than an evaluation. People who oppose abortion do not merely dislike it; they think that it is murder. Even more telling, the unidimensional representation of attitudes blurs important distinctions among those on the same side of an issue. The "same" evaluation can reflect quite disparate, even conflicting, underlying rationales (Fee, 1979). For example, my colleagues and I find that some people oppose welfare because they think that it is mismanaged, whereas others oppose it because they think that it is misconceived (Tourangeau, Rasinski, & D'Andrade, 1991).

Another major drawback to the traditional view is that it is not easily reconciled with theories of the structure of long-term memory (e.g., J. R. Anderson, 1983). If memory is a network of interconnected concepts that form propositions and images, then it is natural to suppose that attitudes are sets of interconnected beliefs, feelings, and images concerning a specific issue (cf. Fazio, 1989; S. T. Fiske & Kinder, 1981; Judd & Krosnick, 1989). Attitudes may include evaluations, but there is no reason to claim that they are restricted to them. The network formalism used in models of long-term memory is ideally suited to representing belief structures like those found by Luker and Fee in which beliefs about one issue are inextricably bound up with those on related issues.

The Attitude Response Process

This view of attitude structure also has implications for our understanding of the process of answering attitude questions. If attitudes are structures in long-term memory, answering an attitude question is likely to involve such component processes as understanding the question, retrieving material about the issue, deriving an answer from what has been retrieved, and reporting the answer (Tourangeau, 1984, 1987; Tourangeau & Rasinski, 1988; for a related model, see Strack & Martin, 1987).

Each of these major components—comprehension, retrieval, judgment, and reporting—consists of more fundamental processes. Comprehension is the process in which respondents interpret the question and identify which attitude issue it concerns. Comprehension includes such steps as parsing the question and inferring exactly what information is sought (Lehnert, 1978).

During the retrieval component, respondents determine what they think about the issue. This entails retrieving relevant material from long-term memory. The material may include beliefs about the issue, feelings, images, memories, or existing evaluations; let us denote such material as considerations. What considerations are retrieved in answering a specific question will be affected by the wording of the question, the nature of the judgment to be made (Wyer & Hartwick, 1984), the instructions given to the respondent (Ottati, Riggle, Wyer, Schwarz, & Kuklinski, 1989; T. D. Wilson, Kraft, & Dunn, 1989), the accessibility of any prior evaluations (Fazio, 1989; Fazio, Sanbonmatsu, Powell, & Kardes, 1986), and the content of earlier items (Tourangeau & Rasinski, 1988).

During judgment, respondents determine the implications of what they have retrieved for the question at hand. Judgment can be a trivial step when respondents already have an overall evaluation of the issue or when the question corresponds closely to an existing belief, but it can get complicated when they do not. When respondents must form a new judgment, such processes as weighing the considerations that they have retrieved and combining them will be needed. During the reporting component, respondents decide how to answer. This component includes such processes as mapping the judgment onto one of the response options and editing the answer for social desirability and consistency with prior answers.

Although it is natural to think of the components of the question-answering process as occurring in nonoverlapping stages, that assumption is not crucial. Although it is probably common for respondents to start by determining which issue the question concerns, next recalling the specific considerations that comprise the attitude, then determining what answer these considerations imply, and finally deciding what to say, there are surely cases in which respondents do not follow this sequence. Respondents often blurt out answers before the interviewer has finished the question, which suggests that the reporting process may have ended while the comprehension phase is still in progress.

The important points highlighted by the response model are that an answer is often based on a judgment that has been created on the spot and that, in any case, the answer is the outcome of a process with multiple components—each one of which may have been carried out unreliably. There is no guarantee that the respondents will invariably interpret an item in the same way or map their judgment onto the same response option. The retrieval component may be especially prone to unreliability. Our results (Tourangeau et al., 1991) indicate that the beliefs on which attitudes rest are often quite numerous; on the other hand, the retrieval process is typically quite superficial. At best, retrieval yields a small sample of the considerations that are potentially relevant (Zaller, 1984); and the sample may not even be a particularly good one, since it is likely to overrepresent whichever considerations happen to be accessible at the time that the question is asked.

Context Effects in Attitude Surveys

Item context, typically in the form of earlier questions in the interview or questionnaire, can affect each component of the response process (Strack & Martin, 1987; Tourangeau & Rasinski, 1988). Prior items can change how respondents interpret the subsequent "target" question, what considerations they retrieve in formulating their answers, which standards or norms they apply in forming the required judgment, and how they report their answers. In addition, different mechanisms producing context effects affect target responses in different ways. Prior items sometimes influence later responses in the direction of consistency, but they sometimes have the opposite effect, producing apparent inconsistencies. Because the term "consistency" carries specific, somewhat misleading theoretical connotations, I prefer the terms "carryover" and "backfire" effects for the two types of context effects. [Other authors is this volume use the terms "assimilation" and "contrast." ED.]

During comprehension, prior items can create carryover effects by providing an interpretive framework for subsequent items (cf. Knowles, 1988). Respondents sometimes interpret items about unfamiliar issues or ambiguous stimuli in terms of the preceding items, inferring that the later items concern the same topic or are drawn from the same category as the earlier ones (Herr, Sherman, & Fazio, 1983; Martin, 1986; Tourangeau & Rasinski, 1988). Backfire effects can also occur during item comprehension. Such effects appear to reflect a misinterpretation of a general item intended as an overall summary of more specific items presented earlier. Respondents apparently infer that the later item is supposed to exclude material already covered by the preceding items. For example, respondents who have already answered an item on marital happiness may exclude their marriages in responding to a later item on happiness in general (Schuman & Presser, 1981; T. W. Smith, 1986a; see Kalton, Collins, & Brook, 1978, for a related example). The respondents take the later item to be asking for new information, for information about aspects of their lives aside from their marriages. Bradburn (1982) suggested that this interpretation reflects the respondents' desire to avoid redundancy, a tendency that some researchers (Strack, Martin, & Schwarz, 1988; Tourangeau, 1984; Tourangeau & Rasinski, 1988) have traced to an even more basic principle of conversation—the principle that each contribution should be informative (Grice, 1975; Haviland & Clark, 1974).

Prior items can also influence retrieval. The process of answering one question can temporarily leave some considerations highly accessible to retrieval. If this material is relevant to a later question, respondents will be prone to use it. In an early demonstration of such an effect, Salancik and Conway (1975) showed that religious attitudes were influenced by answers to prior questions about religious behaviors. The subjects apparently inferred their attitudes from their easily recalled responses to the behavior questions. Later on, I describe two studies that investigate retrieval-based carryover effects in detail. Several investigators have reported backfire effects that apparently reflect the discounting of highly accessible material (e.g., Higgins & King, 1981, Studies 1 and 5; Martin, 1986). Sometimes respondents simply set aside the accessible considerations so that these have no effect on responses to the later item (e.g., Schwarz & Clore, 1983), but sometimes the exclusion of material supporting one response pushes respondents in the opposite direction so that a true backfire effect occurs. In either case, it is thought that respondents reject the highly accessible material because they have become conscious that it is invalid or irrelevant to the question at hand.

By making a particular dimension, norm, or standard of comparison salient, context can also alter how respondents make their judgment. For example, prior items may trigger the application of a norm that is carried over to a later item (e.g., Schuman & Ludwig, 1983). Prior items can also serve as a reference point, or standard of comparison, for later items. For example, Strack, Schwarz, and Gschneidinger (1985) showed that respondents who had recalled positive events from their past rated their present lives as less happy than did those who recalled negative events. The past events (at least when they were not vivid) served as an extreme point of comparison, against which respondents contrasted their current well-being. Higgins and Lurie (1983) and Ottati et al. (1989) reported similar backfire effects that appear to reflect comparison processes operating during judgment.

The reporting component is also susceptible to both carryover and backfire effects. Respondents may edit their answers to maintain logical or psychological consistency, as in McGuire's (1960) "Socratic effect" studies. Although McGuire argued that the process of bringing answers into line required several days, it is now clear that the reduction of inconsistency produces carryover effects within a single questionnaire (Dillehay & Jernigan, 1970; Rosen & Wyer, 1972). Other pressures, such as the fear of taking an extreme or unreasonable position, may lead to backfire effects during reporting. For example, respondents who have already endorsed several items on one side of an issue may reject later items to avoid seeming too partisan (cf. Cialdini, Levy, Herman, & Evenback, 1973).

Retrieval-Based Carryover Effects

The literature tends to be dominated by backfire effects, but my co-workers and I thought that carryover effects were probably common as well and that they were especially likely to arise during the retrieval component of the response process. We thought that retrieval-based carryover effects would occur whenever prior items tended to render considerations favoring one side of a related issue accessible to retrieval.

We recently carried out two studies to provide clearer evidence for such retrieval-based carryover effects (Tourangeau, Rasinski, Bradburn, & D'Andrade, 1989a, 1989b). Both context studies were conducted over the telephone under realistic survey conditions. In both, respondents were asked attitude questions about several social issues, such as abortion, welfare, and the proposed "Star Wars" defense system. Prior to the item on each target issue, the questionnaire included items about related issues. The prior items were designed to increase the accessibility of considerations supporting one side of the target issue. For example, some respondents answered a series of questions about the government's responsibility to the poor before they answered a question on welfare; others answered items about economic individualism before the welfare question. Similarly, some respondents got items about women's rights before an item about abortion; others got items about traditional family values.

Table 4.1 summarizes the designs of the studies. In addition to the context items that preceded the four target questions, the first study manipulated two other variables—the mode of presentation of the context items (i.e., whether the context items were presented in a block placed immediately before the target item or were scattered among unrelated items) and the level of agreement with the context items (some versions of the context items were written to elicit high levels of support; others were written to provoke high levels of disagreement). The second study examined new target and context issues, again compared blocked versus scattered presentation of the context items, and included an open-ended follow-up item. The open-ended item was intended to give some indication of what considerations respondents retrieved in formulating their target answers. Both studies also examined the interaction of context with attitude conflict (whether respondents described their views on the issue as mixed) and attitude centrality (the importance attached to target attitudes).

TABLE 4.1. Design of Context Studies

Issues/Factors	Context Issues
Study 1 (N = 1,052)	
Target Issues	
Abortion	Women's rights vs. traditional values
Star Wars	Soviet threat vs. threat of nuclear war
Nicaragua	Vietnam vs. Cuba
Welfare	Economic individualism vs. government responsibility
Other Experimental Factors	
Mode of presentation (blocked vs. scattered)	
Level of agreement (consensual vs. controversial items)	
Study 2 (N = 1,150)	
Target Issues	
Persian Gulf	Lebanon vs. Iran
Criminal rights	Fear of crime vs. civil liberties
Welfare	Government responsibility vs. economic individualism
Abortion	Traditional values vs. rape
Defense spending	Arms control vs. Soviet threat
Nicaragua	Vietnam vs. Cuba
Other Experimental Factors	
Mode of presentation (blocked vs. scattered)	

There were five major findings from these studies. First, in 7 of 10 comparisons from the two studies, the groups who had answered different context questions differed significantly in their target responses. For example, in both studies the respondents who had answered the items on government's responsibility to the poor were significantly more likely to support increased welfare spending than were those who had answered items on economic individualism. In all 10 comparisons, the differences were in the direction of carryover.

Second, the carryover effects were consistently larger when the context items were presented in a block placed immediately before the target item than when they were scattered among unrelated items. The interaction between the content of the context items and their mode of presentation was significant in Study 1, in the same direction but nonsignificant in Study 2, and significant in a meta-analysis that combined the results of these two studies with those of earlier studies on the effects of "buffering" items placed between the context and target items (Bishop, 1987; Bishop, Oldendick, & Tuchfarber, 1984b; Schuman, Kalton, & Ludwig, 1983). This is not to say that the effects of context disappear entirely when the context items are separated from the target. Although they are reduced, the carryover effects often remain significant (see also Ottati et al., 1989). These reductions are consistent with an explanation based on retrieval processes. The accessibility changes produced by prior items are known to wear off over time (e.g., Posner, 1978). Thus, carryover effects based on such changes should diminish when the presentation of the target is delayed by unrelated material.

The third major finding was that carryover effects were larger when the context and target issues were more closely related. We used the correlation between target and context responses as a crude measure of the connection between the two issues; target–context correlations were computed separately for each set of context items and for the blocked and scattered groups. In Study 1, this yielded 16 observations. The target–context r had a correlation of .74 with the size of the carryover effect. In Study 2, *all* of the context items were chosen to have a high correlation with the relevant target; as a result, the target–context correlations varied over a more restricted range. Even so, in Study 2, the target–context r had a correlation of .19 with the size of the carryover effect (based on 24 observations). When data from the two studies are combined, the correlation between the target–context r and the size of the carryover effect is a highly significant .55. A problem with this analysis is that the target–context correlations may themselves be affected by the context variable. Other analyses, however, ruled out this possibility (Tourangeau et al., 1989a). This finding provided further evidence that the carryover effects in our studies arise during retrieval. According to theories of long-term memory, the degree that retrieving one item from memory affects the accessibility of another item depends on the strength of the connection between the two items (e.g., J. R. Anderson, 1983). Thus, the more closely related two attitude issues are, the more retrieving considerations about the one will affect the retrieval of considerations about the other.

Fourth, attitude importance and conflict interacted to determine susceptibility to context effects: Respondents who regarded their attitudes on the issue as important but who nonetheless reported conflicted beliefs about it consistently showed the largest carryover effects on that issue. As Table 4.2 shows, the effects for such respondents were on the average two or three times larger than the effects for respondents with less important or less conflicted attitudes. This finding is quite counterintuitive; many researchers, beginning with Rugg and Cantril (1944), have argued that respondents who consider an issue important should be *less* susceptible to context effects. It is, of course, possible that the ratings of attitude importance and conflict were themselves affected by the context items. However, the studies included several precautions intended to keep such effects to a minimum. In both studies, the importance and conflict items were administered *before* the context items; in fact, in Study 1, they were administered in a separate interview. Thus, even if prior context did affect responses to the items assessing attitude importance and conflict, such effects would be constant across the different versions of the questionnaires. Still, measures of attitude importance and conflict are no less likely than other attitude measures to be affected by prior context. I suspect that they may be especially susceptible to backfire effects reflecting the use of earlier issues as standards of comparison for judging later ones.

Although counterintuitive, the findings in Table 4.2 are consistent with the idea that prior items affect later responses by facilitating the retrieval of

TABLE 4.2. Context Effects on Each Issue by Attitude Centrality and Conflict

Study and Target Issue	High Centrality		Low Centrality	
	One Side	Mixed	One Side	Mixed
Study 1				
Abortion	2.2	16.1	5.7	−6.6
Star Wars	−0.3	−3.9	2.6	4.5
Nicaragua	10.5	21.6	15.2	14.4
Welfare	13.0	22.9	1.8	20.7
Study 2				
Persian Gulf	−0.8	14.7	8.8	9.9
Criminal rights	−0.2	19.2	9.8	4.1
Welfare	−1.8	7.6	15.8	−3.3
Abortion	7.1	3.6	3.3	−0.8
Defense spending	7.7	36.0	1.9	11.5
Nicaragua	8.8	33.9	8.1	3.9
Mean	4.6	17.2	7.3	5.8
SD	5.4	12.6	5.2	8.4

Note: Negative entries indicate backfire effects. The mean and standard deviation are taken across the 10 issues.

considerations on one side of the target issue. This account implies two pre-requisites for carryover effects. For items on one issue to affect retrieval for items on a second issue, the two issues must be linked in the respondents' memories. The aggregate strength of these links is an important factor in determining the overall size of the effects for different context and target issues. At the individual level, carryover effects require target attitude structures that include strong ties to related issues. Aside from being well developed, respondent attitudes must meet a second condition. For prior items to tip the balance from one side to the other, the attitudes must include considerations supporting both sides on the issue. Central attitudes are more likely to show the necessary structural development; mixed attitudes, the necessary two-sidedness. The two variables should thus interact to determine the size of the carryover effects—a pattern that is apparent in both studies (see Table 4.2). The complexity of the relation between attitude centrality and susceptibility to context effects may explain why past investigations have found such weak and inconsistent results (Krosnick & Schuman, 1988).

The fifth and final major finding was that the level of agreement with the context items was one factor that did *not* affect the overall direction of the context effect. In Study 1, respondents received both sets of context items related to a given target issue (one set before the target and the other set afterward). This feature of the design permitted comparison of the target answers of respondents who showed the same levels of agreement with the context items but who differed in whether the context items preceded or followed the target. The results showed similar context effects for respondents who agreed or disagreed with the context items. For example, even among respondents who indicated overall approval of the U.S. involvement in Vietnam, those who had answered the items on Vietnam *before* the Nicaragua target showed less support for contra aid than did those who answered the Vietnam items *afterward*. Apparently, the items on Vietnam reminded respondents—even those who favored the Vietnam War—mostly of anti-contra arguments. This presumably reflects the association of Vietnam with specific considerations in the debate about Nicaragua, such as the argument that involvement in Nicaragua will eventually prove costly to the U.S. This cuing function of the context items is apparently automatic and does not depend on agreement with the items.

It is significant that the direction of the context effects observed in our two studies was not conditional on responses to the context items (cf. T. W. Smith, 1986a). This finding tends to rule out accounts based on other components of the response process. For example, one alternative focuses on judgment. Context items may trigger a norm for judging the target issue (e.g., Schuman & Ludwig, 1983), or the target issue may be assimilated to the issue raised by the context items. If such processes produced the context effects observed in our studies, the effects ought to depend on responses to the context items (see Tourangeau & Rasinski, 1988, on this point).

Studies of Attitude Structure

The results of the context studies suggest that attitude responses are derived from the considerations that are stored in memory but suggest little about the content or structure of these considerations. We recently carried out a scaling study to examine attitude structure more directly (Tourangeau et al., 1991). The study concerned the structure of attitudes about abortion and welfare. This research proceeded in several stages. First, we conducted intensive, open-ended interviews with small samples on each topic and transcribed the interviews. Next, we compiled a master list of all of the statements about each issue, eliminating those that were unintelligible, redundant, or idiosyncratic. New samples then rated their agreement with statements drawn from the master list for each issue and sorted the statements into groups based on similarity. Finally, both the sorting and agreement data were analyzed using factor analytic, multidimensional scaling, and clustering procedures. Similar methods have been used to study belief structures in many domains, ranging from doctor visits (Bower, Black, & Turner, 1979) to personality types (Cantor & Mischel, 1977).

The scaling studies reveal a general evaluative (or pro–con) dimension, apparent in both the sorting and agreement data; in addition, the sorting data indicate that beliefs about abortion and welfare are organized around distinct topical clusters. For example, one cluster of abortion beliefs concerns the rights of women; another concerns the question of when life begins. Table 4.3 shows the contents of four of the nine clusters derived from a hierarchical cluster analysis of

TABLE 4.3. Example Clusters from Similarity Sorting of Abortion Propositions

Cluster 3: Government Politics and Abortion
9.   (.82) Government officials should not try to impose personal views on the public through abortion legislation.
29. (−.70) Because abortion involves societal values politicians and lawmakers must become involved in the issue.
26. (.02) The major conflict in abortion is whether individual women or society should have the choice of terminating a pregnancy.
18. (.52) Politicians use the abortion issue to get votes.

Cluster 7: Justifications for Abortion
7.   (.75) Abortions are justified in the case of a serious defect in the child.
22. (.76) It is kinder to allow an abortion of an unwanted child than to force it to be born to a life of misery.
23. (−.65) When considering an abortion the woman's first concern should be for the child's welfare.

Cluster 8: Women's Rights
8.   (.90) If a women wants an abortion she should be allowed to have one.
27. (.53) The decision to have an abortion is nobody's business but the woman's.
33. (.35) The life a living woman is more important than the potential life of an unborn child.
35. (.34) In general, each woman is the best judge of how capable she is to have a child.

Cluster 9: When Life Begins
3.   (.75) Aborting an embryo less than three months old is not taking a human life.
31. (.71) A fetus becomes a human life when it actually is surviving outside of the womb.
32. (.76) No one really knows when a fetus becomes human life.
30. (−.82) A fetus becomes human life at conception.
12. (−.90) Abortion is murder.

Note: The numbers in parentheses are loadings on the first factor from principal components analysis of the agreement data.

the abortion sort data; it also shows the position of each item on the pro–con dimension taken from a factor analysis of the agreement data. The topical organization revealed by the cluster analysis was only weakly related to the evaluative dimension. Some clusters represented both sides of the issue (e.g., the cluster of items on the issue of when life begins, which included both pro-life and pro-choice statements); others were nested within one side of the issue (e.g., the women's rights cluster, which consisted only of pro-choice statements).

The scaling results suggest that beliefs about issues such as welfare and abortion have a structure that is too complex to be fully captured by standard dimensional representations based on correlations of agreement with the items (see Judd & Krosnick, 1989, for a detailed critique of the use of agreement correlations to map attitude structures). I do not mean to exaggerate the differences between the sorting and agreement data. Overall, the matrix of similarities derived from the sort data corresponds reasonably well to the matrix of agreement correlations (for welfare, the correlation between corresponding entries in the two matrices is .65). Still, the sort data appear to give a clearer picture of the topical structure of beliefs about abortion and welfare than the agreement data do.

What do these results imply for attitude measurement? There are a number of implications; let me mention just two of them here. First, because attitude items drawn from the same belief cluster tend to trigger the retrieval of the same or closely related considerations (see Table 4.4 below), questionnaires that include multiple items from a single cluster can yield misleading estimates of response consistency—exaggerating both the internal consistency of the attitudes and the reliability of the attitude measures. Questionnaires with multiple items about an issue should therefore include items that tap multiple clusters. Otherwise, all of the answers may be based on the same, not necessarily very representative, sample of considerations. Another implication of the scaling studies is that it may be possible to reduce retrieval-based carryover effects by using items that correspond more closely to respondents' underlying beliefs. Items that allow the direct readout of an existing belief are less likely to be affected by context than are those that require complicated retrieval and judgment processes. The trick, of course, is to identify the underlying considerations and the topical clusters into which they fall.

Attitude Response Times

By themselves, scaling data cannot demonstrate that belief clusters such as those in Table 4.3 represent the memory structures underlying respondent attitudes. At least two other interpretations are consistent with the scaling data. The belief clusters may not correspond to memory structures at all; instead, they may be ad hoc structures generated by subjects in carrying out the sort task. Or the clusters may represent preexisting structures, but ones that are nonattitudinal in character; the clusters may, for example, be based on semantic relations among the items. To address these possibilities, Rasinski, D'Andrade, and I conducted a reaction-time study.

Retrieving one item tends to facilitate the retrieval of related items. This facilitation effect depends on the degree to which the two items are linked in memory, with larger effects when the two items are more closely related (e.g., J. R. Anderson, 1983). Thus, if attitude items require the retrieval of specific considerations about an issue, then respondents should answer more quickly when prior items require the retrieval of related considerations; in addition, this "priming effect" should be larger as the priming item and the subsequent target are more closely related. If the results of clustering accurately reflect the structure of beliefs about abortion and welfare, then the priming effect should be largest when the target and priming items are drawn from the same topical cluster. By the same token, if the traditional dimensional models capture the key relationships among the attitude items, then priming items expressing the same side or viewpoint on the issue as the target should produce the largest priming effects.

Respondents in the study answered eight target items on welfare and abortion. Different targets followed priming items that systematically varied in their distance from the target. The priming items varied in both their topical distance (based on the clustering of the sort data) and their distance along the pro–con dimension from the target (based on the factor analysis of the agreement correlations). The experiment included four levels of topical distance: Some priming items were drawn from the same topical cluster as the target, some were from a different cluster, some concerned an issue related to that of the prime, and some concerned an unrelated issue. (The related-issue primes were items used in our context studies. For example, for the abortion targets, the related-issue primes concerned women's rights or family values.)

To clarify the source of any priming effects, we asked respondents to indicate their agreement with the targets and to classify each one as liberal or conservative. (Task order was counterbalanced across respondents.) If response facilitation results from priming of relevant semantic concepts, it should be equally apparent in the agreement and the classification data, since both tasks require the interpretation of the target items. If facilitation results from priming of considerations related to the target, it should be more apparent for the agreement task than for the classification task, since only the agreement task requires the retrieval and weighing of considerations about the issue.

Table 4.4 shows the main result from the study—a priming effect for the agreement data as a function of topical distance between target and prime. Topical distance had no effect on classification reaction times. Also, there were no facilitation effects for either task when the target item followed a prime on the same side of the issue. (In fact, for welfare, there was some indication that agreement reaction times were *slower* when the targets followed primes on the same side of the issue. Because this effect was restricted to the one task and issue, it is not clear whether it should receive much weight.)

The results indicate that the clusters revealed in the scaling studies are meaningful: Agreement reaction times were significantly faster when the targets followed primes from the same cluster than when they followed primes from a different cluster. Further, the absence of effects for the classification task suggests that the priming effect reflects attitude structure, not semantic structure.

The reaction-time study provides converging evidence that answers to attitude questions are based on considerations retrieved at the time when the question is asked and that prior items can alter the retrieval process. In both the reaction-time and the context studies, prior items appeared to increase the accessibility of specific considerations, thereby altering the retrieval process for a later item—changing its speed (in the reaction-time study) or the overall direction (in the context studies). Both effects reflect the impact of retrieving considerations to answer one question on the accessibility of considerations relevant to another question.

TABLE 4.4. Mean Agreement Reaction Times (Times in Milliseconds)

Cluster or Issue	Abortion	Welfare	Total
Same cluster	3,647	3,640	3,643
Different cluster	3,738	3,703	3,720
Related issue	3,710	3,800	3,755
Unrelated issue	3,993	3,774	3,883

This does not mean that attitude responses are *never* based on existing evaluations (or what Hastie & Park, 1986, call "on-line judgments"); but under a wide range of circumstances, respondents may retrieve specific considerations rather than an existing evaluation. Respondents who are unfamiliar with the issue may not have existing evaluations. Others may have evaluations, but ones that are inaccessible at the time that the question is asked. The work of Fazio et al. (1986) indicates that only highly accessible evaluations are activated automatically. Other respondents may have evaluations that are ordinarily accessible but may nonetheless retrieve a specific consideration because it closely matches the content of the question. For example, respondents who are asked whether a fetus should be considered a human life will, no doubt, often retrieve their specific beliefs about when life begins before they retrieve their overall views about abortion. Finally, even if respondents do have an evaluation and do retrieve it in response to a question, they may still base their answers on more specific material, since the overall evaluation does not provide an adequate basis for an answer. A respondent may endorse an item that asks whether welfare programs are mismanaged even though he or she favors welfare programs overall—despite their management problems. With many items, an overall evaluation simply is not informative enough to answer the question—at least, not accurately.

When an overall evaluation is inaccessible or nonexistent, when it is less relevant than a more specific consideration or uninformative for the question at hand, respondents may retrieve and base their answers on specific considerations rather than on general evaluations about the issue. The structures linking these considerations may determine which ones respondents retrieve and what answers they give. These links may help us predict when asking one question will affect answers to a second question.

5
Constructive Processes as a Source of Context Effects in Survey Research: Explorations in Self-Generated Validity

Jack M. Feldman

Theoretical Background

Within the last several years, there has been an increasing realization that both bias and accuracy in responses to survey measures of many types (e.g., reports of behavior, expressions of attitude and preferences) are outcomes of fundamental cognitive and affective processes (e.g., Bradburn, Rips, & Shevell, 1987; Isen, 1989; Schwarz, 1990; Tourangeau & Rasinski, 1988).[1] This concern with cognition parallels the study of context and framing effects in judgment and decision making (e.g., Hogarth, 1982, 1987; Kahneman, Slovic, & Tversky, 1982) and the general interest in response construction processes within cognition and social cognition (e.g., Barsalou, 1987; Higgins, 1989b; Petty & Cacioppo, 1986b; Srull & Wyer, 1989; T. D. Wilson, Dunn, Kraft, & Lisle, 1989). Research in "contingent decision processes," as exemplified by J. W. Payne (1982), Feldman and Lindell (1990), and Biehal and Chakravarti (1983), is part of the same theme.

In Feldman and Lynch (1988), beginning from the general assumptions of a constructive process approach, we have proposed a preliminary theory of the way in which measurement operations may influence the creation, modification, and expression of beliefs, attitudes, intentions, and behaviors. The present chapter will briefly review some of the major principles of the theory of "self-generated validity" and present three recent studies testing some of its major hypotheses.

We assume, first, the principle of *cognitive economy* (e.g., Wyer & Srull, 1986): Resources are not used in the development of judgments, beliefs, plans of action, etc., unless some reason for doing so exists. Second, we assume that both retrieval and computational or constructive processes occur in response to survey questions about other events in one's life; that is, given some demand for

---

[1]The references included here and subsequently are intended to be illustrative rather than exhaustive.

a response, if a directly relevant judgment, script, affective response, etc., is either unavailable or insufficiently accessible, a response will be constructed based on inputs that *are* accessible (Fischhoff, Slovic, & Lichtenstein, 1980; Lingle, Altom, & Medin, 1984). The effort expended on construction, retrieval, or both (e.g., the integration of recalled episodic information, existing judgments, and immediately present stimulus information) depends on the immediate processing goals, motives, capacity, and skills of the individual and typically can be assumed to meet a "satisficing" criterion, in keeping with the principle of cognitive economy (see, e.g., Devine, 1989).

Third, the individual may or may not be aware of the source or nature of all of the inputs to a constructive process or the origin of the retrieved judgment (see, e.g., Bargh, 1984, 1988; Langer, 1989; Nisbett & Wilson, 1977). The judgment or response generation process (e.g., heuristic) used may vary with the nature of the input and the framing of the question (see Feldman & Lindell, 1990; Feldman & Lynch, 1988).

The Flexibility of Response Generation

Lichtenstein and Srull (1985) illustrate retrieval and constructive processes with the question, "Is the Buick Regal a luxury car?" If a respondent has already made an appropriate categorization, the answer could simply be retrieved. If the respondent has not made a prior judgment, however, a "computational" process involving the retrieval of information about Regals, a "luxury car" representation, and some similarity judgment would be required to compute an answer. Once an answer has been either computed or retrieved, it can be used to answer a subsequent question, for example, "What do you expect a Regal to cost?" "Are power windows standard on the Regal?" "How much do you like the Regal?"

The process used to answer a given question may differ depending on whether a prior question has been answered. If no prior categorization has been elicited, an answer to the "power windows" question may be constructed through retrieval of instances of Buick Regals or Buick advertising. An answer to the "liking" question may be computed by retrieval of instances or attributes, an instance of "piecemeal"-based affect (S. T. Fiske & Pavelchak, 1986). If a categorization has been made, however, the questions may be answered through categorical inference or automatic category-based affect, respectively. Even when existing judgments are used, however, questioning may influence subsequent responding. For example, questions making the "domestic versus foreign" distinction accessible prior to other questions may produce different responses than questions eliciting the luxury *versus* economy dimension, for reasons discussed below.

Studies by both Fazio, Lenn, and Effrein (1983–1984) and Kardes (1986) make the point that attitudes toward specific objects may be formed in response to questioning as well as when other environmental demands are present, but that without either circumstance, they are unlikely to be formed. Similar conclusions can be drawn from Fischhoff et al. (1980) and from research on political attitudes (e.g., Bishop, Oldendick, Tuchfarber, & Bennett, 1980).

Directive Effects of Measurement-Induced Cognitions

Theories of judgment and decision have, until recently, emphasized the role of conscious processes and choice among alternatives (e.g., Fishbein & Ajzen, 1975; J. W. Payne, 1982). Current research, however, leads to the view that much information processing *and* action occur outside of awareness, without volition (Bargh, 1984, 1988; Kimble & Perlmuter, 1970; Lachman, Lachman, & Butterfield, 1979; Langer, 1989; Posner, 1982; Thorngate, 1976). So-called "mindless" behavior, characteristic of much daily life, occurs without deliberate intention or awareness of controlling factors. A script theoretic approach (e.g., Langer & Abelson, 1972), in which one or another course of action is brought to mind, might be more appropriate and parallels the "construct accessibility" theme in judgment research. Which construct or which script is accessible at a given time is a function of active retrieval cues, even though the respondent is unaware of their operation (see, e.g., Cialdini, 1984, on social influence).

Circumstances may, however, force attention to normally unmonitored behaviors or require judgments not made previously. Workers asked about an incentive system, for instance, may consciously consider performance goals that have been habitual for years. In short, behavior is thought to be generated by a process in which volition or thoughtfulness is periodically activated, and then only with respect to some fraction of one's behavior. A survey of beliefs, attitudes, intention, or behavior may cause normally automatic behavior to come under conscious control, at least temporarily. For example, a survey requiring rating of political candidates on various dimensions, overall liking, and voting intentions may well make previously unremarked differences among them accessible; these could serve as inputs to overall liking judgments, which then may guide intention formation, which in turn influences behavior. This is a measurement-induced counterpart of the effects demonstrated by Fazio, Chen, McDonel, and Sherman (1982) and others, in which manipulations that increased the accessibility of a newly formed attitude increased its impact on behavior. Sherman (1980) showed the impact of intention formation on later behavior, and T. D. Wilson, Dunn, Kraft, and Lisle (1989) demonstrated accessibility effects in a nondirective context.

Thus, the form of questioning may influence the construction of beliefs, attitudes, and intentions in ways that would not have occurred under other conditions, and these may subsequently influence behavior. The theory that prompted the construction of the questioning procedure itself may seem to be supported by the data. This is the essence of the concept of "self-generated validity."

It is not the case, however, that measurement *always* determines the responses generated to survey questions. Individual differences in prior knowledge and involvement moderate survey context effects, as will be discussed below. Briefly, direct experience with attitude objects and/or exposure to persuasive communications may create relatively accessible and elaborated attitudes, beliefs, intentions, and habits of behavior (Fazio & Zanna, 1981; Fischhoff et al., 1980; Petty & Cacioppo, 1986b; T. D. Wilson, Dunn, Kraft, & Lisle, 1989), which are retrieved to govern both responses to survey scales and behavior. Under some circumstances, however, measurement operations may strongly influence observed relationships by influencing the occurrence, nature, and contents of construction and retrieval processes (Feldman & Lindell, 1990).

Sources of Influence on Observed Relationships

In contrast to the typical assumption of a fixed causal hierarchy among belief, attitude, intention, and behavior (e.g., Fishbein & Ajzen, 1975; Ray, 1982), the present approach postulates that any of 16 possible causal patterns among these constructs may occur (e.g., belief causing belief, belief causing affect, affect causing belief, behavior causing affect) under appropriate conditions. This has the advantage of integrating theories of "reverse causality" (e.g., Bem's 1972 behavior-causes-attitude model) and reciprocal causality (e.g., L. R. James & Tetrick, 1986) into a single system. For the present purposes, I shall briefly present arguments supporting the contention that measurement may create conditions necessary for particular causal patterns to be observed. These will center around the effects of three interrelated factors—the "diagnosticity" of a prior judgment for a later one, the accessibility of prior judgments in memory, and the accessibility of alternative inputs to judgment—on the likelihood that a response to a measure of a given construct will be based on a prior response to another measure.

Diagnosticity

Perceived diagnosticity of a judgment or decision for a later response is the degree to which the respondent perceives some implication for the second question in the answer to the first. This depends on the nature of both questions, on contextual factors, and on prior knowledge influencing perceived relevance, much as similarity judgments are influenced by context and expertise (Feldman & Lindell, 1990; Holyoak & Koh, 1987; Schuman & Ludwig, 1983; Tversky, 1977). Diagnosticity may also be asymmetric, in the sense that judgment A ("Are any politicians honest?") might be more diagnostic for judgment B ("Is Alan Cranston honest?") than B is for A. Some answers are more diagnostic than others, as well; for example, a "no" to question A would be more diagnostic for B than would a "yes." The phrasing of a question or task instructions may also alter the diagnosticity of existing knowledge or current affective states, changing the basis of people's responses to a question (e.g., Lichtenstein & Srull, 1985; Schwarz, 1990).

Accessibility

Accessibility is the ease with which a given episode, affective response, prior judgment, knowledge structure, or other cognitive/affective construct is brought to awareness. Accessibility is a function of several factors, including the following:

1. The time since the most recent activation of a cognition (Wyer & Srull, 1986)
2. The amount of interfering material encountered in the content domain (Keller, 1987)
3. Elaboration and rehearsal of the original information (Fazio & Zanna, 1981; Ross, Lepper, Strack, & Steinmetz, 1977)
4. Characteristics of the information influencing its rate of decay, such as vividness (Reyes, Thompson, & Bower, 1980) or abstraction and summarizing power (Chattopadhyay, 1986)
5. Motivation and processing goals at initial encoding (Loken & Hoverstadt, 1985; Petty & Cacioppo, 1986b)
6. Retrieval cues, including those internally generated by means of prior knowledge or primed by question or context (e.g., Bettman & Sujan, 1987)

We assume that an interaction exists between diagnosticity and accessibility such that the first sufficiently diagnostic information retrieved is used to answer a given question. Thus an accessible, moderately diagnostic judgment (e.g., an overall evaluation) will be used to construct a response even if more diagnostic but less accessible information (e.g., memory for specific attributes or behaviors) exists in memory.[2]

Accessibility of Alternative Inputs

Cognitions other than those made accessible by prior questioning may also influence responding, either by implying an alternative choice of response or by integrating with them. Three factors influence the accessibility of alternative inputs:

1. Output interference, thought to be produced by associative interference effects (Hoch, 1984). The probability of recalling a new item of information is an inverse function of the amount previously recalled. Thus, answering questions about specific attributes, issues, or values reduces the probability that the respondent will retrieve unmentioned attributes (Fischhoff, Slovic, and Lichtenstein, 1978; Fischhoff et al., 1980).
2. Ability to retrieve more or less diagnostic inputs, which influences the use of the information that is accessible. For example, an easily retrieved overall attitude will guide responding to attitude questions, if one exists. If such an attitude does not exist, respondents will draw attributional inferences from (less diagnostic) memories of past behavior and external circumstances (Bem, 1972). In general, abstract, higher level encodings are diagnostic for a variety of judgments and decay slowly over time (e.g., Carlston, 1980). They are thus very likely to be used unless the framing or context of a question makes them relatively nondiagnostic (see, e.g., Alba

---

[2]This presentation will, of necessity, be highly abridged. Readers are urged to consult Feldman and Lynch (1988).

& Hasher, 1983; Srull & Wyer, 1989, Wyer & Srull, 1986). For example, overall evaluations seem unlikely to be made if the judgment is relative, such as when a choice rather than an evaluation is required (Alba, Hutchinson, & Lynch, 1991).

3. Individual differences in ability to generate alternative inputs, associated with both expertise and affective involvement. Expertise implies a highly organized and elaborated cognitive structure within the relevant domain and highly practiced judgmental processes. Involvement is considered to be similar but coupled with relatively intense affect (e.g., Alba & Hutchinson, 1987; S. T. Fiske & Kinder, 1981; Petty & Cacioppo, 1986b). Both imply the presence of highly accessible context-independent categories and standards of judgment (Barsalou, 1987; Kahneman & Miller, 1986), as well as highly accessible and diagnostic prior judgments and affective responses (or processes for constructing these; see, e.g., Bargh, 1988). "Schematic," involved, and knowledgeable individuals (Markus & Wurf, 1987) are relatively resistant to priming, framing, and context effects (e.g., Bettman & Sujan, 1987; T. D. Wilson, Dunn, Kraft, & Lisle, 1989) although perhaps not absolutely immune (Fischhoff et al., 1978; Schuman & Krosnick, 1988). It is important to note, however, that the effects of expertise and involvement are limited to task domains and tasks within which the person has had experience. As Bettman and Sujan (1987) have shown, when faced with an unfamiliar task (tradeoffs between different product classes rather than within a class), experts and novices alike were influenced by priming manipulations. These arguments apply directly in the domain of political ideology (e.g., Converse, 1964, 1980; Judd & Milburn, 1980).

Illustrative Research

Diagnosticity and Accessibility in Performance Appraisal

The periodic appraisal of employee performance is a ubiquitous form of survey. Its accuracy and potential for bias have been the subject of continuing interest (e.g., Feldman, 1981, 1986; Landy & Farr, 1980), most recently from a cognitive perspective. A laboratory study of appraisal processes (Woehr & Feldman, 1989) provides evidence supporting a central premise of self-generated validity: that judgments may be computed, or recomputed, based on the accessibility and diagnosticity of episodic information and prior judgments.

The respondent's task in a performance appraisal is to rate the quality or frequency of the ratee's behavior on a set of dimensions and to provide overall judgments. It is not dissimilar in this respect to a survey of, say, eating habits, especially when ratings are to be used for research (and fewer deliberate biases may therefore occur). It is reasonable that summary evaluations, being more accessible than specific memories, would be used to construct specific dimensional and overall ratings, *if* they existed. If, however, no summary evaluation existed, it would be necessary to retrieve episodes from memory in order to construct one. Thus, the memory–judgment correlation would be low to zero in the former case and moderate in the latter (Hastie & Park, 1986; Srull & Wyer, 1989).

It is also true, however, that an implicit demand exists to use accessible information, especially where extensive memory search is not required. If a recall task were to be performed prior to rating, the recalled information should be integrated with the existing impression to generate ratings (N. H. Anderson, 1981), especially if the implications of the recalled information are not redundant with the overall judgment.

Our prediction is that when an impression of performance had been formed prior to rating, recall–judgment correlations would be low when recall *followed* ratings but elevated when recall preceded it (because potentially diagnostic information was made more accessible). When, however, no prerating impression had been formed, recall–judgment correlations should be at least moderate across order of recall/rating conditions because recall would be necessary for the rating's construction.

The 472 subjects viewed one of two videotaped economics lectures (Nathan & Lord, 1983), varying performance over five behavioral dimensions such that one taped lecture was evaluated more favorably overall than the other. The actor's performance on three of the five dimensions on the "favorable" tape was, however, worse than his performance on the "unfavorable" tape, as rated by an independent pretest sample. Crossing the "ratee favorability" manipulation were three "processing-objective" conditions designed to influence the formation of an evaluative judgment. The "evaluation" objective required subjects to evaluate the lecturer's performance; the "learning" objective required subjects to learn the lecture material for a subsequent test (with a cash prize for the highest score); the "quality-judgment" objective required subjects to rate the quality of the videotape (lighting, sound, color, etc.) for classroom presentation. The latter two conditions were designed to reduce both motivation and capacity to form evaluations of the lecturer (see Lichtenstein & Srull, 1987). Finally, overall and dimensional judgments of the lecturer's performance and free recall of lecturer behavior were measured in one of two orders: rating/recall or recall/rating.[3]

If the hypothesis is valid, then recall–rating correlations should be higher in the evaluation-objective recall/rating condition then in the evaluation-objective rating/recall condition; recall–rating correlations in the other processing-objective conditions should be moderate, and no differences by recall/rating order or condition should be observed. As Table 5.1 shows, this is the case.

---

[3]Measures of memory organization, rating accuracy, etc., were also obtained but are not of immediate relevance. Also not discussed are the effects of delay on recall and recall–judgment correlations. Recall was scored in terms of "favorability of incident recalled," with a favorable behavior = 1, unfavorable = −1, and neutral = 0. These were summed for each subject, producing a "memory favorability" score.

TABLE 5.1. Correlations between Mean Dimensional Ratings, Mean Overall Ratings, and the Ratio of Positive to Positive Plus Negative Incidents Recalled as a Function of Processing Objective and Rating/Recall Order

| | Rating/Recall Order | | | |
| | Recall/Rating | | Rating/Recall | |
Processing Objective	Dimensional	Overall	Dimensional	Overall
Evaluation objective	.45[*a]	.46[*a]	.11[b]	.10[b]
Learning objective	.42[*a]	.49[*a]	.46[*a]	.40[*a]
Alternate objective	.37[*a]	.38[*a]	.35[*a]	.29[*a]

[a,b] Different superscripted r's in the same row are significantly different ($p < .05$).
[*]$p < .05$.

The critical contrast is significant in the predicted direction. Subsequent structural equation analyses support the causal impact of memory on ratings in the evaluation-objective recall/rating condition. These analyses also show a causal impact of rating (or judgment) on *recall* in the evaluation-objective rating/recall condition, while yielding equivocal results in the other conditions.[4] These results may explain why the zero-order correlations in Table 5.1 are not more supportive of the hypotheses, while providing further evidence for the impact of measurement form and content on subsequent responses.

These results at least make plausible the argument that question order can influence the process of judgment construction through its influence on the accessibility and diagnosticity of information.

The Creation of Cognitive Representations through Questioning: Survey Format Effects on Similarity Judgments

A second central principle of the theory of self-generated validity is that questioning may cause the formation of cognitive representations that did not exist (at least not in a given form) prior to questioning and may promote use of these representations in subsequent judgments. The "ideal" as a category representation is a case in point. Barsalou (1987) has found that ideals, based on extreme values of goal-relevant dimensions, may represent categories (e.g., "foods to eat on a diet"). Ideals are prominent in theories of consumer and worker attitudes and satisfaction (R. M. Johnson, 1971; Locke, 1976) and are central to measurement models requiring comparison of an object's present attribute levels with those that "should" (i.e., ideally) exist (e.g., Porter, 1962). Yet, ideal representations may not exist in some domains without substantial knowledge and involvement, or unless an explicit demand to create an ideal is encountered (Fischhoff et al.,

---

[4] A complete report is available from the author on request.

1980). Feldman and Lynch's (1988) arguments imply that requiring a judgment involving an ideal may cause one's construction, given that one does not exist.

We (Feldman, Wesley, Hein, & Gilmore, 1989) tested this proposition in the context of a similarity judgment by taking advantage of a phenomenon noted in Tversky (1977). His feature comparison model predicts that when a category member (*exemplar*) is compared with a category representation, the resulting similarity judgment will be higher than when the representation is compared with the exemplar. For example, Poland is judged more similar to the USSR than the USSR is to Poland. This is because, in the weighted comparison of shared and distinctive features that determines perceived similarity, features of the subject (Poland vs. USSR, respectively) are weighted more than features of the referent (USSR and Poland, respectively) and because category representations are typically more elaborated—contain more detailed knowledge—than category exemplars, *including more of the distinctive features that reduce perceived similarity*. The exemplar/representation order focuses attention on common features; the representation/exemplar order causes focus on more distinctive (unshared) features.

This is true, however, *only* if an accessible category representation exists. If one does not exist (e.g., an "ideal sports car") but the individual is familiar with a category member ("my old Toyota Celica"), the *reverse* of the asymmetry noted above may obtain. The exemplar in this case has the most elaborated memory representation. If one requires a series of judgments, designed to create an elaborated ideal, of people not likely to have one, subsequent similarity judgments should follow Tversky's original pattern. Judgments requiring the evaluation of a given, familiar exemplar ("my job," "my car") against an ideal on a series of attributes ("pay," "gas mileage") made *before* a global similarity judgment should result in a pattern similar to Tversky's (1977) findings, that is, exemplar/ideal > ideal/exemplar. If the global judgment is made *prior to* attribute ratings, the reverse should obtain, that is, ideal/exemplar > exemplar/ideal.

Classroom instructors were chosen as objects because outcome dependence and frequent interaction would tend to promote elaborated individual representations of these people (M. B. Brewer, 1988). Two different instructors in two classes (introductory social and industrial psychology) were used. Students ($N = 181$) rated their instructor's overall similarity to the ideal classroom instructor on a 20-point scale ("not at all similar" to "as similar as possible") either before or after rating the similarity of the instructor and ideal instructor on 21 behaviors taken from the university's standard course evaluation form (e.g., "uses real-world cases . . . "). The global similarity and attribute judgments were phrased in either the instructor/ideal or ideal/instructor order. Additionally, the behavior ratings were constructed as either an overall similarity judgment or an "is/should be" judgment requiring two separate ratings per behavior. It was felt that this latter format (following Porter's, 1962, satisfaction survey) might constitute a stronger stimulus to the construction of an ideal.

A four-way analysis of variance on overall similarity ratings produced moderate but qualified support for the hypothesis. Rather than the two-way interaction between order of rating (overall similarity first vs. last) and comparison order (instructor/ideal vs. ideal/instructor) expected in the simplest case, a four-way interaction also involving instructor and rating format was significant ($p < .05$). Inspection of this interaction, presented in Table 5.2, shows that for Instructor 1 the expected pattern of ratings was obtained only in the "is/should be" format, whereas for Instructor 2 the hypothesis was supported most strongly in the simple similarity judgment format, where slope differences between order of rating conditions were significant ($p < .05$). The pattern in the "is/should be" format is complicated by a significantly higher similarity rating in the "overall similarity last" condition.

These results may be considered encouraging if an additional factor is considered. Overall, Instructor 1 was rated more similar to the ideal than was Instructor 2 ($p < .01$). Instructor 1's more polarized evaluation may have been sufficiently diagnostic to guide responses to the simple similarity scale, preventing construction of an ideal. Essentially, all of the questions were translated into an evaluative scale by the subjects. The (hypothetically) more powerful "is/should be" scale produced small effects for Instructor 1, consistent with this reasoning. Also consistent are the larger effects for Instructor 2, whose evaluation was close to the scale midpoint on the similarity scale. The high ratings in both comparison orders in the "overall similarity last" condition may be explained by affective polarization produced by rehearsal, as in the research of Tesser (1978). Research is now in progress to test the hypotheses using less affect-laden stimuli, such as consumer products.

Respondent Knowledge and the Locus of Contrast Effects

The theory of self-generated validity makes the claim that, under certain conditions, the form and context of questioning can alter the cognitive representation of stimuli, influencing subsequent judgments. Knowledge in the domain of questioning, however, may render respondents relatively immune to such effects. A study by Lynch, Chakravarti, and Mitra (1989, experiment 2) speaks to both points.

Contrast effects, changes in the rating of a given stimulus as the result of the extremity of other stimuli with which it is rated, are of interest in many specialized areas (e.g., Murphy, Balzer, Lockhart, & Eisenman, 1985; Oliver, 1980; Sherif, Sherif, & Nebergall, 1965; Wexley, Yukl, Kovacs, & Sanders, 1972). Two views of the locus of contrast effects exist: first, that they represent true changes in stimulus perception or representation (Helson, 1964; Sherif et al., 1965); second, that they are simply reflections of differences in response scale usage (or "response language"; Upshaw, 1984). In the former case, one would expect contrast effects to carry over into behavior, whereas in the latter case, one would not.

The constructive process assumed by the present theory takes a different perspective. If a person with extensive knowledge makes judgments about the

TABLE 5.2. Interaction of Comparison Order, Order of Rating, Scale Format, and Instructor

Instructor	Scale Format	Order of Rating and Comparison			
		Overall Similarity First		Overall Similarity Last	
		Ideal/ Instructor	Instructor/ Ideal	Ideal/ Instructor	Instructor/ Ideal
Instructor 1	Similarity scale	13.56	13.38	14.88	13.33
	"Is/should be" scale	14.00	12.33	13.42	14.69
Instructor 2	Similarity scale	10.63	7.50	9.14	13.13
	"Is/should be" scale	10.75	10.20	13.13	14.25

Note: All numbers rounded to two decimal places.

attributes of each of a set of multidimensional stimuli, highly overlearned standard and processes are engaged (Alba & Hutchinson, 1987; Fischhoff et al., 1980; Kahneman & Miller, 1986). Thus, the internal representation of each stimulus is unlikely to be affected by the range of stimuli in the set. These same individuals, however, may be unfamiliar with the rating scale, and thus their interpretation of scale anchors may be influenced, producing response-language context effects (see, e.g., Hutchinson, 1983). A relative novice, however, lacks such specific standards and judgment heuristics; more generalized processes must be used, or a heuristic constructed "on the spot." Thus, changes in the subjective scale value of given attributes may occur and also be reflected in attribute ratings. If members of high- and low-knowledge groups are asked to make overall judgments (e.g., purchase intentions) of the stimuli, however, the correlation between the attribute ratings and the overall judgment (for a constant set of objects) ought to differ between the more and less knowledgeable as a function of the range of stimuli included in the overall set. The range of subjective scale values within the constant set, as reflected in the ratings, would be altered by the range of the attribute within the entire, experimentally manipulated set for the less, but not the more, knowledgeable respondents.

Subjects ($N = 241$) rated the prices of 20 real automobiles on a 1–9 (low–high) scale and ranked the same set in terms of purchase intention from 1 (least) to 20 (most likely to buy). Ten cars (the core set) were low to moderately priced ($6,000–$11,900). The remaining 10 constituted the "context set," either moderately priced ($8,146–$12,750) or expensive ($16,800–$42,700). The high and moderate sets were balanced in terms of car type (e.g., sedan, sports car), origin (domestic vs. foreign), etc. Subject knowledge was defined in terms of price, as the within-subject correlation between the core set's rated prices and their actual prices (range $= -.20$ to .89, $M = .35$, $SD = .18$). Median splits within context condition defined high- and low-knowledge groups. Order of the rating and ranking tasks was also manipulated.[5]

Dependent variables were each subject's mean price rating of the core set cars, the within-subject standard deviation of the core set price ratings, and the correlation between price ratings and purchase intention within the core set. It was expected that both high- and low-knowledge subjects would rate core set prices lower in the expensive context, with less dispersion, but that the less knowledgeable sample would show a lower price–purchase intent correlation than the more expert sample.

These predictions were supported. An analysis of variance showed a main effect of context ($p < .0001$) such that the expensive context produced lower core set ratings ($M = 4.66$) than did the moderate context ($M = 5.09$). There was no significant interaction effect. The standard deviations showed the same pattern: a main effect of context ($p < .005$), with less dispersion in the expensive ($M = 1.48$) than the moderate ($M = 1.64$) context, with an insignificant interaction. The within-subject rank-order correlations (Spearman's rho) *did* reveal a context $\times$ expertise interaction ($p < .02$), however. The simple main effect of context was significant for the less knowledgeable ($p < .05$) but not for the more expert ($p > .10$). In the less knowledgeable sample, Z-transformed correlations were higher in the moderate than the expensive context ($M = -.67$ and $-.45$, respectively), while nonsignificantly reversed in the more expert group ($M = -.38$ and $-.50$, respectively).

These results, coupled with the absence of interactions with task order, suggest that contrast effects on unidimensional ratings have different sources depending on the level of a person's knowledge. The stimulus range may influence the use of unfamiliar response scales (cf. Hutchinson, 1983) for knowledgeable respondents but apparently does not influence the construction of internal representations. The less knowledgeable, however, construct their internal representations on the basis of stimuli salient in the judgment task itself, perhaps because of the absence of context-invariant judgment standards and/or judgment processes. This result is similar in form to Bettman & Sujan's (1987) finding that novice, but not expert, choices among products within a domain were influenced by priming manipulations but that both experts and novices were influenced when performing unfamiliar *between*-domain choices.

Conclusions

Research conducted to date seems to support the usefulness of a constructive process approach in general and the predictions of the theory of self-generated validity in particular, at least to a modest degree. In a survey research context,

---

[5]Order of rating/ranking was manipulated but did not affect the results. Other hypotheses considered in the complete article are not discussed here; readers are urged to contact the author for the complete study.

the directive effects of measurement operations are likely to influence subsequent judgment and behavior in much the same way as do T. D. Wilson, Dunn, Kraft, and Lisle's (1989) nondirective "reasons" manipulations. A wide range of questions remain to be addressed, however.

One of the most important of these is the nature and determinants of "diagnosticity." Why, and under what circumstances, is one judgment or bit of knowledge relevant to another? It is likely that the answer to this question will involve the exploration of existing knowledge structures and the degree to which they are flexible in use (e.g., Barsalou, 1987). The effects of knowledge structures (expertise) and affect (involvement, value systems) also need further exploration. Although it is true that knowledge confers some resistance to the influence of context, question order, etc., it is also true that this resistance is not total (e.g., Bettman & Sujan, 1987; Fischhoff et al., 1978; Krosnick & Schuman, 1988) and may be limited to certain circumstances. Expertise and involvement may apparently be overcome by a sufficiently strong manipulation, which begs the question of what *makes* a manipulation more or less effective. Perhaps some clues may be found in the social-influence literature, as I have discussed in another context (Feldman, 1988).

Whatever the fate of current theories, it seems likely that survey and social-cognition researchers will find many questions of mutual interest for some time to come.

Acknowledgments. Thanks to John Lynch for his many helpful comments and for permission to report Lynch et al. (1989).

6
Question-Order Effects and Brand Evaluations: The Moderating Role of Consumer Knowledge

Barbara A. Bickart

In consumer surveys, questions are often asked regarding an individual's subjective evaluation of a product or service and its features or benefits. For example, in new product research, we obtain a respondent's evaluation of a series of product features, as well as the overall product concept (Urban & Hauser, 1980). We then use this information as one input for deciding whether the new product should be introduced. Likewise, at later stages of the product life cycle we use marketing research to determine how an existing brand might be repositioned in order to gain or maintain market share. Again, we require consumers' evaluations of the product attributes and overall brand evaluations to make this type of marketing decision.

In research for both new and existing products, common practice is to use an "inverted-funnel" question order, where specific questions that rate product attributes are asked prior to a more general brand evaluation (Kahn & Cannell, 1957; Sudman & Bradburn, 1982). Asking the attribute questions first is thought to provide the respondent with a framework for making the brand evaluation. In addition, this approach is recommended to avoid "halo" effects, where an initial positive (or negative) overall evaluation might color responses to later attribute ratings (Urban & Hauser, 1980). Most research from the survey methods literature suggests, however, that general questions, such as overall brand evaluations, are more likely to be influenced by contextual factors than by specific questions, such as attribute ratings (see Schuman & Presser, 1981), thus raising the issue of optimal question ordering.

The pairing of a specific question about one aspect of an object and an overall (general) evaluation of the object has been referred to as a "part–whole combination" (Schuman & Presser, 1981; Strack & Martin, 1987). A substantial amount of work has looked at part–whole question-order effects dealing with evaluations of political issues and life satisfaction (for reviews, see Feldman & Lynch, 1988; Schuman & Presser, 1981; Tourangeau & Rasinski, 1988). However, little attention has been given to evaluations of objects, such as brand evaluations (except see Sudman & Schwarz, 1989). Thus, the nature of these effects and their implications for marketing research are not well understood. The research discussed here examines the influence of rating brand attributes prior to an overall brand evaluation in a marketing survey and the role of product–category knowledge in moderating these effects.

Moorthy (1989) provides an example of how question ordering could impact marketing decisions. Using data from a telephone survey conducted by an office products manufacturer of their institutional customers, he showed that the relative importance weight of an attribute in predicting overall satisfaction varied with question order. In fact, one attribute went from being the least to being the most important depending on the placement of an overall satisfaction question. This is significant because the strategic actions taken by the firm could vary depending on these importance weights. For example, the firm might choose to allocate resources toward improving the area that received the lowest importance weight. To the extent that such importance weights are artifacts of measurement, their usefulness to marketing decision makers is limited.

Product knowledge has been shown to influence consumer judgments and decision making under a variety of conditions (Bettman & Sujan, 1987; Herr, 1989; Rao & Monroe, 1988). Similarly, survey researchers have found that domain expertise and attitude importance influence susceptibility to response effects under certain conditions (Krosnick & Alwin, 1987; Sudman & Swenson, 1985; Tourangeau, Rasinski, Bradburn, & D'Andrade, 1989a). However, results are conflicting on the nature of order effects for respondents differing in domain knowledge and importance. For example, Sudman and Swenson (1985) found that respondents with less crystallized attitudes were more susceptible to response effects than those with well-formed attitudes. Similarly, Krosnick and Alwin (1987) found that less educated respondents were more likely to exhibit response-order effects in a face-to-face interview. In contrast, Tourangeau et al. (1989a) found that people to whom an issue is important are more likely to exhibit carryover effects in surveys. Finally, Krosnick and Schuman (1988) found that issue importance has little effect on a respondent's susceptibility to response effects across a variety of studies.

Direct comparison of these results is difficult because the operational definitions of issue importance, crystallization, and involvement vary across studies. Consumers high in product knowledge are likely to have more information stored in memory about a topic and should have more experience using it (Alba & Hutchinson, 1987). Therefore, it is likely that these consumers' attitudes will be more important and crystallized than those of low-knowledge consumers. Thus, differences in domain expertise may underlie these constructs. In this chapter, I examine the effect of product knowledge on the processes used by consumers to form and report brand attitudes, focusing on the ways in which consumer knowledge might influence part–whole question-order effects. Then, results from an experimental survey regarding these issues are presented, and implications for attitude measurement in marketing are discussed.

Brand Evaluations in Surveys: Computational versus Retrieval Processes

One of the basic assumptions of attitude measurement in marketing is that people have attitudes stored about brands and these attitudes are readily accessible when a judgment is required. Accordingly, it is assumed that respondents will retrieve the appropriate attitude when asked to make a brand evaluation in a survey. However, this simple model may not correctly describe the process (see Bettman, 1979).

Evidence suggests that sometimes people do *not* form overall evaluations or attitudes during exposure to brand information. Instead, attitudes are computed on the spot in a memory-based fashion (Lichtenstein & Srull, 1985). The person's processing objective during exposure to information appears to be a primary determinant of whether judgments are made during exposure to brand information. When people passively view advertising, they are likely to remember some brand information; however, they are not likely to form a brand evaluation unless they have some reason for doing so, for example, if they intend to purchase the product. Therefore, an evaluation must be computed, versus retrieved, when brand information is acquired in a passive manner.

This kind of computational process may be even more prevalent for brand evaluations than for evaluations in other domains. Unlike some social evaluations, consumers often have brand information available to them in the judgment situation. For example, when selecting a pair of athletic shoes, consumers can directly compare brands in the store on most attributes. Under these conditions, the formation of an overall evaluation *prior* to choice would not be necessary; hence, only attribute information may be stored in memory. Then, contextual cues could influence the retrieval of this information from memory during subsequent judgments, such as ratings on a survey. For example, Keller (1987, 1991) has shown that retrieval of brand and advertising information can be influenced by situational cues. In his studies, the use of a pictorial cue on a package resulted in both higher recall of brand-related information presented in an earlier advertisement and differences in reported brand attitudes, depending on the valence of the accessible information.

Even when consumers have made a prior evaluation of a brand on some dimension, they do not necessarily use this evaluation when reporting their attitudes at a later time (Kardes, 1986a; Lynch, Mamorstein, & Weigold, 1988). For example, Kardes (1986a) showed that consumers do not use an earlier attribute evaluation when making a later discrete product judgment. This suggests that consumers make "mixed" judgments, relying partly on an earlier judgment and partly on other information that is either retrieved from memory or available in the context (see Lynch & Srull, 1982). Thus, although people may use an evaluation from memory to make a later judgment, they seem to use other information as well.

Finally, different *dimensions* of an attitude can be retrieved and reported during a survey (Shavitt & Fazio, 1987; Tourangeau & Rasinski, 1988). Shavitt and

Fazio (1987) showed that different attitudes can be retrieved about the same brand depending on the function that the attitude might serve. For example, Perrier water could serve a social function (status) or a utilitarian function (taste). They found that people reported different attitudes about Perrier depending on which of these functions had been activated by a previous series of questions.

Most models of the survey response process (Strack & Martin, 1987; Tourangeau & Rasinski, 1988) suggest that after respondents interpret a question, they retrieve either (a) a prior judgment or (b) relevant information and then compute a judgment. The research discussed above suggests that reporting a brand evaluation might be particularly vulnerable to question-order effects at the retrieval and judgment stages of the response process. First, consumers do not always form an overall evaluation during exposure to brand information. Hence, only attribute information may be available in memory. The retrieval of attribute information could be affected by cues in the context, such as prior questions. In addition, answering attribute questions could lead to the construction of an attitude when none previously existed (Feldman & Lynch, 1988). If a brand evaluation is available in memory, earlier questions could affect the use of this evaluation versus other attribute information. Finally, brand attitudes may be multidimensional in nature. Thus, prior questions could affect the specific dimension of the attitude that is retrieved and reported.

Product Knowledge and Question-Order Effects in Surveys

Contextual factors, such as questions placed earlier in a survey, affect judgments by increasing the accessibility of a given piece of information (Feldman & Lynch, 1988). However, increased accessibility does not guarantee that an input will be used or how it will be used in making a later judgment. Product knowledge is one factor that influences how the accessible information will be used to make a brand evaluation.

Alba and Hutchinson (1987) suggested that consumer knowledge comprises both the actual experience that a person has with a product, or *familiarity,* and the ability to perform product-related tasks successfully, or *expertise.* Increased consumer knowledge about a product category should result in several outcomes, including (a) an improved ability to remember product information, (b) more complete and refined cognitive structures about the product category, and (c) a reduction in the amount of cognitive effort required to perform product-related tasks. I now consider the implications of these outcomes on order effects in consumer surveys.

Information Retrieval

Srull (1983, experiments 1 and 2) provided evidence that expert consumers are more likely than novices to retrieve important information from memory. He showed that product familiarity influenced subjects' ability to recall newly acquired brand information about automobiles. This information was presented to subjects either by brand or randomly. High-familiarity subjects were not only able to recall more information than were novices but were also less affected by the presentation format of the information. Experts, but not novices, appear to have an organizational structure available to them in memory that facilitates recall of brand information.

Because experts should be able to retrieve a prior judgment or additional *important* inputs for making a brand evaluation, they should not have to rely on information made accessible by the context to the same extent as novices (Iyengar, Kinder, Peters, & Krosnick, 1984). This suggests that experts should be *less* influenced than novices by earlier questions in a survey. Novices should be more likely to use information made accessible by earlier specific questions to answer a later, more general one, resulting in an increased correlation between the questions when the specific questions are asked first. Experts, on the other hand, should be less influenced by the context when making judgments at the retrieval stage of the response process.

Knowledge Structure

Product knowledge not only affects individuals' ability to retrieve diagnostic information from memory but also influences their use of this information (Bettman & Sujan, 1987; Herr, 1989; Rao & Monroe, 1988). For example, Herr (1989) showed that priming price categories affected experts', but not novices', judgments about automobiles. He suggested that the primed information increased the accessibility of categories for experts and thus influenced their judgments. Novices presumably did not have such a category structure and, therefore, were not influenced by the primed information.

This suggests that at the judgment stage of the response process experts would be *more* affected than novices by prior survey questions. Prior questions should activate beliefs on one side of the issue for experts because of their better developed cognitive structure. Activated beliefs are then likely to be used in making a later evaluation (Tourangeau et al., 1989a, 1989b). Earlier survey questions would then be more likely to produce carryover effects for experts but should have no effect on novices' judgments.

Cognitive Effort

Finally, experts and novices should differ in the amount of cognitive effort required to answer a brand-related question (Alba & Hutchinson, 1987). This holds two implications for the survey response process. First, Krosnick and Alwin (1987) suggested that if a question is difficult for respondents to answer, they should be more likely to "satisfice," or provide "quick and easy" survey responses as opposed to accurate responses. Supporting this proposition, the authors found that respondents scoring low in cognitive sophistication were more susceptible to response-order effects in a face-to-face survey. Krosnick (in press) found similar results in telephone interviews (also see Krosnick, chap. 14, this volume). Because novice respondents require more cognitive effort to answer survey questions, they should be more likely to satisfice. This would result in the use of activated information, or a carryover effect.

Second, because experts require less cognitive effort to answer a survey question, they should be able to provide more thoughtful answers. Tourangeau and Rasinski (1988) suggested that thoughtful respondents are more likely to be aware of their earlier answers and to assess the relevance of these answers for later responses. Evidence suggests that awareness of an earlier response might be an important factor in a respondent's use of information (Ottati, Riggle, Wyer, Schwarz, & Kuklinski, 1988; Strack, Martin, & Schwarz, 1988). For example, Martin (1986) showed that if people are aware that a concept has come to mind owing to a preceding task, they will intentionally discount this information during interpretation of another concept, resulting in a backfire effect. Martin found that when a concept was blatantly primed in an initial task, subjects would generally avoid the use of the primed concept during a subsequent impression-formation task. According to Martin, a contrast effect occurred because the priming task was blatant and subjects felt that the previous task had made them aware of the concept.

When people are aware of their answers, the use of information should be related to its "diagnosticity." Diagnosticity is defined as the degree to which information enables an individual to attain a processing goal (in this case, evaluate a brand) or the usefulness of the information (Feldman & Lynch, 1988). Respondents should use diagnostic information, but they are likely to discount nondiagnostic information. Therefore, if product knowledge reduces the cognitive effort required to answer a survey question, increased awareness of earlier, *nondiagnostic* responses should lead to a backfire effect, whereas diagnostic responses should lead to a carryover effect.

To summarize, three alternate predictions can be made regarding the effect of consumer knowledge on question-order effects: (a) novice respondents would be positively influenced by prior questions, whereas experts would be less influenced because of their ability to retrieve other inputs; (b) experts would be positively influenced because earlier questions activate beliefs on one side of an issue; or (c) experts would be negatively influenced by earlier questions because they are aware of their answers and want to avoid giving a biased judgment. It is important to note that the processes described above are not independent. In other words, an expert's ability to retrieve alternate inputs is a function of superior knowledge structure, and both of these factors contribute to a reduction in the cognitive effort required to form a judgment. However, different patterns of results are important because they suggest the relative importance of these factors in determining the effect of question order on judgments and may indicate at what stage of the response process such effects are localized (see Strack & Martin, 1987; Tourangeau & Rasinski, 1988).

The objective of the current study is to examine these alternate perspectives on the role of expertise in mediating question-order effects in a marketing context. In order to discriminate among the explanations, the influence of prior attribute questions of varying levels of relevance on an overall brand evaluation is examined with regard to different levels of product knowledge.

Method

A telephone survey about running shoes was conducted to examine the issues described above. Running shoes were selected as the product category for two reasons. First, there is a range of knowledge about running shoes among the general population. Second, a list of runners was available for sampling purposes. This guaranteed a certain number of experts in the final sample.

Sample

The primary objective of the study was to examine the effects of product knowledge on susceptibility to question-order effects. Therefore, two sampling frames were used: (a) a list of members of a running club and (b) the Champaign-Urbana (Illinois) telephone directory. In both cases, the sample was limited to people who were age 16 or older and had purchased a pair of running shoes for their own use in the previous 12 months. For the directory stratum, numbers were systematically selected and the person answering the telephone was interviewed if he or she was eligible. Otherwise, an attempt was made to interview another eligible household member. For the list stratum, all members of the running club residing in the local area were contacted. The final response rate (completes/contacted households) was 77.5% for the general population and 94.2% for the running club, resulting in sample sizes of 100 and 81, respectively.[1]

Design and Data Collection

A survey instrument was developed that included questions about running behavior (e.g., miles run per week, number of events entered), followed by questions about running shoes, including purchase behavior, brand awareness, brand evaluations, and objective knowledge questions about the product category. The final section of the questionnaire obtained demographic information.

Exhibit 6.1 shows the wording used for the key questions. Respondents evaluated both Nike and Reebok running shoes overall and on two attributes. The Nike and Reebok brands were selected because pretesting indicated that respondents of varying levels of knowledge were able to evaluate these brands. In addition to providing their overall impression of each brand, respondents were asked how certain they were about their overall evaluation and how they came to this evaluation.

Four versions of the questionnaire were developed. The versions varied in two ways: (a) the *diagnosticity*, or relevance, of the attributes evaluated and (b) the

---

[1] No call attempts were made once the desired number of interviews were completed. Therefore, the response rates are somewhat lower than would normally be expected.

EXHIBIT 6.1. Question Wording of Key Items

General Questions
1. On a scale of 1 to 7 where 1 is poor and 7 is excellent, overall what is your impression of *(brand)* as a running shoe?
2. How certain are you about your overall impression? (7-point scale)
3. What features did you think about when you made your overall evaluation?

Specific Questions
On a scale of 1 to 7, where 1 is not *(attribute)* and 7 is very *(attribute)*, how would you rate *(brand)* running shoes in terms of . . .
   Low diagnosticity:
      Fashionable styling?
      Number of colors available?
   High diagnosticity:
      Comfort?
      Shock absorption?

---

order in which the specific attribute evaluations and the overall brand evaluation were obtained. Pretesting was used to select two high-diagnosticity (HD) and two low-diagnosticity (LD) attributes of running shoes. In the HD versions of the survey, respondents evaluated both brands in terms of "comfort" and "shock absorption." In the LD versions, respondents evaluated the brands in terms of "fashionable styling" and "variety of colors available." As shown in Exhibit 6.2, in some conditions the specific attribute evaluations were obtained prior to the brand evaluation (S1) and in other conditions they followed the overall brand evaluation (O1).

It was assumed that respondents drawn from the general population would be less knowledgeable than members of the running club about running shoes. Therefore, respondents in the general population stratum comprised the novice category, whereas those from the running club comprised the expert category. The $2 \times 2 \times 2 (\times 2)$ design included two levels of question order (S1 or O1), two levels of diagnosticity (HD or LD), two levels of product-category knowledge (novice or expert) manipulated between subjects, and two brands (Nike or Reebok) manipulated within subjects.

For data collection, each piece of sample was randomly assigned to a questionnaire version. However, in order to maintain relatively equal sample sizes across cells, some pieces of sample were randomly reassigned to versions toward the end of the field period. All interviews were conducted by trained interviewers at the University of Illinois Survey Research Laboratory.

Results

Manipulation Checks

Overall, 82% of the sample indicated that they ran or jogged for exercise, and 74% had jogged in the past month. Therefore, even those who were not running

EXHIBIT 6.2. Question Order by Version

Versions 1 & 3	Version 2 & 4
Running behavior	Running behavior
Purchase behavior	Purchase behavior
Nike specific 1	Nike overall
Nike specific 2	Reebok overall
Nike overall	Nike specific 1
Reebok specific 1	Nike specific 2
Reebok specific 2	Reebok specific 1
Reebok overall	Reebok specific 2
Objective knowledge	Objective knowledge
Demographics	Demographics

club members had some familiarity with the product category. However, as shown in Table 6.1, there were basic demographic differences between the running club members and nonmembers. Nonmembers were significantly more likely to be female (chi-square = 12.34, $p < .001$), were younger, $t(179) = 4.79$, $p < .001$, and less educated (chi-square = 28.04, $p < .001$) than club members.

In order to evaluate the effectiveness of running club membership as a blocking variable for product knowledge, comparisons were made between the groups on several key variables. As shown in Table 6.2, club members reported running more miles per week (28.22 vs. 10.62), $t(131) = 7.52$, $p < .001$, participated in more events per year (9.51 vs. 1.63), $t(98) = 2.81$, $p < .006$, owned more pairs of running shoes (4.07 vs. 1.90), $t(179) = 7.07$, $p < .001$, and purchased running shoes more often per year (2.04 vs. 1.29), $t(179) = 5.11$, $p < .001$, than nonmembers. Four objective knowledge questions and one perceptual measure regarding running shoes were also included in the survey. These questions are shown in Exhibit 6.3. A total score of 12 correct was possible on the objective knowledge questions. Table 6.2 shows that club members scored significantly higher than nonmembers on both the objective knowledge test (6.65 vs. 4.15), $t(179) = 8.17$, $p < .001$, and the perceptual knowledge measure (5.44 vs. 3.69), $t(179) = 8.63$, $p < .001$. Taken together, these results indicate that club members and nonmembers did differ in product knowledge.

The success of the diagnosticity manipulation was assessed by examining ratings of attribute importance and perceived differences across brands, which all respondents rated on a 4-point scale (4 = very important/very different) toward the end of the survey. Diagnostic attributes should be perceived as being important and as being different across brands. As shown in Table 6.3, in both knowledge groups the HD attributes were perceived as being more important and different across brands than were the LD attributes. Thus, the diagnosticity manipulation seems to have worked. However, experts and novices did differ in terms of the *absolute* diagnosticity of a given attribute. Specifically, novices perceived the low-diagnosticity attributes as being more important than did experts.

TABLE 6.1. Demographic Description of Sample, by Club Membership (%)

Demographic	Nonmembers (N = 100)	Members (N = 81)
Gender		
Male	43.0	69.1
Female	57.0	30.9
Total	100.0	100.0
Education		
High school	24.0	7.4
College	47.0	24.7
Graduate school	29.0	67.9
Total	100.0	100.0
Age		
Mean	32.7	41.4
SD	13.8	10.0

TABLE 6.2. Characteristics of Sample, by Club Membership

Characteristic	Nonmembers (N = 100)	Members (N = 81)
Miles run per week		
Mean	10.62	28.22
SD	13.74	13.17
n	(60)	(73)
Number of events per year		
Mean	1.63	9.51
SD	3.33	13.59
n	(24)	(76)
Pairs purchased per year		
Mean	1.29	2.04
SD	0.83	1.13
Pairs of running shoes owned		
Mean	1.90	4.07
SD	1.12	2.81
Subjective knowledge (7-point scale: 7 = very knowledgeable)		
Mean	3.69	5.44
SD	1.52	1.14
Objective knowledge (maximum = 12 points)		
Mean	4.15	6.65
SD	2.29	1.71

EXHIBIT 6.3. Objective Knowledge Questions

Please name all the brands of running shoes that you have heard of. (1 point each to a maximum of 6 points)

What kinds of materials are used to make the midsole of a running shoe? (1 point each to maximum of 2 points)

What kind of running shoe is preferable for a person who overpronates when running? Is it a shoe which is cushioned and flexible or one that provides maximum support? (2 points for "maximum support")

What are the advantages of shoes with "energy return"? (2 points for any reasonable answer)

TABLE 6.3. Attribute Ratings by Product Knowledge

	Novice		Expert	
Attribute	n	%	n	%
	Importance Ratings: % Responding Very/Somewhat Important[a]			
Fashionable styling	55	55.0	21	25.9
Variety of colors	36	36.0	18	22.2
Shock absorption	96	96.0	76	93.8
Comfort	100	100.0	81	100.0
	Difference Ratings: % Responding Very/Somewhat Different[b]			
Fashionable styling	55	57.3	50	67.6
Variety of colors	58	64.4	48	65.8
Shock absorption	78	83.9	67	87.0
Comfort	77	80.2	68	86.1

[a]Rated on a 4-point scale (4 = very important to 1 = not at all important).
[b]Rated on a 4 point scale (4 = brands are very different to 1 = not at all different).

Analysis of Dependent Measures

The two dependent measures of interest were (a) the correlation between attribute ratings and the overall brand evaluation and (b) mean overall brand evaluations. In addition, the overall brand evaluation could affect a subsequent attribute rating. Each of these measures is now examined as a function of the treatment conditions.

The correlations between the specific attribute ratings and the overall brand evaluations were examined first and are shown in Table 6.4 as a function of the treatment conditions. The difference between these correlations across question-order conditions within diagnosticity and product knowledge is of primary interest. In the HD condition, correlations were positive and significant regardless

TABLE 6.4. Correlation between Attribute Ratings and Overall Brand Evaluations as a Function of Treatment Conditions

Product Knowledge	Diagnos-ticity	Brand	Question Order				Diff.
			Specific First		Overall First		
			Corr.	n	Corr.	n	
Novice	Low	Nike 1	.72	24	.01	18	.71**
		Nike 2	.19	22	−.11	17	.30
		Reebok 1	.55	24	.02	18	.53**
		Reebok 2	.43	23	−.19	16	.62**
	High	Nike 1	.65	21	.55	20	.10
		Nike 2	.72	22	.52	20	.20
		Reebok 1	.85	21	.81	18	.04
		Reebok 2	.80	21	.81	19	−.01
Expert	Low	Nike 1	.40	14	.08	16	.32
		Nike 2	−.16	12	−.17	14	.01
		Reebok 1	.24	13	.33	15	−.09
		Reebok 2	−.05	12	.56	12	−.61*
	High	Nike 1	.59	15	.26	19	.33
		Nike 2	.43	16	.41	19	.02
		Reebok 1	.82	10	.85	10	−.03
		Reebok 2	.57	12	.76	10	−.19

Note: Includes only those respondents who answered both overall brand evaluation questions.
* $p < .05$.   ** $p < .10$.

of question order for both novices and experts. Novices' correlations were consistently higher in the S1 that in the O1 condition, but these differences were not significant. Because the attributes rated in the HD condition were important, it is not surprising that these ratings were highly correlated with overall brand evaluations regardless of question order.

Of greater interest is the pattern of correlations in the LD condition. This pattern differed for expert and novice respondents. For novices, the correlation between the items was significantly higher when a LD attribute question preceded the overall evaluation. These differences were significant in three out of four comparisons (Nike 1st: r's = .72 vs. .01, $z = 2.66$, $p < .01$; Nike 2nd: r's = .19 vs. -.11, $z = .86$, NS; Reebok 1st: r's = .55 vs. .02, $z = 2.10$, $p < .02$; Reebok 2nd: r's = .43 vs. .19, $z = 1.76$, $p < .05$). Carryover effects did not occur for experts. In fact, experts actually showed a marginally significant reduced correlation, or backfire effect, when Reebok 2 (number of colors available) preceded the Reebok brand evaluation (r's = −.05 vs. .56, $z = 1.45$, $p < .08$). However, given that a reduced correlation occurred in only one of four conditions, it must be interpreted with caution.

This pattern of findings suggests that novices use inputs made accessible by the context in answering survey questions, whereas experts are able to retrieve alternate inputs. In addition, these results provide some evidence that experts discount earlier nondiagnostic responses when making a later judgment.[2]

Mean overall brand evaluations are shown as a function of treatment conditions in Table 6.5. A repeated measures ANOVA, with two levels of question order, diagnosticity, and knowledge as the between-subjects factors and two brands as the within-subjects factor, showed no significant main effects or interactions involving question order (p's > .10). The only significant results from this analysis were a main effect for brand, $F(1,144) = 49.79$, $p < .00$, such that Nike was rated more positively than Reebok ($Ms = 5.62$ vs. 4.59) and a significant interaction between brand and knowledge, $F(1,144) = 10.56$, $p < .00$. In general, the difference between the experts' brand ratings was greater than the novices, although Nike was rated more favorably by both groups.

The pattern of observed correlations could be accounted for by changes in either the overall evaluations or the specific attribute evaluations. Thus, it is important to examine differences in these ratings too. Mean attribute evaluations are shown as a function of treatment conditions in Table 6.6. A repeated measures ANOVA, with two levels of question order, diagnosticity, and product knowledge as between-subjects variables and two levels of brand and attribute ratings as repeated measures, indicated that question order did not influence attribute evaluations in any way (p's > .10). There were significant interactions between brand and diagnosticity, $F(1,109) = 8.21$, $p < .01$, diagnosticity and knowledge, $F(1,109) = 9.06$, $p < .01$, and rating and diagnosticity, $F(1,109) = 6.73$, $p < .01$. However, these differences were not surprising and are not of substantive importance here.

Summary

Correlations between overall brand evaluations varied as a function of question order, whereas mean attribute ratings and overall brand evaluations did not. These results suggest that asking specific questions prior to overall evaluations can result in correlations that are significantly higher than would be observed otherwise. Given the relatively low importance of the attributes rated in the low-diagnosticity condition, these increased correlations could be misleading to a marketing manager. In the following section, I explore some possible explanations for this pattern of results and discuss implications for survey research and attitude measurement.

Discussion

The findings of this study suggest that expert and novice respondents' judgments are influenced differently by earlier questions. Novice respondents showed an

---

[2]Similar patterns of results were found when comparing unstandardized regression coefficients, representing the impact of the specific evaluation on the overall brand evaluation in each condition.

TABLE 6.5. Mean Overall Brand Evaluations as a Function of Question Order, Product Knowledge, and Diagnosticity

Product Knowledge	Diagnos-ticity	Brand		Specific First	Overall First	Diff.
				Question Order		
Novice	Low	Nike	Mean	5.50	4.94	.56
			SD	1.18	1.52	
		Reebok	Mean	4.88	4.67	.21
			SD	1.65	1.41	
	High	Nike	Mean	5.39	5.90	−.51**
			SD	1.20	.77	
		Reebok	Mean	4.87	4.95	−.08
			SD	1.66	1.69	
Expert	Low	Nike	Mean	6.20	5.63	.57*
			SD	.77	1.41	
		Reebok	Mean	4.13	4.06	.07
			SD	1.60	1.48	
	High	Nike	Mean	5.81	5.74	.06
			SD	.83	.87	
		Reebok	Mean	4.38	4.37	.01
			SD	1.59	1.34	

* $p < .05.$ ** $p < .10.$

TABLE 6.6. Mean Attribute Evaluations as a Function of Question Order, Product Knowledge, and Diagnosticity

Product Knowledge	Diagnos-ticity	Brand	Attribute	Specific First	Overall First	Diff.
				Question Order		
Novice	Low	Nike	Fashion	5.09	5.18	−.08
			Colors	4.27	4.82	−.55
		Reebok	Fashion	5.27	5.35	−.08
			Colors	4.50	4.59	−.09
	High	Nike	Comfort	5.53	6.29	−.76
			Shock	5.53	5.65	−.12
		Reebok	Comfort	5.71	5.35	.36
			Shock	4.88	5.06	−.18
Expert	Low	Nike	Fashion	6.15	5.25	.90
			Colors	4.85	4.33	.52
		Reebok	Fashion	5.62	5.75	−.13
			Colors	4.92	4.83	.09
	High	Nike	Comfort	5.00	5.33	−.33
			Shock	5.10	5.56	−.46
		Reebok	Comfort	4.40	4.33	.07
			Shock	4.60	3.79	.81

increased correlation between a specific and overall evaluation when the specific question was asked first, although the increased correlation was significant only in the low-diagnosticity condition. Thus, it appears that novice respondents have a limited ability to retrieve alternate inputs and must rely on information made accessible by earlier questions, resulting in a carryover effect.

The interpretation is less straightforward for expert respondents. Under most conditions, experts' judgments were not affected by question order. This indicates that experts were able to retrieve alternate inputs when necessary. However, when low-diagnosticity information about the Reebok brand was activated, a marginally significant backfire effect occurred. Although this finding is tentative, there are several possible explanations. First, attributes could hold different evaluative implications across brands for experts. In this case, an attractive appearance might hold positive implications for Nike, but a positive rating of Reebok on this attribute might increase the accessibility of such beliefs as "it's primarily a fashion shoe" or "serious runners don't wear Reebok." The increased accessibility of these beliefs would result in a less favorable overall evaluation of Reebok as a running shoe.

Second, information activated by earlier questions could serve as a cue for categorizing a brand, which could then affect its evaluation. This is likely to occur only if respondents are knowledgeable about the product category *and* if they are uncertain about a particular brand. For example, activating appearance information about Reebok could have resulted in its categorization as a "fashion shoe" and should produce a less favorable evaluation of Reebok as a running shoe. Only 2% of the experts owned Reebok shoes, whereas 49% owned Nike. In addition, experts were less certain about their overall evaluations of Reebok versus Nike ($M = 5.63$ vs. 4.51), $F(1,62) = 24.20$, $p < .01$. This difference was not significant for novices ($Ms = 5.07$ [Nike] vs. 4.72 [Reebok]), $F(1,84) = 1.67$, $p < .20$.

Finally, respondents may discount information of which they are aware, but a variable other than diagnosticity could mediate this process. It is possible that people discount information that seems obvious to them, or that they would normally consider, but use information that is less obvious. Thus, the key factor would be whether the activated information is "spontaneously" used to make the judgment. A respondent must be aware of his or her prior response in order to discount it (Martin, Seta, & Crelia, 1990). Therefore, this effect would occur for experts because they have increased cognitive capacity to answer questions, but it would not occur for novices.

In interpreting these results, several limitations need to be addressed. First, the question-order conditions differed not only in terms of question order but also in terms of the amount of time between the specific and overall questions. In the S1 condition, the overall evaluations immediately followed the specific evaluations, whereas in the O1 condition, there were additional items between the overall and specific evaluations. Thus, the lower correlations in the O1 conditions could be attributed to the amount of time between asking these questions. However, in the high-diagnosticity condition, correlations were positive and significant regardless of question order. In addition, numerous studies support the existence of carryover effects when questions are asked sequentially in both conditions (see Schuman & Presser, 1981). Therefore, although this explanation cannot be ruled out completely, there is some evidence to suggest that it does not account for these findings.

The second limitation of the research is that the order in which brand evaluations were obtained was not counterbalanced across conditions. Thus, it is not possible to determine if the brand interactions are attributable to some higher order question-order effect. It is possible that by asking respondents about Nike first, some type of comparison basis was elicited for experts but not for novices, resulting in the reduced correlation in the low-diagnosticity condition. However, the Nike evaluation preceded the Reebok evaluation in all conditions. Therefore, it seems reasonable that the overall evaluation would be equally affected across question-order conditions, thus minimizing the impact of this problem on the interpretation.

Consumer knowledge plays an important role in mediating question-order effects. The findings indicate that less knowledgeable people are likely to use attribute information made salient by the survey context in generating their overall brand evaluations. Experts are influenced by prior questions in a different way than are novices, primarily because of their increased ability to process brand-related information and superior knowledge structure. Research designed to test for these process differences is needed.

These results bring to question the idea of a "true" attitude, which respondents retrieve and report reliably during an interview. Instead, it appears that attitudes may be multidimensional in structure, possibly organized in terms of the functions that they serve (e.g., Katz, 1960; Shavitt, 1989). Indeed, unless brand familiarity is extremely high, brand attitudes may not exist at all. In this case, it may be more useful to conceptualize brand memory as pieces of brand information and brand-related inferences rather than as an overall impression. Given this model, judgments are likely to be constructed in a memory-based fashion than retrieved and thus are more susceptible to context effects.

These results also suggest that marketing researchers may rely too much on multiattribute models as a diagnostic tool in understanding and predicting brand attitudes. If brand information is not integrated into an overall impression in memory, it is likely that local conditions at the time of choice play a major role in the outcome of decisions. Marketing researchers may want to consider the factors that will be salient to the consumer when he or she makes a purchase decision and then build these factors into the measurement process. In addition, the primary purpose of measuring brand attitudes in surveys is to predict purchase behavior. This suggests that one criterion for evaluating the "accuracy" of an overall evaluation should be its predictive validity. To the extent that reported brand attitudes are measurement artifacts, their predictive ability could be limited.

Finally, it is possible that measuring a brand attitude in a survey could actually affect the representation of the attitude in memory. If this is true, order effects in surveys could influence actual purchase behavior. The work of Wilson and his colleagues (T. D. Wilson, Dunn, Kraft, & Lisle, 1989; T. D. Wilson, Kraft, & Dunn, 1989) provides examples of how explaining attitudes can actually reduce attitude–behavior consistency. Powell and Fazio (1984) showed that repeated reporting of an attitude increases its accessibility, which results in increased consistency between attitudes and behavior. These findings could have important practical and ethical implications for the ways in which marketing research is used and thus require further attention.

Acknowledgments. An earlier version of this chapter received an honorable mention in the 1990 American Association for Public Opinion Research (AAPOR) Student Paper Competition. The reported research was partially supported by a Richard D. Irwin Dissertation Fellowship and by the University of Illinois Department of Business Administration. I would like to thank Tobey Fumento and Chris Horak of the University of Illinois Survey Research Laboratory for their help with data collection and John Lynch, Lenny Martin, Norbert Schwarz, Thom Srull, and especially Seymour Sudman and Carolyn J. Simmons for their input throughout this project.

7
Basking and Brooding: The Motivating Effects of Filter Questions in Surveys

Leonard L. Martin and Thomas F. Harlow

Answer the following questions:

> Q1. Do you happen to remember anything special that your U.S. representative has done for your district or for the people in your district while he has been in Congress? (IF YES): What was that?

> Q2. Is there any legislative bill that has come up in the House of Representatives on which you remember how your congressman has voted in the last couple of years? (IF YES): What bill was that?

If you are like most people, you would find it difficult, if not impossible, to answer these questions. Because people differ in their ability to answer questions like these, such questions have often been included in surveys as filter questions. One's ability (or inability) to answer a factual question is a more valid indicator of his or her knowledge than is a self-report measure (e.g., "How knowledgeable are you about politics?"). By observing what respondents can and cannot answer, we can divide them into groups based on their degree of knowledge. Unfortunately, filter questions may do much more than filter. They may also alter our respondents' answers to other questions in the survey.

In this chapter, we explore the processes engendered in respondents after they answer (or fail to answer) filter questions. We first discuss previous research on the effects of filter questions on survey responses and then research on the processes initiated by the nonattainment of important goals, as well as research on the role of cognitive effort in context effects. After that we discuss an experiment that tested the implications of this research for survey responding. Finally, we consider the implications of our results for survey research.

Previous Research

Filter Questions and Self-Perception

The initial research on the effects of filter questions in surveys was conducted by Bishop and his associates (e.g., Bishop, 1987; Bishop, Oldendick, & Tuchfarber,

1982, 1984a, 1984b). They hypothesized that in answering a self-report question people do not perform an exhaustive search of their memory for all relevant information. Instead, they respond largely in terms of the first relevant information that comes to mind (cf. Wyer & Hartwick, 1980). The ease with which information is brought to mind, however, may be a function of how recently or frequently this information has been used (Higgins, Bargh, & Lombardi, 1985; Wyer & Srull, 1989). Thus, people may report being more interested in politics when they have just been reminded that they voted in the last election than when they have just been reminded that they did not support their candidate by putting a sticker on their car.

Similarly, if one observes oneself failing to answer two questions about politics, and if one does not have a strong attitude about one's interest in politics and if there are no extenuating circumstances, then one may infer that one does not follow what is going on in politics. As Bishop, Oldendick, and Tuchfarber (1984b, p. 510) put it, "What must my interest in politics be if I just told you 'I don't know'?"

Bishop and his colleagues (e.g., Bishop, 1987; Bishop et al., 1984a, 1984b) have shown that in a variety of settings respondents reported significantly less interest in politics when they indicated this interest *after* failing to answer some politically relevant filter questions than when they indicated their interest *before* attempting to answer the filter questions. Presumably, when respondents are unable to answer the filter questions, they categorize themselves as not very knowledgeable about politics. These self-perceptions then become the first relevant information that comes to mind when they report their interest in politics.

The Consequences of Disconfirmed Expectancies

The self-perception interpretation of the effects of filter questions is quite plausible, and the data collected by Bishop and his colleagues accord nicely with that view. There is reason to believe, however, that self-perception theory may not provide a *complete* explanation of the effects of filter questions on subsequent survey responses. Self-perception theory is based on the assumption that individuals come to know their own attitudes and feelings in the same way that they come to know the attitudes and feelings of others, through a cold inference process. One sees oneself eat a great deal and concludes that one must be hungry. One sees oneself fail to answer two questions about politics and concludes that one must not follow what is going on in politics.

We suspect, however, that individuals are not so nonchalant when they have seen themselves perform a behavior that disconfirms a strongly held and valued self-perception. If one sees oneself as the kind of person who generally keeps abreast of politics, for example, and one finds oneself unable to answer two questions about politics, then one may not only *conclude* that one is not as knowledgeable as one had thought, but one may also *feel bad* about one's failure. One may feel embarrassed (cf. Bishop et al., 1984b) or disappointed. One may try to figure out why one thought that one knew more than one did. One may attempt to attribute one's poor performance to some temporary external source and so on.

More generally, it appears that people are motivated to maintain positive views of themselves, and when these views are threatened, people engage in behaviors designed to restore them (e.g., Allport, 1943; Aronson, 1969; Steele, 1988; Tesser, 1988). Thus, "cold" conclusions may have "hot" consequences, and these consequences may influence survey responses in ways that would not be expected if only the "cold" conclusions were operating.

What "hot" consequences might follow the failure to answer filter questions? If we assume that people have a goal to think of themselves as generally intelligent and well informed, then we can see that failing to answer filter questions can threaten to their attainment of that goal. Thus, the failure to answer filter questions can engender processes associated with the nonattainment of goals.

The two effects of goal nonattainment that have been most reliably demonstrated are rumination and suppression (for a review, see Martin & Tesser, 1989). Rumination is *continued thinking* about the nonattained goal, whereas suppression is a *lack of thinking* about that goal. With suppression, however, individuals do not actually "not think" about the goal. Instead, they distract themselves from thinking about the goal by thinking about something else (Nolen-Hecksema, 1986; Wegner, Schneider, Carter, & White, 1987). Thus, the two effects of failing to attain an important goal are continued thinking about the goal and thinking about things other than the goal.

We (Martin & Tesser, 1989) have obtained evidence of both the distracting and the ruminating effects of goal nonattainment and some indication of when each effect occurs. In one experiment, subjects were told that they were to play the role of a corporation president. Their task was to make a series of decisions to make money for their company. The subjects were also told that previous research had found that subjects who make money for the company are much more intelligent than those who do not make money for the company. The purpose of telling subjects this was to ensure that all of them had the demonstration of their intelligence as a goal in the decision task.

All subjects were then led to believe that they had made money for their company. However, some were led to believe that they had done this through their good decisions, whereas others were led to believe that they had done this only through luck. Thus, subjects who had made money through good decisions attained their goal of demonstrating intelligence, whereas subjects who had made money through luck did not. Thus, the former should not engage in distraction and rumination, but the latter should.

Distraction and rumination were assessed in a word-recognition task that followed (either immediately or five minutes after) the success or failure feedback. In this task, subjects were presented with a series of asterisk strings on a computer screen. Every five seconds in random order one of the asterisks in the currently presented string would disappear to reveal a letter. The subjects' task was to recognize the word that was being presented before all of the letters had been uncovered. The time that it took them to recognize each word was recorded, and this served as the measure of rumination/distraction.

If subjects are ruminating about a blocked goal, then information related to that goal should be quite accessible. In this experiment, it means that thoughts related to intelligence should be on the subjects' minds. If, on the other hand, the subjects are distracting themselves by thinking about something other than the blocked goal, then thoughts of intelligence should be relatively inaccessible. This means that subjects who are ruminating should recognize words related to intelligence faster than should subjects who are distracting themselves.

Results indicated that the content of the subjects' thoughts was a function of whether they had succeeded or failed and when their thoughts were assessed. When subjects believed that they had made money through their own decisions, they recognized words related to intelligence faster when the recognition task immediately followed the feedback ($M = 19.1$ secs) than when it followed five minutes after this feedback ($M = 21.4$ secs). When subjects believed that they had made money only through luck, however, they recognized intelligence-related words faster after a delay ($M = 19.1$ secs) than immediately after the feedback ($M = 21.9$ secs).

This crossover interaction suggests that immediately after attainment of an important goal, subjects "bask in success"; that is, they think about the goal, resulting in fast recognition of words related to that goal. This basking, however, quickly fades. The goal has been met, and the subject moves on to another task. Thus, there is a slow down in reaction times with a delay.

When people fail to reach an important goal, their immediate reaction appears to be one of suppression of goal-related thoughts. Presumably, they do this by thinking of things unrelated to the blocked goal. The result is slow reaction times immediately following failure feedback. With a delay, however, the initial emotional reaction to the failure may dissipate, and rumination about the goal surfaces. The result is that failure subjects recognize words related to intelligence faster after a delay than immediately after the failure feedback.

If subjects who have just failed to attain an important goal really are motivated to think of something other than the task that they have just failed, then they should be more distracted by a concurrent task than should subjects who have attained their goal. This is because, unlike successful subjects, failure subjects would rather think about something other than the task that they had just failed, and the concurrent task provides a perfect opportunity for this.

We (Martin & Tesser, 1989) tested this hypothesis using procedures similar to those in our earlier experiment. Subjects were led to believe that they had made money for their company either through their good decisions or through luck. All subjects performed the recognition task *immediately* after receiving the success or failure feedback. Some subjects were allowed to perform the word-recognition task without any distraction, as in Experiment 1. For other subjects, however, a tape recording was played as they tried to recognize the words. The recording presented a review of the movie *Batman,* which had not been released at the time that the study was conducted but which had already attracted a lot of interest in the subject population.

As in the first experiment, subjects took longer to recognize words related to intelligence when they had failed than when they had succeeded. The magnitude of this difference, however, depended on whether the distracting recording was or was not played. When subjects believed that they had made money for their company through their own decisions, the presence of the distracting recording had little effect on their ability to recognize words related to intelligence. They were equally fast regardless of whether the recording was played ($M = 19.9$ secs) or not ($M = 19.1$ secs). Subjects who believed that they had made money only through luck, on the other hand, apparently used the recording as a distractor. These subjects took significantly longer to recognize words related to intelligence when the recording was played ($M = 24.6$ secs) than when it was not ($M = 21.9$ secs).

These results suggest that immediately after receiving evidence that they have attained an important goal, individuals continue to think about that goal; but immediately after receiving evidence that they have failed to attain an important goal, they attempt to distract themselves from thinking about their failure. In terms of survey research, this means that if individuals have a goal to demonstrate their knowledge of a particular issue, then their success or failure in answering filter questions can determine whether or not they continue to think about that issue. Successful subjects may bask on the issue while avoiding unrelated issues (at least as their initial response), whereas unsuccessful subjects may think about unrelated issues in an attempt to avoid thinking about the failure-related issue (at least as their initial response). These differences in type of thinking engaged in by successful and unsuccessful respondents may cause some interesting and important differences in the answers that they give on surveys.

Effortful and Noneffortful Context Effects

One reason that the amount of cognitive effort that respondents exert toward thinking about different topics is important to survey researchers pertains to context effects. Contextual stimuli (e.g., previous questions) are among the most important determinants of answers in surveys (e.g., Schuman & Presser, 1981; Strack & Martin, 1987). It appears, however, that the effect that a given context has on a response depends on the amount of cognitive effort that respondents exert while making their response. A given context can produce either assimilation or contrast depending on whether respondents exert a lot or a little cognitive effort while responding.

We (Martin, Seta, & Crelia, 1990) obtained some evidence to this effect in the area of person perception. In three experiments, we blatantly primed subjects with concepts and then asked them to form an impression of a person described ambiguously with respect to these concepts. This blatant priming procedure typically produces contrast effects (e.g., Lombardi, Higgins, & Bargh, 1987; Martin, 1986; Strack, Schwarz, Bless, Kübler, & Wänke, 1990; Newman & Uleman, in press). Thus, subjects primed with positive concepts should rate the target person unfavorably, whereas subjects primed with negative concepts should rate the target person favorably.

We, however, had some subjects form their impressions while a distracting tape recording either was or was not playing. Subjects who formed their impressions while the tape was playing should have less cognitive capacity to exert toward forming their impressions than should subjects who formed their impressions while the tape was not playing. Therefore, if contrast demands more cognitive effort than does assimilation, then the impressions of the distracted subjects should assimilate toward the implications of the primed concepts, whereas the impressions of the nondistracted subjects should be contrasted with these implications. This is precisely what happened. In other words, distracted subjects formed more favorable impressions after exposure to positive as opposed to negative contextual stimuli (4.7 vs. 2.7, respectively), whereas the reverse was true for nondistracted subjects (2.5 vs. 3.3, respectively).

In a second experiment, we (Martin et al., 1990) blocked subjects on their dispositional tendency to exert cognitive effort (i.e., need for cognition) and obtained results that conceptually replicated the earlier study. Subjects low in need for cognition formed more favorable impressions after exposure to positive as opposed to negative contextual stimuli (6.4 vs. 5.2, respectively), whereas subjects high in need for cognition formed more favorable impressions after exposure to negative as opposed to positive contextual stimuli (6.1 vs. 4.8). Thus, the impressions of subjects low in need for cognition showed assimilation, whereas those of subjects high in need for cognition showed contrast.

Taken together, the results of these experiments suggest that under conditions that normally lead to contrast, assimilation can be obtained if subjects do not exert sufficient cognitive effort. Thus, the possibility is raised that respondents who are distracting themselves (as a result of failing to answer filter questions) will show assimilation under conditions in which respondents who are not distracting themselves show contrast.

Brooding and Basking in Surveys

All of the pieces of our argument have now been presented, and we can summarize our argument as follows:

1. Filter questions do more than filter; they affirm or disconfirm important self-concepts in respondents.
2. The immediate effect of disconfirmation involves attempts to think about something other than the disconfirmation; the immediate effect of affirmation involves thinking of issues related to the affirmation.
3. Contrast demands more cognitive effort than does assimilation. Thus, the amount of cognitive effort that respondents exert can determine the effect of a given context on their responses.

These assumptions not only allow us to make a number of unique predictions regarding context effects but also suggest a way in which the "self-perception effect" of filter questions can be undone. Bishop and his colleagues (Bishop, 1987; Bishop et al., 1982, 1984a, 1984b) found that respondents who attempt to answer difficult filter questions about politics rate themselves as less interested in politics than do respondents who have not attempted to answer these questions. If failing to answer filter questions involves disconfirmation of one's self-concept, then providing respondents with a way to reaffirm their self-concepts should eliminate the rating effect (Martin & Tesser, 1989).

Claude Steele and his colleagues (see Steele, 1988) have shown that merely expressing one's opinions can be sufficient to reaffirm one's self-concept. Thus, allowing respondents to indicate their opinions on political topics after they have failed to answer political filter questions may be sufficient to reaffirm their self-concept. If so, then respondents who have failed to answer political filter questions should indicate less interest in politics than should respondents who have successfully answered these questions, but only when the respondents have not had a chance to indicate their opinion on related political issues.

The Present Study

The theoretical analysis that we have described can be tested by constructing surveys with filter questions that we know respondents either can or cannot answer, then observing the effects of these questions on the direction and magnitude of subsequent rating and context effects. We tested our analysis in this way during the fall of 1989 using as our respondents 101 males and females from introductory psychology classes at the University of Georgia. Each respondent completed one of five versions of a survey.

All versions began with two filter questions, ended with a self-rating of political interest, and had four questions in between (see Exhibit 7.1). In half of the surveys, the filter questions were ones that most participants would have difficulty answering (see Bishop, 1987; Bishop et al., 1982, 1984a, 1984b). In the remaining surveys, the filter questions were ones that respondents with even a minimal degree of political knowledge could answer.

The political interest question was the same as that used previously by Bishop (1987; Bishop et al., 1982, 1984a, 1984b) and in the National Election Study. The four questions between the filter question and the interest rating were composed of two pairs of questions, each in a communication context (see Strack, Martin, & Schwarz, 1988). More specifically, each pair of questions was prefaced by an introduction that indicated that the two questions were related (e.g., "Now we would like to ask you two questions about . . . "), and in each pair the first question was specific and the second was general (see Exhibit 7.2). Respondents answered all four questions by circling numbers on 7-point Likert scales (of either importance or happiness).

Manipulation Check

Before beginning tests of our hypothesis, it was necessary to establish that the easy and difficult questions did significantly differ from one another in terms of how easy or difficult it was for respondents to answer them. This was done by

EXHIBIT 7.1. Filter Questions and Self-Rating of Political Interest

Difficult Filter Questions:

Q1. Do you happen to remember anything special that your U.S. Representative has done for your district or for the people in your district while he has been in Congress? (IF YES): What was that?

Q2. Is there any legislative bill that has come up in the House of Representatives on which you remember how your congressman has voted in the last couple of years? (IF YES): What bill was that?

Easy Filter Questions:

Q1. Do you happen to remember any minority candidates (e.g., black, Hispanic, female) in any recent presidential election? (IF YES): Name one.

Q2. Do you remember why Gary Hart withdrew from the last Presidential election? (IF YES): Give reason.

Political Interest Question:

Some people seem to follow what's going on in government and public affairs most of the time, whether there's an election going on or not. Others aren't that interested. Would you say that you follow what's going on in government and public affairs most of the time, some of the time, only now and then, or hardly at all?

EXHIBIT 7.2. Questions in a Communication Context

Next we would like to ask you two questions about George Bush's performance as President.

First, how happy are you with Bush's recent action to combat the drug problem?
Second, how happy are you with Bush's performance as president in?

Next we'd like to ask you two questions about public transportation.

First, how important is it to provide good public transportation to the elderly?
Second, how important is it to provide good public transportation in general?

Next we would like you to answer two questions that may be related to people's political interests.

First, how happy are you with your social life (e.g., dating)?
Second, how happy are you with your life as a whole?

examining the number of respondents who got the filter questions right in the two conditions. No subject got both of the difficult questions right, and only 2 out of the 52 in this condition were able to answer even one question correctly. In fact, most respondents did not even attempt an answer. The picture was quite different, however, for the easy filter questions. In this case, 50 out of 53 were able to answer both of the questions correctly, and 52 of the 53 were able to answer at least one question correctly. Only one respondent was unable to answer either of the easy questions. Thus, it appears that the difficult filter questions were significantly more difficult than were the easy filter questions.

It should be noted that to make the tests of our hypotheses cleaner, we did not include in our analyses the two respondents who were able to answer the difficult filter questions or the three who were unable to answer the easy filter questions.

Testing for Context Effects

As Strack et al. (1988; see also Strack & Martin, 1987) noted, there are two effects that answering a specific question can have on one's answer to a subsequent general question. It could serve to make information accessible, thus increasing the correlation between respondents' answers to the two questions; or it could serve to initiate the given-new contract. The given-new contract is a tacit agreement among conversants that in answering questions one should provide new, as opposed to old or redundant, information (Clark, 1985). Having just answered a specific question about one's dating life, for example, one can interpret a subsequent question about "life in general" as a request for information about aspects of life other than dating. The result of asking a specific and a general question in a communication context is a low correlation between respondents' answers to the two questions (Strack et al., 1988).

By placing our question pairs in a communication context, we hoped to increase the likelihood that respondents would engage the given-new contract and thus give us a *low* correlation between their answers to the specific and general questions. Note, however, that adhering to the given-new contract may demand more cognitive effort than answering the general question using the information made accessible in answering the preceding specific question. In following the given-new, one must think of *new* information when answering the general question.

If retrieving new information is more effortful than using already accessed information (Martin et al., 1990), then adherence to the given-new contract should demand the expenditure of more cognitive effort than should nonadherence to that contract. Consequently, respondents who exert cognitive effort should show lower correlations between their answers to the specific and general questions than should respondents who exert little cognitive effort.

After successfully answering two filter questions on politics, respondents may bask in success (Martin & Tesser, 1989). Thus, they should exert more cognitive effort when answering political questions than when answering nonpolitical questions. After failing to answer two filter questions on politics, however, respondents may attempt to think about nonpolitical issues to distract themselves from their recent failure (Martin & Tesser, 1989). Thus, after failing, respondents should exert more effort when answering nonpolitical than political questions. Thus, the correlation between respondents' answers to the specific and general questions should be higher for political than nonpolitical issues when respondents have failed but should be higher for nonpolitical than political issues when respondents have succeeded.

Hypothesis 1—Effects on the Political Question

In our surveys, the result of exerting minimal cognitive effort toward answering political questions would be a higher correlation between respondents' answers to the "happiness with Bush's drug policy" question and the "happiness with Bush in general" question in the failure compared with the success condition. These questions were in surveys A, B, C, and D. As can be seen in Table 7.1, the correlations are clearly higher following the difficult filter questions. In the difficult conditions, the correlations are .67 (Form A) and .65 (Form C), whereas in the easy conditions, the correlations are .47 (Form B) and .12 (Form D). The former two are statistically different from 0, whereas the latter two are not. In addition, the correlations in the two difficult conditions differ significantly from the correlations in at least one of the easy conditions, Form D.

These results are consistent with the hypothesis that respondents were exerting more cognitive effort in answering the two questions about Bush after successfully answering filter questions related to politics than after failing to do so.

Hypothesis 2—Effects on Political Topics in General

If the failure respondents really are motivated to avoid thinking of issues related to politics, then a pattern similar to that found for the "drug policy" and "Bush in general" questions should be found for the "dating" and the "life in general" questions. This is because the latter questions were introduced to respondents as "questions that may be related to people's political interest." As can be seen in surveys A, B, E, and F, the dating–life questions do show the same pattern as the drugs–Bush questions. The correlation between happiness with dating and happiness with life in general is higher (.66 and .77) when respondents attempted to answer difficult filter questions than when they answered easy ones (.26 and .19). As with the George Bush questions, the correlations following the difficult filter questions are significantly different from 0, whereas the correlations following the easy filters are not. Furthermore, the correlation in Form E is significantly different from that in Form F. These results suggest that respondents are motivated to stop thinking about their recent failure (i.e., their failure to answer the political filter questions).

Hypothesis 3—Respondents Distract Themselves to Stop Thinking

We argued that respondents do not "not think" about their recent failure. Instead, they distract themselves from it by thinking of something else. This means that failure respondents should exert more effort when answering nonpolitical questions than should success respondents. If so, then the correlations for nonpolitical questions should be lower for failure respondents than for success respondents, a pattern opposite to that obtained for the political questions. In the present set of surveys, this hypothesis can be tested by examining the correlation between respondents' answers to the "transportation for the elderly" question and the "transportation in general" question. These questions were contained in surveys C, D, E, and F.

As can be seen in Table 7.1, the hypothesis is generally supported. The correlations between the nonpolitical questions are lower following failure (.12 and .19) than following success (.49 and .25). Although these results are not as strong as the results for the political questions, they are clearly in the right direction.

TABLE 7.1. Correlations and Political Interest Ratings Following Easy or Difficult Filter Questions

Difficult Filters		Easy Filters	
Form A		Form B	
Drugs–Bush	.67*	Drugs–Bush	.47
Dating–Life	.66*	Dating–Life	.26
Interest	4.30_{ab}	Interest	4.30_{ab}
Form C		Form D	
Drugs–Bush	.65*	Drugs–Bush	.12
Elderly–Transportation	.12	Elderly–Transportation	.49
Interest	4.20_{ab}	Interest	4.20_{ab}
Form E		Form F	
Elderly–Transportation	.19	Elderly–Transportation	.25
Dating–Life	.77*	Dating–Life	.19
Interest	3.70_a	Interest	4.80_b

Note: Interest ratings that do not share at least one common subscript differ from one another at $p < .05$.
*$p < .05$.

Hypothesis 4—Self-Affirmation Can Undo Self-Perception

We hypothesized that failure to answer the difficult filter questions operates as a threat to the respondents' self-concepts. However, if respondents can express who they are by indicating their opinions on issues related to the failure, then the self is no longer threatened. The specific prediction is that respondents will rate themselves as less interested in politics after the difficult compared with the easy filter questions, but only when they have not had a chance to indicate their opinion on the two George Bush questions. This hypothesis can be examined in three ways.

By examining the interest ratings in Forms E and F, we can see the effects of the filter questions without the self-affirmation. What we see is a significant self-perception effect. Respondents indicated that they were significantly less interested in politics following the difficult filter questions (3.70) than following the easy ones (4.80), $t(33) = 2.1$, $p < .04$.

By examining respondents' ratings in Forms A, B, C, and D, we can see the effects of the filter questions when respondents have had a chance to reaffirm their self-concepts. In this case, the pattern of ratings is quite different. There are no differences in rated self-interest regardless of whether respondents had attempted to answer difficult (4.20 and 4.30) or easy (4.20 and 4.30) filter questions. The self-perception effect has been eliminated.

Of course, the most stringent test of the affirmation hypothesis would be a comparison of respondents' ratings following the difficult filter question when they either have or have not had a chance to reaffirm their self-concept. As can be seen in Forms C and E, the ratings are higher following affirmation (4.20) than following no affirmation (3.70). This difference, however, is not statistically significant. Thus, we have little evidence that the self-perception effect has been *completely* eliminated, but we do have strong evidence that it has been at least reduced.

Implications

The results support our hypothesis that filter questions can alter respondents' self-evaluations as well as their self-perceptions. Based on earlier work (Martin & Tesser, 1989), we hypothesized that changes in self-evaluation would be accompanied by changes in the respondents' focus of attention. Immediately after answering filter questions, respondents focus on issues related to the filters. Immediately after failing to answer these questions, respondents focus on issues unrelated to the filters. This shift in attention produces (a) higher correlations between respondents' answers to filter-related questions compared with filter-unrelated questions when respondents have failed and (b) lower correlations between filter-related compared with filter-unrelated questions when respondents have succeeded.

Additional evidence of the operation of self-evaluation processes was obtained in the ratings of political interest. Previous research (Steele, 1988) had indicated that self-concepts can be affirmed even when the behavior that originally disconfirmed the self-concept is not changed. In our study, the respondents had still missed the two filter questions. After indicating their opinions on political issues, however, they apparently did not care as much. Failure respondents indicated less interest in politics than did success respondents only when they had not indicated their opinions on political issues.

We see our theoretical analysis as complementary, rather than as antagonistic, to the self-perception analysis of Bishop (e.g., Bishop, 1987; Bishop et al., 1982, 1984a, 1984b). The brooding and basking that we discussed may come about only after a self-perception process. More specifically, it may come about from observing ourselves engaging in behavior that is inconsistent with what we expected of ourselves. After failing to answer the filter questions, one not only categorizes oneself as less informed than one had hoped to be (self-perception) but also feels bad about being that way (disconfirmation of self-concept). It is the second step, we argue, that motivates the brooding and basking.

It is interesting in this light to examine the procedures previously used by Bishop and his colleagues in their attempts to eliminate the self-perception effect of filter questions. In one case (Bishop, 1987), respondents who had previously failed to answer difficult questions about politics were given a chance to answer an easy question about politics before indicating their interest. This had little effect on respondents' self-ratings. In terms of the present analysis, answering a question may undo the *self-perception* effect, but it may not undo the *blow to the self-concept*. Therefore, it should have little effect.

In other studies (e.g., Bishop, 1987; Bishop et al., 1984a, 1984b), respondents who had failed to answer political questions were given a chance to indicate their opinions on a variety of issues before rating their interest in politics. This also had little effect on respondents' self-ratings. In our study, however, having respondents indicate their opinions on filters eliminated the difference in reported interest of the success and failure respondents. Why did this work in our study and not the earlier ones? In the earlier studies, respondents expressed their opinions on issues unrelated to the filter questions. In the present experiment, it was respondents who indicated their opinions on issues related to politics who also reported equal interest regardless of whether they had or had not been able to answer the filter questions. The affirming effect of expressing opinions is apparently restricted to opinions related to the domain in which the self-concept was threatened.

The present findings also have implications for research on the role of communication rules in determining survey responses. More specifically, these findings extend the work of Strack et al. (1988) in two ways. First, they indicate that successful adherence to the given-new contract demands the expenditure of cognitive effort. We observed low correlations between the specific and general question only when respondents were not distracted by other issues. Second, the results indicate that the way in which two questions are introduced (i.e., related to the filters or not) can determine whether respondents will or will not successfully adhere to the given-new. Respondents will not exert sufficient cognitive effort to search for new information if they believe that the questions pertain to an issue that they do not wish to think about.

Application to Survey Research

The present results have several direct implications for survey research. They suggest, first of all, that conclusions about differences in the attitudes of "informed" versus "uninformed" respondents are questionable whenever the respondents are categorized on the basis of their answers to filter questions. Their ability or inability to answer such questions not only indicates the amount of knowledge that respondents have about a topic but also engenders processes that can influence the way in which they answer subsequent questions. Thus, the differences in informed and uninformed respondents' attitudes about George Bush, for example, may be due to differences in the amount of cognitive effort that they exert and not to any real differences in their attitudes.

Of course, one could argue that most surveys do not use questions in communication contexts, and therefore the effects observed in our study have no relevance to most surveys. It is important to make the distinction, however, between the specific procedures that we used and the general conceptual points being explored. We argue that answering filter questions can change respondents' focus of attention and that focus of attention can determine the effect that contexts have on respondents' answers. Forms of context effects, other than the given-new, are determined by the amount of cognitive effort that respondents exert (cf. Martin et al., 1990).

One could also argue that the effects that we have discussed can be easily circumvented by placing the filter questions at the end of the survey. In this way, both the informed and the uninformed respondents would presumably be exerting the same amount of effort in answering the questions. Although placing the filter questions last may eliminate their effects on other questions in the survey, it does not eliminate the effects of other factors that cause respondents to exert more or less cognitive effort. It is not unreasonable to believe, for example, that informed respondents would find more enjoyment in answering a survey in their area of expertise than would uninformed respondents. If so, then the informed respondents might exert more cognitive effort in answering the survey than might uninformed respondents. If this is true, then it follows that any differences in attitudes indicated by informed and uninformed respondents are just as likely to be due to the differences in effort that they exert as to any real differences in their attitudes.

Similarly, respondents may exert less cognitive effort when survey questions are asked over the telephone as opposed to in person, or respondents may exert more effort to answering questions in the beginning of a long survey than in the middle or near the end. We know also that people exert less effort when they perceive themselves as just another member of a group (Petty, Harkins, & Williams, 1980). Thus, respondents who feel that they are but one of several thousand respondents will exert less cognitive effort than will respondents who feel that their individual responses are needed.

Therefore, although the specific procedures that we have used may not appear directly relevant to survey work, we feel that the general points that we have made are relevant. Contextual stimuli have different effects depending on the amount of cognitive effort that respondents exert. Thus, any factor that motivates respondents to exert more or less cognitive effort could influence their responses and thus produce significant differences in reported attitudes where no actual differences exist.

The Overaccessibility of Accessibility Explanations

Recent attempts to cast survey responding in information-processing terms have helped survey researchers appreciate the complexities involved in the relatively simple act of generating a response to a survey question (see Hippler, Schwarz, & Sudman, 1987; Tourangeau, 1984). This recent work has challenged the assumption that in responding to a survey respondents merely retrieve some inner "true" score and translate it into an overt response. It appears, instead, that respondents construct many of their answers at the time that they are being asked to report them (for a review, see Feldman & Lynch, 1988).

Most of the recent research, however, has explored only the effect of differences in the accessibility of declarative knowledge. Answering a question about dating life, for example, increases the accessibility of memories related to dating, making these memories more influential in respondents' answers to subsequent questions. The present work suggests, however, that the *accessibility-of-*

declarative-memories view fails to capture the full complexity of survey responding. The same declarative information can be used in different ways depending on the procedures that respondents bring to bear (Martin, 1986), and the procedures that are brought to bear may or may not be successfully completed depending on the amount of cognitive effort that respondents exert (Martin et al., 1990). Thus, survey responses are influenced not only by differences in the information that respondents have but also by differences in how they *use* that information.

8
Serial Context Effects in Survey Interviews

Dancker D. L. Daamen and Steven E. de Bie

In survey methods research, the context effects of preceding questions on responses to survey items have been the subject of many interesting studies (see, for instance, Abelson, 1984; Bishop, Oldendick, & Tuchfarber, 1985; Bradburn, 1983; Carpenter & Blackwood, 1979; McClendon & O'Brien, 1988; McFarland, 1981; Perreault, 1975; Schuman, Presser, & Ludwig, 1981; Schuman & Presser, 1981; Sigelman, 1981; T. W. Smith, 1981c; and the chapters in this volume). In particular, effects of question order have been investigated. In most of these studies, the effects of only one or two preceding questions were considered, or the focus was on part–whole combinations of questions. Schwarz and his associates also studied the effects on responses when different ranges of response categories are offered (e.g., Schwarz & Hippler, 1987).

In psychophysics, range effects have often been analyzed in connection with so-called frequency effects (for a review, see Parducci, 1983). Here, however, "range" refers to the range of physical values of presented stimuli (e.g., width of squares in the range from 1 to 15 cm vs. squares in the range from 7 to 36 cm), not to the range of response categories offered to make the judgment. "Frequency" refers to the shape of the distribution of stimulus values in the (preceding) contextual set, achieved by presenting, for instance, more small than large stimuli.

Contrary to the question-order effects in survey methods research mentioned earlier, in these psychophysical experiments (e.g., Parducci & Perrett, 1971) the effects are due to a *series* of preceding stimuli. Ratings are made on scales with verbal categories ranging from, for instance, "very small" through "average" to "very large." According to Parducci and his colleagues, such category ratings of series of objects are a compromise between two tendencies:

1. The *range effect:* The tendency to adjust one's ratings to the range of stimulus values in the series (i.e., the difference between the two most extreme stimulus values). The judge assigns the stimuli perceived to be the most extreme ones to the most extreme response categories and distributes the rest of the stimuli proportionally in between. Thus, if squares of, for

instance, 1–15 cm are presented, they will be rated from very small to very large. In the context of presented stimuli, the stimulus of 15 cm is rated "very large." In a context of squares of 15–40 cm, however, the 15 cm square would be rated "very small." People will tend to use all response categories, no matter which range of physical stimulus values is presented. According to early papers of Parducci and his colleagues (e.g., Parducci, Calfee, Marshall, & Davidson, 1960), this effect depends only on the highest and the lowest physical stimulus values. In more recent work (Parducci, 1983; Parducci, Knobel, & Thomas, 1976), the subjective character of the range is emphasized and the relation with the physical range is assumed to be less direct.

2. The *frequency effect:* The tendency to assign the same number of stimuli to each one of the available rating categories. This tendency can be illuminated by a simple example: 20 stimuli are presented between 2 and 6 cm and only 5 stimuli between 6 and 20 cm, and these stimuli have to be rated on a 5-point scale. If subjects act completely in accordance with this tendency, they will assign 5 items to each category. Thus, subjects differentiate within the group of stimuli with the smallest widths. People try to use the scale in a maximally informative way by differentiating between stimuli as much as possible. This goal is better served by placing 5 items in each category than by placing, for instance, 20 items in one category and the remaining 5 in the other categories: "assigning the same number of stimuli to each category maximizes the number of bits of information transmitted (in the information theory sense)" (Parducci, 1983, p. 269). Thus, the frequency effect depends on the shape of the distribution of stimulus values (determined either by the frequency of presentation of identical stimulus values in the set or by the spacing of stimulus values included in the set). Of course, the "equal number of stimuli per category" rule is not something people are necessarily aware of. In fact, probably no one will actually calculate how many stimuli may be put into one category.

Previous Research on Range and Frequency Effects

In a sophisticated research program covering the last three decades, Parducci and his colleagues quantified range and frequency effects and modeled their combined impact on category ratings in the *range–frequency model* (e.g., Parducci et al., 1960; Parducci & Perrett, 1971; Wedell & Parducci, 1988). The fit of the model in all experiments proved to be very good. Moreover, in a review, Parducci (1983) showed that the model fits data better than range-only models (Gravetter & Lockhead, 1973; Volkmann, 1951) or adaptation-level theory (Helson, 1964).

We will not treat the formal model here, since it is described extensively by Parducci (1983). What is important here is that category ratings are a weighted average of range and frequency effects. To illustrate the impact that range and frequency effects can have on category ratings, Figure 8.1 shows what happens to the mean category rating of one stimulus (S) presented in four different stimulus series. In this example, S is positioned in the middle of some arbitrary continuum (the base lines in the figure). In Figure 8.1A, stimulus S is presented in two contexts differing in the range of presented stimulus values. Both sets (RR and LR) are equally spaced (the differences between the stimulus values are equal). According to the range effect, the most extreme stimuli will be assigned to the most extreme rating categories (1 and 5). This is represented by the solid arrows. The dashed arrows show that owing to the difference in range, the mean rating of stimulus S in the right rectangular (RR) context will be lower than in the left rectangular (LR) context. This is an extreme example because, even in psychophysical experiments, the subjective range may extend beyond the end values of the stimulus series.

In Figure 8.1B, stimulus S is inserted in a right skewed (RS) and a left skewed (LS) set. The skewness of the stimulus distributions in this example is manipulated by altering the spacing of stimulus values.[1] For instance, in LS the stimulus values on the left side of the continuum are more closely spaced than on the right side. If subjects follow only the frequency tendency, they will assign three stimuli to each of the five rating categories while maintaining an ordinal scale. In that case the rating of stimulus S—belonging to the three highest stimulus values—will be 5. However, because ratings are a compromise between range and frequency effects, the mean rating of S will be lower. If we assume in this example that range and skewness effects have an equal impact on the ratings, S will be rated just above 4. Just as both range and skewness effects increase the category rating of S in the LS context, they decrease the rating in the RS context. As a consequence, the mean rating of stimulus S differs considerably between LS and RS. In the rectangular contexts (Figure 8.1A), no skewness effects are to be expected. Differences between the ratings of S in LR and RR, therefore, are less pronounced than between those in LS and RS.

In the extreme example of Figure 8.1B, range and skewness effects affect the mean category rating in the same direction. Of course, both effects could countervail, for instance, in a context with restricted "left" range (low stimulus values) and negative skewness. In such a case, the range effect would have an increasing effect on the rating, whereas the skewness effect would decrease the rating.

It has generally been assumed that scale values are virtually the same irrespective of the number of rating categories (i.e., that scale values on 5, 7, or 9-point scales may be linearly translated into each other). This assumption was challenged by experimental results of Haubensak (1981), Parducci (1982), Parducci and Wedell (1986), and Wedell and Parducci (1988). This research clearly showed that differences in the frequencies of contextual stimuli have more impact on category ratings as the number of rating categories decreases. For example, con-

---

[1] Therefore, we prefer to use the term "skewness effect" instead of "frequency effect."

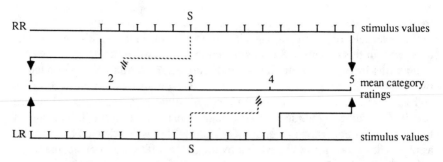

A. RR is a Right Rectangular Distribution with Restricted Range (High Stimulus Values) and Equal Spacing. LR is a Left Rectangular Distribution with Restricted Range (Low Stimulus Values) and Equal Spacing.

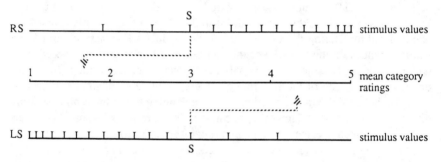

B. RS is a Right Skewed Distribution with Restricted Range (High Stimulus Values) and Negative Skewness. LS is a Left Skewed Distribution with Restricted Range (Low Stimulus Values) and Positive Skewness.

FIGURE 8.1. Mean Category Rating of One Stimulus (S) in Two Different Contexts of 14 Stimuli

textual skewing had a greater effect on the mean ratings of the size of squares when judged on a 5-category scale than on a 9-category scale (Wedell & Parducci, 1988). This phenomenon is called the "category effect."

In one of his articles, Parducci (1982) hints at the possible relevance of range–skewness effects for survey research. Indeed, it is common practice in surveys to group series of questions sharing the same response scale, as, for instance, with Fishbein's belief scales ("very likely" to "very unlikely"). What is more, Dillman (1978, p. 140) advises as part of his widely used Total Design Method to put similar questions directly beneath one another and repeat the wording of the response scale, which very much resembles the task in Parducci's experiments. Range–skewness effects, therefore, are to be expected.

There are at least three important differences between survey items and the aforementioned psychophysical experiments. First, in Parducci's experiments, subjects are confronted with perceptible objects, whereas in surveys, respondents generally are asked beliefs or opinions not linked directly to perceptible objects.

Second, although items in surveys may vary on more than one dimension, stimuli in nearly all range–frequency experiments differed on only one dimension. This dimension mostly was psychophysical—for example, numerical magnitude (Parducci et al., 1960; Parducci & Marshall, 1961), sweetness of taste (Riskey, Parducci, & Beauchamp, 1979), and sizes of geometrical figures (Haubensak, 1981; Parducci, 1982; Parducci & Perrett, 1971; Parducci & Wedell, 1986). Recently "social" stimuli have been used—for example, physical attractiveness of faces shown on photographs (Wedell, Parducci, & Geiselman, 1987), happiness expressed by schematic drawings of faces (differing in the shape of the mouth only) and ratings of happiness of life events expressed by short verbal descriptions (Wedell & Parducci, 1988), satisfaction with test scores and wages (R. H. Smith, Diener, & Wedell, 1989), and "fair" allocations of salaries given merit ratings and "fair" assignments of taxes given salaries (Mellers, 1986; Mellers & Birnbaum, 1983). However, nearly all of these "social" stimuli differed in only one respect. This distinction between variation on one or more than one dimension can be important. For instance, hardly anyone reading the statement, "The small man was stung by the big wasp," will think that the man is smaller than the wasp. The man obviously is judged to be small compared to other men and the wasp is big compared to other wasps. The judgment to call something "big" or "small" is established by comparison with similar objects. More generally, the decision on which *class* a particular object belongs to can have a dramatic effect on the labeling of the extent to which that object possesses a certain quality. The same man, 1.80 meters tall, will be called small or tall depending on how he is introduced: as a professional basketball player or as a successful jockey. Manipulating the selection of basketball players presented (changing the context of judgment) may leave the ratings of jockeys in the same rating task unaffected because these human beings are judged to belong to different domains. In a study dealing with ratings of weights, Brown (1953) found that an anchor weight, in order to influence the subjective rating scale, must be perceived as a member of the same class of objects as the other weights: If the anchor differed in shape from the stimuli in the series, its influence decreased dramatically. Experiments in which circles and squares were presented in consecutive trials showed that subjects were able to keep the square and circle domains separated and to make independent judgments (Parducci et al., 1976). If survey items in a series differ on more than one dimension, respondents may allocate them to different classes. If they do so, contextual manipulation may only affect ratings within the same class of stimuli.

The third difference particularly concerns the present study, in which probability ratings are asked. In the psychophysical experiments, there is always a minimum value for the stimuli (zero point) but no maximum; for instance, there is always a square of a bigger physical size conceivable.[2] According to Zoeke and

---

[2]Only the size of the projection screen in these experiments might serve as a maximum.

Sarris (1983), ratings are influenced more when the stimulus scale is limited only on its lower end and open toward the upper end than when the scale has natural endpoints on both sides. In our experiments, both a minimum (probability of 0%) and a maximum (probability of 100%) are present, so that, in line with their findings, we should expect less influence.

Notwithstanding these differences, range–skewness effects may be expected in surveys with characteristics as described above. To the best of our knowledge, skewness effects have never been studied in a survey-like setting, that is, a setting in which subjects are asked to rate objects of thought instead of perceptible stimuli presented to them by the experimenter. Effects of manipulation of the range of the item series, on the other hand, have been demonstrated in questionnaires. For instance, Fehrer (1952) constructed three scales from the items of a Thurstone scale of attitudes toward war. The two experimental scales had a restricted range: A "militaristic" scale (M) was constructed by omitting the most pacifistic items, and a "pacifistic" scale (P) was truncated at the militaristic end. The control scale had a full range. Fehrer found that her respondents rated the common items on the average more pacifistic in the M-scale condition and more militaristic in the P-scale condition. The shifts were limited to certain items, namely, those near the truncated ends of the experimental scales. Upshaw (1962) and Ostrom (1966) also showed that items included in a set of predominantly favorable statements were rated as less favorable than were items included in a set of predominantly unfavorable statements.

Field Experiment on Range–Skewness Effects

In the present study, the main research question was to what extent range and skewness effects can influence survey results. We chose a scale for subjective probability as the common response scale, just as in the widely used belief scales (Fishbein & Ajzen, 1975). A series of questions was asked about the probability of occurrence of events of a varying nature. In the light of the effects to be investigated, a choice had to be made for one kind of rating task. Of course, our choice was an arbitrary one, and the experiment could have been conducted with other tasks as well.

Preliminary Study

In a preliminary study, sets of stimuli were judged by 120 respondents in a "neutral" context. By "neutral" we mean that the stimuli were presented in "rectangular" sets (equally spaced according to the judgments of three judges), with the full stimulus range of 0%–100%, and that every effort was made to minimize range–skewness effects. Probabilities had to be estimated in either ratios or percentages. Each stimulus was presented on a different page of the questionnaire to avoid insight into previous ratings. After every fourth stimulus, a distraction task was inserted, such as mentioning the last letter of the name of a famous person, to divert respondents from their preceding responses. The mean ratings of this pretest were then used to compose sets with different ranges and spacing of stimuli (conditions). (For a detailed description, see Daamen & de Bie, 1989.)

Hypotheses

Three hypotheses about range–skewness effects were formulated:
- H1. Category ratings of probabilities will be higher if these ratings are preceded by a set of low probabilities than if they are preceded by a set of high probabilities.[3]
- H2. Preceded by a set of low probabilities, category ratings of probabilities will be higher if this set is positively skewed than if this set is rectangular.
- H3. Preceded by a set of high probabilities, category ratings of probabilities will be lower if this set is negatively skewed than if this set is rectangular.

Method

Design

Conditions for the experiments were designed as pairwise counterparts, with an overlap area in the middle. Conditions differed in the midpoint of the range of presented stimuli: In "left" conditions, stimuli were presented with pretest probabilities between 0% and 66%, whereas in "right" conditions, pretest values of presented stimuli ranged from 33% to 100%. Seven items in the overlap area (33% to 66%) were common to all experimental conditions. Together with some other items common to only the "right" or the "left" half of the experimental conditions, these were called "focal stimuli." Included were 17 of these stimuli. All other stimuli were called "contextual stimuli." It will be clear that range–skewness effects can occur only when people have an idea about the distribution of stimuli to be rated. Therefore, ratings of the focal stimuli were always asked at the end of the rating task, after ratings of the contextual stimuli had been given.

In Figure 8.2 the experimental design is visualized. As one can see, the distribution of stimulus values differs per condition. In the upper part of the figure, the left skewed conditions (LS9 and LS5) and the right skewed conditions (RS9 and RS5) are presented; in the lower part, the left rectangular condition (LR) and the right rectangular condition (RR) are shown. The distribution of LS9 and of LS5 is the same, but these conditions differ in the number of categories of the rating scale (9 vs. 5 categories). The same holds for RS9 and RS5.

Three experimental factors were varied systematically in the design:
1. The *spacing* of the stimuli. Skewing was manipulated by offering more

---

[3]Low and high probabilities were determined from mean ratings in the preliminary study.

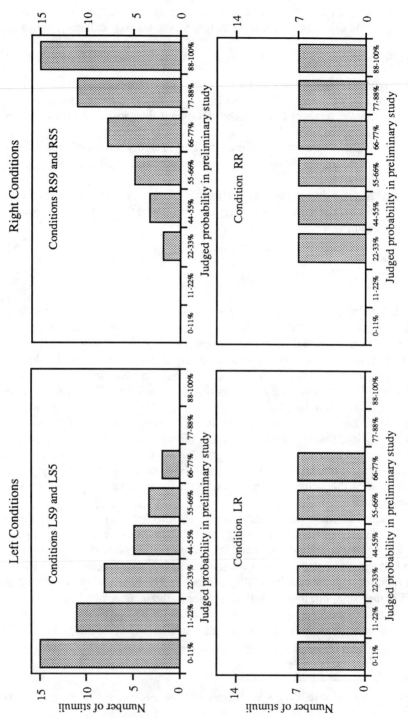

FIGURE 8.2. Experimental Design

stimuli whose pretest values were (very) low (positive skewing in LS9 and LS5) or (very) high (negative skewing in RS9 and RS5). In the rectangular conditions (LR, RR), spacing of stimulus values was equal.

2. The stimulus *range,* defined by the highest and lowest pretest value of stimuli offered in the condition. In "left" conditions, the range was 0%–66%, and in the "right" ones, it was 33%–100%.
3. The *number of rating categories*: 5 in LS5, RS5, LR, and RR; 9 in LS9 and RS9.

Presentation of Contextual and Focal Stimuli

First the contextual stimuli were presented to "set" the context, with a fixed pair of stimuli to start the sequence and one fixed stimulus in the middle of the series. The order of the other contextual stimuli was random and differed for each respondent. The fixed starting pair represented both endpoints of the range of stimuli to come (either 0%–66% in LS and LR or 33%–100% in RS and RR) to establish a notion of the stimulus range as soon as possible. The focal stimuli (see Table 8.1) were presented in two fixed orders in left and in right conditions.[4]

Items were presented on cards. In the 5-point scale conditions, respondents rated the probability of the events by putting the cards down on a sheet with one column for each of the five (verbal) response categories with the labels "high," "rather high," "moderate," "rather low," and "low." In the 9-point scale conditions, four categories were added with the labels "this certainly will happen," "very high," "very low," and "this has no chance at all." Because cards had to be put down like tiles, both the number of stimuli assigned to each category and the content of each stimulus stayed in sight of the respondent. Interviewers were instructed to see that the rating task was completed in one smooth run. Once having finished with the job, respondents were offered a last opportunity to reconsider and maybe change their ratings.

Sample and Fieldwork

Respondents were inhabitants of the city of Leiden (The Netherlands) who had volunteered to cooperate in social science surveys and agreed to have a record of their names and demographic characteristics kept at the University of Leiden. Out of this pool of volunteers, only people with secondary (general or professional) education were invited to cooperate. If education level influences susceptibility to range–frequency effects, this homogeneity assured comparability between con-

---

[4]In a control condition with equally spaced stimulus values and a full range, one half of the 40 respondents were presented the "left" order of focal stimuli, the other half the "right" order. There were no significant differences in mean ratings for the focal stimuli between respondents with one order of presentation and respondents with the other order (none of the F values came even close to significance). Therefore, we may conclude that differences in ratings due to range–frequency effects in this study are not confounded with order effects within the set of focal stimuli.

TABLE 8.1. Wording of Focal Stimuli[a]

All Conditions
  1. John, Peter, and Charles draw straws. What chance has John to draw either the shortest or the longest straw?
  2. In an arbitrary polling booth in the Netherlands, the first one to record one's vote is a woman.
  3. If we in the Netherlands would use coal on a large scale (i.e., 30-40% of total energy needs) to generate electricity, this could cause acid rain.
  4. An arbitrary Dutchman lives in an owner-occupied house.
  5. If the number of TV broadcasting hours is increased, this can cause more children to become addicted to TV.
  6. If we in the Netherlands would use nuclear energy on a large scale (i.e., 30-40% of total energy needs) to generate electricity, this could cause a higher birth rate of abnormal children.
  7. In a school class with 30 pupils, 20 have blond hair. How big a chance is there that a blond-haired pupil has the best mark on a test?

Conditions LS9, LS5, and LR
  8. An arbitrary Dutchman this year takes a coach to go away on holiday.
  9. One time our planet will be attacked by inhabitants of other planets.
 10. An arbitrary telephone number ends with a 3 or 4.
 11. The problem of unemployment will be solved before 1995.
 12. Somebody takes part in a taste test. This person likes Pepsi-Cola better than Coca-Cola.

Conditions RS9, RS5, and RR
 13. Somebody throws a die and has two or more pips.
 14. An arbitrary Dutchman eats bread at least once a month.
 15. An arbitrary person who addresses you turns out to be right-handed.
 16. An arbitrary Dutchman is shorter than 1.95 meters.
 17. A piece of bread with butter and marmalade falls on the floor face down.

[a]Focal stimuli were presented after presentation of 32 (LS9, LS5, RS9, and RS5) or 30 (LR and RR) contextual stimuli. All cards ended up with "This chance is . . . ."

ditions. Of the 352 people invited, 240 were actually interviewed.[5] An equal number of men and women were assigned to each of the six subsamples of 40 people.

Fieldwork was performed by professional interviewers in April–June 1988. Interviews were held face-to-face with respondents in their homes. Interviewers were trained and had to perform pilot interviews before starting the actual interviews. They were not informed of the aim of the study.

---

[5]The number of refusals was 49; the remaining 63 did not cooperate because of other reasons (mostly "not at home").

Results

Range–Skewness Effects: Left versus Right Conditions

Hypothesis 1 implies that category ratings for the seven common focal stimuli will be higher in "left" than in "right" conditions. Multivariate one-way analyses of variance are used to evaluate this. Overall, these category ratings indeed are significantly higher in LS9 than in RS9, $F(7,71) = 2.66$, $p < .01$, one-sided; in LS5 than in RS5, $F(7,70) = 3.51$, $p < .01$, one-sided; and also in LR than in RR, $F(7,72) = 3.32$, $p < .01$, one-sided.

The fact that these three multivariate (Hotelling's) tests are significant does not imply that all seven category ratings are significantly higher in the "left" conditions than in the "right" conditions. In fact, between LS9 and RS9 only two of the seven focal stimuli show, significantly, the expected difference in ratings: Focal Stimulus 2 ($M_L S9 = 6.45$ and $M_R S9 = 5.69$, $F(1,77) = 6.79$, $p < .01$) and Focal Stimulus 4 ($M_L S9 = 6.08$ and $M_R S9 = 5.18$, $F(1,77) = 9.79$, $p < .001$).

Table 8.2 presents results for the seven focal stimuli in LS5 and RS5. On the individual stimulus level, differences for three stimuli are highly significant, for two stimuli not significant but close, and for two other stimuli not nearly significant.

Figure 8.3 illustrates for one focal stimulus the range–skewness effects in LS5 versus RS5. In LS5 subjective probabilities are more often "rather high" or "high" than in RS5. In this last condition, ratings are more often "moderate" or "rather low."

As noted above, a multivariate test shows that, overall, the category ratings for the seven focal stimuli are also significantly higher in LR than in RR. Mainly the ratings of two focal stimuli contribute to this overall difference: Focal Stimulus 2 ($M_L R = 3.38$ and $M_R R = 2.90$, $F(1,78) = 5.79$, $p < .01$) and Focal Stimulus 4 ($M_L R = 3.50$ and $M_R R = 2.93$, $F(1,78) = 11.52$, $p < .001$). These are the two stimuli that also showed the greatest differences between the skewed conditions (LS9 vs. RS9 and LS5 vs. RS5).

Hypothesis 1 can be maintained. It is noticeable that ratings for three focal stimuli never differ significantly between "left" and "right" conditions, namely, Focal Stimuli 3, 5, and 6.

Range–Skewness Effects and Number of Response Categories: 9-Point versus 5-Point Scales

In the first section, we introduced the so-called category effect: a larger effect of contextual skewing when ratings are given on a response scale with fewer categories. Theoretically, this effect is only to be expected when skewing is caused by repeated presentation of stimuli (Parducci & Wedell, 1986). Nevertheless, we evaluated whether the category effect occurred in the present study (in which skewing is caused by unequal spacing). A two-way multivariate analysis of variance was performed with Condition (left vs. right) and Number of Categories

TABLE 8.2. Differences in Mean Ratings for Seven Focal Stimuli between LS5 and RS5

Stimulus Number and Short Description	Mean Category Rating (Scale 1 to 5, Low = 1, High = 5)		F Value	p (One-Tailed Probability)
	LS5	RS5		
1. Draw straws	3.75	3.44	2.16	0.073
2. Woman votes first	4.00	3.26	9.42	0.002
3. Coal causes acid rain	4.00	3.68	1.99	0.081
4. Dutchman lives in owner-occupied house	3.75	3.11	13.08	0.000
5. Children addicted to TV	3.35	3.29	0.06	0.404
6. Nuclear energy causes more abnormal children	2.63	2.82	0.52	0.476[a]
7. Blond-haired pupil has best mark	4.03	3.58	6.66	0.006

[a]Two-tailed probability.

(9 vs. 5) as factors and with the category ratings[6] of the seven common focal stimuli as dependent variables. Of course, a main effect of Condition exists, $F(7,147) = 5.88$, $p < .001$, one-sided: In conformity with Hypothesis 1, category ratings of focal stimuli are higher in left conditions (LS9 and LS5) than in right ones (RS9 and RS5). Also a main effect of Number of Categories exists, $F(7,147) = 2.38$, $p < .05$: Ratings are somewhat higher in the 5-category conditions than in the 9-category ones. However, the Condition × Number of Categories interaction is not significant, $F(7,147) < 1$, NS. Consequently we can conclude that in our study range–skewness effects are not reduced by offering a rating scale with more categories.

Skewness Effects within Left and within Right Conditions

In terms of our experimental design, Hypothesis 2 means that category ratings for focal stimuli have to be higher in LS5 (positively skewed) than in LR (rectangular).[7] LS5 and LR have 12 focal stimuli in common. With multivariate one-way analysis of variance, we evaluated whether category ratings for these 12 focal stimuli on the whole are higher in LS5 than in LR. This is the case, $F(12,65) = 1.82$, $p < .05$, one-sided. In Table 8.3, the results for the individual stimuli are given. Differences in ratings of five focal stimuli are significant. Focal Stimuli 2, 7, and 8 especially contribute to this multivariate overall difference. Differences in ratings for two focal stimuli are close to significance; the

---

[6]In this analysis, the ratings on the 9-point scale of conditions (LS9 and RS9) are linearly transformed into a scale from 1 to 5 to make these ratings comparable with those in LS5 and RS5.

[7]Comparison of LS9 with LR (or of RS9 with RR) is less obvious because of the main effect of Number of Categories described above.

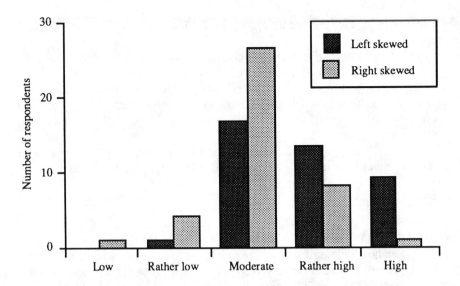

FIGURE 8.3. Range Skewness Effects for One Focal Stimulus in LS5 and RS5. Histogram of Ratings of Focal Stimulus 4 ("An arbitrary Dutchman lives in an owner-occupied house. This chance is...").

TABLE 8.3. Differences in Mean Ratings for 12 Focal Stimuli between LS5 and LR

Stimulus Number and Short Description	Mean Category Rating (Scale 1 to 5, Low = 1, High = 5)		F Value	p (One-Tailed Probability)
	LS5	LR		
1. Draw straws	3.75	3.58	0.65	0.212
2. Woman votes first	4.00	3.40	8.09	0.003
3. Coal causes acid rain	4.00	3.61	2.85	0.048
4. Dutchman lives in owner-occupied house	3.75	3.47	2.06	0.078
5. Children addicted to TV	3.35	3.13	0.58	0.224
6. Nuclear energy causes more abnormal children	2.63	2.71	0.08	0.776[a]
7. Blond-haired pupil has best mark	4.03	3.45	5.59	0.011
8. Dutchman takes coach	3.75	3.11	8.91	0.002
9. Our planet attacked	1.38	1.34	0.06	0.406
10. Telephone number ends with a 3 or 4	3.13	2.79	2.29	0.067
11. Unemployment solved before 1995	1.70	1.32	4.32	0.021
12. Pepsi tastes better than Coca-Cola	3.13	2.97	0.45	0.252

[a]Two-tailed probability.

category ratings for the remaining five focal stimuli hardly differ between LS5 and LR.

Based on these analyses, our conclusion is that within left conditions, positive skewing of the preceding set indeed increases the category ratings.

According to Hypothesis 3, category ratings for focal stimuli have to be lower in RS5 than in RR. Again a multivariate one-way analysis of variance was performed. Since Hotelling's test was not significant, $F(12,65) = 1.44$, NS, there is no support for this hypothesis.

The conclusion is that positive skewing (within left conditions) does affect category ratings, whereas negative skewing (within right conditions) does not.

Discussion

Our results can be summarized as follows:

1. Category ratings of probabilities are higher if these ratings are preceded by (the rating of) a set of positively skewed low probabilities than if they are preceded by a set of negatively skewed high probabilities. The combined effect of different midpoint of stimulus range and different skewness is clearly demonstrated by differences in category ratings of probabilities between left and right conditions. Differences in mean probability ratings of the same event are up to 15% (3/4 scale point on a 5-point scale) due to range–skewness effects. This first conclusion applies to the face-to-face interviews of the present study. In these interviews, respondents were aided in gaining insight into the distribution of their ratings and were offered the opportunity to change the ratings. One could argue that this is not a common task in most surveys. However, in a follow-up study we conducted telephone interviews and replicated the conditions LS5 and RS5. Of course, in these telephone interviews no such visual aid and no such opportunity to change ratings were offered, and we still obtained the same results—ratings of 5 of the 7 common focal items showed significant differences in the expected direction (see Daamen & de Bie, 1990).[8]

2. The range–skewness effects are not reduced when ratings are given on a scale with 9 instead of 5 categories. This result is in line with the extended range–frequency model formulated by Parducci & Wedell (1986): A category effect is only to be expected when skewness is caused by the repeated presentation of identical stimuli, and it will not occur when skewness is caused by unequal spacing. Whenever a series of items in a survey is skewed, it will be because of unequal spacing (of course, frequent repe-

---

[8] We expected range–skewness effects to be stronger in our face-to-face mode (with visual aid) than in the telephone mode. The major reason for this expectation was "the ability to see an entire set of questions in mail and other self-administered surveys . . . and the lack of this ability in telephone surveys" (Tarnai & Dillman, chap. 9, this volume). However, we found no significant mode effects.

tition of the same questions is not a common practice). Thus, in surveys, the number of rating categories will not influence the strength of range–skewness effects.

3. The significant (although small) difference between ratings in LR and RR shows that varying only the range of the preceding set has some impact on probability ratings.

4. A separate effect of positive skewing exists, whereas negative skewing alone has hardly any effect in the present study. Stronger range–skewness effects in positively than in negatively skewed conditions have been previously reported (Haubensak, 1981), but this is the first study in which no effect of negative skewing is found. It is tempting to speculate about the implications for survey research of the absence of this effect. However, because we can not come up with a convincing explanation and because there are numerous studies in which a negative skewing effect did occur, we think that it is wise to suspend these speculations pending further evidence.

One finding is noticeable: the fact that some focal stimuli show no significant range–skewness effects in any of the conditions. Remarkable about these focal stimuli is that they are the "opinion" questions that we added to the set of focal stimuli for comparison with other studies. Owing to this finding, we realized that these stimuli had no comparable items in the contextual set. As can be seen in Table 8.1, focal stimuli can be divided into three kinds: computable stimuli such as Focal Stimulus 1 ("John, Peter, and Charles draw straws . . . "), "frequentistic" stimuli such as Focal Stimulus 4 ("A Dutchman lives in an owner-occupied house"), and "nonfrequentistic" stimuli such as Focal Stimulus 9 ("One time our planet will be attacked by inhabitants of other planets)."[9] The contextual items mainly are "frequentistic" and to a lesser extent "nonfrequentistic." Computable items are a minority. Opinion items such as Focal Stimulus 3 ("Use of coal could cause acid rain"), 5 ("Increasing TV broadcasting hours can cause more children to become addicted to TV"), and 6 ("Use of nuclear energy could cause a higher birth rate of abnormal children"), however, are absent among the contextual stimuli. Ratings of "frequentistic" stimuli show the largest differences between conditions. We believe that opinion items are not affected because they belong to a stimulus class not represented in the preceding set of contextual stimuli. Recently we found some support for this hypothesis of a lack of homogeneity in the set of contextual and focal stimuli.[10]

---

[9]By "frequentistic" stimuli, we mean events that occur in a repetitive fashion and thereby permit specification of likeliness in terms of relative frequency of occurrence. By nonfrequentistic stimuli, we mean events that, while uncertain, are nonrepetitive and unique (Howell & Burnett, 1978).

[10]As part of a follow-up experiment, we interviewed 40 respondents (out of the same pool of volunteers and with the same demographic characteristics as those in the present study). We asked them to judge the dissimilarity between focal and contextual

An alternative explanation might be that for the rating of "frequentistic" stimuli, knowledge about the relative frequency of occurrence is needed. Absence of this knowledge might cause uncertainty and increased proneness to range–skewness effects. Opinions, on the other hand, do not necessarily require knowledge and may be given with more certainty. However, we did not find differences in certainty ratings between "frequentistic" and "opinion" focal stimuli. Moreover, we did not find any influence at all of (un)certainty on the strength of range–skewness effects (Daamen & de Bie, 1989). Consequently we consider this alternative explanation unlikely. Further research on this topic is worthwhile.

Some survey practitioners may consider our demonstrations of range–frequency effects irrelevant because probability judgments are not very common in "normal" surveys or because the series of items is longer than in a typical survey.[11] However, since our research is theory driven, we think the odds are that these effects will show up in other, more common, rating tasks as well. This, however, is a matter for further research. More experiments are needed to investigate the extent to which ratings in "real" surveys with an items-in-a-series format are influenced by range–skewness effects.

How should we deal with range–skewness effects in surveys? One could argue that contextual effects blur the "true" responses. From this point of view, range–skewness effects bias the ratings, cause error, and should be avoided. In psychophysics, Poulton (1979, 1989) takes this stand on the issue (to avoid some contextual effects, Poulton recommends, for instance, that each subject be asked only one judgment). In line with this approach, one could try in surveys to "break" the context: One could spread items that share the same response scale over the questionnaire and insert questions on different issues and with different response scales. The price that one pays for going against Dillman's (1978) good advice is probably confusion and frustration on the part of the respondent. An alternative to decrease error due to range–skewness effects would be to rotate the order of the items within the series: Because range–skewness effects will prob-

---

stimuli. More specifically, we asked them to pick 2 out of 10 focal stimuli that they believed to be the least similar to a specific contextual stimulus (7 of the 10 focal stimuli were the ones common to all conditions in the present study, the 3 other ones were relevant to the follow-up study). Respondents had to perform this task six times: They compared the 10 focal stimuli with 6 contextual stimuli (randomly chosen out of the contextual sets: there were 4 different samples of 6 stimuli, 2 drawn from the "left" contextual sets and 2 from the "right" sets). It appeared that the "opinion" focal stimuli are chosen most often as the most different from the contextual stimuli. These 3 focal stimuli (numbers 3, 5, and 6) were chosen significantly more often than chance (the z scores corrected for continuity are 2.67, 3.96, and 6.38, respectively, all $p < .01$).

[11]We had our focal stimuli preceded by series of 30 or 32 contextual stimuli (depending on experimental conditions), but psychophysical experiments show that range–frequency effects also occur in shorter series.

ably be weak or absent in the beginning and strongest in the end of the series, varying the order will equalize (but not eliminate) the effects.

A totally different stand on contextual effects in psychophysics is taken by, for example, Birnbaum. Context is viewed as "an integral part of the judgment process" (Mellers & Birnbaum, 1982, p. 600). There is no such thing as one "true" response. From this point of view, trying to rule out range–skewness effects in a questionnaire is naive. Ratings are relative, not absolute. There is no reason why the context that is made salient by the questionnaire is worse than the comparisons that a respondent makes spontaneously. Effects such as those of range and skewness of items in a series are lawful and eventually predictable. Knowledge about range and skewness of preceding contextual items is necessary to interpret the responses to a specific question, especially when this question is asked in different contexts in cross-sectional or longitudinal research. When this is the case and the interpretation really matters, it may be worthwhile to vary the context in order to learn its effect, that is, perform a preliminary study in which range, spacing, etc., of preceding items are manipulated (just as in the present study) to investigate the margins between which the ratings vary.

Acknowledgments. This research was partly funded by the Association of Social Research Institutes, Amsterdam. We would like to thank Jaco van Hoorn, Willem Meyer, and Peter van Rooy (students of the first author) for their enthusiastic and valuable contributions to this research and Norbert Schwarz and Roos Vonk for their helpful comments on a previous draft.

9
Questionnaire Context as a Source of Response Differences in Mail and Telephone Surveys

John Tarnai and Don A. Dillman

There are three sources for response effects in surveys: the survey task (mode of administration), the interviewer, and the respondent. Although most research has focused on response differences due to characteristics of the interviewer, and the respondent, research suggests that differences in the mode of administration are the major source of response effects (Bradburn, 1983). However, relatively little is known about the conditions under which response differences can be expected. The literature is mixed with respect to the extent of response differences between mail and telephone survey methods. The general consensus among survey researchers has been that mode of administration has only a modest effect on most survey responses (Singer & Presser, 1989, p. 187), although this view may be changing (Schwarz, Strack, Hippler, & Bishop, in press). Our purpose in this chapter is to present data testing whether some response differences between telephone and mail surveys are attributable to differences in the effect of the context established by the mode of administration.

Theoretical Background

Mail and telephone surveys present very different situations with respect to potential context effects. In telephone surveys, prior questions may serve as influences on questions by changing the meaning of later questions (Schuman & Presser, 1981). However, the influence of context is limited by what the respondent recalls of the questions as they are being asked. In mail and other self-administered questionnaires, respondents are able to look ahead and see what is to come; in fact, they have the capability of viewing the entire questionnaire. Thus, in mail questionnaires later questions as well as prior questions can provide context and can thereby influence responses. This type of context is most evident with questions presented as items in a series of questions using the same response format.

Differences between telephone and self-administered questionnaires that affect the emergence of response effects have been reviewed and summarized elsewhere (Schwarz et al., in press). The major differences between telephone and mail survey modes of administration include differences in (a) the auditory versus visual presentation of questions, (b) the sequential versus simultaneous presentation of questions, (c) the extent to which the pace of the interview is under the control of the respondent, and (d) the presence or absence of an interviewer. Schwarz et al. (in press) show that the impact of question order is greatly reduced in self-administered questionnaires, primarily because questions are available to the respondent simultaneously rather than sequentially as in telephone interviews. However, the impact of the context of related questions is likely to be greater in self-administered questionnaires than in telephone interviews, because respondents have more time to think about the questions as a whole. Respondents are under considerably more time pressure to produce a response in telephone surveys than in the self-administered mode. Under conditions of time pressure, respondents are more likely to show a "top of the head" tendency, that is, to report the first thing that comes to mind (Hippler & Schwarz, 1987).

Krosnick and Alwin (1987) have proposed a theory of response-order effects to explain differences in survey responses. Their theory suggests that visual presentation of questions, as in mail and other self-administered questionnaire formats, should be more likely to produce primacy effects, that is, an increased likelihood of selecting the first response alternative in a list. On the other hand, questions presented orally, as in telephone surveys, should be more likely to produce recency effects, that is, an increased likelihood of selecting the last response alternative in a list. Data supporting this theory come primarily from questions using long lists of response alternatives. It is unclear whether the theory holds for questions with relatively few response alternatives, although preliminary findings are not encouraging. Mingay and Greenwell (1989) failed to find recency effects in a telephone survey in which questions were read at a fast and a slow pace in a split-ballot sample design. It was hypothesized that under the fast-paced condition, respondents would be most likely to show recency effects and report the last response category heard, whereas in the slow-paced condition, it was predicted that respondents would have more time to rehearse the first items presented and be less likely to show a recency effect. Of four questions included in the experiment, no significant differences between the fast-paced and slow-paced conditions were found; additionally, no questions showed a recency effect, and one question showed a primacy effect. This is exactly opposite to the prediction of the Krosnick and Alwin theory.

The position taken here is that telephone survey respondents are more likely than mail survey respondents to show *both* primacy and recency effects; that is, respondents in telephone surveys are more likely than respondents in mail and self-administered surveys to use the end response categories. Mail questionnaire respondents are able to look at full pages of questions. They are able to consider answers to other questions more fully than they otherwise could when they answer individual items. One example of this phenomenon is when question items are presented in series and respondents are asked to use the same set of answer categories in responding to them. A mail survey respondent can see from the visual format of the questions that they will be using the same answer categories in response to several items. The opportunity to see this series of questions is not available to the telephone respondent. We hypothesize that because the entire series of items is available to the mail questionnaire respondent, the choice of response is affected in a way that is different from the telephone survey.

Telephone respondents must commit questions and answer choices to memory, at least for very short periods of time. Mail respondents, on the other hand, may reread items and use clues such as the order in which categories are presented in order to select responses. In telephone interviews the respondent must remember the response categories in order to give an accurate response, whereas in a mail survey the response categories are always in view. The greater the number of response categories that the respondent must remember, the more likely that some will not be remembered. We know that people have a higher probability of remembering the first and last items in a list than items in the middle of the list (Krosnick & Alwin, 1987). If memory plays a role in telephone surveys, then we should expect to find a greater use of extreme response categories in telephone surveys than in mail surveys.

Differences produced by these effects are compounded when vague quantifier answer choices are used in questions. Vague quantifiers are response categories that have no direct empirical referents, such as "strongly agree," "somewhat agree," "somewhat disagree," and "strongly disagree." When the response categories are vague, respondents have greater freedom to interpret the meaning of the choices differently. The boundaries between answer categories are inherently vague. The less clearly the boundaries between categories are defined, the greater the potential for different methods to elicit different answers. The use of vague quantifier answer choices makes it possible for a respondent to shift categories without doing something an outside observer could unequivocally define as lying, as when, for example, one claims to own a Volvo when one actually owns a Chevrolet. A respondent can shift from "strongly agree" to "somewhat agree" without risk of the interviewer being able to detect that the respondent is not telling the truth.

That the meaning of vague quantifiers is influenced by their context is demonstrated in a study by Pepper and Prytulak (1974). In this study, subjects provided numerical estimates of the frequencies implied by various vague quantifier terms, such as "very often," "often," "sometimes," "seldom," and "almost never," under conditions of no context, low-frequency context, or high-frequency context. Low-frequency contexts included earthquakes and airplane crashes, and high-frequency contexts included the occurrence of shooting in westerns (movies). As expected, the results of this study showed that the numerical estimates of frequencies implied by the vague quantifiers increased as the context changed from low- to high-frequency events; that is, the frequency implied by "often" in the low-frequency context was less than that implied in the high-frequency context. The findings of this study suggest that the context provided by questions influences the meaning that respondents give to vague quantifier response categories. Survey respondents given a low-frequency context would be expected to give different responses than those given a high-frequency context.

Additional evidence for such context effects is provided by Daamen and de Bie in chapter 8 (in this volume) on serial context effects in interviews. They investigated to what extent category ratings in surveys are influenced by the characteristics of a series of preceding questions that share the same response scale. Six conditions that varied in the number of rating categories in the series indicated that probability ratings of the same events are higher when preceded by a set of low-probability items than when preceded by a set of high-probability items. They also found this context effect to be stronger for related sets of questions. These findings were obtained in face-to-face interviews where the respondent used cards to see the entire range of response categories. Daamen and de Bie theorize that these results are due to a tendency for respondents to adjust their ratings to the range of stimulus values in a series of items (range effect) and the tendency to assign the same number of stimuli to each one of the available rating categories (frequency effect). These tendencies would be more pronounced in mail and self-administered surveys, where the entire range of questions in a series could be viewed by a respondent, than in telephone surveys, where the respondent would be unaware that a question was a part of a series until after several questions had been asked.

The context provided by questions is more evident in self-administered surveys than in telephone surveys because the respondent is able to see questions simultaneously rather than sequentially (Schwarz et al., in press). In this chapter, we seek to answer the question of whether the ability to scan ahead and see full questions and sets of questions influences responses. Our hypothesis is that the ability to see an entire set of questions in mail and other self-administered surveys is a form of context and the lack of this ability in telephone surveys is a major reason for differences in responses to the two methods.

Over the past few years, we have conducted several studies that compared answers to questions in mail and telephone surveys, and we have demonstrated consistent differences in responses to the same items among respondents from the same populations. The predominant finding of these studies is that differences occur not with all questions but primarily with questions that involve vague quantifier response choices of the kind typically found in attitude or opinion surveys. This difference is characterized by a tendency for telephone respondents to give responses at the extreme end of the response continuum, and often at the positive end of the response continuum. Mail survey respondents, on the other hand, are more likely to use the entire range of the response continuum.

Evidence of Telephone versus Mail Differences

One of the first major studies explicitly to compare mail, telephone, and face-to-face surveys was done by Hochstim (1967), who surveyed a sample of women in one California county about health issues. The design specified that after several attempts to survey respondents by the designated method, follow-ups by the other two methods would be used to increase the response rates. Hochstim found a number of mode differences that he attributed to social desirability bias. For example, he reported that whereas 30% of the mail survey respondents reported being in excellent health (as opposed to good, fair, or poor), 37% of the telephone respondents and 44% of the face-to-face respondents reported being in excellent health. Also, the mail survey respondents, in comparison with the face-to-face and telephone respondents, were more likely to report having discussed medical problems with their husbands. Hochstim explained this finding by suggesting that women might be embarrassed to tell an interviewer of such discussions but could easily check the "yes" box on a mail questionnaire.

Locander, Sudman, and Bradburn (1976) compared telephone with self-administered questionnaires left by an interviewer and picked up later, a technique that has some, but not all, of the qualities of a mail survey. Although differences were quite small, there was a tendency for overreporting of socially desirable behaviors (voter registration and having a library card) and underreporting of socially undesirable behaviors (bankruptcy, not voting in a primary, and being arrested for drunken driving) for telephone respondents in comparison with self-administered questionnaire respondents.

Mangione, Hingson, and Barrett (1982) compared self-administered, telephone, and face-to-face responses from a survey of the general population designed to collect data on drinking behavior and life events. A drop-off/pick-up strategy was used for the self-administered questionnaire. They reported that there were no differences between the self-administered questionnaire and the other methods on 12 demographic characteristics. However, they found that more middle response categories were used in the self-administered questionnaire than in the face-to-face interviews in answering some socially desirable questions about drinking behavior.

Siemiatycki (1979) compared mail, telephone, and face-to-face questionnaires for a health survey of the general population. He reported that fewer of the mail respondents compared with telephone respondents (24% vs. 29%) underreported doctor visits. Also, affirmative responses to some potentially embarrassing questions were more likely to be given by mail than by telephone respondents (39% vs. 31%). He concluded that the mail survey obtained more accurate data than did the telephone survey.

A study by Dillman and Mason (1984) was specifically designed to compare face-to-face, telephone, and mail questionnaires on a variety of questions. The general population survey, which resulted in 900–1,100 respondents completing each questionnaire type, contained a number of questions that used vague quantifiers. In this study, very few differences were found to exist on demographic characteristics and other questions not using vague quantifiers: Mail, telephone, and face-to-face interviews all obtained virtually the same distributions. However, noticeable and systematic differences were found for most of the questions using vague quantifiers.

One of the vague quantifier questions was a series of nine items that required respondents to assess several community issues as not a problem, a small problem, a medium problem, or a serious problem in their community. For *all* nine items, the telephone respondents were more likely to use the "not a problem" category than were the mail respondents. The differences ranged from a 6.7% to a 19.3% advantage for the telephone. Telephone respondents averaged a 15.2% greater endorsement of the "not a problem" category for these nine items than did mail survey respondents. Table 9.1 displays the items and the percentage of respondents choosing the extreme category for the telephone and mail surveys.

Respondents were also asked to respond to a set of semantic differential descriptions of their neighborhood that utilized a scale with endpoints of 1 and 7. The results for this set of items are displayed in Table 9.2. Telephone respondents were more likely to choose the extreme category on the *positive end* of the 7-point scale. Among the nine items, this advantage ranged from 0.8% to 13.8% in favor of the telephone for eight of the items. On the ninth item, there was a small advantage of 0.8% in favor of the mail questionnaire. Overall, telephone respondents averaged a 7.5% greater endorsement of the extreme positive endpoint of the continuum for the nine semantic differential items in comparison with the mail survey respondents.

The conclusion that we draw from this study is that telephone respondents are more likely to select the extreme positive end of the response continuum when making a response than are mail survey respondents, and this is true primarily for questions in a series using vague quantifier response categories. Our hypothesis is that the self-administered survey provides respondents with a context for responding to questions and that this context is lacking in telephone surveys.

Experimental Design

Interpretation of response differences between mail and telephone surveys is often confounded by differences in sample coverage of the population, response rates, respondent selection, and measurement differences (Bishop, Hippler, Schwarz, & Strack, 1988). To control for these factors and to obtain a clearer test of response differences between mail and telephone surveys, we conducted an experiment using university students to see whether the findings of the Dillman and Mason (1984) study on seriousness of community problems and quality of neighborhood could be replicated in a more controlled setting.

Modes of Administration

The design involved three different modes of administration of the same questionnaire. One group of students completed the questionnaire through a typical telephone interview format (Group A). A second group of students also completed the questionnaire through a telephone interview but had a copy of the questionnaire to view as the interview was being conducted (Group B). A third

TABLE 9.1. General Population Respondents Choosing "Not a Problem" in Response to Selected Issues[a] (%)

Issue	Telephone (N = 1,011)	Mail (N = 902)	Difference
1. Police protection	52.4	33.6	18.8
2. Quality of public schools	48.9	32.4	16.5
3. Availability of housing for low-income residents	18.4	10.0	8.4
4. Responsiveness of local officials to the concerns of residents	31.6	12.3	19.3
5. Availability of recreational and park facilities	70.8	53.4	17.4
6. Availability of basic medical services	73.7	58.7	15.0
7. Condition of streets, roads, and sidewalks	40.3	24.3	16.0
8. Residential street lighting	60.1	41.4	18.7
9. Availability of houses or apartments for people to rent	27.9	21.2	6.7
Average of 9 questions	47.1	31.9	15.2

[a]Question wording: "For each issue please tell me whether you believe it is not a problem, a small problem, a medium problem, a serious problem, or you don't know." Based on data reported by Dillman and Mason (1984).

TABLE 9.2. General Population Respondents Choosing "Extreme" Category on the Positive End of 7-Point Scale on Neighborhood Items[a] (%)

Item		Telephone (N = 1,011)	Mail (N = 902)	Difference
A. Noisy	Quiet[b]	25.4	24.6	0.8
B. Friendly neighbors[b] . .	Unfriendly neighbors	36.9	25.4	11.5
C. Buildings are poorly kept up	Buildings are well kept up[b]	32.5	27.8	4.7
D. Safe[b]	Unsafe	39.7	25.9	13.8
E. A lot of road traffic	No road traffic[b]	10.7	9.9	0.8
F. Crowded	Uncrowded[b]	30.1	26.0	4.1
G. Outdoor areas are well kept up[b]	Outdoor areas are poorly kept up	30.6	20.8	9.8
H. A lot of privacy[b] . . .	No privacy	33.6	20.2	13.4
I. Attractive[b]	Unattractive	30.7	21.6	9.1
Average of 9 items		30.0	22.5	7.5

[a]Question wording: "How would you rate your neighborhood and the area around it on a scale of 1 to 7. . . ."
[b]Based on data reported by Dillman and Mason (1984).

group of students completed the questionnaire through a self-administered format similar to a mail survey (Group C). Thus, Groups A and C were like the typical telephone and mail survey modes, respectively. Group B was designed to be like the typical telephone survey but with additional context provided by having a copy of the questionnaire to view at the time of the interview.

The design subdivided the telephone versus mail difference into two parts, so that the influence of both parts can be assessed. One part of the total difference in response is a test of the context effect. The second part is a test of the combined influence of other aspects of the mode difference including the effects of interviewer presence, control over interview pace, and memory.

This design offers three comparisons of interest. The first comparison, which compares Groups A and C, assesses whether telephone and self-administered modes produced overall response differences. This comparison replicates the general population survey results. The second comparison, which compares Groups A and B, is a test of the context effect, since the only difference between the two groups was the additional context provided by the copy of the questionnaire in Group B. The third comparison, which compares Groups B and C, tests whether other factors remain to influence responses after context has been controlled. Since both Groups B and C had a copy of the questionnaire to view, responses by both of these groups could be influenced by context. However, since Group B provided responses by telephone and Group C provided responses directly on the questionnaire, other factors, such as the effects of interviewer presence, control over interview pace, and memory might be involved in causing some of the response differences.

Thus, the experiment was designed to isolate potential context effects from other possible influences. We are particularly interested in the relative differences between Groups A versus B and Groups B versus C. If the A versus B differences are larger than the B versus C differences, then we can conclude that context has a greater effect than other effects. If the opposite occurs, then we can conclude that other effects are more influential than the context effect.

Methods

A brief three-page questionnaire was developed for administration to university students. Three social science classes of undergraduate students were asked to participate in the experiment. We met with the students in each class and randomly distributed envelopes to them. One-third of the envelopes contained instructions for the student to provide us with a telephone number; these students were informed that we would be calling them at home to complete a telephone interview (the telephone interview group). Another one-third of the students also received instructions for a telephone interview; however, this group also received a copy of a self-administered version of the questionnaire in a sealed envelope, which they were to take home and not open until instructed to do so by the telephone interviewer (the telephone interview plus questionnaire group). Last, one-third of the envelopes contained the self-administered version of the questionnaire, which students were asked to fill out in class (the self-administered group).

We attempted to call every student in the two telephone interview groups. Because not all students had telephones and not all students could be reached for the telephone interview, the final completed sample sizes for the three groups were 103 for the telephone questionnaire, 115 for the telephone interview plus questionnaire, and 123 for the self-administered questionnaire.

The questionnaire contained 28 questions. Of these, 4 were objective questions about the respondent's age, gender, year in school, and residence. No significant differences were found among the three groups on these variables.

The 24 remaining questions in the survey all used vague quantifier response choices. Two sets of 5 questions each were set up in a series with the same response choices to test the context effect. One set of 5 questions was an attempt to replicate the questions on the seriousness of community problems from the general population survey described in Table 9.1. For each of five problems appropriate to the student population, students were asked whether they believed it was not a problem, a small problem, a medium problem, or a serious problem for them. In a second set of five questions, students were asked to rank their residence (as opposed to their neighborhood) using a semantic differential 7-point scale as was done in the general public survey and reported in Table 9.2.

Students in all three groups were given the self-administered version of the questionnaire as a posttest approximately one month after the initial questionnaire data had been collected. Thus, we had two sets of data from respondents: an initial pretest version collected by telephone interview, telephone interview plus questionnaire, or self-administered questionnaire alone and a second administration posttest version collected entirely by self-administered questionnaire. The second administration of the questionnaire enabled each respondent to serve as his or her own control. Differences between time 1 versus time 2 responses would thus be affected only by differences in the mode of administration.

Results

The analyses of the questionnaire data focused on three primary issues: (a) evidence of response differences between telephone and mail (self-administered) modes of administration, (b) evidence of a context effect, and (c) evidence for noncontext effects. Tables 9.3, 9.4, and 9.5 present the results that address these three issues.

The first question to be examined was whether we would find response differences between the telephone interview (Group A) and the self-administered (Group C) experimental groups similar to those found between telephone and mail surveys. Therefore, we compared the percentages among the two groups for the response category of "not a problem" for the five questions about problems in the community. The results, reported in Table 9.3, show a very striking similarity to the results found in the general population survey in Table 9.1. For this

set of five questions, the percentage of students giving the extreme "not a problem" response ranges from 12.6% to 38.1% more for the telephone than for the
self-administered questionnaire (difference between Groups A and C). All five
differences are statistically significant by a chi-square test. Thus, the results are
similar and even more extreme in this more controlled setting than for the general population survey. The average difference over all five questions is 24.8 percentage points. Thus, the percentage of telephone respondents who reported that
an issue was "not a problem" in the community is greater by 24.8% than the
percentage of self-administered respondents who reported "not a problem" for
these issues.

We next compared responses obtained from the telephone interview group and
the telephone interview plus questionnaire group. In terms of how the questionnaire was administered, the only difference between these two groups is that the
latter group was instructed to view a copy of the questionnaire as the interview
was being conducted. This was intended to provide, in a telephone interview
situation, the kind of context normally found in a self-administered questionnaire. If context is a factor in producing response differences between telephone
and mail surveys, then we would expect significant differences between Groups
A and B.

For the five questions of Table 9.3, two significant differences between
Groups A and B were found. Both differences are in the hypothesized direction. In
addition, another difference is in the predicted direction but is not significant.
Overall, the average effect of context for this set of five questions is 6.5%,
which is not significant.

Comparisons between Groups B and C are of interest because they involve
two different modes, telephone and self-administered, but with context controlled,
since Group B respondents also had a copy of the questionnaire to view as the
telephone interview was being conducted. Differences found between these
groups would be attributable to noncontext effects because both groups were able
to view the questionnaire. From the last column of Table 9.3, it is clear that
there are large and significant differences between these groups. For the five
questions in Table 9.3, the overall average difference is 18.3%, indicating that
telephone respondents more frequently selected the extreme response category
than did self-administered respondents. All five differences and the average difference are statistically significant by a chi-square test.

Similar results were obtained for the second set of five questions, which asked
respondents to rate their residence on a 7-point scale. Table 9.4 presents the
results of the comparisons for these questions. Overall, the same pattern of differences is observed, although few of the differences are statistically significant.
The telephone interview versus self-administered questionnaire comparisons
(Group A vs. C) are all in the predicted direction. The percentage of telephone
respondents giving extreme responses on the positive end of the scale varies
from 2.8% to 5.6% greater than for the self-administered questionnaire alone.
The average difference between Groups A and C over all five questions is 4.3%.

None of the Group A versus B comparisons in Table 9.4 is significant,

TABLE 9.3. Student Respondents Choosing "Not a Problem" in Response to Selected Issues[a] (%)

Issue	Groups			Differences		
	A	B	C	A – C	A – B	B – C
Quality of shopping alternatives for students	25.0	18.4	7.2	17.8***	6.6	11.2**
Street and sidewalk lighting on campus	38.9	27.6	12.4	26.5***	11.3*	15.2***
Responsiveness of city officials to the concerns of students	20.8	21.8	8.2	12.6***	−1.0	13.6***
The availability of recreational and entertainment facilities	55.6	35.6	17.5	38.1***	20.0***	18.1***
Availability of basic medical services	48.6	52.9	19.6	29.0***	−4.3	33.3***
Average of 5 questions	37.8	31.3	13.0	24.8***	6.5	18.3***

[a]Question wording: "For each issue, please indicate whether you believe it is not a problem, a small problem, a medium problem, a serious problem, or you don't know."
Groups: A—Telephone interview $(N = 72)$.
    B—Telephone interview plus questionnaire $(N = 87)$.
    C—Self-administered $(N = 97)$.
Comparisons: A vs. C = Test of combined effects.
    A vs. B = Test of the context effect.
    B vs. C = Test of other effects.
Significance: * $p < .05$.   ** $p < .01$.   *** $p < .001$.

suggesting very little effect of context for this series of questions. In fact, the largest difference is in the opposite direction. The four other differences are, however, in the predicted direction.

For the Group B versus C comparisons in Table 9.4, the overall average difference is only 4.2%, and only four of the five differences are in the predicted direction. Telephone respondents more frequently selected the extreme response category on four of five questions. Only one of these differences, however, is statistically significant.

Despite the random assignment of respondents to the three experimental groups, there was some attrition of respondents. Thus, it could be argued that some of the observed differences are attributable to differences in the respondents. To address this possible concern, we also compared the questionnaire responses of the first administration with the second administration of the questionnaire. In this comparison, each respondent served as his or her own control. Since all three groups completed the second administration as a self-administered questionnaire, we compared the first and second administrations to see if response differences would be observed.

Table 9.5 presents the results of the first (pre) and second (post) administration of the questionnaire and the differences between the two administrations for

TABLE 9.4. Student Respondents Choosing the "Extreme" Category on the Positive End of 7-Point Scale on Neighborhood Items[a] (%)

Item		Groups			Differences		
		A	B	C	A – C	A – B	B – C
Noisy	Quiet	11.1	10.3	7.3	3.8	0.8	3.0
Friendly	Unfriendly						
neighbors	neighbors	26.8	26.4	24.0	2.8	0.4	2.4
Buildings are	Buildings are						
poorly kept up . . .	well kept up	20.8	16.1	16.7	4.1	4.7	−0.6
Safe	Unsafe	26.4	33.3	20.8	5.6	−6.9	12.5**
Attractive	Unattractive	20.8	19.5	15.6	5.2	1.3	3.9
Average of 5 questions		21.2	21.1	16.9	4.3	0.1	4.2

[a]Question wording: "How would you rate your neighborhood and the area around it on a scale of 1 to 7 . . . ."

Groups: A—Telephone interview($N = 72$).
    B—Telephone interview plus questionnaire ($N = 87$).
    C—Self-administered ($N = 97$).
Comparisons: A vs. C = Test of combined effects.
    A vs. B = Test of the context effect.
    B vs. C = Test of other effects.
Significance: ** $p < .01$.

both sets of five questions. The data in this table were subjected to a chi-square analysis (the McNemar test for the significance of changes; Siegel, 1956). For Group A, which received the telephone interview first and the self-administered questionnaire second, the results are similar to those found for the Group A versus C comparisons. Four of the first set of five questions are statistically significant. All of the differences are in the predicted direction, with a greater percentage of the telephone responses than the self-administered responses being in the extreme direction. For the second set of five questions, none of the differences is statistically significant, although three are in the predicted direction.

We also compared responses to the first and second administration of the questionnaire for Group B, which received the telephone interview plus questionnaire first and the self-administered questionnaire second. The pre versus post differences for the first five questions for Group B in Table 9.5 are all statistically significant. Thus, on these five questions, more extreme responses were given to the telephone pretest than to the self-administered posttest. A similar pattern is observed for the five semantic differential items, although only two of the five differences are significant. All five differences for Group B are in the predicted direction, with the telephone pretest responses being more extreme than the posttest self-administered responses.

Group C respondents completed a self-administered questionnaire on both the first and the second administrations. Thus, there should have been only small differences between the two. As indicated by the last column of Table 9.5, only

TABLE 9.5. Student Respondents Choosing the "Extreme" Category for the First (Pre) and Second (Post) Administration of Five Opinion Items and Five Semantic Differential Items, and Differences between the First and Second Administrations (%)

Item	Group A			Group B			Group C		
	Pre	Post	Diff.	Pre	Post	Diff.	Pre	Post	Diff.
Quality of shopping alternatives for students	25.0	13.9	11.1**	18.4	8.1	10.3**	7.2	3.1	4.1
Street and sidewalk lighting on campus	38.9	16.9	22.0***	27.6	9.2	18.4***	12.4	7.2	5.2
Responsiveness of city officials to the concerns students	20.8	15.3	5.6	21.8	10.5	11.4***	8.2	6.2	2.1
The availability of recreational and entertainment facilities	55.6	27.8	27.8***	35.6	19.8	15.9***	17.5	9.3	8.2*
Availability of basic medical services	48.6	26.4	22.2***	52.9	32.2	20.7***	19.6	15.5	4.1
Average of 5 questions	37.8	20.1	17.7	31.3	15.9	15.3	13.0	8.3	4.7
Noisy . . . . . . Quiet	11.1	11.3	−0.2	10.3	5.8	4.6	7.3	7.3	0.0
Friendly Unfriendly neighbors . . . . neighbors	26.8	22.5	4.2	26.4	18.4	8.1*	24.0	15.6	8.3*
Buildings are Buildings are poorly kept up . . well kept up	20.8	12.7	8.2	16.1	11.5	4.6	16.7	16.7	0.0
Safe . . . . . . Unsafe	26.4	22.5	3.9	33.3	9.5	13.8***	20.8	12.5	8.3*
Attractive . . . . Unattractive	20.8	21.1	−0.3	19.5	17.2	2.3	15.6	16.7	−1.1
Average of 5 questions	21.2	18.0	3.2	21.1	14.5	6.7	16.9	13.8	3.1

Groups: A — Telephone interview ($N = 72$).
   B — Telephone interview plus questionnaire ($N = 87$).
   C — Self-administered ($N = 97$).
Significance: * $p < .05$.   ** $p < .01$.   *** $p < .001$.

3 out of the 10 questions show significant differences. However, 7 of the 10 differences are positive, indicating that more extreme responses tended to be given to the first administration than to the second administration of the questionnaire. This pattern suggests that prior exposure to a questionnaire also serves as a context for responding to the same questions at a later time. This is a particularly interesting finding because of the implications for panel surveys. Changes in response observed from a first administration of a questionnaire to a later administration may in part be attributable to the context provided by the first administration rather than to other causes.

Summary

We began this chapter by suggesting that context was a primary reason for response differences often observed between telephone and mail surveys. We suggested that it was the ability, in the mail or self-administered survey, to scan ahead and see full questions and sets of questions that influenced responses. Our hypothesis was that the ability to see an entire set of questions (context) in mail and other self-administered surveys and the lack of this ability in telephone surveys are a major reason for differences in responses to the two methods.

This hypothesis was tested in an experiment in which students were randomly assigned to one of three survey groups, each of which received the same set of questions but different modes of administration: One group responded by a telephone interview mode; a second group also responded by telephone interview but had a copy of the questionnaire to view as the questions were being asked; and a third group completed the questionnaire in a self-administered setting. We reasoned that if context effects were operating in the self-administered mode, we could reduce response differences if we provided telephone interview respondents with a copy of the questionnaire to look at while the telephone interview was being conducted.

The design of this experiment allowed us to separate the effects of context from other factors involved in mode differences, such as the presence of an interviewer, control over the pace of responding, and memory. Response differences between the telephone and self-administered groups could be partitioned into two components (i.e., $A - C = [A - B] + [B - C]$). The first component, which represents the effects of context, is the difference between the telephone group and the telephone plus questionnaire group. The second component, which represents the effects of other factors, is the difference between the telephone plus questionnaire group and the self-administered group.

In general, the student experiment replicated the results of the general population survey, although even more dramatically. Differences in responses between the telephone and self-administered groups were even greater than those found in the general population survey. However, the results demonstrated that the effect of context are not as powerful as other mode differences. The response differences between the telephone interview and the telephone interview plus questionnaire groups were not as great as the differences between the telephone interview plus questionnaire and the self-administered groups. The results show that the additional context provided by having a copy of the questionnaire available while being interviewed on the telephone makes respondents less likely to use the extreme response categories.

However, even after controlling for context, substantial differences between the telephone interview plus questionnaire and the self-administered modes of administration persist. It is likely that other factors, such as the pace and control over the interview, the social effects of interviewer presence, and short-term memory effects, may be involved in causing some of these differences.

The question of whether survey respondents provide the same answers regardless of whether queried by mail, telephone, or face-to-face interviews has become a critical issue for the advancement of survey research. A major reason for examining the comparability of data collected by different methods is the increased interest in mixed mode surveys (Dillman & Tarnai, 1988). Increasingly, important societal surveys such as the Current Population Survey, the decennial Census, and various agricultural reporting service surveys are being done by mixed methods. A 1981 analysis of surveys approved by the Office of Management and Budget found that the number of mixed mode surveys actually outnumbered those being done by telephone or face-to-face methods alone (U.S. Office of Management and Budget, 1984). What was once posed as a question of whether the results of different surveys using different methods could be compared has now expanded to the question of whether results obtained by different methods from different portions of the same sample can be combined. Another important question is whether information collected from a panel of respondents by one method can be used to measure change from another time when data were collected by another method. This is a critical issue for survey research, since the measurement of change requires that differences in data collection not affect the dependent variable.

The data presented in this chapter suggest that one factor involved in producing response differences between telephone and mail survey methods is the context provided by being able to see the range of questions and response categories. As chapter 8 by Daamen and de Bie also shows, this effect of context is particularly likely for related sets of questions in a series.

10
Context Effects as Substantive Data in Social Surveys

Jaak B. Billiet, Lina Waterplas, and Geert Loosveldt

It has been widely recognized that in personal interviews the response to a specific survey question can be seriously affected by the context of that question, that is, the preceding parts of the questionnaire (Cantril, 1944; Schuman & Presser, 1981, pp. 23–56). More specifically, responses can be affected by a variety of factors: prior questions and their answers, response scales of preceding questions, introductions to questions, and tasks that the respondents have completed (Tourangeau & Rasinski, 1988). Context effects are response effects coming from one or more preceding questions (and answers) or from response scales belonging to previous questions.[1]

For several reasons, the occurrence of context effects is one of the most serious problems in survey research. First, a critical assumption underlying the generalization of survey results from sample to population is that the opinions of the respondents are not systematically altered by their being administered a standardized questionnaire (Dijkstra & van der Zouwen, 1977, pp. 51–52). Any attempt to generalize survey results becomes suspect if results might be a function of a particular question context, since that context is only operative in a specific sample of respondents. Second, the conclusions of trend studies and comparative research based on items in different questionnaires may rest on artifacts if the meaning of identical questions can vary according to the preceding questions. Third, the conclusions of experimental research on particular question wording are confusing if context effects caused by preceding questions intervene (Schuman & Presser, 1981, pp. 23–24).

Schuman's contention that artifacts can be conceived as data that are useful for gaining a deeper understanding of both questions and respondents in their social

---

[1] The term "context effects" is used here in a broader sense than in Schuman and Presser (1981, p. 23), where it refers to question-order effects involving transfers of meaning. For other more mechanical types of artifacts, they use the term "sequence effects."

context (Schuman, 1982; Schuman & Ludwig, 1983) caused a shift in the aim of question-wording experiments. Much more than looking for practical rules to reduce response errors, the *understanding* of the effects became the chief purpose. This is particularly true for context effects, since shifts in meaning are involved.

Cognitive and social psychologists have realized that the analysis of the process of answering attitude questions offers an opportunity to gain insight into cognitive processes (Graesser & Black, 1985). As Tourangeau and Rasinski (1988, p. 301) state, they "try to find the substantive meat in what others may well regard as methodological poison." An imposing number of recent articles in the field deal with question-wording effects in attitude measurement and survey research (Hippler, Schwarz, & Sudman, 1987).

Schuman and Presser (1981, pp. 313–314) were rather skeptical about the relevance of these studies for survey methodology. We do not share their opinion on that point. Although it is true that psychologists mainly use data from small groups out of "captive populations" such as campus cafeteria visitors or medical students (Schwarz, Bless, Bohner, Harlacher, & Kellenbenz, 1991; Schwarz, Strack, Müller, & Chassein, 1988) and concentrate their analysis on cognitive processes, the survey community may well derive important benefits from their theoretical insights. However, since survey researchers have no direct interest in cognitive processes but are concerned with public opinion in its social context, experiments involving large samples and standardized questionnaires that provide ample information about the respondent's social characteristics are indispensable (Schuman & Presser, 1981).

Following the lead offered by Schuman in chapter 2 of this volume, our chapter will show how survey researchers can analyze context effects as substantive data. The first section describes our data, and the second presents the replication of two "classical" question-order effects. The third main section provides a step-by-step, in-depth analysis of one particular and surprising context effect. In the concluding section, we discuss the relevance of this approach to survey research practice.

Method and Data

The context effects presented in this chapter derive from a set of split-ballot experiments with two random samples of 179 and 191 married women from the urban area of Ghent (Belgium), May–July 1987 (Billiet, Waterplas, & Loosveldt, 1988).[2] To the interviewers (all female) and the respondents, the study was

---

[2]Since voting is compulsory in Belgium, we were able to use the electoral registers (per municipality) of the general elections (October 1985), which are exhaustive lists of all adults. These registers include information on age, sex, marital status, occupation, and address of each resident of voting age. A random sample of 1,000 married women between the ages of 21 and 55 was drawn, and 400 sample units were

presented as dealing with aspects of the life situation of married women. The two versions contained 140 questions, of which 38 attitude questions differed slightly in wording or sequence. These experimental questions were separated as much as possible by blocks of common questions.

The aim of the study was to examine to what extent the question-wording effects reported in Schuman and Presser (1981) occurred with questions formulated in Dutch, the official language of Holland and of Flanders, the northern part of Belgium. Therefore, a number of experimental questions were similar to those used in the Survey Research Center experiments (Schuman, 1982; Schuman & Ludwig, 1983; Schuman & Presser, 1981). Other questions were inspired by the ZUMA experiments (Hippler & Schwarz, 1986; Schwarz, Hippler, Deutsch, & Strack, 1985).

The similarity of the respondents in the two experimental groups is essential for split ballots. Apart from random selection, an additional check on the comparability of the two experimental groups is necessary, since the actual samples can be somewhat biased by the dropout of respondents. It appeared that neither the questions on background characteristics nor the other factual questions showed significant differences in response distributions between the two groups,[3] whereas 27 out of 38 experimental questions did yield substantial differences in response distributions.[4] Unintended context effects are present in at least three nonexperimental attitude questions. Possibly owing to the large number of variations in the questionnaires, unintended context effects might also have affected some of the experimental questions. We may conclude that the effects that we found are the result of our experimental manipulation. However, as we show in the third main section of this chapter, some experimental questions that were placed in a different context need special consideration.

Replicating Two Classical Question-Order Effects

Two of the context effects that were tested in our study may be called "classical" because they replicate experiments reported in the United States. These effects are interesting because of their striking similarity to the effects found in the very

---

randomly assigned to one of two experimental conditions (Form A and Form B). In view of the replacement for nonresponse, the other units were matched with the original units using the information about occupation and age. With respect to the replacement, special attention was paid to the comparability of the two experimental conditions. The fieldwork was carried out by the market research institute DIMARSO/ GALLUP BELGIUM. All of the interviews were tape recorded.

[3]None of the differences in response distributions has a probability less than .20 under H0.

[4]We found 23 effects that were significant at the .05 level; 4 others exceeded the .10 significance level.

different social and linguistic context of the United States. The first effect concerns an experiment with a "specific" and a "general" abortion item, well known from the experiments of Schuman, Presser, and Ludwig (1981) and the replications by Bishop, Oldendick, and Tuchfarber (1985). The second effect replicates a set of stable experimental findings over a 40-year period and is related to question pairs evaluating the rights of two competing parties (Schuman & Ludwig, 1983; Schuman, Kalton, & Ludwig, 1983).

The Abortion Items

In version A of our questionnaire, the abortion items appeared in the following sequence:

> Do you think it should be possible for a pregnant woman to obtain a legal abortion if there is a strong chance of serious defect in the baby? *(Birth defect item: specific)*

> Do you think it should be possible for a pregnant woman to obtain a legal abortion if she is married and does not want any more children? *(Woman's right item: general)*

In Form B, this sequence was reversed. Examination of the marginals of the subtables of Table 10.1 shows that the woman's right item received substantially more support when asked first (56.1%) than when asked after the birth defect item (39.7%). The latter item was practically unaffected by its position (89.1% vs. 93.1%).

Schuman and Presser (1981) take this question-order effect to be an example of a "part–whole contrast effect," since the specific–general order increases the difference in marginals between the two items compared with that which would occur if the two items were each asked separately ($89.1 - 39.1$ vs. $89.1 - 56.1$).

According to their interpretation, the woman's right item is the more general item. When it is asked first, respondents take it to include the birth defect item. On the other hand, when the birth defect item is asked first, respondents may think that this specific argument is not included any more in the subsequent general question. It becomes easier to oppose the general item after favoring the specific reason and "subtracting" it from the general item's content (Schuman & Presser, 1981, p. 38).

In trying to explain different types of question-order effects, Strack, Martin, and Schwarz (1987) combine the psychological theory of cognitive accessibility with the theory about the "hidden" rules governing natural conversations. Normally when answering the subsequent general item, the accessibility of the specific content "birth defect" might be enhanced by the prior birth defect question. However, in this case, this would lead to "subtraction" because of a conversational principle stating that questioners only ask for new information (the so-called "given-new contract"). When trying to identify the meaning of the general question, the respondent may consider what the questioner already knows and what the new focus of the question may then be (Strack et al., 1987, p. 9).

TABLE 10.1. Order Effects on Abortion Items (%)

Birth Defect Item	Woman's Right Item		
	Yes	No	Total
	Form A Question Order: Defect/Right ($N = 174$)		
Yes	39.1	50.0	89.1
No	0.6	10.3	10.9
Total	39.7	60.3	100.0
	Form B Question Order: Right/Defect ($N = 189$)		
Yes	55.3	38.1	93.1
No	1.1	5.8	6.9
Total	56.1	43.9	100.0

Woman's right marginals × Order: $\chi^2 = 10.1$, $df = 1$, $p = .001$
Birth defect marginals × Order: $\chi^2 = 1.79$, $df = 1$, $p = .18$

Schuman and Presser (1981, pp. 38–39) checked the possibility that an element of ambivalence was involved, apart from the cognitive redefinition of the general abortion item. Surprisingly, they found that the item used to measure ambivalence was itself affected by the order of the abortion items, although it was placed more than 50 items after the abortion questions.

To measure ambivalence we asked the following question immediately after the abortion items:

Some people are definitely for or against abortion. Others don't really know what to think about it. Do you have a clearcut opinion on abortion or don't you really know what to think about it?

Respondents answering the general/specific question order (Form B) were more likely than those in the other experimental condition to answer, "I don't really know what to think about it" (32.3% vs. 18.3%). This difference comes mainly from the respondents who agreed with the woman's right item (Form B: 36.8% vs. 26.5%; Form A: 17.4% vs. 18.7%). Inspection of the transcripts of the interviews even showed that four respondents who had agreed to abortion on general grounds had asked the interviewer to change their recorded answer from "yes" to "no" after they were asked the subsequent birth defect item. This seems to corroborate the subtraction thesis and to point to confusion.

How can we explain this confusion? When confronted with the birth defect item (Form B) and assuming that the interviewer was asking for new information, a number of respondents may have become aware that they were misled while answering the prior woman's right item because they already had the birth defect argument in mind. Within the survey interview context, this is a problematic situation, since correcting a former answer is unusual and the cognitive redefinition is constrained by the specific content of the birth defect item.

The Norm of Even-Handedness

We now turn to another "classical" question-order effect generated by questions on competing parties. Two questions, analogous to Schuman and Ludwig's (1983) trade-restriction items, were asked:

> Do you think that Europe should be allowed to restrict the import of American products by levying extra taxes on those products? *(Europe item)*

> Do you think that America should be allowed to restrict the import of European products by levying extra taxes on those products? *(America item)*

In Form A, the Europe item came first; in Form B, this order was reversed. Table 10.2 shows clearly that our European respondents are more willing to accept European restrictions on the importation of American products than American restrictions on European imports. When either item is in the first position, approval levels diverge by +34.2 percentage points (48.4% – 14.2%). When either item is moved to the second position, however, support for European restrictions decreases by 24.1 percentage points (from 48.4% to 24.3%), whereas support for American restrictions increases by 22.8 points (from 14.2% to 37.0%). European respondents are more inclined to accept American restrictions if they have accepted European ones first.

According to Schuman and Ludwig (1983), this context effect can be explained in terms of "the norm of even-handedness." This norm states that an advantage given to one of two competing parties should be given to the other as well. Responding according to this social norm, which is activated by the question context, should be seen as the expression of a "real" attitude in life. The attempt to separate fact from artifact is misleading here.

The idea that question-order effects are to be treated as substantive data will be further developed in the next section by means of a third, original, and surprising context effect. We shall also illustrate how interpretations can be tested, using survey data.

A Question-Order Effect in Its Social Context

The context effect that we shall analyze in depth is related to the order of the following pair of specific attitude questions:

> If one of your children decided not to get married but to live with someone without being married, would you approve, disapprove, or not care either way? *(Cohabitation item)*

> If one of your children decided to make only a legal marriage and no religious marriage, would you approve, disapprove, or not care either way? *(Legal-marriage item)*

In Form A, the cohabitation question came first, followed by the legal-marriage item. In Form B, the order was reversed. Some information about the social and religious context in Flanders is needed in order to understand the kind of effect that was expected.

TABLE 10.2. Order Effects on Questions about Import Restrictions by Europe and America (%)

America May Restrict	Europe May Restrict		
	Yes	No	Total
	Form A Question Order: America/Europe ($N = 169$)		
Yes	13.0	1.2	14.2
No	11.2	74.6	85.8
Total	24.3	75.7	100.0
	Form B Question Order: Europe/America ($N = 184$)		
Yes	36.4	0.5	37.0
No	12.0	51.1	63.0
Total	48.4	51.6	100.0

America marginals × Order: $\chi^2 = 22.1$, $df = 1$, $p = .001$
Europe marginals × Order: $\chi^2 = 23.7$, $df = 1$, $p = .001$

The Social Context

Almost all of Flanders is Roman Catholic. In 1987, about 75% of all weddings in Flanders were celebrated in the Roman Catholic Church; 20 years ago, it was 92%. In 1987, 86% of all children born alive were baptized, compared with 96% 20 years ago (Dobbelaere, 1989). In our sample of married women, more than 90% had been married in church.

According to Belgian law, the status of legally married couple can only be conferred by the registrar's office, and all legal formalities have to be accomplished before the religious ceremony can take place,[5] usually the same week or at a later date. The legal ceremony itself is enough to make a marriage lawful. However, not only practicing Catholics but also a large number of unchurched persons have a religious ceremony afterward and consider this to be their "real" marriage. For church-involved Catholics, cohabitation or a legal marriage without a religious ceremony is unacceptable, on not only religious but also practical grounds. Compliance with Church norms very often is a prerequisite to appointment in one of the many Catholic institutions that abound in Flanders (hospitals, schools, welfare services, trade unions, health insurance organizations, etc.) (Billiet & Dobbelaere, 1985, pp. 124–126).

Expected Order Effects

It was assumed that our respondents, having to choose between three alternatives (a religious marriage, a purely legal marriage, or cohabitation), would prefer the

---

[5]In principle before a minister of one of the official religious denominations but in fact nearly always before a Roman Catholic priest.

religious marriage to the legal one and a legal marriage to cohabitation; women approving of cohabitation would also approve of legal marriage. On the other hand, approval of legal marriage would not necessarily imply approval of cohabitation.

On the basis of these assumptions, the following order effects were hypothesized: For both question orders, approval of legal marriage would be higher than approval of cohabitation.

Furthermore, we expected the approval of legal marriage to be even higher if that item followed the cohabitation item because legal marriage would be considered the "lesser evil." Respondents who would, in fact, prefer their children to make a religious marriage might agree to a legal marriage when explicitly confronted with an even less desirable alternative: no marriage at all.

According to the same logic, we hypothesized that approval of cohabitation would drop when that item followed the legal-marriage item because in that case cohabitation would more consciously be perceived as less desirable.

Since we expected the question order to *increase* the difference in marginals between the two items, compared with the difference that would be noted if each item were asked separately, we were looking for a "part–part contrast," in Schuman and Presser's (1981) terms.

The mechanism underlying this context effect is that the respondent, on answering the second question, would be alerted to the difference in social desirability of the offered alternatives. The answer to the first question provides the respondent with a frame of reference for the evaluation of the alternatives offered in the second question, in terms of social desirability.

A Surprising Order Effect

The data in Table 10.3 only partially confirm our hypotheses. The expected context effect does show in the higher acceptance of legal marriage if considered in comparison with cohabitation (30.3% vs. 16.0%) and the lower acceptance of cohabitation compared with legal marriage (23.5% vs. 32.6%).

Contrary to our expectations, no part–part contrast emerges. When each of the two items is in second position, the difference in marginals (approval) is smaller than when they are asked first (6.8 percentage points vs. 16.6 points). This is due to the fact that the acceptance of cohabitation is higher when the item is asked first than when asked second (32.6% vs. 23.5%), whereas the reverse holds for legal marriage (16.0% vs. 30.3%).

If cohabitation and legal marriage are not evaluated in relation to each other, that is, if each item is in first position, cohabitation surprisingly seems to be more acceptable than legal marriage.

Two Different Cognitive Processes?

Our unexpected findings suggest that we wrongly assumed that the female Flemish population takes legal marriage to be a lesser evil than cohabitation.

TABLE 10.3. Response to the Cohabitation and Legal Marriage Questions by Question Order (&)

| Legal Marriage | Cohabitation | | | |
	Approve	Indifferent	Disapprove	Total
	Form A Question Order: Cohabitation/Legal Marriage ($N = 172$)			
Approve	22.1	4.1	4.1	30.3
Indifferent	5.8	27.9	2.9	36.6
Disapprove	4.7	7.5	20.9	33.1
Total	32.6	39.5	27.9	100.0
	Form B Question Order: Legal Marriage/Cohabitation ($N = 187$)			
Approve	12.2	2.7	1.1	16.0
Indifferent	5.4	35.8	7.5	48.7
Disapprove	5.9	5.4	24.0	35.3
Total	23.5	43.9	32.6	100.0

Cohabitation × Order: $\chi^2 = 3.70$, $df = 2$, $p = .159$
Legal marriage × Order: $\chi^2 = 10.98$, $df = 2$, $p = .004$

The question-order effects that we found could be explained by assuming that two different cognitive processes are at work, depending on which question is asked first. If the legal-marriage item comes first (Form B), it alerts the respondent to the fact that legal marriage constitutes a transgression of the norms of the Catholic Church and that no "real" religious wedding has taken place. The respondent keeps this in mind while answering the second question, about cohabitation. This explains why there is a smaller number of positive replies to both of the items in Form B compared with Form A.

The "preference" for cohabitation over legal marriage may be due to the fact that some Catholic women who would wish their children to make a religious marriage consider cohabitation as a provisional state that can still lead to a religious wedding (and legal marriage) in the future, whereas a legal marriage is a definite step. In fact, some youngsters (mostly students) do live together for a while before they ultimately marry in church.

If the cohabitation question comes first, the Church norm is not activated and opposition is not so strong. The first question then serves as a frame of reference for the answer to the second one about legal marriage, which is also rejected less strongly.

Testing the Explanation

Since no direct evidence of what goes on in the respondent's mind is available, our explanation requires testing. It is known that the conformity to Church norms is strongest among older female Catholic churchgoers (Dobbelaere, 1985).

In addition, the two experimental items tend to be more salient for respondents who are 40 years of age or older, since the choices may be real for one of their children. We therefore expect that the group of older Catholic respondents will be most sensitive to the question-order effect. This hypothesis can be tested by analyzing the interaction patterns between each of the two items and question order, church involvement, and age.[6] On the basis of our assumptions, three hypotheses about the interaction effects can be formulated:

H1. The relationship between church involvement and the legal-marriage item will be stronger when the legal-marriage item comes first (Form B), because of the assumed awareness of the Church norm, than when it comes second (Form A). The more zealous Catholic women, especially the older ones, will be least likely to agree to a legal marriage and most likely to disapprove of it when the legal-marriage item comes first.

H2. The relationship between church involvement and the cohabitation item will also be stronger in Form B than in Form A because of the awareness of the Church norm induced by the preceding legal-marriage item.

H3. In Form B, the relationship between church involvement and the cohabitation item will be weaker than the one between church involvement and the legal-marriage item because of the ambiguous attitude of practicing Catholics toward cohabitation.

In order to test the first and second hypotheses, we shall make use of log-linear modeling.[7] Since our hypotheses state that the effect of question order (O) on the response (R) varies according to church involvement (I) and age (A), we expect to fit a model including the three-way interaction term ROI (and possibly ROA). For the third hypothesis, another procedure is used.

The percentages of approval and the gamma coefficients in Table 10.4 give a first descriptive impression of the associations between the two response variables (the legal-marriage and cohabitation items) and church involvement in the categories of age and question order. As was expected, the association is stronger in Form B than in Form A, especially for the women 40 years of age or older.

---

[6]The variable "church involvement" was operationalized by three questions: one about baptism, one about the respondent's actual (subjective) religious or philosophical convictions, and one about church attendance. The categories of the variable are "not catholic," "nonpracticing Catholic," "irregular churchgoer," and "regular churchgoer." Because of the small sample size, for the analysis of multiway tables these four categories are collapsed into two. The irregular and the regular churchgoers are the "practicing Catholics."

[7]We can choose between log-linear modeling, logistic regression, and analysis of variance. Logistic regression uses a logit model based on the cumulative logistic probability function (Pindyck & Rubinfeld, 1981). It is very similar to log-linear analysis with a response variable. For both analysis of variance and logistic regression, we need to code the response variable (legal marriage, cohabitation) into two categories: approval (or disapproval) or not. Because this results in a loss of information ("indifferent"), log-linear modeling is preferred.

TABLE 10.4. Response to the Legal-Marriage and Cohabitation Questions by Age, Church Involvment, and Question Order

Age and Church Involvement	Legal Marriage		Cohabitation	
	% Approve	Total (N)	% Approve	Total (N)
		Form A		
<40				
Nonpracticing	43.8	(64)	39.1	(64)
Practicing	19.2	(26)	34.6	(26)
	Gamma = 0.526		Gamma = 0.228	
40+				
Nonpracticing	29.3	(41)	29.3	(41)
Practicing	15.0	(40)	22.5	(40)
	Gamma = 0.448		Gamma = 0.237	
		Form B		
<40				
Nonpracticing	24.3	(74)	31.2	(74)
Practicing	8.3	(24)	12.5	(24)
	Gamma = 0.664		Gamma = 0.449	
40+				
Nonpracticing	18.5	(54)	24.5	(54)
Practicing	0.0	(36)	13.5	(36)
	Gamma = 0.827		Gamma = 0.554	

The associations between the legal-marriage item and church involvement are also stronger than the associations between the cohabitation item and church involvement, presumably because of the mixed attitude toward cohabitation among practicing Catholics ("It can turn into a religious wedding").

Are the three-way interactions between question order (O), church involvement (I), and the response to the legal-marriage or cohabitation items (R) statistically significant? Log-linear analyses with the expressed attitude toward legal marriage and cohabitation as response variables can provide the answer. In factor-response models, only models in which the associations and interaction between the factors (AOI) are included need consideration (Upton, 1978).[8]

One of the problems of model identification and selection in log-linear analysis is the choice of one model from different competing models. Today, "Akaike's Information Criterion" (AIC) is accepted among statisticians as an

---

[8]In factor-response models, only the associations and interactions in which the response variable is included are considered. The associations and interactions between the factors (AOI) need no test and are included in all of the models. In this way, the 167 possible hierarchical models can be reduced to only 20. Since the models are hierarchical, the three-way interaction term AOI includes the terms A, I, O, AI, AO, OI, and AOI.

adequate and objective criterion for the selection of the "best" model (Sakamoto, 1982; Sakamoto, Ishiguro, & Kitagawa, 1986). The model with the "Minimal AIC Estimation" (MAICE) minimizes the distance between the model and the unknown "true" model (Swyngedouw, 1988; Daemen, 1988).[9]

Table 10.5 provides an overview of the four "best" hierarchical models in ascending order, according to the AIC criterion.[10] The table contains information about the log likelihood ratio (L). This test statistic is often called the "likelihood ratio chi-square." For a particular model, it measures the degree of deviation of the observed multiway table from the expected table. The probabilities are computed from the chi-square distribution with the corresponding number of degrees of freedom (df), and they give an indication of the goodness of fit. Apart from the AIC selection criterion, the probability of the (partial) L^2 contribution of an effect may be used in the model selection. Effects with small probabilities are significant and cannot be omitted from a model.

Let us start with the legal-marriage item (H1). The three-way interaction RIO is present in four of the eight plausible models and in three of the four best models according to the AIC criterion. Similarly, four of the eight models contain RAO, although this interaction is present in only one of the four best models (Model 3). According to our selection procedure, we may select Model 1 (the MAICE model). However, the very small difference between the AICs of Models 1 and 2 makes this choice problematic. If we had used another procedure (stepwise deletion), we would possibly have omitted the three-way interaction RIO, since the p value exceeds .10, but this is on the borderline. There is no discussion about the deletion of RAO. Taking everything together, we find it plausible that, in Form B, the church-involved Catholics are less likely to approve a legal marriage only.

Are the three-way interactions between the cohabitation item (R) and the other variables statistically significant (H2)? This time the MAICE model does not corroborate the hypothesis, since it does not include the three-way interaction RIO. The expected model concerning the interaction between response, question order, and church involvement comes only in fourth place. The probability of the partial L^2 contribution of the three-way interaction RIO exceeds .10. We do not need that effect in order to fit an adequate model.

---

[9] AIC is based on the degree of correspondence between a selected model and the unknown "true" model that is measured by Kullback-Leibler's Information measure (the so-called "negative entropy"). AIC is a function of the number of observations in the multiway table (N), the cell frequencies, the number of cells, the likelihood ratio (L^2), and the degrees of freedom (df). Within the context of a particular table, AIC depends only on L^2 and df, since the other parameters are fixed. In log-linear models, AIC corrects the log likelihood ratio for the number of degrees of freedom (AIC $L^2 - 2df$). Therefore, it may be considered a formalization of the idea of "sparseness."

[10] We use the computer program LOG-SCAN, developed by L. Daemen: *A program to select log-linear models by minimizing Akaike's Information Criterion, Version 1.0*, Department of Sociology, K.U.Leuven.

TABLE 10.5. The Four Most Likely Factor Response Models Applying to the Tables: Response (R) to the Legal-Marriage/Cohabitation Items by Church Involvement (I), Age (A), and Question Order (O)

Model	L^2	Probability	df	AIC
Legal-marriage item (R)				
1. RA,RIO,AOI	2.63	0.853	6	2131.62
2. RI,RA,RO,AOI	7.01	0.536	8	2131.99
(1 – 2) RIO contribution	4.38	0.112	2	Can be omitted
3. RIO,RAO,AOI	2.37	0.667	4	2135.36
(3 – 1) RAO contribution	0.26	0.878	2	May not be added
4. RIA,RIO,AOI	2.45	0.654	4	2135.43
(4 – 1) RIA contribution	0.18	0.914	2	May not be added
Cohabitation item (R)				
1. RI,RA,RO,AOI	7.06	0.530	8	2196.23
2. RI,RA,AOI	11.50	0.320	10	2196.67
(2 – 1) RO contribution	4.44	0.109	2	Can be omitted
3. RI,RAO,AOI	5.26	0.511	6	2198.43
(3 – 1) RAO contribution	1.80	0.407	2	May not be added
4. RA,RIO,AOI	5.41	0.492	6	2198.58
(4 – 1) RIO contribution	1.65	0.438	2	May not be added

Our third hypothesis states that in Form B the relationship between church involvement and attitude toward legal marriage will be stronger than the relationship between church involvement and attitude toward cohabitation. This hypothesis cannot be tested with log-linear models, since the observations in both multiway tables are not independent of each other (same respondents). Inspection of the confidence intervals of the gamma coefficients in the tables collapsed over age (because of the small numbers) reveals that the third hypothesis is acceptable ($p = .092$).

The Context of the Question-Order Effect

After these tests, we can be quite sure that, at least for the legal-marriage item, the differences in response between the two experimental conditions are due to the respondent's *varying awareness* of Church norms, which was in turn related to the order of the experimental items. The question remains if the effect was only caused by the position of the legal-marriage item in Form B or if other differences in the preceding part of the questionnaire affected the response distributions. This question is relevant because our experimental items are preceded by a question about the main reasons for having one's children baptized, which is itself subject to experimental manipulation.

In Form A the cohabitation item immediately followed an open question, whereas in Form B the legal-marriage item was preceded by a closed question with 13 response categories. Several of the reasons proposed refer explicitly to the church or to religious principles.[11] Tests revealed that the relationship between church involvement and the kind of reasons chosen (reference to religious principles or not) was significantly stronger in Form B than in Form A (Billiet, 1989). Table 10.6 shows a three-way interaction between question form (open/ closed), church involvement, and the kind of reasons given. On answering the closed question (Form B), practicing Catholics were more likely to give reasons referring to religious principles. Accordingly, respect of Church norms and religious principles in Form B can be affected by the response categories and answers to the preceding closed question and not by the position of the legal-marriage item.

Was the question-order effect itself an artifact of the context of both experimental questions? The differences in the response distributions and the interactions could very well be explained by such a context effect, since in that case too we might expect a three-way interaction between the legal-marriage item, church involvement, and question order.

This new explanation can be tested by the same procedure that was used earlier. The variable "church involvement" simply has to be replaced by "kind of reasons given for having the child(ren) baptized" (no references to the church or to religion vs. at least one such reference). The test results are given in Tables 10.7 and 10.8.

Table 10.7 contains the descriptive information concerning the interaction between the legal-marriage or cohabitation item, kind of reasons, age, and question order. From the gamma coefficients, it appears that the association between the items and kind of reasons is much stronger in Form B than in Form A, as is to be expected.

The statistical test results (log-linear analysis) are given in Table 10.8. The best (MAICE) model for the legal-marriage item includes the three-way interaction (RBO) between expressed opinion toward legal marriage (R), kind of reasons for baptism (B), and question order (O). According to the test of the partial L^2 contribution, RBO cannot be omitted from the model. This is not the case for the cohabitation item, where a model with RBO comes in second place.

It is very likely that the response effect that we found is not exclusively, or not at all, induced by the position of the legal-marriage item itself but by the response categories of the preceding closed question. If this is the case, the already-invoked attention to the Church norm is transferred to the subsequent legal-marriage and cohabitation question out of a tendency *to be consistent*. We may

---

[11]Form A: "You have had your child(ren) baptized. What were your main reasons for having the child(ren) baptized?" *(Insist: Is there any other reason?)*

Form B: "You have had your child(ren) baptized. On this card (*hand card 3*) there are a number of reasons why parents have their children baptized. We are going to read them together and afterwards I will ask you for the three most important reasons why you had your child(ren) baptized." (Some of the reasons are the following: part of religious community [1]; baptism enables to make . . . a church wedding [4]; to have a religious upbringing [5]; baptism is a sacrament conferring the grace of God [10].)

TABLE 10.6. Respondents Reporting At Least One Religious Reason for Baptism (B), by Form (F) and Church Involvement (I) (%)

Church Involvement	Form A Open	Form B Closed
Nonpracticing	38.7	66.4
Practicing	53.7	90.2

Test of 3-way interaction term BIF: Partial L^2 contribution = 2.86, $df = 1$, $p = .091$ Cannot be omitted. The saturated model is the MAICE model.

TABLE 10.7. Response to the Legal-Marriage and Cohabitation Questions by Age, Reasons for Baptism, and Question Order

Age and Religious Reasons for Baptism	Legal Marriage		Cohabitation	
	% Approve	Total (N)	% Approve	Total (N)
	Form A			
<40				
No reference	44.4	(54)	40.7	(55)
Reference	25.0	(36)	33.3	(36)
	Gamma = 0.184		Gamma = 0.033	
40+				
No reference	26.2	(42)	30.9	(42)
Reference	20.0	(40)	22.5	(40)
	Gamma = 0.169		Gamma = 0.099	
	Form B			
<40				
No reference	38.9	(36)	41.7	(36)
Reference	9.7	(62)	17.7	(62)
	Gamma = 0.551		Gamma = 0.444	
40+				
No reference	30.8	(13)	38.5	(13)
Reference	7.8	(77)	16.9	(77)
	Gamma = 0.514		Gamma = 0.421	

also maintain our hypothesis about the mixed attitude of some Catholic women toward (provisory) cohabitation in that interpretation.

Discussion and Conclusion

The analysis is an application of Schuman's advice to consider question-wording effects as data in order to understand the respondent's expressed opinions in their social context. Throughout our analysis, we looked for the social meaning of the

TABLE 10.8. The Four Most Likely Factor Response Models Applying to the Multiway Tables: Responses (R) to the Legal-Marriage/Cohabitation Items by Reasons for Baptism (B), Age (A), and Question Order (O)

Model	L^2	Probability	df	AIC
Legal marriage item (R)				
1. RA,RBO,BAO	3.14	0.792	6	2157.53
2. RI,RA,RO,BAO	8.54	0.382	8	2158.93
(1 – 2) RBO contribution	5.40	0.067	2	Cannot be omitted
3. RBA,RBO,BAO	1.04	0.904	4	2159.43
(3 – 1) RBA contribution	2.10	0.350	2	May not be added
4. RB,RA,BAO	13.35	0.205	10	2159.74
(2 – 4) RO contribution	4.81	0.090	2	May not be added
Cohabitation item (R)				
1. RB,RA,BAO	7.63	0.665	10	2197.49
2. RA,RBO,BAO	2.24	0.896	6	2200.10
3. RB,RA,RO,BAO	6.51	0.590	8	2200.37
(3 – 2) RBO contribution	4.27	0.118	2	Can be omitted
(3 – 1) RO contribution	1.12	0.571	2	Can be omitted
4. RBA,BAO	6.92	0.546	8	2200.78
(4 – 1) RBA contribution	0.71	0.701	2	May not be added

effects found, by relating them to social characteristics of respondents such as church involvement and age. The plausibility of cognitive interpretations was indirectly tested by analyzing relationships between social characteristics and response patterns. We were not so much interested in the cognitive processes as such as we were in their heuristic value to discover plausible explanations of the interactions between response, background characteristics, and question context.

What did we learn about social reality? We found out that our assumption about the social undesirability of cohabitation in comparison with legal marriage among Catholics was wrong. If there was no experimental manipulation of the order of the two questions and if only the order in Form A was used (after an open question about baptism), then we might conclude that cohabitation is slightly more undesirable than legal marriage (33.1% vs. 27.9% in Table 10.3) and that the relationship between church involvement and the attitude toward the marriage of one's children is moderately strong.

Experimental manipulation revealed a far more complex pattern. The expressed attitude toward the marriage of the children of practicing Catholics can be altered in a conversational context if religious arguments are considered. For some of them, cohabitation seems more desirable than a legal marriage only, presumably because it is perceived as a temporary state that can lead to a religious wedding (and legal marriage) afterward.

After all, we are quite sure about the nature of the context effect that we have detected, namely, *the greater saliency of religious arguments* in the expressed opinion of practicing Catholics. The reason is clear: the presence of verbal cues in the previous closed question. We do not know if the order of the legal-marriage item with a reference to the absence of a church wedding has an effect of its own. We are curious.

Multivariate analysis is an essential tool for our approach to context effects. The restrictions were mainly the small numbers of respondents in our samples and the excessive number of experimental questions in this one study. As a consequence, the full application of the suggested approach needs larger samples (over 600) and experiments within substantial social surveys in general populations. It would then be possible to measure more critical characteristics (i.e., specific attitude-strength measures) and to include more variables in the models.

Acknowledgments. The reported experiments are part of a research project sponsored by the Belgian National Fund for Scientific Research.

11
Qualitative Analysis of Question-Order and Context Effects: The Use of Think-Aloud Responses

George F. Bishop

Understanding how respondents answer survey questions has become a major theoretical objective in public opinion research, in large part because of the need to explain a variety of response effects that have been discovered in experiments on question form, wording, and context (see especially Schuman & Presser, 1981). Stimulated by these experiments, cognitive scientists, social psychologists, and survey researchers have begun to develop theoretical models and research programs to identify the cognitive processes underlying answers to survey questions (see, e.g., Bishop, 1987; Hippler, Schwarz, & Sudman, 1987; Krosnick & Alwin, 1987; Strack & Martin, 1987; Tourangeau & Rasinski, 1988; and Schwarz, Hippler, & Noelle-Neumann, chap. 13, this volume). Finding a way to get at these cognitive variables would be useful, since it would allow researchers to test alternative hypotheses about the psychological sources of response effects in surveys.

In this chapter, I would like to describe and illustrate a method that I and my colleagues have used to get at the cognitions that are evoked by survey questions: having respondents "think out loud" or "talk aloud" as they answer the questions. Cognitive psychologists, such as Ericsson and Simon (1984), have found the think-aloud technique quite useful in understanding how both experts and novices solve various intellectual problems. We assumed that this technique would likewise be useful in revealing how respondents answer survey questions about subjective phenomena such as their beliefs, attitudes, and opinions. In particular, we thought that the technique would help us to explain how responses are affected by the order or context in which a question is asked. We also thought that the technique would have considerable heuristic value as a method of generating alternative hypotheses about specific question-order and context effects, hypotheses that could then be tested, quantitatively, in follow-up experiments.

Here I shall describe the exploratory experiment that we designed to investigate the utility of the think-aloud technique, give some illustrative examples and crude "counts" of open-ended responses in think-aloud protocols, and suggest how the technique can be used to test, as well as generate, alternative hypotheses about order and context effects in public opinion surveys.

Research Design

To begin with, we selected a set of questions from previous experiments on question-order and context effects, such as those involved in the well-known context effect on responses to questions about Communist and American newspaper reporters (Schuman & Presser, 1981), the well-established order effect on responses to the standard question on interest in politics that is asked in the National Election Studies (Bishop, 1987; Bishop, Oldendick, & Tuchfarber, 1982, 1984b), and the well-demonstrated order effect on responses to questions about the abortion issue (see Bishop, Oldendick, & Tuchfarber, 1985; Schuman & Presser, 1981; Scott, 1987b). All of the questions were asked in one of two questionnaire forms. On Form A, for example, respondents were asked the question about abortion in the case of a serious birth defect *before* the question about abortion in the case of a married woman who does not want any more children, whereas on Form B they were asked these same questions in the reverse sequence. Similar split-ballot variations in the order of the questions on Communist and American reporters and the political knowledge and interest items were implemented on Forms A and B of the questionnaire (see Exhibit 11.1).

Think-Aloud Technique

The instructions and warm-up exercise that were used to get respondents in the habit of thinking aloud as they answered the questions are shown in the Appendix. We adapted these instructions and exercises from a set suggested by Ericsson and Simon (1984). The instructions ask respondents not only to think aloud as they answer a question but also to give an immediate retrospective report on what they were thinking about as they answered it. This complementary combination of *concurrent* and *retrospective* self-reports provides a more complete account of what respondents are thinking as they answer a question then would either self-report alone.

Furthermore, as Ericsson and Simon (1984), Loftus (1984), and others have observed, the think-aloud technique, unlike interpretive probing with "why" questions or other after-the-fact procedures (e.g., "thought listing"), does not encourage respondents to guess or make inferences about the "reasons" for their answers. Also unlike postinterview debriefings, it does not force them to rely on *recall* of what they think that they were thinking when they answered the questions earlier in the interview—a difficult, if not impossible, task. Think-aloud protocols, in other words, are more likely to yield evidence of the information that is attended to in short-term memory as respondents answer the questions. The think-aloud procedure, however, does not require respondents to report directly on their cognitive processes—an impossible task—but simply on whatever "comes to mind" as they answer the question, a task that most respondents are quite capable of performing (see Ericsson & Simon, 1984). Inferences about the processes and mechanisms underlying these raw data are the task of the investigator. All that we need assume is that respondents' protocols contain traces of such processes. Provided we get a sufficient sample of protocols, we should be able to detect those processes, however automated they might seem for some respondents.

Respondent Interviews

The findings presented here are drawn from think-aloud interviews with various volunteer respondents who were systematically assigned to either Form A or

EXHIBIT 11.1. Question Forms A and B

Form A	Form B
Communist/American Reporters	
"Do you think a Communist country like Russia should let American newspaper reporters come in and send back to America the news as they see it?"	"Do you think the United States should let Communist newspaper reporters from other countries come in here and send back to their papers the news as they see it?"
"Do you think the United States should let Communist newspaper reporters from other countries come in here and send back to their papers the news as they see it?"	"Do you think a Communist country like Russia should let American newspaper reporters come in and send back to America the news as they see it?"
"Now tell me all that you can remember about your thinking as you answered this question."	"Now tell me all that you can remember about your thinking as you answered this question."
Abortion	
"Do *you* think it should be possible for a pregnant woman to obtain a *legal* abortion if there is a strong chance of serious defect in the baby?"	"Do *you* think it should be possible for a pregnant woman to obtain a *legal* abortion if she is married and does not want any more children?"
"Do *you* think it should be possible for a pregnant woman to obtain a *legal* abortion if she is married and does not want any more children?"	"Do *you* think it should be possible for a pregnant woman to obtain a *legal* abortion if there is a strong chance of serious defect in the baby?"
"Now tell me all that you can remember about your thinking as you answered this question."	"Now tell me all that you can remember about your thinking as you answered this question."

(Exhibit 11.1 continued)

EXHIBIT 11.1. Continued

Form A	Form B
Political Interest/Knowledge	

Form A	Form B
"I'd like to ask you a few questions now about government and public affairs."	"I'd like to ask you a few questions now about government and public affairs."
"Do you happen to remember anything special that your U.S. representative has done for your district or for the people in your district while he has been in Congress?" (IF YES): "What was that?"	"Now, some people seem to follow what's going on in government and public affairs most of the time, whether there's an election going on or not. Others aren't that interested. Would you say that you follow what's going on in government and public affairs most of the time, some of the time, only now and then, or hardly at all?"
"Is there any legislative bill that has come up in the House of Representatives, on which you remember how your congressman voted in the last couple of years?" (IF YES): "What bill was that?"	"Now tell me all that you can remember about your thinking as you answered this question."
"Now, some people seem to follow what's going on in government and public affairs most of the time, whether there's an election going on or not. Others aren't that interested. Would you say that you follow what's going on in government and public affairs most of the time, some of the time, only now and then, or hardly at all?"	"Do you happen to remember anything special that your U.S. representative has done for your district or for the people in your district while he has been in Congress?" (IF YES): "What was that?"
"Now tell me all that you can remember about your thinking as you answered this question."	"Now tell me all that you can remember about your thinking as you answered this question."
	"Is there any legislative bill that has come up in the House of Representatives, on which you remember how your congressman voted in the last couple of years?" (IF YES): "What bill was that?"
	"Now tell me all that you can remember about your thinking as you answered this question."

Form B of the questionnaire. About half of these respondents were graduate and undergraduate students at the University of Cincinnati; the rest consisted of clerical, maintenance, and managerial employees at the University and at a local private hospital, as well as a number of my work associates, friends, and graduate assistants. The first batch of interviews ($N = 14$) was gathered in the spring of

1985 by me and a graduate student assistant, the second batch ($N = 11$) in the fall of 1986 by me and a different graduate assistant, and the third ($N = 36$) in the fall of 1988 by a graduate assistant. With one minor exception in the warm-up exercises, the interview schedule was identical in all three time periods.[1] The typical interview took about 30–45 minutes to complete, each of which was tape recorded and transcribed verbatim into what I refer to below as the think-aloud (TA) protocols.

Illustrative Examples

Let us look now at a few examples of what such protocols can tell us about some well-known context effects, beginning with one that was first demonstrated many years ago by Hyman and Sheatsley (1950) and more recently by Schuman & Presser (1981): an order effect on responses to a related pair of questions about allowing Communist and American newspaper reporters into each other's countries to report "the news as they see it" (see the wording and sequence of the questions in Exhibit 11.1).

Communist and American Reporters

Previous experiments by Schuman and his associates (Schuman & Presser, 1981, chap. 2; Schuman & Ludwig, 1983) have shown that American respondents are more likely to approve of letting Communist reporters into the United States after having answered a similar question about letting American reporters into Communist countries such as Russia; conversely, they are less likely to think that a Communist country such as Russia should let American reporters into their country after answering the question about the United States letting Communist reporters into this country. Schuman and his colleagues have hypothesized that this context effect occurs because the two questions, when they are asked together, evoke a norm of reciprocity or even-handedness that induces the respondent into treating both groups of reporters equally, whereas, when either question is asked alone, or in the first position (which is psychologically equivalent), the respondent tends to answer it by drawing on his or her basic beliefs about communism and the relationship between the United States and the Soviet Union.

---

[1] In the fall 1985 interview schedule, the warm-up exercises began by asking the respondent: "First, I want you to tell me how many different people you talked to yesterday, either on the phone or in person, and tell me what you are thinking as you answer the question." Because some respondents had difficulty with this question, we dropped it and replaced it in the 1986 and 1988 interviews with a question from Loftus' (1984) research: "In the last *12* months, how many times have you gone to a doctor, or a dentist, or a hospital, or utilized any health care specialist or facility?" (See the Appendix for the complete set of think-aloud instructions.)

Is there any evidence for their hypothesis in the think-aloud protocols that we have collected thus far? Indeed there is. Consider the following protocol from a respondent who was asked, first, whether "the United States should let Communist newspaper reporters from other countries come in here and send back to their papers the news as they see it." She answered the question this way:

> Um, well, we shouldn't because, I don't know, I guess it's just because I don't like communism. Having somebody come over here—I feel like it's sort of like, you know, a thief coming over here and getting ideas and stories and finding things out about the United States and taking it back. And, then, just them knowing things about us, that kind of makes me feel, I don't know; it's just I disagree with it. Um, I don't know, they might get something that's pretty important, you know, some kind of important information that, that they shouldn't have got. I guess, I don't know . . . I just don't think they should be able to.

Her TA protocol clearly shows, as Schuman and his associates have hypothesized, that when this question is asked first, it tends to evoke the respondent's attitude toward communism ("I don't like communism"). Her protocol also indicates that the question triggered a related set of fears and beliefs about espionage, a part perhaps of a larger cognitive structure or schema that she had formed about COMMUNIST SPIES.

Consider now another protocol for the same question when a different respondent was asked it immediately *after* the following item:

> Do you think a Communist country like Russia should let American newspaper reporters come in and send back to America the news as they see it?

To which he replied:

> Yes, yeah, because we never get, I don't know, I think they just let out what they want other people to know. So I think if we had kind of an American viewpoint on the Russian way of life, or their government or something, it would be more understandable to and more realistic to people in America to understand. That's all.

When asked next whether he thought "the United States should let Communist newspaper reporters from other countries come in here and send back to their papers the news as they see it," he said:

> I don't see why not. I mean, as long as they weren't going to hurt anybody while they were here, I'm sure they can. They probably do it now anyway, don't you think? I wouldn't mind if they were here. If we're allowed over there, they can come over here; it'd be the *same thing* [italics added]. That's all.

Even though this respondent expressed some negative beliefs about Communist countries in answering the first question ("I think they just let out what they want other people to know") and indicated some concern about letting Communist reporters into the country in reacting to the second question ("I mean as long as they weren't going to hurt anybody while they were here"), his protocol gave clear evidence that the sequence of these two questions triggered a norm of even-handedness, as when he said:

> I wouldn't mind if they were here. If we're allowed over there, they can come over here; it'd be the *same* thing [italics added].

However, not all of the protocols that we have collected with this form of the questionnaire show evidence of such a norm when the questions are presented in this sequence. In fact, when the 31 TA protocols gathered with Form A of the instrument were coded—independently by a trained graduate assistant for expressions of even-handedness— only 19 of them (61.2%) contained such references. Furthermore, the figures for Form B were nearly identical: 18 of 30 protocols (60.0%) included some reference to even-handedness. A test of the hypothesis with such small samples is clearly not conclusive. That, of course, is why the hypothesis should be tested with a much larger sample of protocols, as in any standard split-ballot experiment. If Schuman and his colleagues are correct, we should find that there are significantly more references to a norm of even-handedness in a sample of such protocols when the question about letting Communist reporters into the U.S. is asked second than when it is asked first. Similarly, there should be a significantly larger number of references to even-handedness when the question on letting American reporters into Communist countries is asked second than when it is asked first, although the effect will not necessarily be symmetrical (see the discussion of this point by Schuman & Ludwig, 1983).

General and Specific Abortion Questions

Let us turn now to another illustration of how the think-aloud technique can be used to provide evidence for alternative hypotheses about a well-established context effect on responses to questions about the abortion issue.

Schuman and Presser (1981) have discovered that survey respondents are significantly less likely to approve of an abortion for a woman who "is married and does not want any more children" when the question about it is asked immediately *after* a question about approving an abortion "if there is a strong chance of serious defect in the baby" than when it is asked as the first question of the two. When it is asked in the first position, they hypothesize, some respondents may say "yes" because they have a specific reason in mind, such as rape, incest, or the chance of a birth defect in the child. But, they argue, when the question about abortion in the case of a birth defect is asked first, it may suggest to respondents that the question that follows about a married woman who does not want any more children does not apply to such special circumstances. Respondents, they theorize, may therefore feel freer to say "no" to an abortion for a married woman who does not want any more children after having supported, and "subtracted," the more specific reason about a possible birth defect.

We (Bishop et al., 1985), however, were unable to find any direct evidence for the "subtraction hypothesis" in our analysis of open-ended responses to questions about "why" respondents favor or oppose an abortion for a married woman who does not want any more children (see also Scott, 1987b). Because "why" questions encourage respondents to guess or make inferences about the "reasons" for their answers, the protocols that they produce may not contain any evidence for the subtraction hypothesis, evidence that might be obtained, however, if respondents were asked to give *concurrent* and immediate *retrospective* reports on what they were thinking as they answered the question, as was done in the think-aloud procedure that we have used here. However, in none of the 30 protocols collected with Form B of the instrument (data not shown here) did the coding assistant find any mentions of a possible birth defect as a reason for approving an abortion for a woman who "is married and does not want any more children" when that item was asked in the first position.

Similarly, the think-aloud technique may provide a better test of an alternative hypothesis developed by me and my co-workers (Bishop et al., 1985) about why this well-known context effect occurs: because, as we put it, "the freedom-of-choice rationale implicit in the woman's right item does not seem to be as good a reason for allowing an abortion as is a potential birth defect"—what Tom Smith (1986a) has called the "contrast hypothesis." In fact, one of the protocols that I have collected in this project strongly suggests that some respondents make the implicit comparison of the two reasons for an abortion predicted by the contrast hypothesis. When asked, "Do you think it should be possible for a pregnant woman to obtain a *legal* abortion if there is a strong chance of serious defect in the baby?" one respondent answered it this way:

> Yes, I do, um, I don't really strongly believe in abortion but I see that there are . . . if the child isn't going to be wanted, if it's going to be a really tough time, especially if the child's got some serious defects, I would definitely say yes. I mean why would you want . . . first of all, it's going to be *hard* for the child to live in this world and it's going to be even *harder* on its parents [italics added]. I think they should be allowed to have an abortion.

When asked next, "Do you think it should be possible for a pregnant woman to obtain a legal abortion if she is married and does not want any more children?" he responded:

> Hmm, I think married people, uhm, should not be allowed. I mean, I guess everyone should always have the right to have an abortion. But I think that a married couple, you know, should bring the child up. I don't know, for some reason I think that if they're married . . . unless there's severe *hardship* on the family [italics added]. But I think it's, uh, *if the child's going to be perfectly normal* [italics added], I don't see . . . they're really hurting the child; they're not hurting themselves.

The contents of the latter protocol clearly indicate that the respondent does not think that *not* wanting any more children is a very good reason for having an abortion, especially if the couple is married. Nor does he think it is a very good reason by comparison with the special circumstances of a birth defect, as when he said, "unless there's severe *hardship* on the family. But I think . . . *if the child's going to be perfectly normal*, I don't see . . . ."

Other protocols that we have collected on these questions (not presented here), however, show no trace of such a comparison process. In fact, of the seven most directly relevant protocols from Form A—where a respondent first said "yes" to an abortion in the case of a possible birth defect and then "no" to an abortion in the case of a married woman who does not want any more children—only three of them show evidence of any kind of comparison of the two abortion situations. A much larger sample is obviously necessary to test this hypothesis further.

Interest in Politics

A final illustration demonstrates the utility of the think-aloud technique as a heuristic procedure for generating hypotheses about the psychological factors that mediate order and context effects.

This example is drawn from our previous experiments on question-order and context effects (Bishop, 1987; Bishop et al., 1982, 1984b). The results of those experiments showed that respondents were significantly less likely to say that they followed what is going on in government and public affairs "most of the time" when they were asked about it immediately after some difficult questions about their U.S. representative's record, as in Form A, than when they were asked about it first, as in Form B. This context effect has been replicated a number of times and is highly reliable. It is also quite robust, since it cannot be eliminated or even reduced significantly in magnitude by interspersing a buffer of questions on unrelated topics between the question on Form A about the respondent's knowledge of their U.S. representative's record and the question about how much they follow what is going on in government and public affairs.

Thus we know how this context effect occurs, but we do not understand the cognitive process that mediates it. Is it because respondents infer that they do not follow what is going on in government and public affairs "most of the time" from the fact that they are unable to answer the questions about their U.S. representative's record? If so, how would we account for the fact that many respondents (20–25%) say that they follow what is going on in government and public affairs "most of the time" even though they cannot answer correctly either of the two questions about their representative? Evidently, such respondents must have something else "in mind" when they answer the question. But what is it that they have "in mind"? Asking them to think aloud as they answer the question is a way to get at it. Let us look now at what people tell us when we ask them to think out loud in response to this question.

Let us look first at some of the responses to Form B, in which the question about following what is going on in government and public affairs is asked first. A reading of the protocols that we gathered shows that when this question is asked first, it activates primarily cognitions and memories that the respondents have about how much they keep up with the news by watching TV, reading the newspaper, or listening to the radio. A fairly typical protocol for this question is one that we obtained from a black woman, age 34, who had a bachelor's degree and was employed in a local hospital. She answered the question about following what is going on in government and public affairs this way:

> Government and public affairs . . . well, I guess I follow sort of an overview. I like the news fast, more headline things. And I guess if it interests me I go into it in detail; if it doesn't interest me, then . . . I usually don't, uhm . . . local politics, unless it's a public scandal, I probably don't follow it that closely.

The interviewer then said to her: "Now tell me all that you can remember about your thinking as you answered this question." To which she responded:

> Ah gee, I guess I was just thinking about when I hear the news. I don't have much time to read the newspaper; I bring it in if it's anything in the headlines sometimes that catches my eye. I usually watch cable news, "Around the World in 30 Minutes." And sometimes I listen to the radio on the way to and home from work. So I guess I was just thinking about the few times I hear the news.

Here we see that her think-aloud protocol and her immediate retrospective report are in close agreement regarding the cognitions that were activated by asking the question, namely, those having to do with following the news.

A similar protocol for Form B comes from a young white female, age 23, who also had a bachelor's degree. She answered the question this way:

> Okay, I like to follow it as much as possible . . . so I would say . . . what was the second one you read? Some of the time? Well, I'll make it some of the time, because most of the time probably doesn't apply, since, you know, I may not be around or be able to catch the news because primarily, my major uhm . . . uhm input you know so far as information would be either the TV or the newspaper. So uhm . . . I would just say some of the time. (pause) I feel like I'd like to know more . . . but it's just I'm not real sure that I'm as familiar as I should be with modern news issues because there's a lot to keep up with.

Notice here too the respondent's mention that she is not as familiar with the news as she *should be,* suggesting that the question also activated thoughts and feelings about appearing to be inadequate or ignorant in the eyes of the interviewer.

Not everyone who received Form B, however, mentioned in their concurrent or retrospective reports following the news, probably because they pay little or no attention to the news and thus there is little or nothing of that sort to be activated when the question is asked. Consider, for example, this protocol from an interview with a black woman, age 27, who had a high school education and was employed in a semi-skilled job at a local hospital. She answered the question as follows:

> I have to say some of the time cause I'm not up on political and government, like . . . maybe like not if I should be. And the only time I really get interested is in an election year.

As one might infer from this protocol, this woman probably watches the news or listens to it on the radio only now and then and rarely, if ever, reads stories about government and politics in the newspaper, and thus there is nothing of that sort evident in her report. About all that the question brought to mind for her about politics was a fleeting reference to her thoughts of being interested in politics only during election years.

Furthermore, she talked about not being "up on political and government" as she *should be,* an indication that being asked a question on this subject, about which she knows little or nothing, activated thoughts and feelings about appearing to be a dumbbell in the eyes of the interviewer, something that was clearly evident in her immediate retrospective report in response to the request from the interviewer to "tell me all that you can remember about your thinking as you answered this question." She answered, "About my thinking? Like how stupid I am when it comes to politics."

Keeping these responses to Form B in mind, let us look now at some of the protocols generated by the sequence of the questions on Form A, in which the context effect is known to occur. Recall that on this form respondents are asked first about whether they remember anything special that their representative has done for the district or the people in the district and second about whether they remember how their congressman has voted on any legislation that has come up in the House of Representatives. Not until then are they asked how much they follow what is going on in government and public affairs.

The first of these protocols is from an interview with a college student, a white male, age 19. When asked first if he remembered anything special that his representative had done for the district, he responded by saying, "I don't know who my U.S. district guy is." When asked next if he remembered how his congressman had voted on any legislation, he simply said, "No." And when asked then how much he followed what is going on in government and public affairs, he replied, "Hardly at all, just around elections." Asked, finally, to tell all that he could remember about his thinking as he answered the question, he reported:

> I don't know who the guy is. So I . . . I was thinking maybe it was Luken, but I thought he was retired. And since I just became able to vote when I was 18, I haven't really been around that long to follow.

Notice in this protocol that the respondent made no references to following the news as we found on most of the Form B protocols and that his thoughts while answering the question about how much he followed what was going on in government and public affairs were concerned primarily with his lack of knowledge about his congressman, in particular not knowing his name. This suggests that he had used this information in his short-term memory, largely, if not entirely, to infer that he followed what is going on "hardly at all" except, as he says, around elections, thoughts about which were also activated by asking this question.

We find a similar pattern in the next protocol, this one from a first-year medical student, a white female, age 23. She, too, was unable to answer either of the two questions about her congressman's record, saying "no" to both of them. When asked, then, how much she followed what is going on in government and public affairs, she said succinctly, "Hardly at all." When asked to tell all that she could remember about her thinking as she answered the question, she responded:

Starting at the question about my legislator, well first of all, uhm, if you asked me who my legislator is I probably wouldn't know, not because, just because I can't remember. And as far as bills and that go, I just don't read that stuff in the paper, and uh, it's embarrassing, that you're not up on all this, that I'm not up on all this, and I guess, if you let me think about it for ten minutes I guess I could probably have thought of some stuff, but on the spot I couldn't come up with anything, so . . .

Here again we find that the respondent was thinking largely about not knowing anything about her congressman, especially the name of the "legislator," as she was trying to answer the question about how much she followed what is going on in government and public affairs. Thus she inferred on the basis of that lack of knowledge that she must follow what is going on "hardly at all." Notice too in her report that there was only a brief mention about following the news, that being a negative reference to the fact that she did not read about legislative bills in the newspaper. So even here, following the news is *redefined* by the context of the question to mean following legislative news.

Finally, we see some evidence in her report that her ability to answer the questions about her congressman simultaneously activated feelings of embarrassment. Thinking out loud gives us information, then, not only about cognitions that are activated but about affect as well.

Another protocol, which I shall not present here, shows much the same pattern: The respondent said that she does not follow what is going on in government and public affairs mostly because, it appeared, she could not think of the name of her representative, let alone remember what he has done.

Thus in all of these protocols, there is evidence that the context effect on Form A is created by focusing a respondent's attention on his lack of knowledge about his U.S. representative as the basis for answering the question about how much he follows what is going on rather than on his memories of how much he follows the news about government and public affairs by watching television, reading the newspaper, or listening to the radio. In other words, the context effect occurs by focusing the respondent's attention on the contents of his *short-term* memory, which are created by his response to the first two questions about his representative, rather than on the contents of his *long-term* memory, which are based on his previous experience in following what is going on in government and public affairs.

A more formal content analysis and coding of the think-aloud responses to this question tend to support the memory bias hypothesis suggested by the initial protocols. Of the 48 (multiple) open-ended responses to Form A, 18 (37.5%) indicated an attempt by the respondent to try to think of who his or her U.S. Representative was or gave evidence of some other reference to answering the preceding knowledge questions, compared with none (0%) of the 37 open-ended responses given to Form B. Similarly, of the 48 open-ended responses to Form A, 10 (20.8%) contained expressions of feeling "dumb" or embarrassed for not knowing the answers or other indications that he or she *should* be better informed about politics, compared with 5 of the 37 (13.5%) open-ended responses to Form B—a clear manifestation of the difference in *affect*, as well as cognitions, elicited by the two alternative forms of the question.

Finally, as the memory bias hypothesis would suggest, a noticeably larger percentage of the open-ended responses given to Form B (28 of 37, or 75.7%) mentioned ways in which the respondent normally does follow politics—such as reading the newspaper, watching the news or campaign events like debates, talking to friends or co-workers about politics, and various other political activities—compared with just 14 of the 48 (29.2%) responses given to Form A. There is, then, some crude quantitative evidence to support this heuristically generated hypothesis, which obviously needs to be tested more rigorously with a larger, independently drawn sample.

Conclusion

In brief, I believe the think-aloud technique can be quite useful not only as a heuristic method for generating alternative hypotheses about the psychological sources of context effects in public opinion surveys but also as a way to test such hypotheses given a sufficient sample of protocols. I also think that the protocols produced by this technique can give us some valuable clues about the elusive cognitive processes that mediate various question-order and context effects, and about the nature of the more general theoretical model that needs to be developed. Finally, as I have suggested elsewhere (Bishop, 1986), the think-aloud technique can be used as an intensive, in-depth procedure by survey practitioners not only for pretesting new survey questions but also for reassessing the meaning of older, well-established questions, such as those appearing in the National Election Studies and the NORC General Social Survey. For finding out what respondents "have in mind" as they answer survey questions, the think-aloud technique hardly needs to be emphasized as a useful, theoretical, and practical tool.

Acknowledgments. The author would like to thank Holly Alder, Chad Solomon, and Andy Smith for their assistance in gathering the protocols for the respondent interviews.

Appendix: Think-Aloud Instructions

In this interview we are interested in what you think about when you answer some questions that I'm going to ask you. In order to do this, I am going to ask you to *think aloud* as you answer the question. What I mean by think aloud is that I want you to tell me *everything* you are thinking from the time you first hear the question until you give an answer. I would like you to talk aloud *constantly* from the time I ask the question until you have given your answer to the question. I don't want you to try to plan out what you say or try to explain to me what you are saying. Just act as if you are alone in the room speaking to yourself. It is most important that you keep talking. If you are silent for any long period of time I will ask you to talk. Do you understand what I want you to do?

Good, now we will begin with some practice questions: "In the last *12* months, how many times have you gone to a doctor, or a dentist, or a hospital, or utilized any health care specialist or facility?"

Good, now I want to see how much you can remember about what you were thinking from the time I asked you the question until you gave the answer. We are interested in what you actually can *remember* rather than what you think you must have thought. If possible, I would like you to tell me about your memories in the sequence in which they occurred while you were answering the question. Please tell me if you are uncertain about any of your memories. I don't want you to work on counting visits again, just report all that you can remember thinking about when answering the question. Now tell me what you remember.

Good, now I will give you two more practice questions before we proceed with the interview. I want you to do the same thing for each of these questions. I want you to *think aloud* as before as you think about the questions, and after you have answered it, I will ask you to report all that you can remember about your thinking. Any questions? Here is the next question:

A. *How many windows are there/were there in your parent's house?*

B. Now tell me all that you can remember about your thinking.

C. Good, now here is another practice question.

D. Name *20* animals.

E. Now tell me all that you can remember about your thinking.

F. Good, now keep thinking *out loud* as I ask you some more questions.

12
Thoughts on the Nature of Context Effects

Tom W. Smith

Despite over 40 years of study, question order is probably the least developed and most problematic aspect of survey research. As Schuman and Presser (1981) remarked in their work on survey methodology:

> Overall, order effects . . . constitute one of the most important areas for methodological research. They can be very large [and] are difficult to predict. . . . At this point research needs to be aimed not merely at producing more examples, but at understanding why those already obtained occur. (p. 77)

This perplexity is shared by Bradburn (1983), who observes, "No topic in questionnaire construction is more vexing or resistant to easy generalization than that of question order" (p. 302), and by Groves (1989), who notes that "there seems to be no general theory that predicts when such effects are to be expected and when they should not be expected" (p. 479). There is a temptation to blame our collective befuddlement on a dearth of experimental studies. Although we, like Oliver Twist, would like "more," the paucity of data is not the main cause for our ignorance. There have been nearly 100 studies of order effects, most involving split-ballot experiments.

First and most fundamentally, understanding has been limited because the topic is extremely complex. It now appears that there are many distinct types of order effects. Until recently we have been like 19th century physicians, who used the term "a cancer" to cover many separate diseases. We are now only beginning to distinguish, sort out, and study the different types of order effects and their causes. We are not even sure at this point if we have identified the main causal processes or correctly specified the major types of order effects. We are beginning to realize that a knowledge of social psychology (e.g., attitude change) and cognitive psychology (e.g., memory recall and linkage) will be required to understand order effects.

Second, development has been hampered by an atheoretical focus. Most early studies have lacked explicit (and a number even implicit) explanations for the effects under investigation. The development and testing of competing hypotheses has typically been ignored, and even when the previous literature is cited by later studies, there is often no cumulativeness of research. Studies are cited as examples, but we have not tended to learn from these examples.

Third, there has been a major underanalysis of existing empirical data. The majority of experiments merely compare the marginal distribution of B under orders AB and $\overline{A}$B. Reciprocal marginal effects, interitem associations, conditional effects, and interactions with other variables have rarely been examined.

In brief, we have been trying to understand a complex problem without adequately applying either the theoretical or empirical tools of the social scientific method. As a result, we have been able to demonstrate repeatedly the existence or nonexistence of various particular order effects with little cumulative understanding of the causes and conditions involved.

This chapter (a) examines the use of conditional order effects as a method for understanding the nature of context effects, (b) considers how common context effects are, (c) evaluates the related issues of scattering and buffering, and (d) reviews various systems for classifying context.

Conditional Order Effects

Conditional order effects are one of the most commonly overlooked yet most important aspects of context effects. Almost all studies prior to Schuman and Presser's (1981), as well as many since, have assumed that it is the prior question or questions themselves that have induced order effects in subsequent questions. This holistic assumption appears likely for certain types of order effects (see section later in this chapter on Classifications and Causes) but not for other types. Implicitly (and rarely explicitly) in the early literature, there is an indication that the order effect rests not only on the context of a prior question but also on how one responded to the antecedent question. This interaction between question order and response to the antecedent question is what I call a "conditional order effect." I focus on this aspect of order effects because (a) I believe that conditional effects are common among order effects and (b) understanding the conditional relationship between antecedent and subsequent responses greatly facilitates comprehending the nature and causes of context effects.

Prior to the work of Schuman and Presser (1981), not one study tested for conditional effects. This makes conditional effects the most neglected aspect of order effects. In contrast, other aspects of order effects beyond unidirectional, marginal effects, such as interitem associations, reciprocal marginal effects, and interactions with other variables, have been measured in various studies. To study conditional order effects, I was able to draw on three examples from Schuman and Presser: general and specific abortion, Communist and American reporters, and general and specific job discrimination; five examples from the General Social Surveys (GSSs): tax and spending, alienation and institutional confidence, marital and general happiness, national service for men and women, and anomia; one example from the Greater Cincinnati Surveys: political interest and congressional knowledge; and four examples from NORC's Chicago context effects surveys: welfare spending and economic individualism, welfare spending and government responsibility, Cuba and aid to the contras, and Vietnam and aid to the contras. The GSSs are based on full probability personal interviews and the rest on random-digit-dialed (RDD) telephone surveys. The Schuman and Presser and GSS experiments are based on samples of the national adult population conducted between 1976 and 1982 by, respectively, the Survey Research Center at the University of Michigan or the National Opinion Research Center at the University of Chicago (for more details, see Schuman & Presser, 1981, and Davis & Smith, 1989). The Greater Cincinnati experiments were conducted in the Cincinnati metropolitan area in 1983–84 (Bishop, 1987), and the NORC Chicago context effects surveys were carried out in Chicago in 1987 (Tourangeau, Rasinski, Bradburn, & D'Andrade, 1989a).

Table 12.1 shows six cases in which context effects were conditional on responses to the antecedent question (see Davis & Smith, 1989, and Schuman & Presser, 1981, for wordings). In the first example, the overall context effect is for the appearance of the marital happiness question immediately before the general happiness question to increase general happiness.[1] Looking at the conditional context effects, we see that the effect is largely confined to those rating their marriages as very happy. Mentions of marital happiness increase general happiness, since most married people rate their marriage as very happy; but among the unhappily married, there is no nuptial bliss to spread to general happiness.

In the second example, placing alienation items before confidence items reduces the confidence rating of major companies. This effect is, however, entirely confined among those who agreed with the proposition that "the rich get richer and the poor get poorer." Similarly, asking about allowing Communist reporters to gather news in the United States first reduces support for allowing an American reporter to cover a Communist country such as Russia only among those opposed to allowing Communist coverage of the United States.[2] Likewise, in the tax/spending example, fiscal conservatives (people rejecting most current spending levels as too high) do not vary their opinions on taxes, whereas spending moderates and liberals are less likely to object to taxes after the spending items. Next, people who favor national service for women do not differ in their attitudes toward national service for men by whether the item on men or women is asked first, but those opposing national service for women show less support for national service for men when the men question follows the women question. Lastly, the asking of two anomia items in a row increases the anomic responses

---

[1]A result that is at odds with Schuman and Presser's similar experiment (1981; Schuman, Presser, & Ludwig, 1981).

[2]The Communist/American reporters example is actually more complicated than the others because the marginal effects are reciprocal. As a result, the distribution of the conditional controls varies by order.

to the second item. This response occurs among those who agree with the first statement that the lot of the average man is getting worse and does not occur among those disagreeing with that statement. (For more analysis of this experiment, see T. W. Smith, 1983b.)

TABLE 12.1. Six Examples of Conditional Context Effects

Item	Order		Context Effect
	General Happiness by Marital Happiness by Order		
	Marital/General	General/Marital	(Order 1 – Order 2)
	Marital Happiness = Very Happy		
	56.1 (421)	47.5 (177)	8.6
General happiness (% very)			
	Marital Happiness = Not Very Happy		
	11.5 (192)	8.8 (91)	2.7
	Confidence in Major Companies by Alienation by Order		
	Alienation/ Confidence	Confidence/ Alienation	(Order 1 – Order 2)
	Rich Get Richer = Yes		
	11.9 (528)	22.6 (541)	−10.7
Major companies (% great deal)			
	Rich Get Richer = No		
	38.9 (175)	39.2 (169)	0.7
	American Reporters by Communist Reporters by Order		
	American/Communist	Communist/American	(Order 1 – Order 2)
	Communist Reporters = Allow		
	99.0 (100)	96.2 (130)	2.8
American reporters (% allow)			
	Communist Reporters = No		
	21.6 (74)	40.0 (40)	−18.4
	Tax Approval by Spending Preferences by Order		
	Spend/Tax	Tax/Spend	(Order 1–Order 2)
	Spend Scale = Antispending		
	59.7 (144)	61.0 (141)	−1.3
Tax (% taxes too high)			
	Spend Scale = Not Most Antispending		
	68.0 (400)	49.4 (389)	18.6

(Table 12.1 continued)

TABLE 12.1. Continued

Item	Order		Context Effect
	National Service for Women by National Service for Men by Order		
	Men/Women	Women/Men	(Order 1 – Order 2)
	National Service for Women = Favor		
	98.3 (464)	98.9 (443)	0.6
(% favor, strongly favor for men)			
	National Service for Men = Oppose		
	39.0 (246)	28.4 (282)	–10.6
	Anomia by Anomia		
	Clustered (Lot Getting Worse/ Not Fair to Have Child)	Scattered	(Order 1 – Order 2)
	Lot Getting Worse = Agree		
	50.9 (475)	31.6 (455)	–19.3
Not fair to have child (% agree)			
	Lot Getting Worse = Disagree		
	21.8 (211)	19.8 (232)	–2.0

For two of these examples, I was able to examine conditional effects in greater detail by looking at seven levels on the alienation scale and four spending levels (Table 12.2). First, in both cases the overall order effect (less confidence in business after alienation items and less opposition to taxes after spending questions) is not merely absent under certain conditions but reverses at one pole. The outlook of the extreme antispending and unalienated groups differs so much from the majority that the spending and alienation items have an opposite impact on them than for the majority. This means that the gross order effect across individuals is substantially greater than the net effect observed among the aggregate population.

The second similarity is more surprising. The largest order effect in the main direction does not occur at the opposite pole on alienation but in the middle. The middle conditional order effect is also large on the tax/spending example. In both cases this effect occurs among the median group, those with 3 agrees and 3 disagrees on the alienation scale and those with an average score of 2 (spending about right) on the 11 spending items. I hypothesized that the effects might increase among the median groups because those groups contained a large share of people with weak attitudes on the issues whose median scores were more a product of nonattitudes and random responding than a reflection of a considered middle position. Being without fixed attitudes, they were more swayable by

TABLE 12.2. Detailed Conditional Effects

Item	Order		Context Effect
	Confidence in Major Companies by Alienation Scale by Order		
	Alienation/ Confidence	Confidence/ Alienation	(Order 1 − Order 2)
	Alienation Scale = 0		
	51.5 (68)	40.0 (40)	11.5
	Alienation Scale = 1		
	27.9 (61)	34.9 (83)	−7.0
Confidence in major	Alienation Scale = 2		
companies	20.9 (86)	34.5 (94)	−13.4
(% great deal)	Alienation Scale = 3		
	10.1 (89)	33.0 (94)	−22.9
	Alienation Scale = 4		
	24.1 (87)	28.7 (108)	−4.6
	Alienation Scale = 5		
	10.0 (110)	13.5 (104)	−3.5
	Alienation Scale = 6		
	6.2 (97)	12.1 (91)	−5.9
	Tax Approval by Spending Preferences by Order		
	Spend/Tax	Tax/Spend	(Order 1 − Order 2)
	Spend Scale = Most Antispending		
	57.8 (90)	65.2 (89)	−7.4
Tax	Spend Scale = Low Spending		
(% taxes too high)	69.8 (182)	49.4 (168)	20.4
	Spend Scale = Moderate Spending		
	65.4 (208)	55.0 (191)	10.4
	Spend Scale = High Spending		
	65.6 (64)	40.2 (82)	25.2

question order (Tourangeau & Rasinski, 1988; Tourangeau, Rasinski, Bradburn, & D'Andrade, 1988).

I tried to check this by examining whether this group showed less interest, knowledge, or involvement. The median group did not overrepresent less educated respondents or those giving "don't knows" to other attitude questions. On the spending questions, however, the median group had the highest level of nonvoting (32.8% vs. 22.3% for everyone), but on the alienation items, no difference appeared. These minimal results probably occurred because the median group contained both random responders and those with moderate positions and because of the difficulty of finding general items that would predict random responding to a particular scale. The one confirmation on the voting item may indicate that my explanation for why middle order effects were high is plausible.

The next two examples (Tables 12.3 and 12.4) show conditional effects occurring in combination with general context effects. In Table 12.3, the general

TABLE 12.3. Respondents Who Follow Politics "Most of the Time," by Congressional Knowledge and Context (%)

| | Order | | |
Congressional Knowledge	Follows/ Cong. Items	Cong. Items/ Follows	Context Effect
Knows about Congress = Both (2)	74.0 (50)	66.7 (36)	−7.3
Knows about Congress = Partial (1)	55.3 (199)	38.3 (162)	−16.9
Knows about Congress = Neither (0)	30.7 (651)	21.4 (669)	−9.3

Source: Adapted from Bishop (1987, Table 3). Order compares Forms A and B and collapses over and ignores item about knowing governor.

effect is for prior questions asking about the actions and votes of one's representative in Congress to lead to fewer reports of following politics and public affairs "most of the time." This effect occurs regardless of how much knowledge one professed. The context effect is not uniform, however, but also conditional, being much larger among those claiming partial knowledge than among those with full or no knowledge. This resembles the pattern appearing in Table 12.2, with the median group showing a larger effect than the extremes. Unlike the other cases, the trigger questions measure knowledge rather than an attitude. Perhaps those responding to the two difficult congressional questions include a number of labile respondents who had randomly responded to the knowledge questions (for more on this experiment, see Bishop, 1987).

The example in Table 12.4 shows the results from four of the NORC Chicago context effects studies. In each case, there are main effects (support for welfare spending is shifted by prior items on both economic individualism and government responsibility and favoring contra aid is influenced by the earlier items on Cuba and Vietnam) as well as conditional effects. The context effects are typically twice as large among those with high agreement with the trigger items as among those with low agreement with these items. For example, among those with low agreement with the Vietnam items, the context effect is −9.1 percentage points, whereas those with high agreement show an effect of −19.1 percentage points (for more analysis of these experiments, see Tourangeau & Rasinski, 1988; Tourangeau et al., 1988, 1989a).[3]

The final two examples (Table 12.5) show no evidence of conditional order effects, but actually both underscore the importance of checking for these specifications. As Schuman and Presser note, the lack of a conditional effect on the abortion questions is surprising, since their prime explanation of the effect (a

---

[3]These results are contrary to those reported by these authors. They generally report no such conditional effects. For example, "Similarly, the effects of context did not depend on the respondent's initial opinion about the target issue" (Tourangeau et al., 1988, p. 30).

TABLE 12.4. Endorsement of Welfare and Nicaragua Target Items, by Context and Level of Agreement with the Context Items (%)

Context Set	Low	High
	Favor Increased Welfare Spending	
	Agreement with Government Responsibility Items	
Economic individualism	42.4	52.5
Government responsibility	52.3	78.1
Context effect (bottom – top)	+9.9	+25.6
	Agreement with Economic Individualism Items	
Economic individualism	56.5	40.7
Government responsibility	66.8	58.8
Context effect (bottom – top)	+10.3	+18.1
	Favor Increased Welfare Spending	
	Agreement with Cuba Issue	
Cuba	26.2	57.9
Vietnam	17.2	38.5
Context effect (bottom – top)	–9.0	–19.4
	Agreement with Vietnam	
Cuba	40.4	41.6
Vietnam	31.3	22.5
Context effect (bottom – top)	–9.1	–19.1

Source: This table is adapted by permission from Tourangeau et al. (1989a, Table 4). Copyright © by Academic Press. The N for each row is approximately 500.

Note: Respondents received both sets of context items (e.g., the items on economic individualism and those on government responsibility), with one set coming before the relevant target item and the other set coming afterward. The context set variable indicates the items that preceded the target.

subtraction effect) implies such an effect. They argue that people who are presented with the popular, specific reason for abortions in case of possible defects in the unborn child first tend to exclude this reason from the subsequent general abortion question and thereby lower their support for the general abortion item. This scenario works nicely for the majority of people who approve of abortions in cases of possible birth defects, but it fails to explain why people who opposed abortion for birth defects are also less likely to approve of general abortions when the specific birth defect item comes first. Presumably since birth defects have been rejected as a good reason for an abortion, there is no positive component to subtract out of the general abortion question. Either there is a general

TABLE 12.5. Six Examples of Conditional Context Effects

Item	Order		Context Effect
	General Abortion by Specific Abortion by Order		
	Specific/General	General/Specific	(Order 1 – Order 2)
	Specific Abortion (Defect) = Yes		
General abortion (no more children = Yes)	56.1 (246)	69.2 (253)	–13.1
	Specific Abortion (Defect) = No		
	6.4 (47)	19.2 (52)	–12.8
	General Job Discrimination by Specific Job Discrimination by Order		
	Specific/General	General/Specific	(Order 1 – Order 2)
	Specific Discrimination (Avoid Friction) = Favor		
General discrimination (in principle) = Favor	18.7 (32)	13.3 (30)	5.4
	Specific Discrimination (Avoid Friction) = Oppose		
	9.6 (157)	3.2 (158)	6.4

explanation other than the subtraction effect proposed by Schuman and Presser, or we have two distinct conditional effects that happen to be equal in magnitude.

Alternative explanations include a contrast effect. The general reason may not seem as attractive when compared to the highly attractive birth defect reason, and therefore fewer people may endorse the general abortion question. This contrast effect could work either among people opposed to abortions for birth defects or among those in favor of it, since even those opposed to abortions for birth defects might recognize it as a better reason than general abortion and therefore reduce their approval of the general item.

Another possible explanation has similarities to the subtraction effect, a redefinition effect. When the general question appears first, some people think of the various reasons for not having another child, and since some of the reasons are attractive (e.g., the prevention of birth defects), they approve of the general abortion question. When it comes second, they realize that it does not mention birth defects and may infer that it does not include any other extenuating circumstances either. It thus changes from being a general abortion question to being a specific question about unwanted children. The specific/general ordering clarifies that the so-called general question does not include any extraordinary reasons for not wanting another child but simply a desire to avoid more children. Thus, even someone opposed to abortion for birth defects would be less likely to support general abortion not because birth defects are excluded from the question but because the question is seen as excluding all special circumstances. Since the context redefines what the general question is asking about, it changes how everyone responds to the question regardless of their attitude on the birth defect item.

Although either of these general explanations may explain the lack of an interaction within the birth defect question, it is also possible to come up with particular explanations for those opposed to abortions for birth defects. From a Guttman scaling perspective, those who say "no" to abortion for birth defects but "yes" to abortion for preventing more children represent an error group.[4] Perhaps these cases do represent error by people who are confused by or inattentive to the abortion question. Although the specific-to-general (easy-to-hard) order reduces error, the opposite order permits more random error on the general question. Perhaps the appearance of the general question second allowed respondents more time to sort out their thoughts on abortion and therefore to give consistent rather than inconsistent response patterns. This would leave among the error cases those most confused about the abortion issue and a group whose true pattern deviated from the predominant pattern (e.g., those who thought defective children were God's special children and a blessing in disguise but that unwanted normal children would be raised without love and thus best prevented).

The situation about job discrimination is similar to abortion. No conditional effect is observed, but as Schuman and Presser note, this is counter to the consistency explanation suggested by the marginal shifts. I shall not go through possible alternative explanations for the absence of a conditional order effect but instead reiterate that the absence of such an effect is often as informative as its presence.

In 8 of 10 examples available, order effects were concentrated in whole (6 cases) or in part (2 cases) among certain categories of the antecedent question. It was not the mere mention of a prior topic that induced a marginal shift in the subsequent question but a respondent's position on the antecedent variable and the order that induced the order effect. In fact, from the tax/spending and alienation/confidence items, we see that even the direction of the order effect is dependent on the position on the antecedent item. This information can not only be used for a better understanding of the particular observed order effects (along with other empirical analysis of reciprocal marginals, interitem correlations, and interactions with other variables) but also perhaps allow a refined classification of order effects, better theory, and improved predictions of when order effects are likely.

Of course, context effects that are conditional on one's attitudes toward prior topics but not conditional on one's responses to prior questions may also occur. As I shall suggest in a later example, a prior question may lead one to access memories and beliefs that specify later questions (see section on Classifications

---

[4]Looking at the six abortion items on the GSS, which include the two items used by Schuman and Presser, we find that the general abortion item is the hardest item to approve, while the birth defect item is the second easiest. The coefficients of reproducibility and scalability are .94 and .81.

and Causes), but the prior question may not be framed in a way that allows recording expressions of those memories and beliefs so as to permit the measurement of a conditional order effect. It is unknown whether actually expressing an attitude in response to a prior question or merely accessing (but not expressing in a response to a prior question) the relevant memories and beliefs would create a similar context effect. One suspects, however, that actual expression of the conditional attitude in a prior question might exert a greater effect than activation without explicit expression.[5]

Commonness of Context Effects

There is some disagreement on how common context effects are. Tourangeau et al. (1988) conclude that "the literature on survey context effects may create the impression that such effects are relatively rare, involving items on a few scattered issues. These results here indicate otherwise" (pp. 22–23). This impression of pervasiveness is supported by numerous instances in which changes in question order have upset time series or caused other undesired measurement variations (Astin, Green, Korn, Schalit, & Berz, 1988; Cowan, Murphy, & Wiener, 1978; Gibson, Shapiro, Murphy, & Stanko, 1978; T. W. Smith, 1986b, 1988c; Turner & Martin, 1984). Schuman and Presser (1981), on the other hand, reach a conclusion that at least differs in emphasis: "Question-order effects are evidently not pervasive, . . . but there are enough instances to show they are not rare either" (p. 74). This nonpervasive impression is supported by numerous failures to produce context effects in experiments designed to do so (Schuman & Presser, 1981; T. W. Smith, 1983a; Turner and Martin, 1984) and by the ability of different houses to produce similar marginals when the same questions, but different question content (and other variations), existed (Turner & Martin, 1984; T. W. Smith, 1978, 1982).

Two studies have conducted general searches for context effects.[6] Schuman and Presser (1981) examined the 1971 Detroit Area Study (DAS). The DAS used split ballots in order to accommodate various experiments in either question order or wording. They looked at 113 attitude items that were not the designed objects of these experiments but appeared after the experiments and thus varied in

---

[5]In terms of the cognitive framework of Tourangeau and Rasinski that we explore later, there are several ways that conditional order effects could be created. Even if no relevant attitude was directly expressed, a retrieval carryover effect could occur if a prior question triggered selective memory sampling and people differed in their affect toward the primed memories. In addition, the expression of a relevant prior attitude could create a conditional order effect by causing judgmental carryover or consistency editing during the response selection stage.

[6]Also see Bradburn and Mason (1964), which tested for 14 differences in marginals across four forms and found no statistically significant variation.

context due to the prior experiments. Apparently using simple random sample (SRS) assumptions, they found eight significant differences at the .05 level, just two above what chance would predict. Their inspection of these eight suggested that three probably represented real effects and the rest were due to sample variation.

I have examined the 1988 GSS (T. W. Smith, 1988a). In 1988 the GSS switched from an across-years rotation scheme to a within-year split-ballot design (T. W. Smith, 1988b). That meant that three split ballots were employed. Each ballot represented a year under the old across-years rotation scheme. Demographics typically appeared on all three ballots, and attitudes and other items usually appeared on two of the three ballots. In the vast majority of cases, the items appearing on different ballots appeared in very different orders. I tested both for context effects across the ballots and for evidence of context effects by grouping together earlier years that largely duplicated the same orders that appeared in the 1988 ballots. Among 358 questions that varied in context across the ballots, 9.2% were found to vary significantly using SRS assumptions, but only 3.6% varied significantly when adjusted for design effects. Close examination of the 14 statistically significant adjusted results suggests that 6 probably represent real context effects and the remaining 8 are chance occurrences.

These studies suggest that unanticipated context effects might occur once out of every 40–60 questions. However, this is probably an underestimate, since on the GSS, and presumably on the DAS, batteries of questions on one topic (e.g., the seven abortion items) were asked in a block and not varied across ballots. Since context effects are most likely to occur between closely related items, the failure to vary items experimentally within topical blocks probably underestimates the frequency of context effects.[7]

Buffers, Scattering, and Context Effects

Almost all early research on context effects placed the experimental variation in order immediately prior to the target item. In recent years, however, several studies have been conducted that have varied the placement of the trigger question(s). One approach inserts a buffer of unrelated items between the trigger and the target, and the other presents the trigger items either in a block or scattered among unrelated items. In the buffering approach, investigators have taken a well-known context effect and tested its power by inserting a buffer of items between

---

[7]The abortion example discussed above is a prime example of what can occur when the order within such a block is disturbed. See also Schuman and Presser's (1981) discussion of same. For other examples, see Astin et al. (1988) and T. W. Smith (1984). I suspect that within-scale context effects are rather common, probably even typical. Since such scales tend to be replicated as units without changes to their internal order, these effects are rarely studied, and whatever context effects exist generally remain fixed across administrations of the scale.

the trigger and the target (Bishop, 1987; Schuman, Kalton, & Ludwig, 1983). These studies indicate that context effects are quite robust and work with little or no diminution even when a large buffer intervenes. In the block/scattered approach, the investigators test whether concentration in a block is needed to affect respondents or perhaps is so obvious that it creates a backfire effect (Tourangeau et al., 1988, 1989a). Despite some early indications that scattering might be more effective than blocking, Tourangeau and his colleagues now believe that scattering diminishes and may eliminate context effects. Their meta-analysis of the buffer and scattered/blocked experiments showed that intervening items do diminish context effects (Tourangeau et al., 1988).

This conclusion is supported by my research on context effects that suggests a first-only effect (T. W. Smith, 1981a, 1988a). In this research, I found three examples of context effects influencing only the first item on subsequent scales. For example, alienation items reduced the confidence rating of the first item in the 13-item confidence items but had no significant impact on the distributions of the following 12 items (T. W. Smith, 1981a). This suggests not only that scattering or a wide buffer can reduce a context effect but that a single item may absorb the effect. The very robust effects detected by some investigators may be because they tested particularly strong context effects, and these results may be the exceptions rather than the rule.

Classifications and Causes

In order to advance in the study of context effects, we need to develop theories about what causes such effects. Two approaches have been used that might facilitate this process. The first is the classification of context effects into different types according to their cause and effect. The second is to delimit the cognitive steps involved in answering questions and to relate how context might operate during each of these steps. Although these two approaches have developed independently and are distinct, they overlap. The classification approach largely evolved out of an attempt to explain existing or known context effects by applying relevant social-psychological and cognitive theories. The cognitive-steps approach came from a general attempt to apply cognitive theory first to the survey process in general and then to context effects in particular.

Schuman and Presser (1981) and Bradburn (1983; Bradburn & Mason, 1964) have formulated two similar classifications schemes for question-order effects[8] (see Table 12.6). Both refer to psychological or cognitive processes by which order influences subsequent questions. Schuman and Presser's classification is more detailed and more hierarchically organized than Bradburn's but mainly differs by using question-type distinctions (part and whole) within the consistency

---

[8]Here, as elsewhere in this chapter, we exclude the related matter of response-order effects (see Schuman & Presser, 1981, pp. 56–74).

TABLE 12.6. Classification of Order Effects

Schuman and Presser	Bradburn
I. Context effects (transfers of meaning)	
A. Part–part consistency	
1. Normative principles	
2. Logical inference	1. Consistency
B. Part–whole consistency	
C. Part–part contrast	
D. Part–whole contrast	
1. Subtraction	2. Redundancy
2. Simple contrast	
E. Salience	3. Saliency
II. Sequence effects (more mechanical types of artifacts)	
A. Rapport	4. Rapport
B. Fatigue	5. Fatigue
C. Initial frame of reference	

Source: Schuman and Presser (1981), Bradburn and Mason (1964), and Bradburn (1985).

and contrast categories and the addition of the initial frame of reference and simple contrast classes.

Tourangeau, Rasinski, and others (Tourangeau & Rasinski, 1988; Tourangeau et al., 1988; Strack & Martin, 1987) have more recently described the various steps and processes involved in answering survey questions and how context could effect each step and process. Tourangeau and Rasinski (1988) describe the four steps in answering a survey question: (a) interpretation, (b) retrieval, (c) judgment, and (d) response selection. At each stage they posit two types of context effects: carryover and backfire.[9] Carryover effects involve the usually automatic or unconscious influence of prior questions on subsequent questions (except for editing during the response selection stage). In some general sense, a prior question shapes responses to a later question during one or more of the answering stages. Backfire effects are a more conscious rejection of the influence of prior questions when answering later questions. In addition to these eight types of possible context effects, Tourangeau and Rasinski subdivide the response selection stage into the processes of mapping attitudes into response categories and editing for the sake of either consistency or self-presentation.

The Tourangeau-Rasinski approach has the decided advantage of grounding context effects in cognitive theories. Their work is an excellent example of intellectual, hybrid vigor, since it uses the results from psychological experiments to illuminate survey research. But in explaining and illustrating their differing types of context effects, they may draw too heavily from diverse literatures in experimental psychology at the expense of underexamining survey research's own experiments on context effects.

---

[9]The authors sometimes refer to these as assimilation and contrast, respectively.

In the following sections, I shall use a slightly modified version of the Schuman-Presser/Bradburn classifications[10] to review the extant survey literature on context effects (see T. W. Smith, 1986a, for the literature) and then consider how this standard scheme meshes with the cognitive approach of Tourangeau-Rasinski.

Order effects come in many variations. Some context effects are unrelated to the substance of the prior questions, others are related to the prior substance but not to prior responses, and still others are related to both the substance and one's response to the prior question. First, there are Schuman and Presser's sequence effects (also called "position effects"). These are sometimes described as "mechanical" and are believed to be completely unrelated to the substance of the preceding question(s). A rapport effect argues that a more trusting and open exchange of information occurs after the interview has developed. Less mentioned and perhaps sometimes subsumed under rapport effects are learning effects. Learning effects suggest that respondents, in general, learn their role as respondents better as the interview unfolds and in particular become more familiar with response scales and other tasks (e.g., the use of 7-point scales or sorting tasks). This reduces measurement error. At the opposite pole, a fatigue effect stipulates that, after a long series of questions, a respondent grows tired and gives less complete and more perfunctory answers. Another less commonly mentioned position effect is what Schuman and Presser (1981, pp. 51–52) call an "initial frame of reference effect." Within a battery of questions rating or comparing topics on a common criterion, an item will tend to receive either its lowest or highest mean rating when it appears first.

Second, there are what Schuman and Presser call "context effects," which involve some transference of meaning between the antecedent question and the subsequent question. Some of these context effects depend only on the topics raised in the prior questions and not on a respondent's affect toward or responses to these items. One example is a stimulation effect (akin to priming) in which questions about a subject stimulate more reports of behavior related to or interest in the topic. For example, attitude questions about crime lead to more reports of criminal victimization (Cowan et al., 1978; Gibson et al., 1978), and questions about politics increase reported levels of interest in politics.[11] Three quite distinct explanations have been offered for these increases: improved memory search leading to more complete reports, increased telescoping of behaviors causing exaggerated reports, and intentional exaggeration because of role fulfillment pressures. Although improved memory search is usually the favored explanation, it is quite possible that all three processes can be at work either in different situations or even simultaneously in the same situation (e.g., some of the increased

---

[10]The basic categories are employed, but (a) some additional refinements and distinctions are added, along with some new terminology, and (b) the part–whole distinction is not utilized (T. W. Smith, 1986a).

[11]But for an exception, see Bishop, Oldendick, & Tuchfarber (1982, 1984a).

crime reports may come from a more thorough memory dragnet, whereas some come from increased telescoping).

Another effect that depends on the substance of prior questions is a redefinition or clarification effect (similar to redundancy and subtraction effects). For example, as part of a series of questions about the brand of washer, TV, etc., you own, an inquiry about "And what kind of car do you own?" would elicit more model names than the same question appearing alone, which would get more references to vans, sedans, convertibles, etc. Similarly, I posited above that the general–specific abortion effect might involve a redefinition of the general question. When the redefinition effect eliminates a specific element from the subsequent question, we have a subtraction effect as discussed earlier.

Closely related to the redefinition effect is redundancy. As Bradburn describes it, a person mentioning certain behaviors at an earlier point may consider it repetitive to mention them again. The respondent may believe that these elements are excluded from the subsequent question (redefinition) or simply be reluctant to go over the same ground twice even if the respondent realizes that the same information is applicable to the later questions.

Finally, simple contrast effects may fall into this category. Here one judges the desirability of the second question in light of the first. If the first represents a highly positive situation and the other a less attractive situation, the relative merit of the second item may seem even less because it is contrasted to the first and pales in comparison. This effect necessitates that a respondent recognizes a contrast between the desirability of two propositions but not necessarily that he endorses the attractive proposition. One need only recognize that, in general, such a distinction is seen.

Next there are context effects that depend not only on the substance of the prior question but also on responses to the antecedent question constraining response to the subsequent question. One such constraint or consistency effect involves the establishment of a normative principle between two questions. This is exemplified by the Communist/American reporters question. This type probably represents the strongest of context effects and usually, if not always, will cause reciprocal marginals effects (i.e., both A and B distributions will differ in orders AB and BA).

A second constraint effect establishes a logical connection between questions. This would include the tax/spending example. Although not too distant from normative effects (especially if we consider logic as a norm) and also involving, like the former, a conscious attempt to bring responses into line, the logical connection effect does not rest on a general social norm separate from the main substance of the items.[12]

Next comes a rather large and fairly amorphous category of focus effects (similar to salience effects). These focus attention on some topic that relates to the subsequent question. Questions about children preceding an abortion question

[12]For example, where context failed to induce logical constraint, see T. W. Smith (1981a, 1981c).

might reduce support for abortion, since the salient images of children might focus attention on unborn children rather than on women when considering the abortion questions.[13] Unlike logical connection effects, focus effects do not come from strictly logical propositions but rather from more subtle pressures and inclinations, and the impact is seen as working through memory access rather than through conscious reconciliation of response patterns.

It is, however, often difficult to determine whether responses involve conscious logical constraint ("I am very happily married. My marriage is the most important part of my life. Therefore, my life is very happy") or patterns of cognition (in thinking about general happiness, R has most ready access to the marital happiness memories that have just been recalled). In either case, being very happy on marriage will lead to increased reports of happiness on the general question, but the causes or processes are not the same. In the former case, general happiness responses are being consciously reconciled with the prior marital happiness response, which comes from the accessed memories of marital happiness, whereas in the latter case, the effect comes directly from the memories.

Third, although involving conditional effects in a general sense, it may not be possible to demonstrate conditionality because the antecedent questions may not have an item that explicitly records the attitude that specifies the order effect. A focus effect is conditional in that it is what you feel toward the topic covered by the antecedent question that determines your subsequent response. This may not be discernable, since the antecedent question may not inquire about feelings toward the topic. For example, in the classic dress-advertising example (American Marketing Association, 1937), "questions regarding dresses" preceded attitudes toward advertising. I do not know just what dress questions were asked but suppose that these questions covered such matters as place of purchase, styles favored, and the like. Subsequent attitude questions revealed that after the dress questions (a) ratings of advertising was more favorable and (b) dress advertising was the main type of advertising thought of. The factor that leads the increased focusing on dresses to improve advertising ratings is that women like dresses and as a result presumably like dress advertisements. Among the presumably small proportion of women who disliked clothes in general or dresses in particular, we would presumably not find an increase in favorable ratings of advertisements. Although there are distinct differences in the processes involved in these two classes of effects, they are differences of degree and specific examples may involve blends of both.

Table 12.7 compares these standard categories of context effects on the Tourangeau-Rasinski scheme. The fitting of the standard types into this framework was a difficult, but useful, exercise. It revealed strengths and limitations of both systems, showed when conceptualizations were similar and when they were divergent, and raised the possibility of developing a better overall understanding of order effects by drawing on elements of both classifications.

---

[13]I found little support for this particular example (T. W. Smith, 1983a).

TABLE 12.7. Comparison of the Tourangeau and Rasinski Categories with Traditional Classifications of Context Effects

Question-Answering Steps	Reactions to Prior Questions	
	Carryover	Backfire
A. Interpretation	Redefinition/clarification	Redundancy
B. Retrieval	Stimulation	
	Focus/salience	Simple contrast?
C. Judgment	Constraint (normative & logical)	Simple contrast
D. Response selection		
1. Mapping		
2. Editing		
a. Consistency	Constraint (normative & logical)	Simple contrast?
	Focus/salience	
b. Self-presentation	Focus/salience	

First, sequence effects are hard to relate to the Tourangeau-Rasinski scheme. It is possible to associate them with the various steps, but because sequence effects are not related to substance, the carryover versus backfire distinction seems to apply well. For example, fatigue effects in general lead to less accurate and less thoughtful response. Retrieval would tend to be less thorough and less accurate, and judgments would tend to be less considered and more labile. These effects result from the number of prior questions but do not seem to represent either carryover or backfire effects as Tourangeau and Rasinski conceptualized them.[14] The same would seem to apply to rapport, learning, and initial frame of reference effects.

Second, for substantive context effects, the matching of standard types to the Tourangeau-Rasinski scheme is more appropriate and useful. For the interpretation stage, there seem to be standard types that closely match both carryover and backfire effects. Redefinition/clarification effects are carryover interpretation effects whereby prior questions change or create meaning for a following question. Redundancy effects are backfire interpretation effects where a topic covered by a prior question is excluded from consideration in responding to a later question.

Carryover effects at the retrieval stage would seem to cover two types of traditional effects: stimulation effects and some, but not all, focus and general salience effects. Stimulation effects either result from more thorough memory searching or lead to overreporting through telescoping. Focus/salience effects at this stage come about from biased sampling of memory due to selective prim-

---

[14]Tourangeau and Rasinski (1988) explicitly admit that their framework is not comprehensive and separately discuss sequence effects.

ing. Backfire retrieval effects occur when respondents "discount or actively suppress information [created by prior questions] that they regard as suspect or irrelevant" (Tourangeau & Rasinski, 1988, p. 305). It is not clear if any of the standard categories are examples of this process, although some simple contrast effects may be of this type.

In the judgment stage, normative and logical constraint effects represent carryover effects, as do some of the more amorphous focus effects. For example, context may create or enhance in people's minds the norm of even-handedness as a standard for judging later questions. Simple contrast effects can represent backfire judgment effects where one's evaluation of a subsequent question is contrasted to an earlier standard of judgment.

The response selection stage covers some rather distinct processes that might well be thought of as involving different steps. The mapping process of figuring what response represents a respondent's attitude does not appear to be related to any of the standard types of context effects. (Learning effects would presumably lead to less error at this step.) At the editing stage, carryover effects are once again represented by both normative and logical constraint effects and more diffuse focus/salience effects. Whether a normative effect belongs in this category rather than in the judgment stage depends on whether the acknowledgment of the norm resulted from a perhaps unconscious and sincere application of a norm or the conscious and strategic decision to follow a norm in order to appear consistent. In the case of the even-handedness norm on the Communist/American reporters questions, a judgmental carryover effect exists if a norm is created in a respondent's mind that shapes attitudes toward a later question. A consistency response selection effect occurs if the norm does not really shape one's attitude toward allowing Communist reporters but one changes one's response in order to appear consistent with the norm. Although logically distinguishable, empirically separating these two types of normative effects would be difficult. Self-presentation/social desirability effects during editing involve related strategic responding and also cover some forms of focus/salience effects.

For backfire editing effects, there again do not appear to be any examples from the standard classification or survey literature. Tourangeau and Rasinski do describe a hypothetical example, which they call a "moderation effect." Consider the case of a person who has a self-perception as being a moderate on an issue (e.g., abortion). If that person has answered several questions in a pro-abortion direction, he or she might answer subsequent questions in an anti-abortion direction in order to maintain a moderate image, even though the respondent's true attitude on the individual subsequent questions might be pro-abortion.

What has the marrying of standard survey research classifications to the Tourangeau-Rasinski scheme suggested? First, the exclusion of sequence effects from their scheme indicates that their scheme is not comprehensive. Second, the lack of clear survey examples for several of their types suggest that these may be rare effects. Third, the splitting of several traditional effects across more than one of their categories shows that some existing types clearly involve different processes, and employing the Tourangeau-Rasinski framework clarifies the difference.

Fourth, the appearance within their categories of different standard effects (e.g., stimulation and focus among carryover retrieval effects) suggests that there are useful divisions within their stages (similar to those in the response selection stage). Fifth, the difficulty of empirically distinguishing between what stage or stages are involved indicates that great challenges await in identifying the processes that create context effects. Finally, combining elements of the standard classification scheme with the Tourangeau-Rasinski scheme will probably create a better framework than either alone.

Order effects can be induced by a variety of cognitive and social-psychological processes. These processes can intercede at various steps in the question-answering process and can impinge on later questions in at least two ways (carryover and backfire). Sometimes position alone is sufficient to create an effect, whereas other effects are stimulated by the substance of prior questions and often by a respondent's implicit or explicit attitude toward the prior substance.

In addition, many types of order effects can interact and commingle. For example, fatigue effects can be reduced or increased by question form and the topics covered. Although there may be a general fatigue curve associated with time or number of responses, the slope of this curve may be increased or decreased by such factors as the format of the questions and the interest and difficulty of the questions involved. In fact, two or more different (and even conflicting) effects may be relevant in the same instance. For example, extended discussions of a topic usually result in more interest in that issue being subsequently reported. Bishop (1987), however, found that when the discussion included several difficult knowledge questions about which most people lacked information, interest decreased. In this instance, it appears that the stimulation effect was overcome by a logical connection effect that linked low knowledge with low interest. It is probably such interactions that explain various failures to replicate order effects or to generalize to apparently similar circumstances (Schuman & Presser, 1981; Tourangeau & Rasinski, 1988; Turner & Martin, 1984).[15] Order effects, alas, are not of Horatian simplicity.

Conclusion

Refining our understanding of order effects will not be an easy task given (a) the large number of different processes involved; (b) the difficulty of distinguishing between competing explanations; (c) the interaction of order effects with such other factors as question type (e.g., behavioral, affective), question specificity (T. W. Smith, 1988a), question vagueness (Turner & Martin, 1984; Zaller, 1988), question centrality (Turner & Martin, 1984; Krosnick & Schuman,

---

[15]As Tourangeau and Rasinski (1988) note, "Context effects are often unstable; this instability may reflect the number and complexity of the processes that are responsible for the effects, as well as the large number of variables that can influence the size and direction of the context effects" (p. 311).

1988), response type (substantive response vs. nonresponse), history (e.g., the Communist/American reporters and parental/student party identification—Willick & Ashley, 1971; Schuman & Presser, 1981; Hyman & Sheatsley, 1950), mode and pace of administration (Tourangeau & Rasinski, 1988), ambivalent or conflicted attitudes (Tourangeau & Rasinski, 1988), and other factors; and (d) interactions between different types of effects.

One key to further progress is simply to apply theoretical models, setting up experiments to test specific hypotheses about the causality of order effects and clearly choose between competing explanations. In particular, experiments need to be devised that can determine which stages in the question-answering process are involved. This will necessitate moving beyond simple split-ballot experiments. Useful as split ballots are with their experimental controls, we shall have to apply even more elaborate designs to gain a better understanding of the mental processes that cause order effects.

One useful approach is the think-aloud procedure, by which respondents are asked to relate their cognitive processes orally while these are occurring. Limitations are that it probably works best for conscious mental processes and that verbalization may significantly alter the mental process being employed.

A second promising approach would be the addition of a follow-up question after the antecedent and subsequent questions that would inquire about what the respondent was thinking about (Bishop, 1985, and chap. 11 of this volume; Tourangeau & Rasinski, 1986). Take Kalton's example (Kalton, Collins, & Brook, 1978), in which evaluations of driving standards were rated more positively immediately after a similar question about the driving standards of young drivers. Kalton et al. hypothesize that the more positive evaluation of drivers in general resulted from a subtraction effect that excluded young drivers from consideration in the second question. We should be able to test for this effect by asking after the general driving condition either an open-ended question about what type of driver one had in mind or a more focused closed question such as, "When you answered the question about general driving standards, were you thinking mostly about young drivers, middle-aged drivers, or older drivers?" If a subtraction effect were operating, there should be a reduction in references to young drivers when the general question was preceded by the question about young drivers. Other follow-up questions could be used to test the operation of other effects.

Another possibility is the use of questions probing other dimensions besides affect: importance, salience, information, knowledge, and commitment (Gallup, 1947; Schuman & Presser, 1981; T. W. Smith, 1981c). By learning with what dimensions and conditions order effects interact, we should better understand their causes (Tourangeau & Rasinski, 1986). Similarly, attributes of the questions, such as vagueness and response categories, could be explored.

Another useful approach would be a test/retest design in which four orders could be used (A1B1A2B2, A1B1B2A2, B1A1B2A2, and B1A1A2B2). This would allow a comparison of the consistency of each item in each order (Hayes, 1964; T. W. Smith & Stephenson, 1979). Given certain assumptions, it would also permit an intrarespondent analysis of order effects. Alternatively, one might ask respondents the subsequent question later in the same interview in a different context. Interviewers could then reconcile discrepancies in responses. Through these and other elaborations of the basic split-ballot technique, it should be possible to examine directly the causes of context effects and gain a deeper understanding of the mental processes involved.

By more fully analyzing split-ballot order experiments, by elaborating these experiments with specific inquiries about mental processes and other auxiliary items, and by greater grounding in appropriate cognitive and social-psychological theories, we should be able to advance our understanding of order effects. Although the natural complexity of language and human cognition will undoubtedly hinder precise and comprehensive generalizations about order effects, thorough and cumulative analysis of sophisticated theory-driven experiments should greatly advance the art of ordering questions.

Acknowledgments. Parts of this chapter are adapted from T. W. Smith (1986a). This research was done for the General Social Survey project directed by James A. Davis. This project is supported by the National Science Foundation, Grant No. SES-87-18467.

Part III
Response-Order Effects
in Surveys

13
A Cognitive Model of Response-Order Effects in Survey Measurement

Norbert Schwarz, Hans-J. Hippler, and Elisabeth Noelle-Neumann

Survey researchers have long been aware that the order in which response alternatives are presented to respondents may profoundly affect the obtained results (cf. S. L. Payne, 1951). However, the exact nature of the impact of response order is not well understood. Theoretically, *primacy effects,* that is, higher endorsements of items presented *early* in the list, as well as *recency effects,* that is, higher endorsements of items presented *late* in the list, may be obtained. Moreover, the conditions under which either of these effects may emerge are not well specified, and the area is characterized by a large number of apparently inconsistent findings.

We suppose that the apparent inconsistency of the available findings reflects the contribution of several different processes to response-order effects. As all researchers have noted, response-order effects are in part a function of respondents' memory of the alternatives provided to them. However, they also reflect respondents' opportunity to think about the implications of the response alternatives, as was pointed out by Krosnick and Alwin (1987). Moreover, under some conditions, judgmental contrast effects may emerge, which may dilute the impact of other influences. In the present chapter, we shall summarize a model that addresses these different cognitive processes, paying particular attention to the complexity of the emerging interaction effects. Although experimental data that bear directly on the assumed mediating processes are not yet available for some key aspects of the model, the model generates a number of nonobvious predictions that are consistent with the available findings. Most importantly, it allows us to predict the direction of order effects and to specify some of the conditions under which they will or will not emerge.

Response Alternatives and the Limitations of Memory

Response-order effects have frequently been attributed to respondents' memory limitations. As a large body of psychological research on the learning of long lists of verbal expressions indicates, the recall of verbal material depends on its serial position in the list and the time delay between learning and testing (see Smyth, Morris, Levy, & Ellis, 1987, for a review). Material presented at the beginning of the list is more likely to enter long-term memory than is material presented later because the first few items "suffer less competition for time and space in immediate memory from other items" (Smyth et al., 1987, p. 123). On the other hand, although material presented at the end of the list is less likely to enter long-term memory, it may still be in short-term memory if recall follows learning without much delay. This results in an interaction effect of serial position and the delay between learning and recall: Without delay, material presented at the end of the list is much more likely to be recalled than is material presented at the beginning, reflecting the ability to recall the later items from short-term memory. Accordingly, recency effects are typically obtained under no-delay conditions, and they are more pronounced if the material is read to subjects rather than presented visually (e.g., Murdock & Walker, 1969). If recall is delayed, however, material presented at the beginning of the list is more likely to be remembered than is material presented at the end, reflecting the entrance of the early items into long-term memory, whereas the later items can no longer be recalled from short-term memory. This results in primacy effects under delayed recall conditions. Material presented in the middle of the list is least likely to be recalled under any conditions.

Applied to survey measurement, these considerations suggest that we should typically observe the emergence of *recency effects* in long lists of response alternatives. Given that respondents report their answer immediately after exposure to the response alternatives, no delay between "learning" and "recall" is introduced. Accordingly, response alternatives presented at the end of the list should be easily accessible in short-term memory. Because recall of late items from short-term memory is better than recall of early items from long-term memory under no-delay conditions, this should result in pronounced recency effects. *Primacy effects* should only be obtained if a delay is introduced between exposure to the response alternatives and respondents' reports. This is typically *not* the case in survey interviews. Nevertheless, primacy effects have typically been reported in survey experiments with long lists of response alternatives (e.g., Krosnick & Alwin, 1987; Mueller, 1970; S. L. Payne, 1951; Ring, 1975), suggesting that memory limitations are *not* the primary source of response-order effects in survey measurement.

In fact, long lists of response alternatives are usually presented on show cards that remain available until respondents report their answers, thus placing little burden on their memory to begin with. Moreover, response-order effects have been observed on questions that present only two or three response alternatives (e.g., Hippler, Schwarz, & Noelle-Neumann, 1989; S. L. Payne, 1951; Schuman & Presser, 1981). This limited number of response alternatives, however, should be easily accessible in short-term memory under the no-delay condition of survey interviews, thus rendering the emergence of order effects unlikely unless the alternatives are overly complex. Accordingly, it seems that we need to consider other processes if we want to account for response-order effects in survey measurement.

In summary, memory limitations are most likely to play a role in the emergence of response-order effects when numerous or complex response alternatives are presented without the help of show cards, thus taxing respondents' memory. In this condition, psychological theorizing about memory limitations predicts the emergence of recency effects. Primacy effects, however, would only be predicted under delayed recall conditions, which are atypical for survey interviews.

Cognitive Elaboration and the Likelihood of Endorsement

If memory limitations do not account in a coherent manner for most response-order effects in survey measurement, what other processes do we need to consider? One relevant process is suggested by cognitive research in the area of persuasive communication. Assume that a respondent is asked an opinion question and is provided several response alternatives that reflect different views about the issue. We propose that each of these response alternatives may be portrayed as a short persuasive communication. If so, the processes that are known to determine the impact of persuasive communications may also determine respondents' reactions to the items presented to them.

As a large body of research has demonstrated, the impact of a persuasive argument is determined to a large degree by recipients' "cognitive responses," that is, by the thoughts that recipients generate in response to the presented argument (see Petty & Cacioppo, 1986a, 1986b, for reviews). The more positive, agreeing thoughts that the argument elicits, the more the recipient is influenced by it, resulting in a positive attitude change. Conversely, if the argument elicits negative, disagreeing thoughts, the recipient is likely to show a boomerang attitude change, moving away from the implications of the message. Applied to response alternatives, this suggests that response alternatives that elicit positive thoughts will be endorsed by respondents, whereas response alternatives that elicit disagreeing thoughts will not be endorsed.

However, the number of thoughts elicited by a given argument is not only a function of the content of the argument but is also determined by the recipients' ability and motivation to process the content of the argument—and by the opportunity that the situation provides them to do so. Thus, a plausible argument is more likely to elicit agreement the more the respondent can think about its implications, whereas an implausible argument is more likely to elicit disagreement under these conditions. Accordingly, conditions that interfere with recipients' cognitive elaboration of the implications of a presented argument, such as distracting recipients while they listen to the message, have been shown to eliminate the advantage of plausible over implausible arguments (e.g., Bless, Bohner, Schwarz, & Strack, 1990; Harkins & Petty, 1981; see Petty & Brock, 1981, for a review). Applied to response alternatives, we assume that a plausible response alternative is *more* likely to be endorsed the more cognitive elaboration it receives. Conversely, an implausible response alternative is *less* likely to be endorsed the more cognitive elaboration it receives.

However, as Krosnick & Alwin (1987; see also Krosnick, chap. 14, this volume) have argued in a very persuasive paper that strongly influenced the present approach, the degree of cognitive elaboration that a given response alternative receives is likely to be influenced by the *order* and *mode* in which the response alternatives are presented. Whereas Krosnick & Alwin focused on the implications of these variables for the recall of items from memory, we emphasize their implications for respondents' opportunity to think about the implications of the response alternatives.

Assume, for example, that a long list of response alternatives is presented to respondents in a *visual* format, either on a show card as part of a face-to-face interview or in a self-administered questionnaire. Under these conditions, "items presented *early* [italics added] in a list are likely to be subjected to deeper cognitive processing," as Krosnick and Alwin (1987, pp. 202–203) noted. "By the time a respondent considers the later alternatives, his or her mind is likely to be cluttered with thoughts about previous alternatives that inhibit extensive consideration of later ones" (p. 203). Accordingly, items presented early in the list are more likely to be endorsed under a visual presentation format than are items presented late in the list, resulting in *primacy* effects—provided that the items are plausible to the respondent.

Assume, however, that the items are not presented visually but are *read* to respondents by the interviewer, either under face-to-face or telephone interview conditions. In this case, respondents have little opportunity to elaborate on the items presented early in the list, since the time that is available for processing is restricted by the speed with which the interviewer moves on to read the next item. "Under these circumstances, respondents are able to devote most processing time to the *final* item(s) read, since interviewers usually pause most after reading them" (Krosnick & Alwin, 1987, p. 203). In addition, respondents may find it difficult to keep all response alternatives in mind without visual helps, as discussed above. Accordingly, items presented near the end of the list should be more likely to be endorsed under an *auditory* presentation format than are items presented early in the list, resulting in *recency* effects—again provided that the items are plausible to the respondent.

In summary, these cognitive-elaboration hypotheses predict an interaction effect of presentation order and presentation mode. Specifically, primacy effects are predicted under a visual presentation mode and recency effects under an auditory presentation mode, always assuming that the response alternatives are plausible to the respondent. If the response alternatives are implausible, on the other hand, the opposite predictions hold. In that case, recency effects should emerge under a visual and primacy effects under an auditory presentation format. Moreover, these interaction effects should be most likely to be observed under conditions that do not tax respondents' memory, thus limiting the impact of the recall processes discussed above.

As a first observation, we note that the predicted primacy effect under a visual presentation mode is in line with the bulk of studies that obtained primacy effects in long lists of response alternatives, which are always presented in a visual mode, usually on show cards (e.g., Krosnick & Alwin, 1987). Unfortunately, however, data bearing on an auditory presentation of long lists are not available. Thus, we have to limit ourselves to questions that present only two or three response alternatives because these questions may be administered under both presentation modes. As a further limitation, we have to add that data bearing on the plausibility prediction are not yet available because survey researchers usually avoid implausible response alternatives.

Questions with Two or Three Response Alternatives

To reiterate the key prediction, the degree of elaboration that a given item receives is assumed to depend on its serial position and the administration mode used: If the response alternatives are presented on show cards or in a self-administered questionnaire, items presented early in the list are more likely than items presented later to be extensively processed, resulting in primacy effects (for plausible items). In contrast, if the items are read to respondents, the last response alternatives are more likely than the first ones to be extensively processed, resulting in recency effects (again, for plausible items).

Our data base is provided by a large number of split-ballot experiments conducted since the early 1950s by the Institut für Demoskopie Allensbach, Germany, under the direction of Elisabeth Noelle-Neumann. Each experiment is based on a quota sample of about 2,000 adult respondents in West Germany. The selected examples are typical for a larger number of experiments that are currently subjected to a quantitative meta-analysis. All examples involve the use of so-called "dialogue questions," in which different opinions are attributed to different fictitious individuals and the respondent is asked which opinion is closer to his or her own. If a show card is used, it provides a schematic portrayal of two individuals, with two diverging opinions presented in speech bubbles.

Visual Presentation Format

The first group of experiments involves the use of these show cards, with the restriction that the response alternatives are *only* shown to respondents but are *not* read to them at the same time. Under this condition, a primacy effect is most likely to be obtained. For example, in one study conducted in the early 1960s, respondents were given a show card that presented two different opinions on the role of government in social welfare, one emphasizing the role of government and one the role of private charity. They were asked to read both opinions and to report if they agreed with the opinion presented in the upper or in the lower part of the page—a wording that avoided labeling the opinions with political catchwords (see Appendix, Example 1). As shown in the first part of Table 13.1, pronounced primacy effects of 14 and 6 percentage points emerged, and the same holds true for other studies that followed this format.

TABLE 13.1. Response-Order Effects in Dichotomous Questions as a Function of Presentation Mode (%)

Presentation Mode	Response Order	
	Presented First	Presented Second
Visual Presentation		
Example 1:		
Welfare is responsibility of		
State	64	50
Private charity	34	28
Auditory Presentation		
Example 2:		
Form of government:		
Authoritarian	15	26
Democratic	58	67
Example 3:		
Preferred novel		
Serious	31	35
Humorous	48	53
Mixed Presentation		
Example 4:		
Second TV channel		
Same management	41	48
Different management	24	36

Note: Question wordings and data sources given in the Appendix.

Auditory Presentation Format

On the other hand, if both response alternatives are *read* to respondents without the help of show cards, recency effects are likely to emerge. For example, in an experiment that was conducted in the summer of 1960, two opinions about different forms of government were read to respondents. One opinion favored an authoritarian form of government and the other a democratic form of government (see Appendix, Example 2). As shown in Table 13.1, pronounced recency effects of 11 and 9 percentage points were obtained.

Moreover, this finding is not restricted to response alternatives that are particularly lengthy and complicated but is also obtained with response alternatives that are presumably easy to process. For example, in an experiment conducted in the spring of 1957, respondents were asked whether they would rather read a serious or a humorous novel (see Appendix, Example 3). As shown Table 13.1, recency effects of 4 and 5 percentage points emerged on this rather simple question. By and large, the available data suggest that recency effects in an auditory presentation format are more pronounced for lengthy and complicated questions, but they are definitely not restricted to these conditions (cf. Noelle-Neumann, 1974), as this example illustrates.

Visual and Auditory Presentation Format

In some experiments, a combination of visual and auditory presentation formats was used. Specifically, the response alternatives were read to respondents *before* they were presented on a show.card to facilitate the respondent's answer. In experiments of this type, recency effects were most likely to emerge. For example, in one experiment, two different opinions about the introduction of a second TV channel were first read to respondents and then presented on a show card (see Appendix, Example 4). As shown in the ·bottom part of Table 13.1, recency effects of 7 and 12 percentage points were obtained, despite the presentation of a show card. This and related findings suggest that respondents process the response alternatives while they are read to them by the interviewer, without too much attention to either the accompanying or subsequent presentation of a show card. Accordingly, the data pattern follows the pattern that is observed under a purely auditory administration mode.

We conclude from this sketchy review of the Allensbach findings that response-order effects do in fact emerge in dichotomous questions and that they do so more frequently than one would assume on the basis of the available literature. In contrast to Schuman and Presser's (1981) conclusion, based on their literature review, the Allensbach data suggest that response-order effects in dichotomous questions are all but a rare phenomenon. Specifically, they are obtained in about 40% of our sample of the Allensbach split-ballot experiments—which, of course, does not mean that they are obtained in 40% of all dichotomous questions. Even though the Allensbach researchers conduct a large number of split-ballot experiments in their surveys, they are more likely to introduce a split when intuition and experience suggest that response order may be important. Accordingly, the available split-ballot data do not reflect a representative sample of survey questions, although they cover an amazing variety of content domains.

In summary, the available data are compatible with the predictions generated by the elaboration-likelihood assumption. If a purely visual presentation format is used, primacy effects are more likely to be obtained than are recency effects. If a purely auditory presentation format is used, however, recency effects are more likely to emerge than are primacy effects. Moreover, the obtained recency effects seem more pronounced when the response alternatives are lengthy and complicated, presumably reflecting that these response alternatives tax respondents' memory. However, this aspect awaits more detailed analysis. Finally, if visual and auditory presentation formats are combined, the auditory format is likely to dominate, resulting in recency effects. We hasten to point out, however, that these conclusions are drawn on the basis of different questions used under different administration modes. Most obviously, controlled experiments that use the same questions under all administration modes will be needed to test the validity of these conclusions.

From an applied point of view, the most problematic finding is certainly that the direction of response-order effects may depend on administration mode. Most importantly, this finding suggests that face-to-face interviews with show cards may yield results that are quite different from the results of telephone interviews without show cards, given that the primacy effects that operate in one mode may combine with the recency effects that operate in the other.

Eliminating Order Effects

In addition to accounting for the reported findings, the assumption that the likelihood of endorsement depends on the degree of processing that a response alternative receives suggests conditions under which response-order effects should *not* be obtained. Recall that we assume that respondents' answers are based on the thoughts that are elicited by the response alternatives. If so, we should be able to reduce response-order effects by stimulating respondents to think about the respective content area while they answer preceding questions. This should increase the cognitive accessibility of other relevant thoughts and should therefore decrease the relative impact of the thoughts that are elicited by the response alternatives. Accordingly, response-order effects should be *less* pronounced when preceding questions bear on the same issue than when they do not. Experimental findings support this hypothesis.

In a modified replication of S. L. Payne's (1951) oil supply question (also used by Schuman & Presser, 1981), 91 adult citizens of Mannheim, Germany, were read the following question:

> Some people say that we will still have plenty of oil 25 years from now. Others say that at the rate we are using our oil, it will all be used up in about 15 years. Which of these ideas would you guess is most nearly right?

The order in which the two opinions were presented was reversed for half of the sample.

As shown in the first part of Table 13.2, Payne's original finding replicated well in the German sample. As predicted by our previous generalizations, pronounced recency effects of 33 percentage points were obtained for both response alternatives in an auditory presentation format. For half of the sample, however, Payne's question was preceded by two questions that tapped the same content domain and should therefore trigger cognitive elaborations bearing on the oil supply issue. These questions concerned the respondents' attitudes on restrictions in oil consumption and on the development of alternative sources of energy. As expected, introducing these context questions not only affected respondents' overall attitudes but also completely eliminated the response-order effect.

This finding supports the general hypothesis that response-order effects are, in part, a function of the cognitive elaboration of the response alternatives: If respondents are induced by preceding questions to elaborate on the issue before being exposed to the response alternatives, response-order effects may be largely reduced, or even eliminated. At the same time, the impact of the preceding questions on respondents' reports indicates that having respondents elaborate the content domain may elicit pronounced shifts in the reported attitudes. Accordingly, this finding bears on the theoretical rationale offered here but is not intended to imply that researchers should replace response-order effects with question-order effects.

TABLE 13.2. The Elimination of Response-Order Effects as a Function of Preceding Elaboration of the Content Domain (%)

	Response Order	
Context	Presented First	Presented Second
Without preceding questions		
25 years	36	69
15 years	31	64
With preceding questions		
25 years	73	71
15 years	29	27

Note: The percentage of respondents who endorsed a given response alternative is reported. $N = 91$.

Let us now turn to the implications of the cognitive-elaboration assumption for long lists of response alternatives.

Long Lists of Response Alternatives

Long lists of response alternatives are nearly always presented on show cards, that is, in a visual presentation format. Accordingly, the present model predicts the emergence of primacy effects. The available literature is in line with this prediction (e.g., Krosnick & Alwin, 1987; Mueller, 1970; S. L. Payne, 1951), which is also supported by our analysis of the data available in the Allensbach archive (Schwarz, Hippler, Noelle-Neumann, Ring, & Münkel, 1989).

However, the conclusion that primacy effects dominate the field, whereas recency effects are rare in a visual presentation format, is potentially misleading. In all studies that we could locate in the literature, only two response orders were compared; that is, the presentation order was simply reversed, making the first item of List A the last item of List B. Accordingly, a recency effect *could* only be detected if no primacy effect emerged to begin with, or if the recency effect was stronger than the obtained primacy effect. It is, therefore, conceivable that primacy and recency effects operate simultaneously but that primacy effects are more pronounced, thereby diluting the weaker recency effects.

A series of studies conducted by Erp Ring (1974, 1975) of the Institut at Allensbach bears on this possibility. Unfortunately, these studies have received little attention in the literature. In three surveys, each based on representative samples of about 2,000 adult West German citizens, respondents were presented a list of 18 famous individuals and were asked to select the ones whom they liked best. A different list of names was used in each survey, thus providing three stimulus replications, and the names were presented in four different order conditions. The results clearly indicate the simultaneous operation of primacy *and* recency effects, as shown in Table 13.3. Specifically, across all three surveys, a given person was more likely to be selected if presented in the first posi-

TABLE 13.3. Average Endorsement of Stimulus Persons as a Function of Presentation Order

Stimulus Person Presented in Position			
1	9	10	18
17.2%	13.6%	13.4%	15.5%

Note: The percentage of respondents who selected a given person in each order condition is reported. $N = 5,901$ for each order condition. Data adapted from Ring (1975).

tion on the list than if presented in the middle of the list (positions 9 or 10), reflecting an average primacy effect of 3.7%. However, compared with the average endorsement if presented in the middle of the list, the likelihood of being selected increased if the same person was presented in the last position, reflecting an average recency effect of 2%.

This pattern of findings has two important implications. First, it indicates that response-order effects in visually presented long lists do *not* reflect memory limitations. Note that the memory research reviewed above would predict a pronounced recency effect under conditions where exposure to the list is immediately followed by the recall task: Recall of the late items from short-term memory would be much better than recall of the early items from long-term memory, resulting in a reversal of the data pattern obtained here.

In addition, the present findings draw attention to the methodological shortcoming of studies that involve only two order conditions. If we restricted ourselves to a comparison of the first and last positions on the list, we would conclude that a small primacy effect of 1.7% emerged, and we could not observe the simultaneous operation of a recency effect because the latter is diluted by the larger size of the former. Accordingly, we conclude that the size of primacy effects in long lists has typically been *underestimated* in the literature.

So far, the reviewed data are consistent with the elaboration-likelihood assumption. However, this assumption captures only part of the processes that mediate response-order effects. Specifically, response-order effects not only are a function of respondents' memory limitations and the cognitive elaboration of the response alternatives provided to them but are also a function of other judgmental processes elicited by the items. To introduce these processes, we first have to highlight an important distinction between two different types of response alternatives.

Dimensional and Nondimensional Response Alternatives

One type of response alternatives simply consists of a list of heterogenous possibilities. For example, respondents may be asked, "What did you do last Saturday?" and may be offered alternatives such as "sleeping in," "working," and "shopping." The possibilities presented are not clearly related to one another and do not bear on a single underlying dimension. For lack of a better term, we call sets of this type "nondimensional." We assume that response-order effects in the endorsement of nondimensional response alternatives are primarily a function of their elaboration likelihood if only a few alternatives are presented. If a large number of response alternatives are offered, limitations of respondents' memory may add to the emergence of order effects, as discussed above (see also Krosnick, chap. 14, this volume; Krosnick & Alwin, 1987).

Other response alternatives, however, bear on a single underlying dimension. For example, respondents may be asked, "Which of the following drinks do you consider to be typically German?" and may be offered "vodka," "wine," "beer," etc., as target stimuli. In that case, all response alternatives are to be evaluated along a single dimension. Accordingly, we call them "dimensional." Note in this regard that dimensionality is not determined by the content of the response alternatives per se but rather by respondents' task. If respondents were to report if they ever bought the respective drinks, these drinks would make up a set of nondimensional response alternatives. Evaluating the typicality of these drinks, however, introduces a dimension along which these drinks have to be ordered. This task gives rise to other judgmental processes that may dilute the impact of cognitive elaboration. We will now turn to the nature of these processes.

Asymmetric Contrast Effects

Specifically, if a given item is preceded by an item that is more extreme on the dimension of judgment, a contrast effect may emerge. Suppose, for example, that respondents were asked to select persons that they liked well, as was the case in Ring's (1974, 1975) studies. Suppose further that an extremely well liked person was presented in the middle of a list. If so, moderately liked persons who were presented in the second part of the list would seem *less* likable by comparison. They would therefore be less likely to be selected as "liked" under this order condition. If we compared two orders of this list, the judgmental contrast effect would therefore lead us to conclude that a pronounced primacy effect emerged. On the other hand, if the person presented in the middle of the list were extremely *dislikable,* the same mechanism of judgmental contrast would increase the endorsement of moderately liked persons presented in the second half of the list. In that case, a comparison of both order conditions would lead us to conclude that a pronounced recency effect emerged. Note, however, that the underlying cognitive process of judgmental contrast is quite different from the cognitive-elaboration processes discussed above.

A classic example for such a contrast effect was reported by Noelle-Neumann (1970). Specifically, respondents were presented a list of food items and were asked to select the ones that are typically "German." Respondents were more likely to consider a number of food items, such as noodles or potatoes, as typically "German" when they were preceded by rice than when they were not. Thus, introducing rice as the first item resulted in pronounced contrast effects in the perception of the other food items. Finally, the evaluation of rice itself was unaffected by order manipulations.

Although primacy and recency effects in lists are presumably a function of the cognitive elaboration that a given item receives in different positions, contrast effects are thought to be a function of the items' extremity on the underlying dimension of judgment. Introducing a more extreme item results in a wider "perspective" regarding the set of stimuli, thus affecting their evaluation as described in Ostrom and Upshaw's (1968) perspective theory. Accordingly, contrast effects should also emerge under conditions in which each item is likely to receive about the *same degree* of attention and elaboration. To explore this possibility, we used a rating rather than a selection task in a laboratory experiment. Specifically, we asked subjects to rate each of a number of drinks according to how typically "German" they are (Schwarz & Münkel, 1988). As expected, all drinks were rated as more typically "German" if an atypical drink, namely vodka, was presented as the first rather than as the last item. The rating of vodka, on the other hand, was not affected by the order manipulations. That is, an asymmetric contrast effect emerged, as predicted by Ostrom and Upshaw's (1968) perspective theory. According to that model, respondents use the most extreme stimuli that come to mind to anchor the response scale. In the present case, presenting vodka as the first item resulted in a shift of the moderate stimuli away from the anchor. Vodka as the most extreme stimulus in the set, however, is itself unaffected by the order manipulation because the most extreme stimulus is assigned the extreme scores under any order condition—except if preceded by a more extreme stimulus.

Moreover, contrast effects of this type do *not* require that the items are presented on the same list. They have also been shown to emerge if the extreme item is presented as part of a preceding question, provided that this question taps the same dimension of judgment. For example, in a study by Schwarz, Münkel, and Hippler (1990), we asked some respondents to estimate the percentage of Germans who drink vodka and asked others to estimate the percentage of Germans who drink beer. Subsequently, they were asked to rate the typicality of various drinks. As expected, subjects who estimated the percentage of Germans who drink vodka rated subsequent drinks as more typically German than did subjects who estimated how many Germans drink beer. This replicates the contrast effects obtained when all stimuli were presented on the same list. Other subjects, however, were asked as part of the preceding questions to estimate the *caloric content*, rather than the consumption, of vodka or beer. Although this question also serves to render these drinks highly salient in the interview context, it does not tap the typicality dimension that underlies estimates of the consumption of these drinks. Accordingly, estimating their caloric content did *not* influence subsequent typicality ratings. Thus, we conclude that contrast effects can emerge as a function of preceding questions *if* these questions tap the same underlying dimension of judgment.

This emergence of contrast effects bears in important ways on the emergence of primacy and recency effects in general. Specifically, it accounts for data sets that do *not* follow our predictions of primacy and recency effects as a function of elaboration and memory processes: If an extremely *positive* item is presented as part of the stimulus set, it will *decrease* the endorsement of subsequent moderate items. If an extremely *negative* item is presented, on the other hand, it will *increase* the endorsement of subsequent moderate items. These judgmental effects may lead the researcher to conclude that the data show pronounced recency or primacy effects. Accordingly, the phenomenon of judgmental contrast may dilute the emergence of elaboration phenomena, thus contributing to the mixed findings that characterize this area.

Conclusions

In summary, we propose that order effects in nondimensional sets of response alternatives are a function of their cognitive elaboration and of the limitations of respondents' memory. The processes that underlie order effects in dimensional sets of response alternatives, however, are more complex and require a consideration of judgmental contrast in addition to a consideration of cognitive elaboration. Based on the data that we have seen so far, we feel that this set of assumptions accounts in a reasonably coherent manner for the emergence of response-order effects in survey measurement.

Most importantly, the elaboration-likelihood assumption provides a rich set of predictions that have only partially been tested. First, it predicts an interaction of serial position and administration mode that is well supported by the available data, although more controlled experiments using the same questions under visual and auditory presentation modes are urgently needed and currently under way. Second, it predicts conditions under which response-order effects should be more or less pronounced, and these predictions have been supported in at least one experiment. Third, it predicts a reversal of response-order effects if the presented response alternatives are implausible rather than plausible. Although data bearing on this issue are not yet available, this consideration suggests that response-order effects may go in different directions, depending on respondents' attitudes. Accordingly, primacy and recency effects may cancel one another in heterogeneous samples. Finally, the elaboration-likelihood assumption points to a host of other variables, such as respondents' ability and motivation to elaborate on the implications of the response alternatives, that have been explored in research on persuasive communications (see Petty, Ostrom, & Brock, 1981, and Petty & Cacioppo, 1986a, 1986b, for reviews) but have not been systematically addressed in the context of response-order effects. Needless to say, these predictions deserve systematic testing, both in sample surveys and in the cognitive laboratory, with a careful assessment of the cognitive responses that are assumed to mediate the observed effects.

In addition, the assumptions about the impact of respondents' memory limitations and the emergence of judgmental contrast effects point to conditions under which the impact of cognitive elaboration may be diluted. Regarding the impact of memory limitations, our analyses suggest that a straightforward application of findings from the psychological literature on list learning cannot account for the pattern of response-order effects observed in survey research. Most importantly, this literature predicts recency effects in the absence of a delay between learning and recall, as is typical in survey research, and provides no mechanism for the emergence of primacy effects under these conditions. However, memory limitations may contribute to the size of recency effects under auditory presentation conditions (e.g., when the response alternatives are lengthy and complex). Moreover, they may dilute the size of primacy effects under visual presentation conditions if one assumes that time pressure prevents respondents from going back over the list before reporting their answer, thus introducing some memory burden into the task. Finally, judgmental contrast effects may further dilute the operation of the previously discussed processes if a dimensional set of response alternatives is presented and some response alternatives are considerably more extreme than others.

Accordingly, it comes as little surprise that the emergence of response-order effects seems to follow the rule, "sometimes you see them, sometimes you don't." When we consider the above predictions, it becomes obvious that there is not a single main effect. Instead, the emergence and direction of response-order effects seem to depend on a complex interaction of serial position, presentation mode, item plausibility, complexity and extremity, and respondent ability and motivation. Although we believe that the underlying processes are systematic and their effects ultimately predictable, the complexity of these interactions promises to provide a rich set of surprises in future studies.

Acknowledgments. The reported research was supported by grant SWF0044-6 from the Bundesminister für Forschung und Technologie of the Federal Republic of Germany to the first author.

Appendix: Question Wordings

Example 1 (Table 13.1):
Source: HB 1064, Institut für Demoskopie Allensbach.
Presentation order of statements on show card manipulated.

> Here are two men talking with one another. Would you please read what the two of them say? (Interviewer gives respondent time to read show card.) Which of the two would you rather agree with? With the upper one or with the lower one?

The show card presents two individuals with the following statements in speech bubbles:

> I feel it is the responsibility of the state to make sure that there is no social misery. Retirement payments, social welfare, and sick leave compensation must be sufficient for one's living. That is the only adequate way to eliminate social misery.

I feel that the state cannot ease all social misery. There are many individual cases where state payments are not all that is needed. One often needs to consider the individual circumstances. Therefore, each individual should help through donations and personal commitment to ease social misery.

Example 2 (Table 13.1):
Source: HB 1044, July 1960, Institut für Demoskopie Allensbach.
Presentation order of statements manipulated; no show card used.

Two men talk about how a country should be governed.
- One says: I prefer that the people put their best politician at the top and delegate all power to him. Then he and selected experts can make clear and fast decisions. There isn't much talking and things are really going to happen.
- The other says: I prefer that several people have some influence in the state. That results in some talking before anything gets done, but it makes sure that power cannot be abused that easily.
Which of these two opinions is closer to your own—the first one or the second one?

Example 3 (Table 13.1):
Source: HB 445, March 1957, Institut für Demoskopie Allensbach.
Presentation order of "serious"/"humorous" manipulated.

If you had the choice to read either a serious or a humorous novel, what would you rather read these days: The serious or the humorous novel?

Example 4 (Table 13.1):
Source: HB 1051, Institut für Demoskopie Allensbach.
Presentation order of statements read to respondents, and shown on card, manipulated.

Here are two men talking about who should manage the second TV channel: the same groups who are already managing the current program, or a new broadcasting organization. With whom would you rather agree, with the one shown at the top or the one shown at the bottom?

The show card presents two individuals with the following statements in speech bubbles:

I'm in favor of founding a new broadcasting society for the second TV program. That results in competition between the first and the second program to see who does a better job. One organization alone would never strive that hard.

In my opinion, the organizations that run the first program should also run the second program. They have the most experience. If both programs are in the same hands, they can also be better coordinated. Moreover, building a new broadcasting organization would cost unnecessary amounts of money.

14
The Impact of Cognitive Sophistication and Attitude Importance on Response-Order and Question-Order Effects

Jon A. Krosnick

In a paper published in *Psychological Review,* Greenwald, Pratkanis, Leippe, and Baumgardner (1986) argued that the most useful and effective method of theory development is to seek the limiting conditions of known findings, what Greenwald et al. called "condition-seeking." That is, Greenwald and his colleagues argued that the best way to understand why a phenomenon occurs is to identify when it does not occur. This is a way to determine the conditions that are necessary in order for a particular effect to appear, thus increasing the precision of one's theoretical account of it. More importantly, condition-seeking can be a very effective way to identify the mechanisms by which a particular effect occurs.

The goal of the research reported in this chapter was to identify the cognitive mechanisms of two classes of response effects in surveys through the method of condition-seeking. In the first study reported below, I explored the mechanisms of four response-order effects; and in the second study, I explored the mechanism of a question-order effect. I did so not by systematically altering circumstantial or situational factors but rather by exploring heterogeneity among respondents in terms of their susceptibility to these effects. Specifically, I examined whether respondents differing in levels of cognitive sophistication and attitude importance would reveal stronger or weaker response effects. In doing so, I tested particular a priori hypotheses regarding the mechanisms of the effects.

Study 1

The focus of the first study was response-order effects, which are defined as changes in respondents' answers to a closed-ended survey question that result from alterations in the order in which response alternatives are presented. Many such effects have been documented to date (Becker, 1954; Belson, 1966; Brook & Upton, 1974; Carp, 1974; Mueller, 1970; Quinn & Belson, 1969; J. D. Payne,

1972; S. L. Payne, 1951; Rugg & Cantril, 1944; Schuman & Presser, 1981). Some of these demonstrations identified primacy effects, where response choices presented early were most likely to be selected. Other studies have found recency effects, where response choices presented later were more likely to be selected.

In Krosnick and Alwin (1987) we offered a cognitive theory of the mechanisms underlying such response-order effects. In short, this theory ascribes response-order effects to inadequate memory search and superficial evaluation of response options. Exactly how these two factors have effects depends on whether the response choices are presented visually or orally to respondents.

When response alternatives are presented to respondents visually, either on a show card or in a self-administered questionnaire, primacy effects are most likely to occur. When respondents are asked to indicate which of a list of national problems is most important for the country, for example, they are likely to begin at the top of the list and consider each response alternative individually; and when they think about each response alternative, their thoughts are likely to evidence a confirmatory bias (Hoch, 1984; Klayman & Ha, 1984; Koriat, Lichtenstein, & Fischhoff, 1980; Tschirgi, 1980; Wason & Johnson-Laird, 1972). In the present example, respondents are likely to try to think of reasons why each alternative could be the nation's most important problem and not reasons why it is *not* the most important problem. Given that survey researchers typically include in questions only response choices that constitute reasonable answers, this confirmatory-biased thinking is likely to generate at least a reason or two in favor of selecting almost any alternative that a respondent thinks about.

After considering one or two response alternatives to a closed-ended question, the potential for fatigue becomes significant. Those respondents who do become fatigued can cope by thinking only superficially about later response alternatives; the confirmatory bias would thereby give the earlier items an advantage. Alternatively, fatigued individuals could simply terminate their evaluation process altogether once they come upon a response alternative that seems to be a reasonable answer to the question. Again, because most answers are likely to seem reasonable, these respondents are likely to end up choosing response alternatives near the beginning of a list. Thus, cognitive fatigue seems likely to produce primacy effects under conditions of visual presentation.

When response alternatives are presented orally, depth-of-processing issues and memory issues come into play. Consider first depth of processing. When response alternatives are read aloud, respondents are not given the opportunity to process the first alternative extensively. Presentation of the second alternative usually terminates processing of the first one relatively quickly. Therefore, respondents are able to devote the most processing time to the final item(s) read, since interviewers usually pause most after reading them. Thus, deeper processing dominated by generation of reasons supporting selection is more likely to be accorded to the last option, so that a recency effect would be expected. However, if the list of alternatives is short, some respondents may simply listen to the list and then begin thinking by evaluating the first option and progressing through the alternatives in the order in which they were read. Given that cognitive fatigue may set in for some respondents relatively quickly, this response strategy would presumably produce a primacy effect.

This tendency toward both primacy and recency effects will be enhanced by the effects of memory. Items presented early in a list are most likely to enter long-term memory (e.g., Bruce & Papay, 1970; Crowder, 1969; Dreben, Fiske, & Hastie, 1979; Rundus, 1971), and items presented at the end of a list are most likely to be in short-term memory immediately after the list is heard (e.g., N. H. Anderson & Hubert, 1963; Glanzer, 1972; Waugh & Norman, 1965). Therefore, when a list of response alternatives is long, items presented at the beginning and the end of the list are more likely to be recalled and thus more likely to be available for selection. However, if a list of response alternatives is relatively short, memory is unlikely to exert an effect.

Taken together, these arguments suggest that both primacy and recency effects would be expected in response to orally presented questions. Furthermore, given that primacy and recency effects in memory are typically of roughly equal magnitude, the ratio of people who begin evaluating alternatives at the beginning of the list versus people who begin evaluating alternatives at the end will determine whether a primacy or a recency effect will appear for the sample as a whole.

Regardless of whether a primacy or a recency effect occurs in a particular instance, the reasoning offered above suggests that the effect should be greater under conditions that enhance inadequate memory search and superficial evaluation of responses. Specifically, these two processes should be enhanced among respondents for whom complex, abstract, and extensive cognitive activities are difficult and therefore not enjoyable. Krosnick and Alwin (1987) referred to these individuals as being low in cognitive sophistication.

In Krosnick and Alwin (1987) we examined two sorts of measures of cognitive sophistication. The first was the years of formal schooling that respondents had completed, and the second was respondents' scores on a vocabulary test. As might be expected, these two measures were very strongly correlated with one another. Consistent with the hypothesis offered above, we found that a primacy effect in the context of visual presentation was stronger among respondents low in formal education and vocabulary test scores than among respondents high in education and vocabulary test scores. This negative association between educational attainment and strength of the response-order effect has also been observed in a number of other investigations (Cochrane & Rokeach, 1970, Table 2; McClendon, 1986; Schuman & Presser, 1981, p. 71).[1] Therefore, this evidence provides some support for the claim that response-order effects are greatest

---

[1] Schuman and Presser (1981, p. 71) indicated that their data revealed that less educated respondents tended to show stronger response-order effects but that none of the interactions with education that they examined approached statistical significance. However, no quantitative results were formally reported, and a meta-analysis might well have revealed a significant overall effect when the various experiments were combined in a single analysis. I am therefore reluctant to accept the conclusion of no association between the size of response-order effect and education.

among individuals for whom the costs of effortful cognitive processing are greatest, thus lending support to the inadequate memory search and superficial evaluation explanations.

It is important to recognize that measuring the number of years of formal education that a respondent has attained indicates not only cognitive sophistication but also many other related constructs. Education imparts values about appropriate and inappropriate standards of behavior, factual knowledge about the world, practice with multiple-choice tests and other similar exercises, and so on. Furthermore, some individuals are more likely than others to be admitted to college and graduate school, so that differences in formal educational attainment partly reflect these preexisting selection factors that determine access to education. In sum, then, differences between survey respondents in terms of formal education attainment almost certainly reflect an array of constructs in addition to cognitive sophistication. In order to be more certain that response-order effects are truly greater among respondents with less cognitive sophistication, it is necessary to examine whether such effects vary according to a more direct measure of cognitive sophistication.

This is precisely what this study was designed to accomplish. For it, four response-order effects identified in previous research were experimentally replicated among a sample of college students, thus holding level of educational attainment constant. It was then possible to examine whether these response-order effects were greater among respondents who were lower in cognitive sophistication, as measured by students' college grade point averages.

Method

Respondents and Data Collection

Respondents were a representative sample of 396 undergraduate students at The Ohio State University (OSU). The students were interviewed by telephone between January and March of 1988 by trained, experienced survey interviewers. Each respondent was randomly assigned to one of two versions of the questionnaire. In total, 195 respondents received Form A, and 201 received Form B.

Measures

Prior to the four target questions of present interest, respondents were asked approximately 100 questions, most of which addressed their political attitudes and beliefs. Many of these items addressed candidates and issues prominent in the 1988 U.S. Presidential election campaign, which was just getting under way at the time of the interviewing. The remaining prior questions measured demographics and respondents' needs, attitudes, and beliefs regarding child care facilities at OSU. This large number of preceding questions undoubtedly rendered respondents quite fatigued by the time that they reached our four target questions.

The four target questions used in this experiment were adapted from prior research on response-order effects by Schuman and Presser (1981) and Krosnick and Alwin (1987). The wordings of each question on the two forms were as follows:

Oil Supply, Form A: Some people say that we will still have plenty of oil 25 years from now. Others say that at the rate we are using our oil, it will all be used up in about 15 years. Which of these ideas would you guess is most nearly right?

Oil Supply, Form B: Some people say that at the rate we are using our oil, it will all be used up in about 15 years. Others say that we will still have plenty of oil 25 years from now. Which of these ideas would you guess is most nearly right?

Divorce, Form A: Should divorce in this country be easier to obtain, more difficult to obtain, or stay as it is now?

Divorce, Form B: Should divorce in this country be easier to obtain, stay as it is now, or be more difficult to obtain?

Housing, Form A: Some people feel that the federal government should see to it that all people have adequate housing, while others feel each person should provide his own housing. Which comes closest to how you feel about this?

Housing, Form B: Some people feel each person should provide his own housing, while others feel that the federal government should see to it that all people have adequate housing. Which comes closest to how you feel about this?

Child Qualities, Form A: If you had to choose, which of the following would you pick as the most important for a child to learn to prepare him or her for life—to obey or mind his parents, to be well-liked or popular, to think for himself or herself, to work hard, or to help others when they need help?

Child Qualities, Form B: If you had to choose, which of the following would you pick as the most important for a child to learn to prepare him or her for life—to help others when they need help, to work hard, to think for himself or herself, to be well-liked or popular, or to obey or mind his parents?

At the end of the questionnaire, respondents were asked to report their current cumulative grade point average at OSU. This served as the measure of cognitive sophistication used in the analyses reported below. Respondents with GPAs less than 3.00 were labeled the "low cognitive-sophistication group," and respondents with GPAs of 3.00 and greater were labeled the "high cognitive-sophistication group." Of respondents who received Form A, 44.0% fell into the high cognitive-sophistication group, whereas 40.1% of the respondents who received Form B fell into the high cognitive-sophistication group. This slight difference between the Form A and Form B samples was not statistically significant.

Results

When the full sample was examined, the oil supply and child qualities questions revealed the previously documented response-order effects. In response to the oil supply question, 74.5% said "plenty" when that response option came second, compared with 59.1% saying "plenty" when it came first. Thus, this item revealed a recency effect of 15.4% overall (chi-square(1) = 9.14, p = .003). The child qualities question revealed a primacy effect. A total of 40.8% of respondents chose either "to work hard" or "to help others when they need help" when these options appeared first, whereas only 33.7% of respondents selected one of these response options when they appeared last (chi-square(4) = 9.83, p = .043). These results suggest that most respondents began their evaluations of the oil supply response alternatives with the last one, whereas most began their evaluations of the child qualities alternatives with the first. The other two items did not reveal statistically significant order effects for the full sample, but both revealed trends in the expected directions (divorce: chi-square(2) = 2.05, NS; housing: chi-square(1) = 0.08, NS).

In order to explore whether these effects were greater among less cognitively sophisticated respondents, these analyses were repeated separately within the high- and low cognitive-sophistication groups (see Table 14.1). In the cases of the two questions that revealed order effects for the full sample, the expected interactions did indeed appear. For the oil supply question, the order effect was 20.9% for the low cognitive-sophistication group (chi-square(1) = 9.40, p = .002) and only 8.2% for the high cognitive-sophistication group (chi-square(1) = 0.79, NS). The difference between these two effects approaches marginal statistical significance (chi-square(1) = 1.73, p = .19). For the child qualities question, the order effect was 20.2% for the low cognitive-sophistication group (chi-square(4) = 15.24, p = .004) and nonsignificant and, in fact, in the reverse direction for the high cognitive-sophistication group (−11.00, chi-square(4) = 6.53, NS). The difference between these two effects is significant (chi-square(4) = 12.31, p = .015). Thus, in these two cases, the cognitive-sophistication hypothesis receives consistent support. For the two items that showed no order effects in the full sample, there was no evidence of an interaction between response by form and cognitive sophistication in the two subsamples either (divorce: chi-square(2) = 0.27, NS; housing: chi-square(1) = 0.06, NS).

Discussion

This experiment provides support for the cognitive-sophistication hypothesis. For the oil supply and child qualities items, there were significant response-order effects for the full sample, and those effects were confined exclusively to respondents who were low in cognitive sophistication. This finding is consistent with previous evidence that response-order effects are greater among respondents with less education (Cochrane & Rokeach, 1970, Table 2; Krosnick & Alwin, 1987; McClendon, 1986; Schuman & Presser, 1981, p. 71), and the present evidence suggests that these associations are attributable at least partly to differences between highly educated and less educated respondents in terms of cognitive sophistication. Finally, the present results lend some support to the argument offered above that response-order effects are due to inadequate memory searches and superficial evaluation of response alternatives; that is, these response-order

TABLE 14.1. Response-Order Effects for High and Low Cognitive-Sophistication Subsamples (%)

Response	High Sophistication			Low Sophistication		
	Form A	Form B	Difference	Form A	Form B	Difference
Oil Supply						
Plenty	63.2	71.4	8.2	58. 3	79.2	20.9
Used up	36.8	28.6	−8.2	41.7	20.8	−20.9
Total	100.0	100.0		100.0	100.0	
	($N = 76$)	($N = 70$)		($N = 96$)	($N = 106$)	
Child Qualities						
Obey	4.9	2.7	−2.2	8.8	8.0	−0.8
Well-liked	0.0	5.3	5.3	0.0	0.9	0.9
Think	49.4	57.3	7.9	65.7	45.5	−20.2
Work hard	25.9	18.7	−7.2	22.5	29.5	7.0
Help others	19.8	16.0	−3.8	2.9	16.1	13.2
Total	100.0	100.0		100.0	100.0	
	($N = 81$)	($N = 75$)		($N = 102$)	($N = 112$)	
Divorce						
Easier	12.5	11.1	−1.4	13.9	13.5	−0.4
More difficult	22.2	31.9	9.7	29.7	35.1	5.4
Same	65.3	56.9	−8.4	56.4	51.4	−5.0
Total	100.0	100.0		100.0	100.0	
	($N = 72$)	($N = 72$)		($N = 101$)	($N = 111$)	
Housing						
Government	56.0	54.3	−1.7	52.6	48.1	−4.5
Each person	44.0	45.7	1.7	47.4	51.9	4.5
Total	100.0	100.0		100.0	100.0	
	($N = 75$)	($N = 70$)		($N = 97$)	($N = 104$)	

effects are greatest among respondents for whom the cognitive costs of complete memory searches and careful evaluation of response alternatives are presumably greatest.

For the divorce and federal housing items, there was no evidence of any response-order effect in the full sample or in the high or low cognitive-sophistication subsamples. Because our manipulations of these items did not produce reliable response-order effects at all, these items did not provide an opportunity to test the cognitive-sophistication hypothesis.

In sum, this condition-seeking exercise has clarified the interpretation of previous findings regarding educational attainment. It has also lent further support to the claim that response-order effects are the results of inadequate memory search and superficial response alternative evaluation.

Study 2

The focus of the second study was a question-order effect involving the magnitude of the false-consensus effect. The false-consensus effect was first documented by Ross, Greene, and House (1977) and has been demonstrated in a variety of ways by many investigators since then (see Marks & Miller, 1987; Mullen et al., 1985; Mullen & Hu, 1988). In general, the effect involves the overestimation of the proportion of others who share one's own attitude toward an object, or an overestimation of the similarity between one's attitude and the attitudes of others.

In reviewing the false-consensus literature, Marks and Miller (1987) suggested four possible mechanisms by which the false-consensus effect might operate. First, it could be the result of selective exposure and cognitive availability. Because people tend to associate with others who are similar to themselves (Berscheid & Walster, 1978; Newcomb, 1961), images of similar others should be readily accessible in memory and should come to mind easily and automatically, thus enhancing their prominence in judgments. Second, individuals may focus their attention on their own attitude position and may overestimate its prevalence among others as a result. Third, because people perceive most of their behavior to be the result of situational factors (Jones & Harris, 1967; Jones & Nisbett, 1972), they may assume that most others would be similarly affected by those situational forces and will therefore share their attitudes. Finally, people may intentionally distort their perceptions of others in order to "bolster perceived social support, validate the correctness or appropriateness of a position, [and] maintain self-esteem" (Marks & Miller, 1987, p. 73). Thus, the false-consensus effect may be the result of a self-enhancement motive.

In the present study, I set out to explore the validity of these various possible mechanisms. To do so, I examined the effects of two variables: the order in which the self-perception and others-perception questions are asked, and the personal importance of the issue to the respondent. As Table 14.2 illustrates, the effects of these variables on the magnitude of the false-consensus effect can be used to assess the viability of each possible explanation for it.

If the self-enhancement explanation is true, the effect ought to be greater when the self-perception question comes first and makes one's own attitude salient (see the first row of Table 14.2). This increase in impact under the self/others orders ought to be greater among high-importance subjects than among low-importance subjects, because the former individuals should presumably be more invested in their attitudes and should have a greater need for self-validation on the issue.

If the focus-of-attention explanation is true, the false-consensus effect ought again to be greater under the self/others order than under the others/self order. This is because the former order presumably enhances focus on the self at the time that the others judgment is made. Highly important attitudes that may attract an individual's attention are more accessible than low-importance attitudes (Krosnick, 1989), so that the basic false-consensus effect would presumably be

TABLE 14.2. Predicted Effects of Attitude Importance and Question Order According to the Four Possible Explanations of the False-Consensus Effect

Explanation	Importance Main Effect	Question-Order Main Effect	Importance by Question-Order Interaction
Self-enhancement	Hi imp > Lo imp	Self/others > Others/self	Hi imp > Lo imp
Focus of attention	Hi imp > Lo imp	Self/others > Others/self	Hi imp > Lo imp
Selective exposure	Hi imp > Lo imp	None	None
Attribution	None	None	None

greater among high-importance subjects. Focusing attention on one's attitude may be more consequential among high-importance subjects, so that the effect of the question-order manipulation may also be larger among these individuals.

If the explanation emphasizing selective exposure to similar others is true, there is no reason to expect that manipulating the order of the questions would alter the magnitude of the false-consensus effect. However, under both question orders, there is strong reason to expect high-importance respondents to show a stronger false-consensus effect than low-importance respondents. This is because high-importance respondents are substantially more likely to affiliate with others who share their attitudes (Krosnick, 1988; Tedin, 1980).

Finally, if the attribution explanation is accurate, there is no reason to expect that a manipulation of question order would alter the size of the false-consensus effect. Similarly, there is no reason why high-importance respondents should evidence a stronger or weaker false-consensus effect than low-importance respondents.

In order to test these various explanations, I conducted an experiment involving a series of political issues. For each issue, the order of the self-perception and others-perception questions was systematically varied. Furthermore, respondents were asked to report the personal importance of their attitudes on each issue. This design makes it possible to examine whether any one of the patterns described in Table 14.2 is actually obtained.

Method

Respondents and Data Collection

The data analyzed in this study were also collected during the telephone survey described above in Study 1. About two-thirds of the way through that survey's interview, respondents were asked the nine questions analyzed below.

Measures

Three political issues were examined in this study: U.S. government aid to the contra rebels fighting the Nicaraguan government, U.S. defense spending, and legalized abortion. In each case, respondents were first asked how important the issue was to them personally. All three importance questions were embedded in a battery of questions measuring attitude importance. Nine questions later, respondents were asked to indicate whether they favored or opposed each policy and what proportion of American citizens they guessed would favor each policy. The exact wordings of the questions were:

> *Attitude Importance:* How important is (U.S. government policy toward Central American nations/the issue of U.S. defense spending/the issue of abortion) to you personally—extremely important, very important, somewhat important, not too important, or not at all important?

> *Self-Perception:* Do you favor or oppose (U.S. government aid to the contra rebels fighting the Nicaraguan government/a substantial cut in U.S. defense spending/legalized abortion in the U.S.)?

> *Others-Perception:* What percent of American citizens would you guess favor (U.S. government aid to the contra rebels fighting the Nicaraguan government/a substantial cut in U.S. defense spending/legalized abortion in the U.S.)?

Respondents were randomly assigned to one of two forms of the questionnaire. In one form, self-reports preceded reports of perceptions of others; and on the other form, self-reports followed reports of perceptions of others. Thus, on one form, the question order was self/contras, others/contras, self/defense, others/defense, self/abortion, and others/abortion. On the other form, the order was others/contras, self/contras, others/defense, self/defense, others/abortion, and self/abortion.

Of primary interest here are differences between respondents who attached a great deal of personal importance to an issue and respondents who attached relatively little importance to that issue. To explore these differences, the full sample was divided into a high-importance subsample and a low-importance subsample for each issue. The high-importance subsample was composed of respondents who said that the issue was "extremely important" or "very important" to them personally. The low-importance subsample was composed of respondents who said that the issue was "somewhat important," "not too important," or "not important at all" to them personally. On Form B, the low-importance group was 65.2% of the sample for the contras, 37.8% of the sample for defense spending, and 29.5% of the sample for abortion. The comparable figures for Form A were 60.4%, 43.1%, and 17.2%. There were no statistically significant differences in these figures across the two forms.

Results

Before examining the false-consensus effect directly, I determined whether the distributions of responses to the self and others questions varied across the questionnaire forms. Surprisingly, when the full sample was considered as a whole, there were no statistically significant or even marginally significant differences between the two forms for any of the six questions. Analyses conducted separately with the high- and low-importance groups of respondents yielded comparable results. Thus, whatever effects the question-order manipulations had were not apparent in the marginal distributions of responses to the individual questions. However, this does not preclude effects of question order on the magnitude of the false-consensus effect.

The false-consensus effect was assessed by computing the difference between the mean perceived proportion of citizens favoring a policy among respondents who favored that policy and the mean perceived proportion of citizens favoring a policy among respondents who opposed that policy. As the figures displayed in Table 14.3 illustrate, there were significant false-consensus effects for all issues under both orders for the full sample. The effects range in magnitude from a 5.28-unit difference to a 12.74-unit difference.

Table 14.3 also illustrates a statistically significant effect of question order on the magnitude of the false-consensus effect. However, the direction of this interaction is completely unexpected. Across the three issues, the false-consensus effect was consistently larger under the others/self order than it was under the self/others order. When the results for the three issues were combined through meta-analytic procedures, the question-order effect was clearly statistically significant ($z = 1.77$, $p = .038$). Thus, this finding definitely challenges the self-enhancement and focus-of-attention explanations.

When we turn to differences between high-importance and low-importance respondents, we find further surprises (see Table 14.4). In particular, we cannot reach a single conclusion about whether the false-consensus effect is different in magnitude for the high- and low-importance respondents. Under the self/others order, the false-consensus effect is sizable and significant among the low-importance respondents and is smaller and nonsignificant among the high-importance respondents (interaction: $z = 2.67$, $p = .004$; see Table 14.5). However, under the others/self order, the false-consensus effect appears to be of the same magnitude in both the high- and low-importance groups (interaction: $z = 1.01$, $p = .156$). When examined through meta-analysis combining the three issues, the two-way interaction between order and importance is almost marginally significant ($z = 1.17$, $p = .121$). Because of the simple effects results, I am inclined to view this interaction as a real one. Thus, this seems to be a case where the substantive implications of an empirical investigation regarding the relation between attitude importance and the false-consensus effect vary depending on the order in which the questions are asked. Regardless of this inconsistency, however, the failure to find any evidence that the false-consensus effect is greater under high importance clearly contradicts the self-enhancement, focus-of-attention, and selective-exposure explanations.

Finally, we can examine whether the question-order manipulation had a greater effect among the high-importance respondents than among the low-importance respondents as the self-enhancement and focus-of-attention explanations predict. As Table 14.4 clearly illustrates, this prediction is confirmed. The question-order manipulation had a highly significant impact among the high-importance respondents ($z = 2.35$, $p = .009$) and no impact among the low-

TABLE 14.3. Unstandardized Regression Coefficients Estimating the False-Consensus Effect for the Full Sample

Question	Order Self/Others	Others/Self	Significance of Difference
Aid to contras	5.28*	10.61*	z = 1.60
	(N = 154)	(N = 164)	p = .055
Defense spending	8.20**	12.74**	z = 1.24
	(N = 183)	(N = 188)	p = .108
Abortion	6.73**	7.56**	z = 0.22
	(N = 180)	(N = 183)	p = .280
Combined			z = 1.77
			p = .038

*$p < .05$.   **$p < .01$.

TABLE 14.4. Unstandardized Regression Coefficients Estimating the False-Consensus Effect for the High- and Low-Importance Subsamples

Question	Order Self/Others	Others/Self	Significance of Difference
High Importance			
Aid to contras	−1.40	10.41**	z = 2.51
	(N = 60)	(N = 61)	p = .006
Defense spending	5.79*	11.79**	z = 1.27
	(N = 102)	(N = 113)	p = .102
Abortion	4.08	5.61	z = 0.29
	(N = 86)	(N = 92)	p = .386
Combined			z = 2.35
			p = .009
Low Importance			
Aid to contras	9.30**	11.00**	z = 0.37
	(N = 94)	(N = 103)	p = .356
Defense spending	11.56**	14.50**	z = 0.48
	(N = 81)	(N = 75)	p = .316
Abortion	10.05**	12.01**	z = 0.34
	(N = 94)	(N = 91)	p = .367
Combined			z = 0.69
			p = .245

*$p < .10$.   **$p < .01$.

TABLE 14.5. Significance Levels for Tests of the Differences between the False-Consensus Effects in the High- and Low-Importance Subsamples

Question	Order		Significance of Difference
	Self/Others	Others/Self	
Aid to contras	$z = 2.45$	$z = 0.12$	$z = 1.65$
	$p = .007$	$p = .452$	$p = .050$
Defense spending	$z = 1.02$	$z = 0.52$	$z = 0.35$
	$p = .154$	$p = .302$	$p = .363$
Abortion	$z = 1.16$	$z = 1.11$	$z = 0.04$
	$p = .123$	$p = .134$	$p = .484$
Combined	$z = 2.67$	$z = 1.01$	$z = 1.17$
	$p = .004$	$p = .156$	$p = .121$

importance respondents ($z = 0.69$, $p = .245$). Therefore, an interaction did appear involving attitude importance in the direction expected. However, because the direction of the question-order effect is opposite to that predicted by the self-enhancement and focus-of-attention explanations, this significant interaction involving importance cannot be viewed as offering support for those explanations.

Discussion

Taken together, these results cast serious doubt on all four of the possible explanations for the false-consensus effect offered by Marks and Miller (1987). Not one of the predictions presented in Table 14.2 was confirmed by these data. Although disappointing in this regard, these results make it clear how condition-seeking can be a useful way to assess the validity of hypotheses regarding the psychological mechanisms of well-documented effects.

Before considering possible alternative explanations suggested by the present findings, it is useful to note that these findings are consistent with those of a variety of previous investigations that explored the main effects of either question order or attitude importance on the magnitude of the false-consensus effect. For example, Campbell (1986) used only the self/others question order, and as is true in the present results, she found a weaker false-consensus effect among high-importance respondents than among low-importance respondents.[2] Also, two

---

[2]Instead of measuring attitude importance, Crano (1983) manipulated it by altering the perceived relevance of an issue for subjects. Increased importance was associated with an increase in the magnitude of the false-consensus effect. I suspect that the difference between this result on the one hand and Campbell's (1986) and the present findings on the other is due to the different operationalizations of attitude importance.

meta-analyses and many experimental studies have found that the false-consensus effect was greater under the others/self order than under the self/others order (Baron & Roper, 1976; McCauley, Kogan, & Teger, 1971; Mullen et al., 1985; Mullen, Driskell, & Smith, 1989; Mullen & Hu, 1988), just as Table 14.3 reveals.[3] Because none of these previous studies examined variation in the impact of the question-order manipulation across levels of attitude importance, they were unable to offer the definitive disconfirmation of the four explanations afforded by the present investigation.

Given this correspondence between the results of these prior investigations and those of the present investigation, it seems reasonable to view them as robust. It therefore seems appropriate to speculate about what these results suggest in terms of alternative cognitive mechanisms underlying the false-consensus effect. I say mechanisms here because the present results suggest that there are almost certainly different mechanisms at work among high- and low-importance respondents. This is because the impact of the question-order manipulation is different in these two groups.

In the high-importance group, the false-consensus effect is robust under the others/self order and essentially nonexistent under the self/others order. This result is consistent with the following scenario. When high-importance respondents are first asked to report their own attitudes on the issue, they do so easily and reliably because these attitudes are associated with strong, clear, and highly accessible internal cues (Krosnick, 1986, 1988, 1989). When these respondents are next asked to report their perceptions of others' attitudes on the issue, they may recognize the temporary salience of their own attitudes and their tendency to perhaps overly assume that others agree with them. In order to compensate for this, these individuals may correct for the impact of their own attitudes on their perceptions of others' attitudes (see, e.g., Martin & Harlow, chap. 7, this volume; Strack, Martin, & Schwarz, 1988). Because their perceptions of others' attitudes may be relatively weak and malleable, it is relatively easy for respondents to adjust their report of others to be more dissimilar from their own than they would have stated otherwise. This effort to differentiate may thus eliminate the impact of respondents' own attitudes on their perceptions of others' attitudes. This process is akin to Schuman and Presser's (1981) subtraction effect, where respondents intentionally subtract their own attitudes out of their reports of their perceptions of others' attitudes. This scenario, of course, predicts exactly the results obtained in the present study.

When high-importance respondents are asked the others question first, their own attitude is likely to come to mind spontaneously and automatically (Krosnick, 1989) and is therefore likely to be a highly salient anchor influencing their responses. Because these individuals' perceptions of others are again probably relatively malleable, the self-anchor is presumably capable of exerting a substan-

---

[3]Weinstein (1984) failed to find a stronger false-consensus effect under the others/self order compared with the self/others order. This inconsistency with the preponderance of published results is difficult to explain.

tial effect on them. When these respondents are next asked to report their own attitudes, they again probably feel some pressure not to be redundant and therefore to differentiate themselves from others. However, because the internal cues associated with their own attitudes are quite strong and unambiguous, no differentiation can take place. Furthermore, there is no clear reason why these respondents should subtract their perceptions of others out of their reports of their own attitudes. Therefore, the false-consensus effect would be expected to be readily apparent under this question order, just as it was.

In the low-importance group, the false-consensus effect is equally strong under both question orders. This suggests that the false-consensus effect does not occur because these individuals' attitudes are salient perceptual anchors that pull assessments of others' attitudes toward them. Instead, neither these individuals' own attitudes nor their perceptions of others' attitudes are likely to be associated with strong and clear internal cues. In this case, respondents may be forced to go through a reasoning process described by Bem's (1972) self-perception theory. That is, regardless of whether they are asked the self question or the others question first, these respondents may ask themselves: "What would a reasonable position be for a smart person to take on this issue?" Then, when the next question is asked, regardless of whether it addresses self or others, these respondents are likely to apply the same reasoning and therefore reach a comparable response. This would lead to the appearance of an equally strong false-consensus effect under both question orders. The reason for it would be that the same speculative reasoning process is used to generate both answers. Of course, all of this reasoning is post hoc and highly speculative, so that it should not be taken too seriously before additional empirical evaluations are conducted.

In addition to the specific finding of this study, the results reported here support some broad conclusions about the nature of response effects in survey questionnaires. First, effects of question order were present here even though the marginal distribution of answers to the relevant questions were unaltered. This supports the growing consensus that analyses of marginal distributions are not sufficient for ruling out effects of question form, wording, or ordering on the substantive conclusions of research (see, e.g., Kinder & Sanders, 1990; Krosnick & Alwin, 1988). The findings from this study also demonstrate that the substantive findings of correlational research can vary depending on question order. The impact of attitude importance on the magnitude of the false-consensus effect was different depending on which question order was examined. Question-order effects may similarly limit the generalizability of other psychological effects.

The data in this study indicate that the magnitude of an experimental effect decreases across replications of the experiment in the same survey. Specifically, the effects of question order become weaker moving from the top to the bottom of Table 14.3. This presumably occurs because respondents began to anticipate the questions that they would be asked later, thereby eliminating any potential effects of question order. This suggests that investigators interested in question-order effects (and also perhaps other response effects) should not attempt to conduct more than one or two parallel experiments in a row during an interview.

A third general conclusion that receives some support from the data in this study involves the cognitive mechanisms underlying response effects. I argued above that different psychological processes produced the false-consensus effects shown in the various cells of Tables 14.3 and 14.4. Thus, effects that appear to be comparable on the surface may in fact reflect quite different underlying dynamics. This possibility should be borne in mind by investigators of response effects in the future.

Conclusion

Both of the studies reported here illustrate the value of condition-seeking research. In Study 1, I found that response-order effects were greater among respondents with less cognitive sophistication. This finding reinforces previous interpretations of the findings in earlier studies and lends additional support to a particular cognitive explanation for these response-order effects. In Study 2, I found that the magnitude of the false-consensus effect depends on both the importance of the attitude to respondents and the order in which the self-perception and others-perception questions are asked. The specific pattern of results obtained clearly challenges the four explanations for the false-consensus effect that are currently prominent in the relevant social-psychological literature. The obtained results also led to the generation of a set of speculative alternative explanations that can be subjected to testing in future empirical research.

Part IV
Order Effects in Psychological Testing

15
Order Effects within Personality Measures

*Eric S. Knowles, Michelle C. Coker, Deborah A. Cook,
Steven R. Diercks, Mary E. Irwin, Edward J. Lundeen,
John W. Neville, and Mark E. Sibicky*

The Measurement Encounter

As early as 1692, Christian Thomasius had developed 12-point rating scales to measure psychological character (McReynolds & Ludwig, 1984). In the ensuing three centuries, our measurement theories have been refined and have markedly improved the quality of the information that we obtain (F. M. Lord & Novick, 1968; Hulin, Drasgow, & Parsons, 1983).

Most personality measures use the general form where the test maker provides a stimulus to which the test taker provides a response. The stimulus may be a self-description ("I cry easily") that the respondent endorses or disavows, a general statement ("Most things in this world occur by chance") to which the respondent agrees or disagrees, a problem ("Find the picture that doesn't belong") for which the respondent seeks a solution, or even an ambiguous representation (e.g., a TAT picture, a Rorschach inkblot, or an incomplete sentence stem) to which a respondent constructs a story. Current theories of measurement allow test makers to select and develop inquiries that maximize the information that the test maker receives from the inquiry–reply process.

The inquiry–reply measurement strategy engages the respondent in a social interaction with the test maker. Into this social interaction the test maker brings the inquiry and the test taker brings the reply. Out of this interaction the test maker takes information that, with proper scaling and comparison to norms, informs the test maker about the personality of the respondent.

What does the respondent bring out of measurement interaction? At the most general level, a person who engages the test material brings away two things from the encounter:
1. An awareness of and involvement with the issues and constructs employed by the test maker, and
2. A confrontation with self as the respondent attempts to integrate the encounter into the self-concept.

Measurement Reactivity

The question of how the respondent reacts to the measurement encounter has been largely neglected in measurement theories (D. W. Fiske, 1967). When addressed, the question is often framed as a problem of measurement reactivity, defined as "error," and treated primarily as a nuisance for the test maker. Webb, Campbell, Schwartz, and Sechrest (1966), for instance, found that

> The most understated risk to valid interpretation is the error produced by the respondent. Even when he is well intentioned and cooperative, the research subject's knowledge that he is participating in a scholarly search may confound the investigator's data. (p. 13)

Webb et al. (1966) employed a motivational perspective where measurement errors were tied to the self-presentational concerns of the respondent. The respondent, apprehensive about evaluation, was thought to hide the true self or to construct a situationally appropriate (but untrue) identity.

Two things are missed by focusing on measurement anticipation and self-presentation. First, this focus of attention frames issues at a very molar level, using the test as a whole and the entire testing encounter as the units of analysis. Second, the attention on the anticipation and preparation for measurement neglects other interesting issues having to do with how measurement alters the respondent's understanding of the measure or the self.

This chapter focuses on the cognitive rather than the motivational consequences of measurement, in particular on how the measuring process alters the respondent's understanding of the questions and issues addressed in the test. From this perspective, the context effects in which we are interested represent *meaning changes* in the comprehension of the test or of the self and not simply self-presentational strategies. The test item is the appropriate unit of analysis for this inquiry. Specifically, we shall look at how considering one question alters the kinds of answers that are given to the subsequent questions.

Consequences of Being Asked a Question

The cognitive processes initiated by question probes are beginning to be understood, as many chapters in this volume illustrate. Most authors adopt the models proposed by Rogers (1974a) and Tourangeau and Rasinski (1988), who divide the cognitive processes involved in inquiry–reply measurement into a four-stage sequence that includes (a) question interpretation, (b) information/memory retrieval, (c) judgment formation, and (d) response selection. These four stages and the many component processes are described in the other chapters in this volume and in Tourangeau and Rasinski's (1988) thorough review.

From these presentations, it is clear that the task of considering a single question and formulating an answer has many identifiable consequences. Ten of the more important consequences for personality measurement are listed below. These effects are important because they are the sort that may persist and influence answers to subsequent questions.

1. Questions may force an answer to be created where none previously existed (Getzels, 1982; Salancik & Conway, 1975; Sandelands & Larson, 1985)!
2. Respondents construe a question in one particular way, so that one meaning or one interpretation becomes salient and other possible interpretations fade into the background (C. G. Lord, Lepper, & Preston, 1984).
3. Detailed questions may alter the respondents' level of action identification and may make them more susceptible to changing their view of self (Wegner, Vallacher, Kiersted, & Dizadji, 1986).
4. Thinking about an issue tends to polarize the judgments that are made about that issue (Higgins & Rholes, 1978; Sadler & Tesser, 1973; Tesser, 1978; Tesser & Conlee, 1975).
5. Information, memories, and/or attitude structures that are activated by a memory search become more available, more easily accessed, and more influential for subsequent judgments (Bargh & Pratto, 1986; Fazio, Powell, & Herr, 1983; Higgins, King, & Mavin, 1982; Posner, 1978).
6. Declaring an intention or producing an overt answer makes the respondents more committed to their position (Feldman & Lynch, 1988; Kiesler, 1971). Subsequent behavior is then more likely to be consistent with the judgment (Sherman, 1980).
7. A judgment, once rendered, serves as an anchor point against which further considerations may be assimilated or contrasted (Higgins & Lurie, 1983; Strack, Schwarz, & Gschneidinger, 1985).
8. Formulating a judgment and rendering a response themselves activate a post hoc memory search. The search is biased in favor of information that supports the response (Petty & Cacioppo, 1986a). This search can produce entirely new cognitions (Sadler & Tesser, 1973) and can allow existing evidence to be reinterpreted as consistent with the judgment (Tesser & Cowan, 1977).
9. Merely thinking about a complex issue may increase the coherence and interconnectedness of the various facets of the issue (McGuire, 1960; Millar & Tesser, 1986).
10. Considering difficult questions may make respondents develop more complex conceptual structures through which to view issues. For instance, La Rue and Olejnik (1980) found that questions that demanded formal operational thought led young respondents to employ more formal operational responses on a later reasoning test.

These 10 consequences of considering and answering questions suggest the many profound ways that someone's view of an issue and of self may be affected by the measurement process. We need, however, a methodology to study the impact and generality of these influences on personality measurement.

Serial-Position Analysis of Accumulating Effects

Personality tests are particularly useful areas for studying measurement consequences and context effects. A test that inquires about self-descriptions rather than about abstract opinions should engage a deeper and more involved level of processing (Burnkrant & Unnava, 1989; Petty, Rennier, & Caioppo, 1987). Also, a single-factor personality test should make the consequences identified above accumulate as the respondent considers the same dimension again and again with each additional item. Specifically, (a) respondents should become more confident, committed to, and polarized in their judgment; (b) respondents should become more efficient at making their judgments; (c) respondents should become more consistent and reliable in determining their judgments; and (d) respondents should have a fuller and more organized schema for the construct being measured.

Accumulating reactions have two advantages for studying context effects. First, effects based on a large number of items should be stronger and therefore more evident than would effects based on a single item. Second, the accumulation of reactions should be directly evident as linear trends over the number of items considered. This second property has been particularly important to our research.

The printing press has been a boon to personality research because it has allowed many copies of a questionnaire to be duplicated efficiently. One of the costs of duplication, at least for the study of context effects, is that the printed form confounds the content of an item with its serial position. The first item is always the same, as is the last, and as is every item in between.

This confounding of content with context creates a problem for interpreting item answers. The answer to any particular item on the test includes reactions to the content of that item and reactions that carry over from the previous items. When we inspect answers to the last item on a test, we usually cannot disentangle how much of the answer is due to the content of that particular item and how much is due to the context provided by the previous items.

Of course, interpretation is clouded only at the level of the item answer. Interpretations of the scale score, which is the focus of most personality measurement, is not compromised by the confounding of content with context. However, coming to understand the cognitive processes involved in personality measurement requires a focus at the item level and attention to this confounding.

To investigate the accumulating reactions that people have to thinking about and answering personality test questions, we have had to disentangle the content from the context of the previous items. We have done this by using a randomized latin square to counterbalance item content across the serial positions in a test. For instance, with a 30-item personality measure, we create 30 different forms such that each item (a) appears in each of the 30 serial positions, (b) is preceded and followed by each of the other items approximately half of the time, and (c) is separated by random distances from each of the other items.

Table 15.1 presents a simple randomized latin square for a 7-item measure.

TABLE 15.1. Counterbalance Design for a 7-Item Measure

Test Form							

Test Form	1st	2nd	3rd	4th	5th	6th	7th
Form #1	D	A	B	G	F	C	E
Form #2	E	B	C	A	G	D	F
Form #3	F	C	D	B	A	E	G
Form #4	G	D	E	C	B	F	A
Form #5	A	E	F	D	C	G	B
Form #6	B	F	G	E	D	A	C
Form #7	C	G	A	F	E	B	D

Note: The letters "A" through "G" refer to items of different content. Each form presents each item in a different serial position. Over the block of 7 forms, each item (a) appears in each of the seven serial positions, (b) preceeds and follows each other item, and (c) is placed at random distances from each other item. In a sample, equal numbers of subjects receive each form.

The 7 items, labeled A through G, were first placed in a random order, for example, 1st = D, 2nd = A, 3rd = B, 4th = G, etc. This was the order of items used on the first form of the test. For the second form, each letter was increased by one value, except for the highest value (G), which was returned to the lowest (A), for example, 1st = E, 2nd = B, 3rd = C, 4th = A, etc.

This procedure is preferable to a simple rotation scheme in which the last item on Form 1 becomes the first item on Form 2 but the order and distance of items otherwise remain constant. Although our random latin square randomizes these orders and distances, these confounds can be even better controlled by following the prescriptions in Ostrom, Isaac, and McCann (1983). In practice, a microcomputer randomly assigns up to 40 items and then composes and prints multiple copies of each of the counterbalanced forms. We distribute forms to respondents in a random manner but make sure that we have completed replications of the latin square design; that is, with a 30-item measure, we have 30 different forms of the measure, each with a different order of the 30 items, and submit this to some multiple of 30 respondents (e.g., 90, 120, or 150 subjects).

Context Effects within an I-E Test

Counterbalancing item content over serial positions in a test allows the effects of item content to be disentangled from the effects of context. We will illustrate these effects with the results from a data set obtained from 120 respondents to an Internal-External Locus of Control scale (Knowles, 1988, Study 1). The respondents received one of 30 forms composed from W. H. James's (1957) 30-item I-E scale. The answers were prepared in several ways. First, the scores of any negatively worded items were reversed so that positive scores indicated the same end of the scale (Externality). Second, item means and variances were equated by standardizing the answers given to each content item.

Several estimates of context effect are particularly informative.

Mean Shifts

Since the different content items appear in equal proportion in each position, the mean answer at each serial position provides an estimate of the mean test score. If the context created by previous items has no effect, then this mean will remain the same for each serial position. Systematic shifts in this mean, from the beginning to the end of the measure, reflect reactions to the earlier measurement.

The mean answers to James's I-E scale showed no systematic change from beginning to end of the measure, $F(29, 2610) = .86$, NS. Also, the serial position did not interact significantly with item content to affect some items differently from others, $F(812, 2610) = 1.06$, NS. Thus, the mean answers on the I-E test showed no evidence that later answers were affected by earlier answers. We shall show later that (a) some measures do show shifts in mean answers and subjects even in this study systematically polarized their later judgments. For many authors, mean shifts are the only context effects that are measured. Although the I-E test showed no mean shifts, it did show other clear context effects.

Reliability Shifts

The scores at each serial position can be correlated with the sum of the remaining scores. Since all items appear at each serial position, the resulting coefficient is an estimate of the internal consistency of the measure as a whole. If the context created by previous items has no effect, then this correlation will remain the same for each serial position. Systematic shifts in this reliability estimate reflect reactions to earlier measurement.

The reliability estimates did show a significant increasing linear relationship with serial position. Figure 15.1 presents this serial-position effect. The 30 correlations, one for each serial position, were transformed into Fisher's z scores and inspected to make sure that they met the assumptions of a parametric data set. These Fisher z scores themselves were then correlated with the serial position to describe the trend evident in Figure 15.1. The positive linear relationship between serial position and reliability was highly significant, $r(28) = .51$, $p < .01$.

A regression equation ($Y' = .4054 + .0062 \times$ Serial Position) provided a best estimate of the reliability of items in the first position as .390 (Fisher $z = .412$) and of items in the last position as .531 (Fisher $z = .592$). Since the same item content appeared in the first and the last position, this significant increase reflects a reaction to the earlier measurement.

Polarization of Reactions

The total scores on the measure can be used to differentiate respondents into high-, medium-, and low-scoring subgroups. For this analysis, we combined two data sets to obtain 270 subjects (Knowles, 1988, Study 3). Across subgroups,

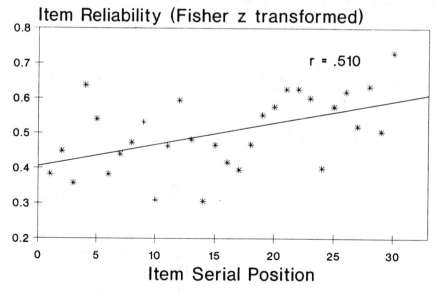

FIGURE 15.1. Reliability Shift on James I-E Scale

the mean answers to the items at each serial position show a consistent spreading apart. As shown in Figure 15.2, the low-scoring Internal subjects gave mean answers that systematically decreased with the serial position of the item ($r = -.64$). The regression equation estimated Internals' answers to the 1st item to be $Z = -.43$ and answer to the 30th item to be $Z = -.63$. In contrast, the answers given by External subjects were positively but nonsignificantly correlated with serial position ($r = .25$). The regression equation estimated External subjects' answers to increase from $Z = .50$ on the 1st item to $Z = .60$ on the 30th item. Subjects, especially the Internal subjects, became more polarized in their ratings as they thought about and answered more and more of the I-E questions.

Other Consequences of Measurement

We know from other studies that respondents are able to answer later items more quickly and more knowledgeably. In one study (Knowles & Diercks, 1988), 270 respondents were seated at a computer to answer questions from a personality inventory. After familiarizing themselves with the computer procedures by answering a variety of demographic questions, subjects read a screen that described the Personal Reaction Inventory as containing 60 items that concerned a variety of topics, for which there were no right or wrong answers and to which large numbers of people agreed and large numbers disagreed. Following this description, they read and answered 0, 1, 3, 9, or 27 items from either Rokeach's (1956) Dogmatism scale or Taylor's (1953) Manifest Anxiety scale.

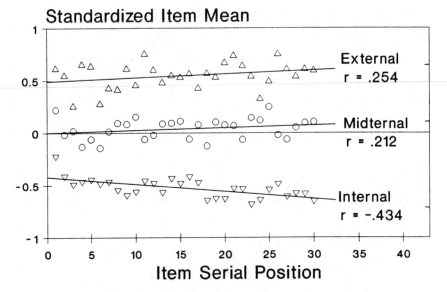

FIGURE 15.2. Polarization of Answers

After finishing this first phase of the study, all subjects were shown eight new items and asked to judge how likely each item was to belong to the Personal Reaction Inventory. The eight items included four that were prototypic of the scale construct and four that were distractor items. In preparation for this experiment, psychology faculty and graduate students rated each of the original test items in terms of how prototypic it was of the test construct. The four items with the highest prototypicality ratings were saved for this second phase of the study and were interspersed with four items from unrelated scales. Respondents entered on the computer keyboard their 9-point ratings of how well the items belonged to the scale. After making these ratings, subjects continued to answer the remaining 27 items from the personality test.

Judgment Accuracy

Exposure to more test items increased subjects' accuracy at recognizing the items that belonged to the scale, $F(4, 260) = 5.46$, $p = .001$, but did not affect their ability to detect the distractor items, $F(4, 260) = 0.60$, $p = .66$. Although anxiety prototypes were judged more accurately than dogmatism prototypes, the effects of exposure to items were identical for the two tests. Figure 15.3 presents the effects of experience on these belongingness judgments, averaged across the two types of personality measures.

Response Time

In this study, we also recorded the response interval from initial display of the personality test item until a response key was pushed. The condition had no

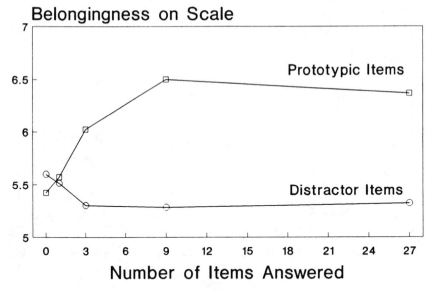

FIGURE 15.3 Learning the Test Construct

main or interactive effect on these response times. As is shown in Figure 15.4, the response times for both personality tests continuously decreased across the 27 items. Of course there are many possible explanations for this decrease in response time. Subjects may have become more efficient judges, may have had the relevant cognitions more available, or may have been lazier. Nonetheless, this study suggests that as subjects answer more and more test items, they answer them both more quickly and more knowledgeably.

Generalizability of Reliability Shifts

Our studies of serial-position shifts in reliability have extended to other measures besides I-E. Knowles (1988) reported equivalent reliability shifts across serial position for measures of I-E (W. H. James, 1957), Dogmatism (Rokeach, 1956), Anxiety (Taylor, 1953), and Social Desirability (Crowne & Marlowe, 1964). In other research we have replicated these findings for I-E (Knowles, Cook, & Neville, 1989a; Knowles, Lundeen, & Irwin, 1988) and Anxiety (Coker & Knowles, 1987; Neville & Knowles, 1990) and extended them to measures of self-acceptance (Knowles, Cook, & Neville, 1989b).

We have not found serial-position changes in item reliability for Snyder's (1974) self-monitoring scale (Knowles, Lundeen, & Irwin, 1988), Beck's (Beck, Rush, Shaw, & Emmery, 1979) Depression Inventory (Knowles, Coker, & Diercks, 1988), or for several extracted MMPI scales (Neville & Knowles, 1990). Although we have not found this context effect universally, we have found it with enough regularity and generality to suspect that it is a widespread phenomenon. We suspect that multifactor measures, where it is more difficult to

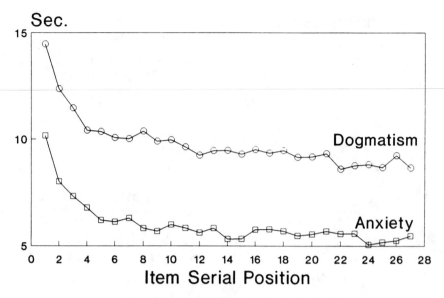

FIGURE 15.4. Response Times to Items

discern a consistent theme to the test, may be less likely to produce the reliability shift (Neville & Knowles, 1990).

Applications to Test–Retest Effects

Retests on a measure have shown two kinds of differences from the original test: reliability shifts and mean answer shifts.

Test–Retest Reliability Shifts

More than 50 years ago, Pintner and Forlano (1938) observed that odd–even reliabilities on several personality measures tended to increase over four testings. Since then many researchers have found that people answer a personality retest more consistently than they answered the first test (D. W. Fiske, 1957; Goldberg, 1978; Howard, 1964; Howard & Diesenhaus, 1965; Schubert & Fiske, 1973; Windle, 1955). Many test developers, including Taylor (1953) for her anxiety measure, report that retests have higher internal consistency than first tests. The greater internal consistency on retest with the same or similar items seems to be a normal consequence of the reliability shifts that we have observed within tests (Coker & Knowles, 1987). The retest elevation in reliability merely perpetuates the changes that occur within the first test.

Test–Retest Mean Answer Shifts

Windle (1954) compiled test–retest data from numerous personality inventories and concluded that a variety of "adjustment" scores showed significantly better adjustment on retest, especially with retest intervals of less than two months. This intriguing mean answer shift on retest continues to be observed for various tests (Chance, 1955; Goldberg, 1978; Payne, 1974; Perkins & Goldberg, 1964; Windle, 1955).

We find that the increased scores on retest are not really a test–retest phenomenon but an item-to-item reaction that is also apparent within the first test. We (Coker & Knowles, 1987) studied two 25-item alternate forms of an anxiety test using the latin square design. The mean answer shift observed within the first testing continued unabated throughout the second testing given a week later, as shown in Figure 15.5.

The shift in mean answers is most often interpreted as an impression management phenomena in which respondents try to present themselves on the retest as more adjusted and socially desirable (Goldberg, 1978; Payne 1974). In Neville, Coker, and Knowles (1988) we interpreted this impression management theory as implying that the subjects who were most anxious would change the most. We divided our Coker and Knowles (1987) sample into high-, medium-, and low-anxiety subgroups, based on the sum of their test and retest scores, and found that each subgroup showed equivalent serial-position decreases in mean answers, both within and between the two test administrations. Since subjects with the most desirable scores changed as much as the subjects with the least desirable scores, the impression management theory did not seem particularly useful. We (Knowles et al., 1989b) recently observed a similar increase in self-acceptance scores within a test, increases that were also equivalent for high-, medium-, and low-scoring subgroups.

Although many personality measures do not show a mean shift within or between test administrations, tests of adjustment, including anxiety and self-acceptance, seem to be susceptible to these context effects. The fact that adjusted and unadjusted respondents show this effect equally is less suggestive of a social desirability explanation and more consistent with a meaning-change interpretation. Answering earlier items may alter the interpretation, recall of relevant information, and meaning of later items in ways that shift the respondent's answer.

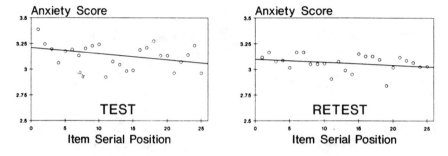

FIGURE 15.5. Mean Answer Shift on Anxiety Test and Retest

Implications for Factor Structure of Measures

One way to conceptualize the meaning-change explanation is that respondents learn through experience to interpret the scale-relevant content of an item and to disregard surplus meanings. Consequently, answers to later items better reflect the scale construct than do earlier items. In Knowles, Lundeen, and Irwin (1988) we used this reasoning and factor analyses to explore the degree to which items saturated the I-E scale construct.

Using counterbalanced orderings of James's (1957) 30-item I-E scale, 150 subjects were tested and then two weeks later were retested. The item responses were standardized for each item content but left in the order in which they had been answered. In a novel use, factor analysis was employed to identify serial-position changes in item saturation.

The scores at each *serial position* were factor analyzed for test and retest. Each serial position included answers from all content items. Since all items contributed equally to the scores at each serial position, the factor analysis of serial positions revealed one large factor representing whatever was measured by all of the items. Figure 15.6 presents the factor loadings of each serial position on the single factor identified at test and retest.

For the first testing, the factor loadings were positively correlated with serial position of the items, $r(28) = .66$, $p < .001$. Based on regression line estimates, items in the first position had an estimated factor loading of .348. The same items appearing at the end of the test were estimated to have a loading of .540 on the same factor.

For the retest, serial position made little difference. All of the factor loadings were high and fairly consistent. However, on this retest, the serial positions had significantly higher average loadings (.495) than did the original test (.444), $t(28) = 2.46$, $p < .05$. The average retest loading (.495) was not significantly different from the estimated loading at the end of the first test (.540), $Z = .73$, NS.

Since every item appears at every serial position, these factor loadings do not represent content differences. Instead, they seem to represent "saturation" differences (Harris, 1975), that is, the degree to which the underlying construct is reflected in the item set. It seems that for the single-factor I-E scale, an item

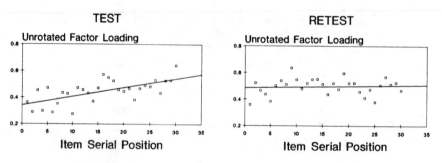

FIGURE 15.6. Saturation of Items at Each Serial Position

engages less of the test construct when it appears at the beginning of the test than when it appears at the end. Experience with the intervening items clarifies the construct being measured, eliminates surplus meanings from the item, and alters the response characteristics of the item.

Modifiers of the Reliability Shift

Most recently, we have turned our attention to another question: Who shows the reliability shift most strongly? In Knowles et al. (1989a) we investigated the role of cognitive and motivational mediators of the reliability shift. Specifically, we assessed whether people who had a higher Need for Cognition (Cacioppo & Petty, 1982) and higher conceptual ability (as measured by the vocabulary sub-test of the Shipley Institute of Living Scale; Zachary, 1986) were more likely to show this serial-position increase in reliability on a 40-item Locus of Control scale.

We found that verbal ability strongly modified the serial-position effect on item reliability, but it was opposite to the one that we had expected. The correlation between serial position and item reliability was $r = .69$ for subjects low in verbal ability but only $r = .18$ for subjects high in verbal ability. This difference in correlations was significant, $Z = 2.85$, $p < .01$.

Figure 15.7 presents the scatter plots and regression lines for these two relationships. Low Verbal Ability subjects showed a much steeper increase in item reliability than did High Verbal Ability subjects. Their later answers apparently profited from the repeated encounters with earlier test items. The High Verbal Ability subjects answered even the first question with a moderately high level of reliability and showed only a slight increase over the 40 serial positions. It seems that their ability to answer a question was barely affected by the previous questions.

We conducted a similar analysis to look for the moderating influence of the Need for Cognition. High Need for Cognition subjects were significantly more internal than Low Need for Cognition subjects $F(1, 398) = 16.79$, $p < .0001$, but showed no difference in the reliability shift, $Z = 0.73$, NS. As shown in Figure 15.8, both subgroups showed the benefits of answering earlier items.

In the Knowles et al. (1989a) study, the subjects' vocabulary ability, more than their cognitive motivation, modified the reliability shift. We assume that the less verbally able subjects answered early items unreliably but, with continued experience, came to discern the test construct more clearly, finally matching or surpassing the reliability that more verbally able subjects exhibited even on the first items. We think that the more verbally able subjects could extract the implicit meaning of the items from the beginning of the test.

Conclusions

This program of research shows that respondents' reactions to tests changed systematically in several ways as they moved from the beginning to the end of

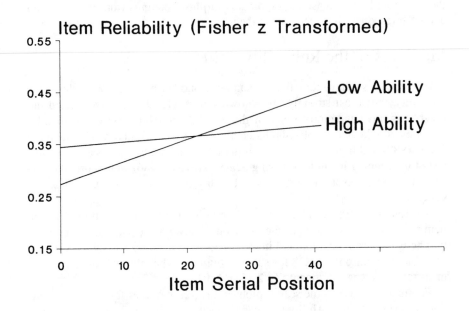

FIGURE 15.7. Verbal Ability and Reliability Shift

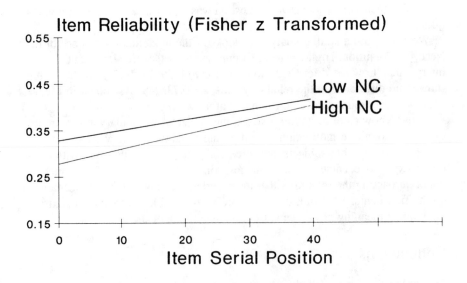

FIGURE 15.8. Need for Cognition and the Reliability Shift

the test and from test to retest. Respondents typically answered questions in more extreme, more consistent, and more reliable ways. These more consistent answers were achieved more quickly and with more understanding of the test construct, particularly by those subjects who would have the most difficulty discerning the implicit meaning of the early items.

Meaning Change

We think that these results are most consistent with what we call the "meaning-change hypothesis." This is an explanation that relies on the cognitive processes involved in considering and answering questions. The four-stage process involved in considering a single item—interpreting its meaning and implications, retrieving relevant information, forming a judgment, and making a response—has a variety of consequences that feed forward to influence the processing of the next item. Consequently, for later items, the construct relevant content is more easily discernible and accessible; construct irrelevant associations can be ignored. Information retrieved and created for earlier items is more available for later items. The early judgments formed for specific items become a generalized judgment concerning the latent construct. Consequently, the response generation process becomes less an information integration task and more the calibration of a generalized judgment to the particular scale values represented by the question and response scale. In short, answers to later items become more informed, more efficient, and more confident.

Alternative Explanations

The meaning-change hypothesis guided this research and, we believe, is most consistent with the results. There are several rival explanations that still need to be considered.

Social desirability is a persistent alternative explanation for instances of measurement reactivity (Goldberg, 1978; Webb, Campbell, Schwartz, Sechrest, & Grove, 1981). Social desirability does not seem to offer a reasonable alternative explanation for the reliability shifts, response polarization, or construct learning effects that we have found. However, we believe that social desirability plays a part in the mean shifts that have been found for tests of adjustment (e.g., Windle, 1954). Social desirability is likely to influence (a) the content of the thoughts that are retrieved in response to each question, (b) the arguing and counterarguing that occurs during and after considering a question, and (c) the ease with which questions and thoughts are assimilated into the self-concept. Although there certainly are situations where people decide to "fake good" or "fake bad," we believe that the more general influence of social desirability is fairly subtle and has its impact early in the response process.

Cognitive laziness is another possible rival explanation (Israelski & Lenoble, 1982; Krosnick, in press). In this view, respondents become fatigued or bored with repeatedly considering similar questions and simplify the strategy that they employ to formulate answers. Rather than fully considering and integrating their information about questions, respondents come to adopt a strategy that "satisfices"; that is, one that produces, with minimal effort, a just adequate rather than optimal response. Krosnick (in press) provides a careful and provocative review of how satisficing strategies might be employed in answering questions.

We have concluded that respondents become more efficient in answering later personality items and are able to neglect the irrelevant meanings of an item to concentrate more directly on the abstracted test construct. These effects, seen through a cynical eye, may have the look of laziness.

The meaning-change and satisficing alternatives involve more than whether one is looking at the same phenomenon through pollyanna or jaundiced eyes. Several tests between these alternative explanations are possible. One test would look at the effects of ego involvement. Ego involvement should increase the motivation to process the items and should reduce the reliability shift, but in different ways according to the meaning-change and satisficing hypotheses. Under meaning change, increased motivation should raise the reliability of early-appearing items; but, if the satisficing hypothesis is correct, motivation should reduce the reliability of later-appearing items. A second test would look at the effects of task demands or distraction. Increasing the cognitive task load should reduce the reliability shift under the meaning-change explanation but should increase the reliability shift under the satisficing theory (Krosnick, in press).

Ambiguity of Measurement

These studies have an intriguing implication: They bring the Heisenberg (1958) principle to personality measurement. The act of measurement alters the meaning of the measure as the respondent becomes educated about self and about the test construct. When these changes occur at the item-to-item level, it is very difficult to tease apart how much of the answer reflects the personality before measurement and how much reflects an interaction with the measurement.

Measurement that engages the respondent in an inquiry–reply encounter is not "objective" in the sense of being outside of and apart from the respondent. It is a subjective and interactive process, in which both the respondent and the test taker bring something into the encounter and both take something away from it.

16
Context Influences on the Meaning of Work

Gerald R. Salancik and Julianne F. Brand

Order effects in surveys are a special class of context effects on opinions. In this chapter, we examine context effects on a job reaction survey and show that context can be manipulated to study how individuals use information about their job experiences to generate job descriptions.

Researchers who study job reactions propose that individuals are more or less motivated to do their work and more or less satisfied with their jobs when those jobs possess certain features. In particular, a job is said to be motivating (or satisfying for the individual) if the work is organized to allow the individual *autonomy* and discretion as to how to do it, if it lets the individual use a *variety* of his or her talents and abilities, if it permits the individual *identification* with the outcome, if the individual can see the *significance* of his or her work for others (customers, co-workers), and if the individual gets *feedback* from the work about how well or poorly it is going. The general relationship between job reactions and these characteristics has been well established. Jobs characterized by autonomy, identification, variety, significance, and feedback are typically rated by those who do them as more satisfying and more motivating (Hackman & Oldham, 1980).

Less is known about how individuals characterize their work along these dimensions. The authors of one instrument for describing jobs, the Job Diagnostic Survey (JDS), used in several hundred studies, assume that workers' responses are simply reports on objective features of their work (Hackman & Oldham, 1980); that is, the individuals are reporting on what they know about their jobs. One indication that this might be the case is that observers will often describe jobs in the same way as they do their occupants. Other research, however, has shown that job descriptions are affected by social suggestions (e.g., Griffin, 1983; O'Reilly & Caldwell, 1979) and various response and method artifacts (Glick, Jenkins, & Gupta, 1986; Idazak & Drasgow, 1987).

Consistent with both positions, we argue that survey instruments asking persons to characterize their personal experiences along a set of dimensions—such as the Job Diagnostic Survey—are influenced necessarily by both content and context. We assume this because such instruments, by design, ask persons to translate their experiences into specified descriptions. If the task is taken seriously, then in fulfilling its request they would review their knowledge of the situation and derive interpretations meaningful for that context (Salancik, 1982). Respondents, of course, may repeat descriptions given to previous inquiries, but their earlier views will reflect the knowledge and interpretations then available. Whenever views are generated, anything affecting the recall or use of information about the situation will affect judgments.

Theoretical Framework

There are at least four influences of context on responses. One arises if a context directly primes a response, as is common when a person acknowledges how nice another looks before going on a date. Another occurs when a context makes information salient, which in turn affects a response, as might happen when a person going out the door with a date is prompted to remember whether the gas tank is filled. These two effects are commonplace biases that are also easily detected because they affect most respondents in the same way. Two additional effects, however, are conditioned by a person's own experiences or knowledge. One effect comes from the differential relevance that a person attaches to knowledge in different contexts even when it is readily available in each. In evaluating a person in the context of a date, one might consider the knowledge that the person wears glasses as important information for the evaluation but might easily overlook such trivia when evaluating the person in the context of a marriage. A related effect arises from the differing implications derived from a particular knowledge rather than from its relevance. Knowledge that a person wears glasses may entail either negative or positive implications in different circumstances.

These latter influences are closely related to the kinds of order effects noted for survey questions. As an illustration, consider a person with considerable knowledge about his preferences and experiences with several fruit juices. This person really loves orange juice, easily recalls its taste and aroma, and readily sees himself reaching for it on entering a grocery store. In contrast, he has only a mild regard for grapefruit juice and fleeting experiences. Finally, he has a definite dislike for apple juice, quivers at its pungent odor and the bland, flat, untextured residue that it leaves in his mouth as it is swallowed. Suppose asking this person two questions: "Do you like orange juice?" and "Do you like fruit juices?" We might expect such a person to have a lower probability of answering "yes" to the second question if it were asked after the first than if it were asked before. We would expect this because having confessed his passion for orange juice to the first question, a repetition might seem a bit out of place for the second, especially since it might imply he likes all juices when he clearly does not. If asked about fruit juices first, however, he might surely wish to speak out strongly for his favorite. For this individual, context differs from one order to another and would be revealed by comparing them.

Yet, because different individuals have different experiences and knowledge, the order-effects paradigm will be limited for revealing such effects as a general rule. A person with the opposite preferences would not be similarly affected. Hence, we may be unable to observe real context differences when they are present simply by seeing how different orders of questions influence responses. Equally important, we shall be unable to learn how individuals generate their opinions in the first place.

To study context effects that are conditioned by personal knowledge requires a different kind of paradigm. The one that we use here is the context-priming paradigm. In this paradigm (Salancik, 1982), an investigator assumes (or knows) that certain knowledge is in the domain used by individuals in coming to their opinions. To study how opinions are generated and how context affects them, one varies the context in some way that is theoretically relevant to hypotheses about the opinions under study. For example, in the theory of job reactions, job characteristics are assumed to be stable properties of the way in which a person's work is organized and directed in an organization. If a person is free to do a job in whatever way he or she deems appropriate, he or she should attribute autonomy to it. If the job directly and visibly affects the welfare of others, it should be invested with great significance. As former Governor Jerry Brown of California said of university professors, "They should be paying the State for the privilege of having such wonderful jobs," alluding to the possibility that professors can do whatever they like whenever they like and have a great time playing in their research labs while admiring students writing down their every word. Yet, in this job, as in others, there are contradictions. Passing gems of wisdom every day can consume energy and time far in excess of the doting affirmations received. Such consumptions could clearly diminish a sense of significance. We expect that these and other feelings would depend severely on whether one thought about teaching in a context of oneself or one's students. From the point of view of theories about job reactions, such an outcome would question assumptions that jobs have stable properties that spawn motivations and satisfactions.

Thus, our purpose for the study described here was to evaluate how opinions about jobs are affected both by content and by context. In brief, workers were queried about their job content, primed by one of two context cues, and then asked to characterize their jobs on the Job Diagnostic Survey (Hackman & Oldham, 1980).

Overview of Study

The jobs studied were the teaching jobs of University of Illinois graduate assistants, which vary widely in the instructional, administrative, evaluative, counseling, and social activities involved. To ensure that all respondents were aware of their jobs' content, we first gave them a list of teaching assistant (TA) activities and ask them to place a checkmark by the ones that applied to their jobs.

This also gave us specific knowledge about the tasks comprising their jobs. An underlying assumption was that individuals will process knowledge of their job activities to derive meaning but that the meaning derived will vary with context. The design was constructed to allow us to evaluate the alternative influences that context might have on job descriptions. If the context affected relevance or meanings, then job activities would associate with JDS characteristics differently in different contexts. If, on the other hand, task content directly implied certain job descriptions, then the same job activities would imply the same characteristics regardless of context. And if job interpretations differed regardless of job activities, then context affected either information recall or response biases.

Context was manipulated by focusing the TAs' attention on themselves or on their students, a choice based on pilot interviews and our own experiences. Interviews suggested that the TAs held their jobs in contradictory regards. They vacillated between thinking of the job's effects on their students and on their own lives and obligations. Thus, at times, teaching was viewed as a good opportunity to gain experience in organizing and integrating knowledge from one's field, but at other times, it was a drag that kept one away from academic goals. These variations in meaning from the same content were consistent with our theoretical views.

Method

Forty graduate teaching assistants at the University of Illinois were interviewed about their jobs. The individuals were sampled randomly from the University's list of graduate TAs stratified to cover major branches of studies—the physical, biological, and social sciences, the humanities, the performing arts, and engineering. All were graduate students employed half time. TA jobs differ greatly, ranging from independently teaching entire undergraduate courses, through leading discussion sections of a large course, to assisting in setting up demonstrations for a professor-taught course. Interviews were arranged by contacting the TAs and meeting them at convenient locations on campus, their places of work, or their homes. The interviewer was a female graduate student who also taught undergraduates. Each interview lasted one to three hours. Respondents had no knowledge of the study before being solicited and interviewed.

Procedures

The study was introduced to respondents in a straightforward manner:

We are doing this study to find out more about what graduate teaching assistants at the University do in their jobs, how the jobs of instructors in different departments vary, and how instructors feel about their jobs.

Interviewing was in three stages. First on a list of 95 activities each TA checked off those that were typically and regularly part of his or her job, then answered a question that manipulated context, and finally assessed the job on the JDS and evaluated his or her job satisfaction.

Job Activities

The list of 95 activities was constructed during a two-month pilot study of a sample of 15 University teaching assistants. The individuals free associated about the activities that made up their jobs. Several hundred items resulted. These were edited to incorporate similar activities under the same description. Editing was repeated until the final 95 were settled on. For ease of presentation, the items were grouped into five general categories: (a) instructional activities, (b) counseling activities, (c) administrative activities, (d) maintenance activities, and (e) evaluative activities. Four examples of the most common activities in each are presented in Table 16.1.

To collect information from each respondent about the activities comprising his or her job, the interviewer handed out the list of activities and asked the respondent to read each item and judge if the indicated activity was something done as a regular or normal part of the job. It was explained that "regular" meant "the activity is something you normally do in your particular job even if it is done only once during a semester." Illustrations were then provided indicating that an activity such as "grading final exams" might only be done once in a semester but was a regular part of the job if done each term. It was also explained that our interest was in the job as it was actually done rather than as others might do it or as the University might have defined it. The TA was then left alone to check off the activities, and the interviewer sat nearby to answer questions. Questions were minimal. After marking the activities list, the respondent was asked if any items were unclear or puzzling. The purpose of this question and the checklist was to ensure that the respondent's job activities were salient and accessible from memory.

Context-Saliency Manipulation

After reviewing the activity list, the interviewer injected the context manipulations with

> Now, we'd like to ask you about some of the effects that your job has had. Specifically, we would like to know how you do your job, what you do in your job, how this benefits (you/your students).

The parenthetical variation in the last sentence constituted the context manipulation. The respondent was asked to think about such effects and describe them. Reports lasted about three to five minutes, and the interviewer took notes but said nothing during them except affirmations ("Uh-uh" or "I see"). Conditions were assigned by alternating interview schedules between conditions until about 20 respondents were available for the "self" and "student" contexts. Each condition served as a control for the other.

TABLE 16.1. Illustrative Activities Checked by TAs, Grouped by Category

---

1a. Instructional Activities
  Eliciting questions for class discussion
  Summarizing readings to the class
  Paraphrasing student comments in class discussion
  Skimming media for class relevant ideas or materials (e.g., TV)

1b. Counseling Activities
  Offering course advice
  Counseling students about academic matters outside of your course of program study
  Giving advice on personal development, growth, or time management

2a. Administrative Activities
  Ordering books through publisher or University system
  Putting readings on reserve in library or elsewhere
  Ordering lab or classroom supplies (e.g., chemicals, paper, paints)
  Keeping attendance records

2b. Maintenance Activities
  Attending ongoing seminars for TAs held by the course supervisor
  Consulting with administration about class management issues
  Selecting wardrobe for class or laboratory presentations
  Going for drinks with those associated with class

3. Evaluative Activities
  Defining grade criteria
  Scoring the homework problems or exercises
  Providing critiques or constructive comments of the quality of work to students
  Preparing test or quiz questions

Job Characteristics

Following the context manipulation, respondents described their jobs according to the JDS scales of Hackman and Oldham (1980). The job characteristics part of the survey included five questions that directly asked the respondent to assess the extent to which the job possessed autonomy, identification with the work, variety in the use of skills, significance or importance of the work for the well-being of others, and feedback from the work itself about performance. These assessments were requested on 7-point scales with appropriate verbal descriptions for the ends and middle of the scales. In addition, respondents marked on a scale from 1 to 7 how accurately each of 14 sentences described their jobs. Skill variety was assessed in the first case with "How much *variety* is there in your job? That is, to what extent does your job require you to do many different things at work, using a variety of your skills and talents?" and in the second case by "The job requires me to use a number of complex or high-level skills" and "The job is quite simple and repetitive." All scales were used, aggregated, and scored as recommended by their authors.

Job Satisfaction and Motivation

Respondents also answered the job satisfaction questions asked in the JDS procedure, which ask about several facets (see Table 16.2). It was expected that job satisfaction judgments would follow from the job characteristics generated during the job description phase of the study. As such, the manipulated context should have affected job satisfaction if it affected job attributions.

Analyses and Results

Means of the various scales used in the study for each context are presented in Table 16.2. Contexts did not differ by the number of reported job activities, suggesting that they were not accidentally confounded with job content reports. However, TAs induced to think of their jobs in terms of themselves reported less "internal motivation" ($t = 3.13$), more "significance" ($t = 2.10$), and less "feedback" from the job ($t = 2.16$). These effects, we shall see, were primarily the result of context-manipulation effects on the TAs' use of job activity information to infer job features. As required by our assumption that job characteristics are related to knowledge about job experiences, a significant canonical correlation (.578) was observed between the set of job activities and the set of job characteristics (chi-square $= 42.97$, $df = 25$, $p = .014$).

Our main analysis concerned the effects of context on the relationship of job activities to the characteristics that respondents attributed to their jobs. To test whether JDS characterizations were the result of the content of the job activities alone, the number of activities reported in each category was regressed against the JDS categories. To test whether the context induced TAs to use the information about their job activities differentially, interaction terms were regressed in a similar manner. Interaction terms were constructed by coding context subgroups +1 and −1 and multiplying these codes with the job activities of each respondent.

Job activities were assessed as the number of items that the individual checked summed across categories of instructional, counseling, administrative, maintenance, and evaluative activities. The first two were added together to form a category of "educational" activities, and the second two were added to form a category of "maintenance" activities. This grouping reduced the activity categories to a smaller but logically meaningful set so that stable regression analyses could be performed.

Test of the argument that context affects how respondents interpret their jobs, given their activities, involves comparing regression coefficients for the activities independently of context and when they interact with context. If interaction terms are significantly associated with JDS reactions, we can conclude that the context affected respondents' use of job activity knowledge in forming opinions about their jobs. If only the coefficients for activity reports are significant, it indicates that the respondents were affected only by their job experiences.

TABLE 16.2. Means for Self/Student Context Groups on Job Activities, Job Characteristics, and Attitudinal Measures

| | Context | | p-Level |
	Self ($n = 21$)	Student ($n = 19$)	Difference
Reported Job Activities			
Instructional	10.57	12.84	
Counseling	1.42	1.00	
Administrative	12.33	13.00	
Maintenance	7.81	7.84	
Evaluative	12.57	13.05	
Reported Job Characteristics			
Autonomy	3.75	4.02	
Identification	4.37	4.67	
Variety	4.64	4.46	
Significance	4.22	3.89	.05
Feedback	4.35	4.65	.05
Attitudinal Measures			
Internal motivation	5.58	6.21	.01
General satisfaction	5.43	5.60	
Job satisfaction	5.05	5.29	
Security satisfaction	4.81	4.74	
Compensation satisfaction	3.91	4.34	
Supervisor satisfaction	4.17	4.42	

Table 16.3 presents the unstandardized regression coefficients predicting JDS characteristics from the activities in each category and their interactions with the self/student context. Since the interaction terms were uncorrelated with job activities (the nine r's range between +.15 and −.05), a stepwise analysis was done, with variables selected according to their significant contributions in reducing variance. In the case of every JDS characteristic except "autonomy," one or more interaction terms entered the regression first and was significantly associated with the characteristic.

Three of the 10 significant coefficients in Table 16.3 relate activities with job characteristics independent of context. Respondents attributed more "autonomy" to their jobs when the job involved them more in instructional and less in maintenance activities, and they attributed less "significance" to their work when they were involved in evaluation.

Seven of the 10 coefficients relate activities with job characteristics dependent on context. These indicate respondents from each condition reacted differently in forming interpretations about their jobs, given their similar experiences. Since the probability was only .14 $(1 - .95^3)$ that at least one of the three activities would have been significantly related to a job characteristic, the fact that four of the five characteristics had significant interactions suggests that context had a powerful effect on the meanings that the TAs derived from their experiences.

TABLE 16.3. Significant Coefficients from Stepwise Regression of Job Activities and Their Interaction with Context (IC), on Job Characteristics

Job Activities	Job Characteristics				
	Autonomy	Identification	Variety	Significance	Feedback
Educational	.112**	—a	—	—	—
Maintenance	−.071**	—	—	—	—
Evaluative	—	—	—	−.058*	—
IC-EDUC	—	—	—	−.098**	—
IC-MAIN	—	−.025**	.035**	.035*	—
IC-EVAL	—	—	−.050**	.052*	−.041*
R^2	.27	.25	.19	.38	.13

a— = NS (not significant).
* $p < .05$.   ** $p < .01$.

Although the results in Table 16.3 tell us that the context subgroups differed in the way in which they formed job opinions, they do not tell us exactly what meanings each subgroup derived from their job experiences. To assess these, we regressed job characteristics simultaneously on context, the job activities reported for each area (educational, maintenance, and evaluative), and the interaction of context with each activity category. The equation estimated is

$$JC = b_0 + b_1 I + b_2 M + b_3 E + b_3 C + b_4 I*C + b_5 M*C + b_6 E*C + e,$$

where JC is the job characteristic; C is the context coded 1 or −1; and I, M, and E are the numbers of instructional, maintenance, and evaluative job activities reported. The overall effect of activities on the characteristics attributed to the job is determined by their partial derivatives, which

$$\text{Educational effect} = b_1 + b_4*C;$$
$$\text{Maintenance effect} = b_2 + b_5*C;$$
$$\text{Evaluative effect} = b_3 + b_6*C.$$

Note that the effect of each job activity is moderated by context. Since the contexts were coded +1 and −1, the overall effect of an activity in the self context is the sum of the coefficients; in the student context, it is their difference. We did this analysis for each of the job characteristics. The statistically significant results are summarized below.

TAs in the self condition who reported that their jobs involved educational activities saw those jobs as having autonomy but lacking significance, whereas those in the student condition who reported doing educational activities saw their jobs as having both autonomy and significance. The respondents from the self context who reported doing maintenance activities saw their jobs as lacking identification, whereas those reporting maintenance activities from the student context saw their jobs as lacking autonomy and variety. The respondents from the self context who reported evaluative activities described their jobs as lacking variety, whereas those reporting evaluative activities from the student context saw their work as providing feedback but detracting from identification and significance.

In short, context seemed to play a major role in determining the meanings that respondents derived from their work experiences. As an indication of its relative importance, Table 16.4 presents the amount of variance associated with the job activities alone and the incremental amounts associated with context and its interaction with activities. The results are from hierarchial regressions of each job characteristic, constrained to enter the main effects first and interactions last. Although this evaluation is conservative, the results reinforce our interpretation of Table 16.3. Only in the case of "autonomy" did job activities by themselves account for a significant amount of variance. Although the context manipulation appears to have had a direct and independent effect on "feedback," most of its effects were through interactions with job activities. Significant increments to explained variance were contributed by interaction effects for respondents' views on "significance," "variety," and "identification."

The results from Tables 16.3 and 16.4 are particularly striking because responses to the five job descriptors did not themselves correlate much for this sample; only "autonomy" and "feedback" correlated significantly ($r = .386$). Correlations for the other nine pairs of job characteristics ranged in absolute value between .006 and .271.

A final indication that context affected respondents' interpretations of their work experiences comes from analyses of the satisfaction measures. TAs who were induced to think of the job in terms of themselves reported less "internal motivation." However, this effect was mainly due to the differential importance of educational and maintenance activities for these respondents. They reported less "internal motivation" when they were more involved in maintenance activities ($b = -.52$; $p < .01$). Recall that these subjects also reported feeling less identified with their jobs when they were involved in maintenance. If we control for these effects, the direct association of context with "internal motivation" vanishes.

Discussion and Conclusions

The data are clear in suggesting that context had a strong effect on the way in which TAs derived meaning about their teaching jobs from their experiences. The data are also clear in suggesting that knowledge about the content of their jobs was insufficient as a basis for their interpretation of its features. Using the TAs' reports of their specific work activities as indicators of the content of their work experiences, we found that these activities bore little systematic direct relationship to the TAs' descriptions of their jobs on the Job Diagnostic Survey. Yet this lack of relationship is not because the job activities were irrelevant for their job descriptions. The reported activities were, in fact, systematically related to job descriptions, but the particular relationships were dependent on the context primed for a respondent. When the TAs were primed to think of their work in

TABLE 16.4. Incremental Variance Results from Forced Hierarchial Regression of Job Activities and Context on Job Characteristics

Job Characteristics	(1)	(2)	(3)	Overall R^2
Autonomy	.30*	.02	.03	.352**
Identification	.09	.03	.22*	.337**
Variety	.02	.02	.15*	.225
Significance	.07	.07	.35*	.490**
Feedback	.03	.14*	.11	.285
df	3/36	1/35	3/32	7/32

*Indicates significant ($p < .05$) increment in explained variance over previous step.
**Indicates significant ($p < .05$) overall R^2.
Step (1)—Adds job activities content.
Step (2)—Adds "self/student" context.
Step (3)—Adds interaction of context × content.

terms of their students, they tended to derive positive meanings from their instructional and evaluative activities and negative meanings from their administrative duties. The TAs primed to think of their work in terms of themselves derived negative meanings from each area of work activity.

Interpreting these results is helped by the unique design used in this study, the context-saliency paradigm (Salancik, 1982). In this design, context differences that are believed to influence the knowledge that individuals use in forming their opinions or how they use that knowledge are manipulated independently of the knowledge. Such a design allows a very explicit evaluation of context effects and enables one to determine if context has a general biasing effect on opinions or influences the way in which individuals form opinions from the knowledge available to them. For the present study of TAs, for instance, it is clear that the context manipulations primarily affected the relevance that respondents attached to their various job experiences. Overall, seven of the coefficients relating job activities to job descriptions were significant (alpha set to .05) for the student context, whereas only four were significant in the self context. Moreover, three of the seven coefficients for TAs primed to think about their students related to their evaluative activities, indicating that these activities were very relevant for deriving the meaning of their work. Finally, in only two cases did the two context groups relate the same activity to the same job descriptions, and only for one of these were the signs of the coefficients opposite. In short, context seemed primarily to have affected what knowledge the TAs used in forming opinions rather than the implications that they derived from that knowledge.

Acknowledgments. We thank the Office of Instructional Resources, University of Illinois at Urbana-Champaign, for help in various stages of the study, and Greg Oldham, Joe Porac, Carol Kulik, and Ellie Weldon for comments on earlier drafts.

17
The Psychometrics of
Order Effects

Abigail T. Panter, Jeffrey S. Tanaka, and Tracy R. Wellens

The chapters in this volume and its predecessor (Hippler, Schwarz, & Sudman, 1987) attest to a broad interest in item-order effects. A better understanding of their causes and implications has come from perspectives in cognitive psychology, social cognition, and survey methodology. The importance of contemporary psychometric theory for evaluating order effects has been overlooked. We believe that recognition of psychometric contributions can help researchers better understand item-order effects. One obstacle faced thus far has been that many of the latest psychometric developments have not been readily accessible (or comprehensible) to researchers in this area. The goal of this chapter is to show how such contributions logically relate to testing and interpreting item-order effects. In doing this, we define some necessary preconditions that should exist for the effects obtained to date, and for those obtained in future research, to be interpreted unambiguously.

In the first section, we introduce and review some basic principles of modern psychometric theory that are relevant in understanding item-level response processes. More specifically, we consider item-order effects as they occur within a single construct, as well as across constructs. Throughout these discussions, we illustrate our thinking with examples, including the General Social Survey (GSS) abortion items. Finally, we discuss how psychometric theory allows researchers to specify the characteristics of items, thus better informing research on item-order effects.

The Relevance of Psychometric Theory for Understanding Item-Order Effects

Consider a simple examination of an item-order effect. Two items, A and B, are presented to a respondent in either order AB or order BA. An effect is considered to be present if the response to item A or the association between items A and B is changed in some way by the order manipulation. Built into this strategy are certain assumptions about the nature of the items, A and B, and the nature of the construct (or constructs) that are presumed to underlie these items. More concretely, this order manipulation can be illustrated in survey research employing the classic Schuman and Presser paradigm (e.g., Schuman, Presser, & Ludwig, 1981). Distinctions are made between "general" items, which are thought to assess a respondent's broad underlying attitude, and "specific" items. The specific item can either represent an item drawn from the same construct as the general item or from a different, but potentially associated, construct. Researchers select specific items to tap an ostensibly narrower context than general items.

One relatively robust effect reported in this paradigm occurs when a general item is juxtaposed with a specific item. This presentation creates an item-order effect (as defined above), where the proportion of respondents who agree with a general item is changed (reduced) when the specific item is presented first. One prominent explanation of this effect draws from communication rules and states that the findings are compatible with given-new contracts in information processing (e.g., Strack & Martin, 1987).

What has been generally missing from this research is a psychometric perspective. Measurement issues often play handmaiden to the "more interesting" substantive questions of this research. An investigator may carefully consider what construct will be measured, whereas comparatively less effort may be devoted to the determination of the multiple ways in which a construct can be measured. This approach often results in measures with unknown reliability and an ambiguous relation to the underlying constructs of interest. The selection of measures is typically guided by pragmatics, the history of a research literature, or investigator assumptions and "intuitions."

We explicate later in this chapter the psychometric assumptions that must hold true when inferring order effects based on comparisons between items. To interpret an item-order effect, a number of preconditions must exist within the data. When these assumptions are not met, the interpretation of these empirical findings is obscured, since there is no formal evaluation of how the units of analysis (i.e., items) relate to their underlying hypothesized construct(s). We begin, however, with an overview of developments relevant to the understanding of order effects from a psychometric perspective.

Historical Psychometrics Perspectives

As reviewed by Leary and Dorans (1985), there has been a relatively extensive history of research on item-rearrangement effects in the educational measurement literature. Adopting their structure, the study of item-order effects can be classified into three periods of research emphasis. In the first period, which parallels the initial interest in order effects in the survey methodology literature, the presence of order effects when individuals read and respond to self-report items was simply acknowledged. The key studies during this period investigated item-order effects by manipulating order in three conditions: (a) easy-to-difficult, (b) difficult-to-easy, and (c) random (cf. Mollenkopf, 1950; MacNicol, 1956). These different presentation orders can be thought to be analogous to the general/ specific–specific/general item orderings, although the item content and assessment goals in the educational literature clearly are different.

The second phase of the rearrangement research began to address more process-related issues in interpreting item-order effects. Work on this domain with educational tests considered individual difference variables such as test anxiety or achievement level as possible moderators of observed item-order effects (e.g., Hambleton & Traub, 1974; Smouse & Munz, 1968). For example, an individual high in anxiety might show different patterns of item response when difficult items were presented first followed by progressively easier items than the converse. The experimental manipulation of item order or response context represents another way to understand process issues (e.g., Tourangeau & Rasinski, 1988). In the latter case, focus is directed toward characteristics of the response situation and away from properties of the individual.

The final stage outlined by Leary and Dorans (1985) uses modern psychometric theory in conjunction with psychological process theories to characterize the mechanisms underlying order effects (see also Whitely & Dawis, 1976; Yen, 1980). From our perspective, we concur with the work of Leary and Dorans in their suggestion that a more appropriate emphasis in understanding these effects may not be the single-item juxtapositions but rather the rearrangement of intact test subsections (or "testlets"), each reflecting different item characteristics (e.g., item specificity). Drawing on logic that we have developed more fully elsewhere (Tanaka, Panter, Winborne, & Huba, 1990), we argue that the availability of multiple indicators to demonstrate order effects is preferable to the more typical single-item approaches. This focus concentrates on comparisons at the construct level.

Items and Their Relations to Underlying Construct(s)

If responses at the item level are to be compared, then it is of primary importance at the outset to understand the relation of target items to their respective underlying construct(s). In certain research contexts, the investigator may be comparing the item order of two items from the same construct. This emphasis often is seen in educational or personality assessment, where interest may be in a single underlying attribute (e.g., ability or trait). In this case, item-order effects would occur within a given construct. The work of Knowles and his colleagues (Knowles, 1988; Knowles et al., chap. 15, this volume) exemplifies this approach. Alternatively, the two items being evaluated may be hypothesized to represent two different, but potentially related, constructs. This emphasis is more characteristic of survey methodology applications, where order effects are likely to occur between constructs.[1]

---

[1] We thank Norbert Schwarz for making this distinction.

Although empirical tests regarding the relation of the target items to their respective constructs are possible, they are rarely conducted. Instead, investigators tend simply to accept the assumption that the items are assessing the constructs that they think they are, to the degree that they think they are, because the items superficially reflect the relevant domain. Invoking this "face validity" criterion (e.g., Anastasi, 1988) has always been inappropriate psychometrically for establishing the relations of items to a common underlying construct. For the psychometric models that we are proposing, we need to consider models that account for within-construct (intraconstruct) versus between-construct (interconstruct) order effects. We discuss intraconstruct effects first.

Intraconstruct Item-Order Effects

To illustrate how intraconstruct item-order effects can be evaluated, consider the abortion items from the GSS. Order effects have been reported for these items by juxtaposing single items that assess possible reasons for obtaining an abortion and finding that endorsement rates vary as a function of the order in which the items are juxtaposed. We shall assume in this particular discussion that each of the GSS items is hypothesized to be tapping a *single* unobserved abortion attitude. Under this assumption, one might assess the "strength" of a respondent's abortion attitude by summing across all presented abortion items or establish the reliability of such a measure by using an internal consistency measure such as the alpha coefficient.

Items may or may not be equally good indicators of a single abortion attitude. Such differences may be due to characteristics of the items (e.g., Hippler & Schwarz, 1987), characteristics of the person responding to the items (e.g., Judd & Lusk, 1984; Leone & Ensley, 1986; Tesser, 1978), or the interaction of person and item (e.g., Panter, 1989). If items do not tap this dimension to the same degree, then order effects will be confounded, as will be demonstrated in our consideration of psychometric models. Items may also be hypothesized to represent different components of abortion attitudes, but we shall treat this case in the next subsection on interconstruct order effects.

The logic of the intraconstruct approach to testing item order parallels the one made about subjects. There it is assumed (but again typically not tested) that, through random sampling mechanisms, individuals are interchangable units of analysis, and individual differences are ignored. In the case of items, it might be assumed (but again not tested) that the two presented items (i.e., the general item and the specific item) are sampled from the universe of all possible items that might be thought to measure a single underlying attitude toward abortion. Of course, this metaphor breaks down because items are generally not considered as random variables.[2] In attitudinal research, individual items are often used in research contexts on the basis of content alone, without regard to the specific

---

[2]Of course, this logic does not apply for random effects designs such as those assumed in generalizability theory (Brennan, 1983).

properties and characteristics of the items themselves. Item selection from a larger pool of items is a process that requires both content considerations and empirical analysis, since either alone can be misleading (Jackson, 1971; Wainer & Braun, 1988).

Interconstruct Item-Order Effects

In contrast to the prior case where we assumed that items assess the same uni-dimensional construct, item-order effects can also be conceptualized as occurring across different constructs. This research emphasis typifies the situation in sur-vey applications where practical considerations may preclude administering mul-tiple items that assess a domain of research interest. For example, instead of assuming that the GSS abortion items tap a single dimension of attitudes toward abortion, we might assume for this case that each item assesses unique and mul-tiple dimensions of abortion attitudes.

More concretely, the general and specific items would be hypothesized to measure distinct (and, ideally, independent) dimensions of abortion attitudes. Although there is clearly a conceptual relation among the GSS abortion items (i.e., they all ask respondents to express endorsement of situations under which a woman could obtain an abortion), this perspective underscores the distinct (as opposed to common) aspects of what these items are assessing. Given that these items are thought to tap distinct constructs, we can expect the internal consis-tency reliability among these items (as might be assessed by coefficient alpha) to be low.

The difference between intra- and interconstruct approaches might best be illustrated by example. Consider a sample of respondents who are presented with items concerning how much they like different films. The listed films are *Star Wars, The Wizard of Oz, The Sound of Music, Lawrence of Arabia, Annie Hall, ET,* and *West Side Story*. If the obtained responses to these items across subjects reflected the single dimension of "liking movies," we would expect items to demonstrate strong internal consistency, reflecting their common dependence on "liking movies." On the other hand, the item responses might reflect a more complicated process such as a two-dimensional clustering (representing, for example, "liking musicals" and "liking nonmusicals"). In either case, we believe that whatever item associations are obtained in data reflect some implicit or-ganizational structure that characterizes an average respondent's understanding and interpretation of the presented items.

From the perspective of the psychometric models to be discussed in this chapter, we can account for either an intra- or interconstruct representation for items. The choice between these representations is an investigator's prerogative and will be guided by theoretical concerns. However, given these distinctions, the choice between these alternatives must be specified and empirically validated. From the predominantly intuitive perspective that has characterized much of the item-order research to date, this choice has been arbitrated simply by assumption and has not always been stated and tested explicitly.

The use of items without specifying the hypothesized relations to underlying constructs is one aspect of this problem considered from a psychometric perspective. In addition to model specification, we believe that a more systematic understanding of item properties can be obtained through empirical tests. Such tests evaluate the equivalence of items as they relate to underlying construct(s). We shall draw on both classic and modern psychometric theories for these tests.

Psychometric Issues

In the methods that we discuss, latent variables describing unobservable processes are invoked. In test theories, latent variables have been described under the rubric of "true" scores. Before we proceed in outlining the statistical preconditions, we draw some distinctions about the implications of belief in true scores or latent variables.

Are True Scores "True"?

The assumptions that underlie the theory of "true" scores in measurement models have had their critics (e.g., Cliff, 1983; Knowles, 1988; Lumsden, 1976; Schönemann & Steiger, 1976; Strack, personal communication, October 1989). Among methodologists, the idea of "true" scores or latent variables has been attacked on the basis of the indeterminacy associated with relating indicators to latent variables and the lack of parsimony from introducing a higher level of abstraction than necessary for characterizing empirical relations. Substantive researchers claim that the psychometrician's conceptualization of "true" score differs from the subjects' phenomenological perspectives that they may (Ericsson & Simon, 1984) or may not (Nisbett & Wilson, 1977) be able to report on with accuracy.

From the psychometric and statistical viewpoint, we also feel some discomfort in postulating a classical test theory true-score model for measured variables. After all, it is tautological reasoning that decomposes an observed variable into two unobserved components (true score and error). From the perspective of psychologists interested in substantive issues, high premiums are generally placed on having high-quality behavioral data that are free of the potential biases of other methods of data collection (e.g., self-report). As empirically trained scientists, we have learned to value that which we can observe.

On the other hand, in much of contemporary psychology, interest is not in behavior per se but in behavior as an index of some underlying construct. The response to an attitude item is of interest only to the extent that it is a reliable indicator of the generating attitude structure within the individual. As we have argued elsewhere (Tanaka et al., 1990), most current psychological theories employ unobservable constructs (e.g., personality, attitudes, cognitive processes) that are operationalized in terms of specific observable measures.

The importance of the underlying construct is particularly true of current process-oriented models that dominate the literature on order effects. Psychometric theories can formalize and evaluate the links between observed measures and unobservable constructs. Thus, psychologists can move away from the idea of attitude assessment by assumption toward formal mathematical and statistical models and can evaluate the validity of their indicators.

"True" scores may or may not be true in any phenomenological sense. However, in the psychometrically based framework adopted here, formal testable models are considered preferable to implicit untestable models. The "true"-score concept as we use it in our discussions represents the association of measured variables as indices of unobservable constructs such as personality, attitudes, and cognitive processes. We next describe how effects can be empirically modeled when items are thought to tap a single dimension.

Intraconstruct Effects and Classical Test Theory

A major contribution to explaining the different kinds of relations that might exist between items and an underlying unidimensional construct was provided by Jöreskog (1974), who formalized a set of testable models of relations among measures of a construct. Specifically, a taxonomy of different models was described for how a group of items might relate to a hypothesized single underlying construct, such as an abortion attitude. In the Jöreskog hierarchy, each level implies increasingly stringent assumptions about relations between observed measures and the underlying construct.

The weakest of the model assumptions states that all items within a set are indicators of a single dimension. These items may be differentially related to the underlying construct; that is, some items may be more strongly related to the underlying construct, whereas others may show weaker relations, but all items are assumed to reflect the same underlying dimension. Such items are said to be "congeneric." Differences among congeneric items in terms of their relation to an underlying construct might be caused by wording, question length, or other such properties (e.g., Hippler & Schwarz, 1987). Thus, if the GSS abortion items are congeneric, they might have relations of different magnitudes to the underlying single abortion attitude, but they all would be reflections of that dimension.

A stronger assumption than congeneric measurement is that target items are related in a uniform way to the underlying attitude, in addition to relating to the same dimension. Thus, in this case, if one were able to compute the zero-order correlation between any particular item and the underlying construct, then these correlations would be identical for all items. Such measurements are called "tau-equivalent," following from the classic psychometric evaluation of "true" scores (tau) for a construct.

The most stringent version of the assumption regarding item equivalence is that, beyond a common homogeneous relation to a single underlying construct, all items are equally reliable. Thus, items would be related to the underlying construct in identical ways, and their errors of measurement would also be constant. From the classic psychometric perspective, groups of such items are referred to as "parallel" measures.

Jöreskog (1974) described a statistical framework to evaluate each of these assumptions that employs linear structural equation modeling techniques, which are well suited for testing process hypotheses (e.g., Tanaka et al., 1990). However, there is one problem in the direct adoption of the Jöreskog framework for testing item order in many measurement situations in the survey literature. The approach was intended initially for interval-level continuous measurement. In our example with the GSS items, the unit of analysis is the single item. As has been suggested by Muthén (1984) and others, the application of statistical methods for continuous data to what are essentially ordered categories or even dichotomies of item responses may lead to conclusions that are not correct. Thus, to apply the Jöreskog approach, we must look to developments in modeling of ordered categorical and/or dichotomous data and item response theory.

Factor analysis (cf. Harman, 1976) is the most well known method for evaluating the congeneric model. In factor analysis, a matrix of interitem correlations is modeled empirically to discover (in an exploratory framework) or test (in a confirmatory framework) the underlying dimensionality of constructs generating the responses to the measures. However, the dichotomous nature of the GSS items poses a problem for the traditional factor model. Research in the factor analysis of dichotomous items (e.g., Ferguson, 1941 [summarized in Comrey, 1973]) has suggested that the simple factor analysis of correlation coefficients for dichotomous items may lead to inappropriate conclusions, with a tendency to suggest more dimensions than necessary for explaining the intermeasure structure of the data. Fortunately, recent psychometric developments have presented alternative methods for examining the structure of dichotomous data.

One proposed approach is an extension of work by Bock and Lieberman (1970) and Bock and Aitken (1981). This approach is implemented in the computer program TESTFACT (D. Wilson, Wood, & Gibbons, 1984). An alternative approach (Muthén, 1978, 1987; Muthén & Christoffersson, 1981) also provides a method for factor analyzing dichotomous data and is implemented in the computer program LISCOMP (Muthén, 1987).

Some broad distinctions can be made between the approaches for dealing with noncontinuously measured data. For example, the LISCOMP model is flexible and can be adapted for exploratory or confirmatory factor analyses, whereas the TESTFACT model is appropriate only for exploratory factor analysis models. Moreover, the TESTFACT model is best suited for a large number of variables (and a small number of hypothesized factors), whereas LISCOMP is limited in the number of variables that it can analyze. Finally, extensions of the LISCOMP model to ordered categorical, truncated, and censored variables are quite easy, whereas TESTFACT is limited to dichotomous data. Further comparisons and contrasts between these two approaches can be found in Mislevy (1986).

Evidence against the Congeneric Assessment of the Abortion Items

In the research conducted to date on order effects in the GSS abortion items, it has been assumed that all items measure the single underlying construct "attitudes toward abortion." As such, responses to the juxtaposed GSS abortion items are hypothesized to be cognitively influenced by the way in which subjects encounter, process, and judge these items on a single attitudinal structure.

In considering the factor structure of these dichotomous GSS abortion data, it is fortuitous that Muthén has employed this data set in multiple analyses to demonstrate his techniques for dichotomous and ordered categorical data (e.g., Muthén, 1978, 1981; Muthén & Christoffersson, 1981). In all of these analyses, he easily rejects the hypothesis of unidimensionality for these items, interpreting a two-factor solution with abortion for social reasons (e.g., the item asking whether a legal abortion should be possible "if she is married and doesn't want any more children") and abortion for medical reasons (e.g., the item asking whether a pregnant woman should be able to obtain a legal abortion "if there is a strong chance of serious defect in the baby") comprising the two factors. Interestingly, in some of the work on order and context effects with these items (e.g., Schuman et al., 1981), the two items that have been juxtaposed experimentally come from these two domains. To draw appropriate conclusions about order effects where an intraconstruct situation is assumed, it must be shown empirically that the same domain or knowledge structure is being assessed by all presented items. Yet, the Muthén results disconfirm the hypothesis that the item set is unidimensional.

Items Must Be Uniformly Related to the Underlying Construct

If the unidimensionality assumption can be met within a set of items for which an order effect has been demonstrated, other conditions also need to hold true if such effects are to be interpreted unambiguously. The previously discussed psychometric assumptions suggest other conditions could be tested. Because of its flexibility in testing some necessary constraints on the model, we frame our discussion in the context of Muthén's LISCOMP model. However, we acknowledge the models that we present here and those discussed in Jöreskog (1974) in classical test theory models. At the item level, our development focuses not only on the relations of items to their underlying construct but also on possible homogeneity of what have been termed "item difficulties." We believe that these points are best considered through another popular psychometric model, item response theory (IRT). We do not intend to provide an extensive review of item response theory here but refer interested readers to other sources (e.g., Hambleton & Swaminathan, 1985; F. M. Lord, 1980).

Developed in the context of educational testing, IRT relates the conditional probability of an observed item response to both item characteristics and person "ability." Although the "ability" interpretation of the person parameter has predominated in the IRT literature (given its use in educational domains), this parameter refers to any unidimensional latent construct, such as a trait or an attitude. In the context of attitude or personality items, the parameter may be conceptualized as an individual's proclivity to respond to items assessing the unidimensional construct (e.g., Reise & Waller, 1990; Reiser, 1980).

In one standard representation of the IRT model, the two-parameter model, two item parameters are hypothesized to relate to the conditional probability of an observed response given an individual's standing on the underlying attribute. Item discriminations refer to the strength of the relation between the observed response and the unobserved construct. Thus, item discriminations might be viewed as analogous to factor loadings in the more familiar factor analysis model.

Item difficulties characterize the tendency of respondents to endorse a particular item. Considered from the perspective of ability applications of the IRT model, items ordered on their difficulties might be indicative of increasing mastery of the domain. From the perspective of attitudinal or survey items, item difficulties might be conceptualized as representing the response extremity of presented items. For example, a set of Guttman-scaled attitude items would represent a set of items ordered in terms of their item difficulties from difficulties small in magnitude to those large in magnitude.

The hypothesis of item-order effects can be viewed as hypotheses about item difficulties. Thus, if cognitive processing is affected by item order, then effects should be observed at the level of item difficulties (i.e., the relative response proclivity to an item given a particular ordering). However, to establish such effects for item difficulties, it must first be demonstrated that the items relate to the underlying attitudinal construct in the same way across treatment conditions (e.g., equal item discriminations). Context should not change the relation of the item to the construct. We shall describe in the next subsection how this is accomplished using latent variable modeling procedures.

Although requiring equal discriminations might be viewed as rather stringent, it is essentially the same as the homoscedasticity assumption in the analysis of variance, in which hypotheses about mean differences between groups cannot be evaluated formally without assuming equal dispersion across those groups.

Assessing the Preconditions for Item-Order Effects

We next describe how to develop testable models of item-order effects. In discussing these ideas, we rely on the Jöreskog (1974) discussion of congeneric, tau-equivalent, and parallel models. These models can be easily adapted to an IRT perspective, in which the unit of analysis is the item. Thus, in this development, we take advantage of the unique properties of dichotomous or ordered categorical data.

Congeneric models reflect the least restrictive of these measurement models in the classical test theory framework for unidimensional phenomena. Discussions of item unidimensionality in the IRT framework are discussed, for example, by Reckase (1979, 1985). Previous work with, for example, the GSS abortion items would appear to suggest that they are not congeneric assessments.

Although we suggested that the GSS abortion items may not be congeneric, let us assume that a set of congeneric items could be identified and that the assumption of unidimensionality was found to be plausible. Two further assumptions would then have to be shown to hold true to allow unambiguous conclusions about item-order effects. First, following the tau-equivalence assumption, items would have to be shown to relate in a uniform way to the underlying construct, since context could not change the relation of the item to the underlying construct. Having met the congeneric and tau-equivalence preconditions, we could then test the null hypothesis of equal item difficulties or the assumption of parallelism. We elaborate each of these precondition tests in turn.

Tau-equivalence requires that measures are uniformly related to the underlying construct. Another way of stating this characterization is that the zero-order correlation between any measure (item) and the underlying construct is constant for all items. In the IRT framework, this is the assumption of equal item discriminations as found in the Rasch (1980) model. It is interesting to note that the sociologist Duncan (1984) has been a major proponent for the use of the Rasch model as an operating measurement model in social measurement. The tau-equivalence assumption, although quite stringent empirically, could be addressed in a number of ways. For example, items might be pretested, so that the zero-order relations between items and the construct were constant. Dichotomous response format items might be written in such a way to maximize variance; in other words, items would be worded so that endorsement rates would be approximately 0.5 for each response alternative. If observed data were consistent with the Rasch model, tau-equivalence could be established by testing the equality of item–total correlations. However, it is probably not safe to assume that any set of items will have properties such that the tau-equivalence assumption will be routinely met.

In the development of his model, Muthén suggests that latent response variables reflect underlying normally distributed variables that have been cut at some threshold to generate the observed dichotomous (or ordered categorical) process. This is the same logic that calculates tetrachoric correlations for dichotomous variables. These correlations form the data foundations of Muthén's model.

The tau-equivalence assumption is still only a necessary precondition for the interpretation of order effects. The most stringent hypothesis to be tested to establish that such order effects exist depends on a rejection of the null hypothesis of parallel assessments, given the existence of tau-equivalent assessments. To establish that item-order effects exist, it is necessary to operate under the assumption that items are equally good measures of the underlying construct, in terms of both their difficulty and their relations to the underlying construct or discriminability. If this is true, then the items are said to be parallel with no differences at either the mean or covariance level. We believe that it is only in this context that the issue of item-order effects can be addressed.

Items versus Item Clusters in the Examination of Context Effects

Despite the stringent evaluation of how items are related to an underlying attitudinal construct, information at the item level will generally be of limited utility. As indices of underlying attitudes (and all other things being equal), single items are more likely than multiple items or item clusters to be unreliable and to elicit inconsistent responses. Hence, a preferable method might be to aggregate (reliable) items within a particular question type (e.g., the general-type or specific-type questions) and then see whether effects currently being interpreted at the item level might also appear when looking at these aggregated item clusters. In the educational literature, a number of authors (e.g., Wainer & Kiely, 1987; Wainer & Lewis, 1990) have made similar observations to help clarify context effects involving ability items. We shall outline the logic of this aggregate approach or the use of "testlets," as they are referred to in the educational measurement literature.

Testlets are subsets of items, which are placed together and treated as units on the basis of some theoretical or content specifications. Wainer and Lewis (1990) review three examples of testlets. For example, all items that directly refer to a single reading-comprehension passage might be viewed as a testlet. Similarly, items that are hypothesized to be general might be clustered together with the assumption that their "generality" is their dominant, shared attribute. Such a "general" testlet might then be compared to a "specific" testlet constructed in an analogous manner. There are a number of reasons why item-order research might want to begin considering testlets instead of single items.

Conceptualizing items in terms of testlets or units of related items rather than single pieces of information changes item-order analysis. First, well-constructed testlets are comprised of items that are related to one another according to some content specification such as topical similarity or content balance and will necessarily be psychometrically more reliable units of analysis than will single items. Second, testlets can be evaluated in terms of the parallelism hypothesis that we previously discussed. Although this may be an unreasonably stringent assumption, parallelism of items within a testlet can provide researchers with relative security about (a) the properties of testlet items, testlets, and their underlying dimensions and (b) how items are perceived by respondents compared with other items within the testlet. Thus, as Wainer and Kiely (1987) note, "Each item is embedded in a predeveloped testlet, in effect carrying its own context with it" (p. 190). It might be desirable to create testlets whose components (items) have known relations to one another to control for item-rearrangement effects, particularly when certain items are deemed critical.

Finally, once testlets are constructed and treated as the unit of analysis, hypotheses based on context effects or the invariance of item and/or attribute parameters can be examined between testlets. The advantage in this case is that the tau-equivalence of the testlets (i.e., whether each testlet equally relates to the underlying construct) can be determined and tested in a straightforward manner.

Beyond the psychometric strengths that we perceive in employing the testlet strategy to investigate item-order effects, we feel that a claim for the superiority of this approach can also be based on theoretical and conceptual foundations. Consider, for example, the frequency-of-activation models in social cognition and social judgment reviewed by Wyer and Srull (1989). In these models, the frequency with which a construct is activated increases its accessibility. This increased accessibility, in turn, has demonstrated robust effects on social judgment and decision making. In the present context, the availability of multiple items in a testlet should repeatedly activate the construct that the items are presumed to measure. In moving from a general to a specific testlet (as opposed to single items), this increased activation level should predict a larger effect than has been previously obtained, given the results of these models.[3] Thus, we believe that testlets represent one way to begin interpreting these order effects with the confidence of reliability and unambiguous interpretation.

Interconstruct Item-Order Effects

In addition to the intraconstruct case, where items being compared are hypothesized to represent the same latent dimension, a theoretical model involving items from different (potentially related) constructs may be developed. In this interconstruct case, item-order hypotheses can be tested using extensions of the framework of assumptions described above, with some modification. We can show that although, by definition, the assumption of congeneric assessments would not apply in the interconstruct case, the increasingly stringent assumptions of tau-equivalence and parallel models can be evaluated in item-order investigations examining multiple constructs, and the concept of testlets can be incorporated.

Consider the simple case where responses to two items (or testlets), each tapping conceptually different constructs, are compared in one order versus another. Owing to the factor analytic developments of Muthén and others discussed previously, we need not make assumptions about the exact measurement scale of the items under consideration; they may be continuous, ordered categorical, censored, truncated, or dichotomous. In the interconstruct case, models can be tested by making explicit statements about item relations with their hypothesized construct in one condition versus the second condition. Two out of the three model assumptions described for the intraconstruct case are relevant with multiple constructs.

The assumption of congeneric measurement questions whether items reflect the same underlying construct. As noted, the GSS abortion items employed in our examples were shown to reject the congeneric assumption and to reflect two conceptually different constructs, representing subcomponents of abortion attitudes, Medical Reasons for Abortion versus Social Reasons for Abortion. To the extent that these constructs represent theoretically interesting distinctions, they can (and should) be treated as such. Thus, with failure to find support for a congeneric model for these items, the available evidence suggests future models should be tested in an interconstruct framework.

When items from two constructs are compared, the tau-equivalence assumption could test whether the strength of each item's relation to its underlying construct (the item discrimination) varies as a function of order condition. Note that this emphasis is not on whether each item relates to its underlying construct

---

[3]It must also be noted that, given a frequency-of-activation model for these effects, it is possible that the conditions under which these effects might be obtained would be delimited (e.g., Herr, Sherman, & Fazio, 1983).

to the same degree; instead, the investigator seeks to determine the extent to which these relations between observed variables and latent constructs are invariant across order conditions. If invariance as a function of condition cannot be demonstrated, we are again in a position where noncomparable elements are being contrasted. However, this noncomparability may be diagnostic in that across-group comparisons of differences among individual parameters can be inspected to determine what differences emerged in item order.

Finally, the assumption of parallelism focuses the equivalence of relations to underlying constructs across conditions, as well as equal error variances for each item with respect to its construct. By adding the constraints on error variances, this assumption becomes quite stringent. Although this ensures metric comparability in an across-condition comparison, the particular goals of an investigation might arbitrate whether such criteria are necessary.

A multiple-sample analysis of these assumptions permits evaluation of whether the patterns describing the relations in order AB for item A and item B is the same (or fairly close) to that describing order BA in a between-subjects design (cf. Jöreskog & Sörbom, 1989). Clearly, the comparison of models between treatment conditions changes as a function of the choice of assumptions to be tested (i.e., tau-equivalence assumption).

As we have suggested in the context of intraconstruct hypotheses, investigators can begin to define concepts such as "general" or "specific" in terms of groups of items, or testlets, hypothesized to be similar along these dimensions. Testlets can function as items, although their use carries the additional benefit of aggregated itemmetric responses.

An example of this interconstruct hypothesis in the personality domain is given by Osberg (1985). In this study, he considered variations in responses to the Self-Consciousness Scale (SCS) of Fenigstein, Scheier, and Buss (1975) as a function of where this measure was placed in a group administration of this and other personality measures in a large sample. In the between-subjects design that he employed, Osberg administered the SCS in different serial positions along with other personality inventories (e.g., Locus of Control, Need for Cognition) to test hypotheses about level differences as a function of order. From the perspectives of the psychometric models proposed here, level differences in the SCS would be maximally relevant if it could be shown that (a) the SCS's psychometric properties do not change as a function of the order of presentation and (b) the tests in which the SCS is embedded (e.g., Locus of Control, Need for Cognition) also do not change in terms of their psychometric properties.

Concretely, these conditions would imply a model where items or testlets were linked to the SCS construct in each different order condition under the tau-equivalence or parallelism assumptions. Similarly, the items or testlets of the other personality measures would be linked to their respective constructs. The interconstruct hypothesis of level differences would be evaluated at the construct level. This hypothesis would address the issue of whether, at the construct level, differences could be observed.

It is interesting to note in passing that current research in the interconstruct tradition is implicitly assuming a Rasch measurement model for items assessing the constructs. In a simple two-construct case, this operating model assumes equal links between items and constructs for each of the two (unidimensional) constructs. Further, individuals' total scores accurately reflect their position on the distribution of the unobserved construct. It is in this case only that a between-group comparison of total scores would be psychometrically appropriate.

Summary

There are strong parallels between the sequence of research issues for evaluating order effects in the educational and ability literatures and issues that we have identified in the survey literature. In their review, Leary and Dorans (1985) identified three major stages of research on item-order effects. During the first stage, the phenomenon of item order was described and might be considered analogous to effects in the tradition of Schuman et al. (1981). The second phase of research attempted to identify processes responsible for these effects. In the survey literature, this is paralleled by the substantive contributions in this volume and its predecessor (Hippler et al., 1987) and the work of investigators modeling the survey response process using principles in cognitive and sociocognitive psychology. The focus of this chapter parallels the third stage identified by Leary and Dorans. In this stage, item-order effects are evaluated only after the psychometrics of the items has been considered.

In this chapter, we presented the strong conditions under which item-order effects can be interpreted. We outlined some preconditions that, from a psychometric standpoint, must hold true to allow for interpretation of order effects. Differences were established between the intra- and interconstruct cases. The intraconstruct case, where items are thought to be tapping the same underlying construct, involves three testable models of increasing stringency. In the interconstruct case, only two of these models are applicable. Finally, we introduced the notion that researchers might begin to concentrate on item clusters or testlets to test for order effects. The use of testlets will serve to increase the reliability of obtained effects by creating a better controlled within-testlet context.

We recognize that it is unlikely that researchers will always operate under these stringent conditions. We hope that we have raised issues for investigators in this literature to consider. In designing future research on item-order effects, an awareness of the psychometric issues involved in item (or testlet) comparisons is crucial, and these issues must be considered before order effects can be interpreted.

Acknowledgments. We wish express our thanks to the conference organizers, Norbert Schwarz and Seymour Sudman, for allowing us to participate in the exciting intellectual exchange at the conference and to contribute to this volume, as well as for providing critical comments on a previous version. We also thank Bill Chaplin for carefully reading and commenting on a previous version. This chapter may represent different perspectives on the evaluation of order effects in survey and psychological testing, and the views expressed (and any remaining errors) are our own. Order of authorship of this chapter was determined alphabetically because all of the authors made unique contributions to the work.

Part V
Social Judgment

18
Information-Processing Functions of Generic Knowledge Structures and Their Role in Context Effects in Social Judgment

Galen V. Bodenhausen

Social scientists have long recognized the possibility that research data may be affected by seemingly theoretically irrelevant contextual factors such as the ordering of response items in multiple-measure designs. There are many situations in research in which the ordering of measures or manipulations is theoretically uninteresting, but the results obtained may nevertheless be significantly affected by these contextual variations. Although an obvious concern in survey research (e.g., Fienberg & Tanur, 1989; Schuman & Presser, 1981; Sudman & Bradburn, 1982), inadvertent context effects can arise in most social and psychological research, including such diverse topic areas as personality testing (Knowles et al., chap. 15, this volume), lateralization of brain function (van Eys & Mc-Keever, 1988), and countless others. One obvious motivation in seeking to understand the causes of context effects is the desire to control their influence or eliminate their occurrence. Indeed, the procedure of counterbalancing measures and manipulations is a staple of experimental design that is intended to control order effects. Although they have frequently been regarded as a nuisance factor in research, context effects can also be viewed as providing information about the processes involved in the generation of behavioral responses in experiments and surveys. From this perspective, they constitute a potentially important source of data about human thought processes (cf. Loftus, Feinberg, & Tanur, 1985). Understanding the psychological underpinnings of context effects thus becomes more than just a methodological issue.

In this chapter, I explore one approach to understanding context effects in psychological research, based on the concept of generic knowledge structures, a commonly invoked theoretical construct in cognitive and social psychology. Generic knowledge structures (GKSs) are organized sets of beliefs about the social environment that summarize, in a general (abstract) and functional way, previous direct and vicarious experience with the stimuli encountered in this environment. These knowledge structures reside in long-term memory and are thought to be organized by stimulus domain. For any given topic, the GKS includes a specification of the elements or basic attributes of the stimulus domain and their interrelationships (for comprehensive reviews, see W. F. Brewer & Nakamura, 1984; S. T. Fiske & Taylor, 1990). In essence, GKSs are the means whereby the social perceiver constructs the meaning of current experience. They provide a basis for making sense of the world by providing information about the elements of the environment and their interrelationships, as well as their significance for the perceiver. GKSs occupy a central position in most theories of social cognition and include such well-known theoretical entities as scripts (Abelson, 1981), schemas (Rumelhart, 1980), categories (Lingle, Altom, & Medin, 1984), and stereotypes (Hamilton & Trolier, 1986). Although the content and structure of these types of mental representation have been a matter of heated debate (see, e.g., E. E. Smith, 1988; Solso, 1989), there is abundant evidence suggesting that the idea of abstract knowledge structures is a useful theoretical tool for understanding human information processing, especially information acquisition and retrieval (see Alba & Hasher, 1983, and S. T. Fiske & Linville, 1980, for respectively pessimistic and optimistic analyses of the usefulness of the GKS approach).

To understand the role that GKSs may play in context effects, it is necessary to elaborate the information-processing functions that these structures are thought to serve. Below I describe four of the main functions that GKSs perform in the cognitive system and provide examples of these functions by referring to research on social judgment and survey question answering. Then, I review and critically evaluate recent research that provides evidence addressing the comparative importance of these functions.

Four Cognitive Functions of Generic Knowledge Structures

Generic knowledge structures are usually assumed to play a powerful role in many types of information-processing routines. The first function of GKSs is *information acquisition;* that is, generic knowledge about the objects and events of the social environment directs the social perceiver's attention to a subset of the panorama of stimuli available for consideration. This subset receives greater attention, rehearsal, and elaboration than does other stimulus information and is therefore more likely to be stored in long-term memory. It is usually proposed that GKSs establish expectancies for the stimulus environment and direct the perceiver toward expectancy-relevant data. When entering a restaurant, to use a hackneyed example, one's "restaurant script" guides one's attention to stimuli and events that are relevant to the elements of the script. Many other aspects of the situation may be ignored or screened out. Thus, what we attend to and encode is affected by the knowledge structures operating at the time that we encounter a stimulus. This, of course, implies that the activation of a particular knowledge structure *before* one encounters a specific stimulus can affect what is learned and retained about that stimulus, perhaps dramatically. Consider a man who is told that his blind date is a librarian. Stereotypic beliefs about the personality characteristics of librarians may lead him to be more likely to notice and encode those of her attributes that match his schematic expectations about librarians but to overlook other features (Cohen, 1981). By constraining what is learned, GKSs must also constrain what can subsequently be recalled and used in rendering judgments.

Second, generic knowledge structures play a role in *information interpretation*. Inevitably, much of what we see in the social environment is ambiguous in its meaning and open to multiple interpretations. GKSs provide a set of expectations that can be used to disambiguate such stimuli. Is a child who pokes another child with a pencil being playful or aggressive? Sagar and Schofield (1980) provide evidence that if the child doing the poking is black, he is seen as aggressive, but if the child is white, he is seen as playful. As is evident from this finding, stereotypic preconceptions about the behavior of blacks can lead to a more negative interpretation of ambiguous behavior. Research on "priming" has also documented that having a certain frame of reference activated *before* one encounters ambiguous information can have a powerful effect on the interpretation that is given to that information (e.g., Higgins, Rholes, & Jones, 1977; see Wyer & Srull, 1989, for a comprehensive review). However, several studies suggest that once the information has been interpreted, providing a new frame of reference (or a different schema) may have little effect on judgments that are made of the stimulus (e.g., Massad, Hubbard, & Newtson, 1979; Srull & Wyer, 1980). Thus, as with information acquisition, the information-interpretation effects of GKSs generally appear to require the activation of the knowledge structure(s) prior to encountering the stimulus in order for the effects to occur.

A third important function of GKSs is *information retrieval*. As noted above, to the extent that knowledge structures bias what is learned about a stimulus, they also bias what can be recalled. Beyond this, it has been suggested in several studies that GKSs selectively direct retrieval processes, leading to better recall of schematically consistent material when both consistent and inconsistent materials have been stored in memory. This effect depends on the nature of the GKS that is activated at the time that a judgment is to be rendered or a memory is to be reported rather than on the nature of the GKS(s) that had been activated at the time that the stimulus was initially encountered. Thus, if a different GKS becomes activated subsequent to encoding and storing information about another person, it can have effects on subsequent memory and judgments about the person. As a hypothetical example, consider once again a person going on a blind date with a librarian. Because of the information-acquisition function, we would expect the person to be particularly likely to attend to and remember aspects of the librarian's behavior that exemplify stereotypic qualities of librarians (e.g., intelligence, introversion). However, if it were subsequently learned that the librarian was moonlighting as an exotic dancer, the person might, in thinking back to the date, selectively recall data that jibes with this new GKS. This function is particularly important from the standpoint of survey research, because it implies that any GKS that is activated by the survey instrument itself may affect the retrieval of information undertaken in answering the survey questions.

The fourth function of generic knowledge structures is *inference generation*. GKSs allow us to go beyond the information available and generate inferred data about a stimulus that seem probable, based on past experience. This function does not appear to be crucially dependent on the timing of GKS activation: Inferences can easily be generated on the basis of a GKS that is not activated until *after* one has already encoded a set of stimulus information. For example, suppose a person has formed a very positive impression of a politician based on his voting record, speeches, etc. If the person subsequently learns that the politician is a homosexual, the activation of this new GKS may lead to the generation of inferences about the politician that might have a dramatic effect on impressions of him, depending on the individual's stereotypic beliefs about homosexuals. It is clear that this function is highly relevant in survey research contexts (cf. Bradburn, Rips, & Shevell, 1987), because it implies that any GKS that is activated by the survey instrument may lead to the generation of inferences that are then used in answering questions. Consider a questionnaire about consumer product preferences. If respondents are led (by item wording or other contextual factors) to think of the products being evaluated as "gourmet" or "luxury" items, their evaluations of the products may be inflated by inferences about the quality typically associated with such items. Their judgments may be based more on this momentary mindset than on the actual attributes of the products, or memory of these attributes. It may simply be easier for respondents to use an inference rule such as "if it's gourmet, it's good" or "luxury = quality" than to search through memory for their past experiences with the product in question. Generic knowledge about luxury items provides the basis for a quick and easy answer to the query.

Pre- and Post-Information Effects

As the above discussion implies, there are many ways in which the activation of GKSs can affect memory and judgment processes. Because the effects occur at different points in the stream of information processing, order effects related to the timing of the activation of these knowledge structures become an important issue in understanding context effects. Some of these mechanisms require that the GKS be activated at the time that information about the target of the judgment is first encountered, whereas others may be influential even if it is not activated until much later, at the time that a judgment is requested. For the sake of simplifying verbal descriptions of these considerations, I shall refer to effects that occur when a schema is activated prior to other material as "pre-information effects," and those that occur when a schema is activated later as "post-information effects."

Consider an informal survey conducted by a radio station in which respondents were asked: "Do you believe Jim Bakker, the TV evangelist, is guilty of tax fraud?" Results indicated that a sizable majority indeed believed him to be guilty, as the actual jury subsequently also did. It is interesting to speculate about the ways in which stereotypes about TV evangelists may have affected the outcome of this poll or the trial itself. Since Bakker was virtually always identified as a TV evangelist, it is quite possible that beliefs about this group affected the acquisition and interpretation of information about Bakker all through the course of his well-publicized fall from the PTL leadership and subsequent trial. Stereotypic inferences may have been generated about him throughout the course of the media coverage or at the time that the judgment was requested. Moreover, since stereotypes about TV evangelists were undoubtedly activated at the time that the question was posed to respondents, they may have selectively retrieved evidence from memory and used this biased data base in rendering their judgments. Which of these processes are the crucial ones through which GKSs produce biases in judgments, when such biases exist?

A review of the social-psychological literature reveals considerable evidence of the pre-information effects of GKSs but very little unambiguous evidence of post-information effects (cf. S. T. Fiske & Taylor, 1990). One study allowing a comparison of the two types of effects was conducted by Massad et al. (1979). They had subjects view a film of abstract geometric figures moving dynamically around the screen. In one condition, one of the figures was described as a "bully and rapist," whereas in the other condition, the identical figure was characterized as a "guardian" protecting a treasure. Obviously, two very different types of GKSs were activated by these characterizations. The type of GKS that was activated affected not only subjects' evaluations of the figures but also their perceptual organization of the events shown in the film. When the initial descriptions of these targets were reversed *after* the information had been received (under the pretense that an error had been made), the "correct" descriptions had no influence on subjects' judgments. The initial description of the figure apparently influenced the representation that was formed on-line from the information, and this representation was used as a basis for subsequent judgments, notwithstanding the experimenter's "corrections." Thus, a GKS activated prior to information presentation had a strong effect on judgments, but when a different GKS was activated after the initial processing, no effects were evident.

Another comparative test was conducted by Srull & Wyer (1980). In their experiments, subjects were "primed" to think about abstract trait concepts such as "hostile" or "kind" by completing an experimental task in which one such concept was repeatedly activated. Then, as part of an ostensibly unrelated task, subjects were asked to read an ambiguous description of a person and form an impression of him. Under such conditions, judgments of the target person were clearly affected by the nature of the concept that had been activated prior to reading about the target. This was true regardless of whether the judgment was reported immediately, one day later, or one week later. However, when the order of events was changed, so that the subjects first read about the ambiguous target person, then completed the priming task, and then reported their judgments, the priming task had no influence on impressions of the target. Once again, evidence of pre-information effects was clearly documented, but no evidence of post-information effects was found.

A study by Rothbart, Evans, and Fulero (1979) is more informative with respect to the effects of GKSs on memory. In this experiment, subjects read about the individual behaviors of 50 members of a social group. Either before or after reading these behaviors, the group was characterized as either intellectual or friendly. In all cases, an equal number of intelligent and friendly items were incorporated into the behavior descriptions. When the characterization preceded the presentation of information, subjects were subsequently better able to recall behaviors that were consistent with the characterization (and they rated such behaviors as having occurred more frequently). This pattern was not found, however, when the trait concept was activated *after* the initial presentation of behaviors. Thus, the results of this study, like those of Massad et al. (1979) and Srull and Wyer (1980), suggest that the effects of activating generic concepts at the time of encoding are considerable but that the effects of activating such concepts only at the time of retrieval and judgment seem to be negligible at best.

Finally, a research study that I conducted (Bodenhausen, 1988) deserves attention because it sought not only to distinguish pre-information effects from post-information effects but also to determine the precise nature of the robust pre-information effects of GKSs described above; that is, it sought to determine the relative importance of the information-acquisition function and the information-interpretation function. This study involved ethnic stereotypes as the GKSs of interest and exploited the possibility of order effects as a means of diagnosing the processes producing stereotype-based discrimination in judgment. The basic logic of the experiment was as follows: If stereotypes bias judgments primarily through their influence on information acquisition and information interpretation, then, in order to observe biases, it would be necessary to activate the stereotypes *before* other information about a person is encountered. This would be in keeping with the literature summarized above. On the other hand, if stereotypes bias judgments primarily because they lead to the generation of inferences or the selective retrieval of evidence at the time of judgment, then it should not be necessary to activate them before the evidence about the person is encountered. As long as they are activated at the time of judgment, these other biases could operate.

This experiment used a mock juror decision-making format. Subjects were asked to take the role of a juror and to read the case evidence with a goal of determining the defendant's guilt or innocence in a case of criminal assault. In some cases, the assailant was assigned a Hispanic name. For purposes of comparison, the defendant was given an ethnically nondescript name in other conditions. The evidence presented to subjects was mixed in its implications, some implying guilt, some implying innocence. The crucial independent variable was the order in which the ethnicity information and the evidence were presented. For half of the subjects, the defendant's name (conveying his Hispanic identity in some cases) was presented at the outset, *before* the case evidence. For the remainder, the defendant's name was not presented until *after* the case evidence.

One of the primary dependent variables was subjects' ratings of the defendant's guilt. As suggested by previous research, stereotypes about Hispanics were found to bias these judgments only when they were activated prior to initial consideration of the evidence; when activated later, no discriminatory bias was found. These results suggest that we can rule out information retrieval and spontaneous inferences as the principal vehicles through which stereotypes lead to discrimination in the guilt judgment task. It does not, however, provide a way of comparatively testing information acquisition and information interpretation as the crucial processes involved. The information-acquisition hypothesis proposes that when stereotypes are activated at the time that the evidence is initially presented, subjects will attend to, elaborate, rehearse, and retain that portion of the evidence that is consistent with their stereotypic beliefs to a greater extent than they will inconsistent evidence. In contrast, the information-interpretation hypothesis suggests that some or all of the evidence will be interpreted more negatively (i.e., seen as more incriminating) when a stereotype has been activated prior to its consideration of the evidence.

Two types of dependent measures were collected in an attempt to evaluate the contribution of each of these processes. First, subjects were unexpectedly asked to recall the case evidence (after a brief distractor task). In keeping with the notion of biased information acquisition, subjects tended to recall stereotype-consistent material (i.e., the incriminating evidence) better, but only when the stereotype had been activated prior to consideration of the evidence. As a second source of evidence, subjects were also asked to make ratings of the probative implications of each piece of evidence presented to them. Specifically, each item presented in the case was presented again, and subjects rated how incriminating it was on an 11-point scale ranging from –5 (extremely unfavorable) to +5 (extremely favorable). According to the information-interpretation hypothesis, when a stereotype is activated prior to presentation of the evidence, the evidence will be interpreted more negatively. Contrary to expectations, this pattern did not emerge. Instead, there was no indication that activation of stereotypes differentially affected the interpretation given to the stimulus material, under either pre-information or post-information conditions. Thus, the results of this study point to biases in information acquisition as the mechanism through which GKSs affect memory and judgment.

To bolster faith in this conclusion, a second experiment was conducted to determine if selective acquisition of evidence is a necessary condition for stereotypic discrimination to occur. The second experiment was similar to the first in most respects. In fact, the only difference was that subjects were required to evaluate each piece of evidence as it was initially received. This was a significant change in procedure, however, because it required subjects to attend to and think about each piece of evidence at some depth. In this way, it should have undermined the tendency to learn stereotype-consistent material better and subsequently to base one's judgments on this biased set of material. However, the procedure did not prevent the other possible effects of stereotype activation from occurring. It would still have been possible to interpret the evidence more negatively, to retrieve stereotype-consistent material selectively at a later time, or to generate stereotypic inferences about the defendant.

Results can be described very succinctly. Even though the same case materials were used as before, the procedure of having subjects individually rate the implications of each piece of evidence as it was initially received completely eliminated the previously observed biases in guilt judgments and recall, nor were any effects found in the ratings of the evidence items. It was apparent that by preventing selective attention to stereotype-consistent information, the impact of the stereotype was, in essence, eliminated.

Taken together, the results of these sets of experiments very consistently suggest that GKSs are influential only when they are activated at the time of information acquisition and can selectively guide attention and learning of the material. They provide no evidence that GKSs that are only activated at a later time can influence judgments. This latter possibility is probably of greater interest and concern to survey researchers. If GKSs that are activated, perhaps inadvertently, at the time that questions are asked can influence responses involving previously acquired information, they constitute a potent source of bias in survey responses.

Post-Information Biases in Question Answering

The research described above may be somewhat reassuring in that survey researchers are primarily concerned with post-information effects, or cases in which the survey instrument itself may bias retrieval and judgment processes. The research that I have summarized implies that once memories are established, subsequently activated GKSs may do little to bias recall of the information or judgments based on it. Yet, there are a few well-known studies that seem to support the information-retrieval function of generic knowledge structures that are activated after the basic data base has been provided and initially processed. These studies warrant close attention.

Perhaps the best known study showing post-information effects is one conducted by Snyder and Uranowitz (1978), who presented subjects with a biography of a fictional character named Betty K. As described, Betty K. had some characteristics that are stereotypical of heterosexual women and some that are stereotypical of lesbians. However, her sexual orientation was not revealed prior to the presentation of this biographical sketch. Instead, it was revealed immediately before subjects took a multiple-choice test on the material contained in the biography. It was found that subjects tended to "forget" the stereotype-inconsistent items (e.g., failing to recognize items that were stereotypical of lesbians when they had been told Betty was a heterosexual), but they tended to recognize accurately the stereotype-consistent items. This pattern was interpreted as a case in which stereotypes guided retrieval processes in a selective fashion.

Bellezza and Bower (1981) suspected that the pattern of results obtained by Snyder and Uranowitz was not a product of selective retrieval but was instead due to a guessing bias; that is, subjects may have been responding on the basis of general stereotypes about lesbians and heterosexual women rather than on the basis of retrieved or unretrieved memories. In the terminology that I have adopted, they suggested that the pattern observed was due to the inference-generation function of generic knowledge structures rather than to the information-retrieval function. They provided compelling proof for this proposition by conducting a replication of Snyder and Uranowitz's (1978) study in which they adopted a signal-detection framework to analyze subjects' responses. This procedure allows a direct assessment of the impact of response bias (or guessing) on subjects' recognition performance. They were able to document this response bias empirically, concluding that no evidence was available to support the information-retrieval hypothesis favored by Snyder and Uranowitz. Thus, although the Snyder and Uranowitz study does not provide evidence of post-information effects of stereotypes on information retrieval, it does clearly provide evidence for post-information effects of stereotypes on inference generation. Since it is unclear whether such inferences would have been made in the absence of a forced-choice recognition task, the implications of this study for naturalistic impression formation are somewhat uncertain. However, the results have undeniable implications for survey researchers. Activating stereotypes or other sorts of GKSs at the time of questioning can lead respondents to rely on their generic knowledge of the world, rather than on specific memories, in answering survey questions.

Another well-known study that provided suggestive evidence of post-information effects of generic knowledge structures on information retrieval was conducted by R. C. Anderson and Pichert (1978). In this study, subjects read a very short story describing two schoolboys and their activities in one of the boys' homes. The bulk of the story was a description of the house. In reading the story, subjects were instructed to take the perspective either of a homebuyer or a burglar. Information was included in the story that was relevant to each perspective (e.g., the location of valuable possessions, structural weaknesses of the house). In a recall task, subjects remembered more of the information that was relevant to the perspective that they had taken at the time of encoding. However, subsequent to this first recall task, they were asked to take the alternate perspective and try to recall the story again. This time subjects recalled more information that was relevant to the new perspective than to the encoding perspective, including information that had not been previously recalled. Thus, the post-information perspective seemed to direct retrieval processes, even overriding the effects of the pre-information encoding perspective.

Baillet and Keenan (1986) raised a number of concerns about Anderson and Pichert's study. The study is of particular interest to cognitive psychologists because it contradicts one of the more well established principles of memory, namely, Tulving's principle of encoding specificity (Tulving, 1983; Tulving & Thompson, 1973). This principle states that a match between the conditions at encoding and at retrieval facilitates information recall. In showing that a new perspective at the time of retrieval can facilitate recall, Anderson and Pichert's results cast doubt on the notion of encoding specificity. Of foremost concern to Baillet and Keenan was the possibility that Anderson and Pichert stacked the deck against the encoding specificity principle by using an extremely short story and a very brief delay between presentation of the story and the perspective shift. Since some research shows that even the surface structure of a text can be retained for as long as 20 minutes after reading (e.g., McKoon & Keenan, 1974), it is possible that the dominance of the encoding perspective on what is retrieved will only show up after a longer delay or when longer stories are used. Baillet and Keenan (1986) repeated the experiment, in some cases using a considerably longer delay period (one week) and longer stories (in some cases, more than five times longer). Under the conditions that most closely approximated Anderson and Pichert's study, comparable results were found, but when the longer delays and stories were used, no post-information shift in retrieval was documented. Instead, the encoding framework continued to dominate recall. Baillet and Keenan (1986) concluded that a framework that becomes available at the time of retrieval can indeed make certain information more accessible for output, but it is "ultimately constrained by the accessibility of information as determined by the encoding framework" (p. 247). Thus, the pre-information activation of GKSs once again appears to be where most of the action is. As far as survey research goes, this study also appears to imply that the activation of a new or different framework or schema at the time of questioning is unlikely to lead to radically different patterns of information retrieval.

As we have suggested elsewhere (Bodenhausen & Wyer, 1987), however, it is premature to conclude that survey researchers can safely ignore the possibility of distorted retrieval processes due to the activation of GKSs. One factor of obvious importance that has not been systematically investigated is the nature of the memory structure that is being accessed. Much of the research that I have reviewed has involved information presentation conditions that are likely to result in highly organized mental representations in which the elements are associated with one another (in the case of stories, see van den Broek, 1988; in the case of social impressions, see Srull & Wyer, 1989, and Wyer & Srull, 1989). Retrieval of information from these types of representation is probably least likely to be influenced by post-information activation of GKSs because of the integrated nature of the representation. On the other hand, many of the types of memory structures that survey researchers want to tap may be less organized and more diffuse (e.g., memory for mundane behaviors, information pertaining to global judgments that incorporate data from several different life domains, etc.), and accessing such structures may be more appreciably influenced by the post-information activation of GKSs. This possibility certainly warrants empirical investigation.

In conclusion, the research that I have reviewed implies that when generic knowledge structures are activated prior to the presentation of other material, they can have a profound impact on the learning of the material and on judgments that are based on it. However, there is very little evidence that the activation of generic knowledge structures after relevant information has already been encoded has any appreciable effect on retrieval of the information from long-term memory. Instead, the biases that occur under post-information conditions appear to be the result of the inference-generation function of generic knowledge structures. In other words, schemas, scripts, and stereotypes that are activated at the time of questioning may not affect recall of previously learned or experienced events, at least when this information is contained in highly integrated memorial representations.

On the other hand, the considerations raised in this discussion point to at least two ways in which GKSs may affect subjects' responses in social survey research. First, it seems clear that GKSs can provide the respondent with a means for answering the question that bypasses an effortful search of long-term memory (i.e., the inference-generation function). Second, the interpretation function of GKSs suggests that a schema that is fortuitously activated by the survey instrument or the social context of its administration may affect the way in which a question is interpreted, to the extent that its wording permits multiple interpretations (see Hippler & Schwarz, 1987). Theories and data about the cognition of abstraction thus provide us with a greater understanding of the multiple processes involved in question answering as well as methodological cautions about the specific nature and source of context effects in the conduct of survey research.

19
Context Effects and the Communicative Functions of Quantifiers: Implications for Their Use in Attitude Research

Linda M. Moxey and Anthony J. Sanford

Description under Uncertainty

Many descriptions of states of affairs or beliefs are quantified. Quantification in its most general sense involves the use of numbers and proportions (e.g., 3, 2%) and more typically a whole host of natural language expressions, including quantifiers (a few, some, most), quantifying frequency adverbs (sometimes, often, usually), and probability expressions (possibly, likely), among others. It may be the case that when they are used, such expressions play the role of numerical descriptions without requiring the exactness of numbers. Sometimes this is true, and such an approach has led to research on how the mapping between verbal descriptions and decisions under risk, particularly using probability or likelihood expressions (e.g., Budescu, Weinberg, & Wallsten, 1988; Rapoport, Wallsten, Erev, & Cohen, in press). The results of these studies show that numerical information is more accurate than that information conveyed by a verbal expression and is consistent with the view that quantifiers do not denote single values but instead specify ranges, which are describable as membership functions on probability or frequency continua. Obviously, the same argument can be made for the importance of ranges with quantifying determiners (see Moxey, 1986): A word such as "many" can be thought of as denoting a range that the user has in mind, for instance.

In some ways, then, the use of natural language quantifiers seems like a second-best in data collection situations using questions and questionnaires, as it is when people are allowed to use them as possible responses in other data-gathering situations such as interviews. However, it is often difficult to ask questions without using them, and people are often reticent about using numbers when answering questions because of uncertainty inherent in their knowledge (see Wallsten, 1990, for a review of varieties of uncertainty), or because they just do not like numbers. What we wish to argue in this chapter is that people like to use natural language expressions because they can and often do convey more than is implied by accounts based on the denotation of proportion, even if they are elaborated through a membership-function treatment. Our view is that quantifiers convey pragmatic and rhetorical aspects of meaning. We shall illustrate the case using data from a variety of studies on quantifiers, making the argument that by using this extra expressive power, people can more properly convey a message about their beliefs. By the same logic, when a person uses a quantifier (or a related natural language expression) in response to a question, or to express an opinion, the pragmatic and rhetorical aspects of use have to be taken into account, as well as the denotational aspect. Finally, the same sort of argument applies to how people interpret questions that are expressed through the use of natural language quantifiers. Indeed, it is claimed that particular quantifiers might have an impact on formulating attitudes that a question may be attempting to probe.

The chapter begins with coverage of the denotational aspect of quantifiers and then shows how quantifiers can control attentional focus and how they may convey information about common expectations.

Mapping Linguistic Expressions to Numbers

Much work has been aimed at providing a precise mapping between linguistic expressions of quantity and their numerical denotations. The benefits of this are obvious. If a researcher wishes to examine the relationship between social status and anxiety, it would suit him better if subjects would indicate what percentage of the time they felt anxious (for instance) as a numerical percentage. In many situations, however, including this example, subjects find it easier to use linguistic descriptions—for example, "occasionally"—because language allows us to convey vague information, whereas numbers require precision. If our knowledge is lacking, or the facts themselves are vague, then language is not only more appropriate but also a more precise means of conveying the information.

Problems with Obtaining Accurate Mappings

Work up until 1981 in this area has been described by Pepper (1981). The basic problem highlighted is that quantifiers and similar terms are interpreted differently by different subjects and in different situations. Even the assumption that the average interpretation represents the "normal" interpretation of a term cannot be justified given the differences in denotation that appear across different studies. Pepper (1981) attributes the cross-study variation to three basic sources. First, researchers do not tend to attempt replicating previous research. They use different expressions and different tasks, utilizing different measures of subjects' interpretations and reporting different aspects of their data. Second, terms are found to vary because researchers have tended to present them in different contexts, a more interesting discovery. In fact, a number of studies have been aimed at discovering how the interpretation of various quantity expressions depends on context. The results suggest that there are at least some reliable, and controllable, contextual effects, which we discuss more fully below.

The third basic source of variation, according to Pepper (1981), is individual differences between subjects. For a given situation, the proportion denoted by a quantifier will vary from person to person, often quite greatly. Goocher (1965, 1969) showed that subjects who do not like an activity, or do not participate in it, will use higher denoting expressions to describe the same frequency of the activity as subjects who like the activity, or participate in it. Thus, if a subject does not like dancing, he will think that dancing 3 times a month is more than normal and will describe this amount using a larger quantity expression than will someone who likes dancing and who goes dancing 20 times a month. This phenomenon appears to be related to the dependence of quantifier choice on expectation of what is normal, where it is the concept of what is normal that is the source of systematic individual bias. This result foreshadows our later discussion of how quantifiers can carry presuppositional information about expectation.

One important problem with many studies of quantity expressions is that investigators have presented subjects with a list of expressions and have invited numerical correspondences to be drawn. Hence, any one expression is interpreted in the context of several others. Estimates of mean values and other moments of distributions are heavily influenced by such a procedure (see, e.g., Poulton, 1973, for seminal work on range phenomena; also Daamen & de Bie, chap. 8, this volume, for further work on range and distributional effects). The problem may be overcome by using large groups of independent subjects, each of whom sees only one of the expressions; but there is little work that has used this methodology, apart from some of our own to be discussed below.

Influence of Context on Quantifier Scaling

Other contextual effects are not so easy to control and are of greater interest. Hörmann (1983), for example, found that the interpretation of a quantifier depends on the size of the overall set accompanying it and on spatial aspects of the situation depicted. For example, "a few" is a smaller number of hills than it is of people, and "a few" people standing in front of the town hall is more than "a few" people standing in front of a hut. Other research has shown that the proportions denoted by such expressions also vary with overall set size (see, e.g., Newstead & Pollard, 1984). Bass, Cascio, and O'Connor (1974) attempted to investigate the effect of importance of topic on interpretation but failed to find any effects. Other work on frequency terms (such as "often") and probability expressions (such as "possibly") shows that the baseline frequency of an event influences the interpretation of expressions used to describe the frequency of that event (e.g., Pepper & Prytulak, 1974; Wallsten, Fillenbaum, & Cox, 1986). For example, if an event has a low baseline frequency, frequency expressions will generally be interpreted as lower than if the event has a high baseline frequency.

In fact, Wallsten, Fillenbaum, and Moxey (1986) and Pepper and Prytulak

(1974) found that the relationship between baseline frequencies and expressions used to describe frequencies is slightly asymmetrical; that is, expressions that normally denote large frequencies are apparently interpreted as denoting smaller frequencies when they are used to describe events that have low baseline frequencies. It is not clear that the reverse is true, since expressions that normally denote lower frequencies appear to have more robust interpretations. As Pepper and Prytulak (1974) have argued, large-denoting expressions have larger variances. We (Moxey, 1990) have found similar results using quantifiers rather than frequency or probability terms.

In one of the conditions of a large-scale study of quantifiers, independent groups of subjects were asked to indicate their proportional interpretation of the following expressions: "few," "a few," "very few," "only a few," "quite a few," "not many," "many," "very many," "a lot," and "quite a lot." One-third of these subjects saw their quantifier in a context where the expected proportion was high (the proportion of guests who enjoyed a party), another third saw it in a context where expectations were neither high nor low (the proportion of an audience influenced by a speech at a conference), and the remainder saw their quantifier in a context where expectations were low (the proportion of female doctors in the local area). Quantifiers that normally denote large proportions (many, very many, quite a lot, a lot) were interpreted as less when in the third context, where baseline expectations were low. However, the interpretation of quantifiers that denote small proportions did not vary significantly over contexts. The results obtained with an independent groups design are shown in Figure 19.1.

The asymmetrical interaction between context and quantifier interpretation has been explained in terms of the entailments of situations depicted by quantified statements (see Moxey, 1990). If "many people went to the party" is true, then the situation entails the state of affairs that "a few," "few," "quite a few," etc., people went to the party, just as if 10 people went to the party, the situation entails that 2 did. The reverse is not true: "A few people" attending does not entail the situation where many people went to the party. In this sense, smaller denoting quantifiers are dependent on the interpretations given to larger denoting quantifier, and this gives them less room for maneuver.

In this chapter's final main section on Quantification and the Elicitation of Attitude Data, we shall discuss the implications of this research for the use of quantity expressions in surveys and questionnaires. First we turn to further, less explored aspects of quantifier meaning, which may also have some bearing on the issue of question asking and answering.

Quantifiers as Controllers of the Focus of Attention

Is the following statement true or false?

(1) Few of those who say that abortion is wrong have experienced an unwanted pregnancy.

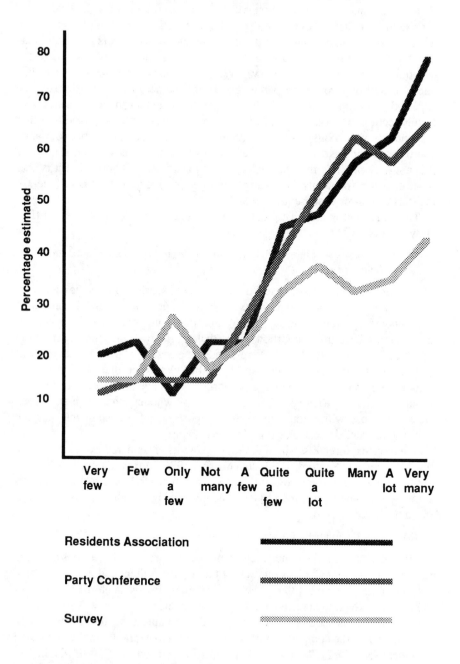

FIGURE 19.1. The Mean Percentage Interpreted by Subjects in Each of the Quantifier and Context Conditions

Clearly, responses to this question will be influenced by a number of factors—for example, beliefs about stereotypical anti-abortion lobbyists, beliefs about what constitutes an unwanted pregnancy, and one hopes, beliefs about the relationship between these two. However, responses also depend on answers to the question, "What proportion is few?" We argued above that the answer to this question will depend on the perceived size of the set of anti-abortionists, the expected proportion of them who have experienced an unwanted pregnancy, etc. In this section, we argue that the above item also increases the probability that respondents will focus on or pay attention to the (large proportion of) anti-abortionists who have *not* experienced an unwanted pregnancy. If this is so, then it is not only possible that the shift in focus influences responses, but it is also possible that respondents will change their perspective on the issue sufficiently to affect responses to subsequent items.

This argument is intuitively defensible in that (2) is interpreted very differently from (1):

(2) A few of those who say that abortion is wrong have experienced an unwanted pregnancy.

The factors influencing responses to this statement are the same as they were for (1). Previous work shows that the proportion denoted by "a few" is similar to that denoted by "few" (Moxey, 1986), and the same contextual decisions are likely to influence this proportion. Nevertheless, the two statements seem quite different, and it is easy to imagine respondents answering "true" to one of them and "false" to the other. Why should this be? We argue that (1) focuses the respondents' attention on the large proportion who have not experienced an unwanted pregnancy, whereas (2) focuses on those who have had such an experience. For those with strong opinions, the phrasing of this statement has the power to produce defensive or sympathetic responses.

We have explored elsewhere the focus patterns engendered by "few" and "a few" (Moxey and Sanford, 1987; also Moxey, 1986; Moxey, Sanford, & Barton, 1990), along with those of related expressions. In several experiments, subjects were presented with quantified statements, followed by the plural pronoun "they" (as in the example below):

(3) Few of the football fans were at the match. They . . .

Their task was to continue the "they" sentence in a way that made sense. On the assumption that "they" picks out the set that is most salient and in focus for the subject, it was concluded that "few" leads subjects to focus on the negation of the predicate (e.g., the fans who did not go to the match) about 60% of the time. This subset of the set of fans is known as the "complement subset" or COMPSET, since it is the complement of the set referred to explicitly in the quantified statement (REFSET). "A few" led subjects to focus on the COMPSET in less that 1% of sentence completions.

The tendency for "few" to focus on the COMPSET is not simply due to "few" drawing attention to the smallness of the subset involved. "Only a few" clearly signals a comment on the small number, yet continuations to examples such as (3), where "only a few" is the quantifier, show that this expression typically results in a very small number of COMPSET references in comparison with those resulting from the use of "few," "very few," or "not many."

A number of studies by us and our colleagues have examined the focusing properties of several quantifiers and quantifying (frequency) adverbs. The general results are shown in Table 19.1, which includes an indication of the strength of the tendency for each quantifier to lead to COMPSET focus, where the numbers are the percentages of COMPSET continuations, elicited under the same conditions.

The significance of the COMPSET may be summarized as follows: The stronger the tendency for readers to focus on the COMPSET, the more likely it is that information relating to the negation of the written predicate will influence the reader's thoughts. For example, the statement "Not many students voted conservative" is likely to lead readers to think of those students who did *not* vote conservative and the politics of those nonconservative students. Note that very small proportions expressed as percentages (numbers) do not result in COMPSET focus, although it is possible that COMPSET focus of a weak kind may result from saying "Only x% .... " (For further details on the focus-shift studies, see Moxey & Sanford, 1987.) In the next section, we argue that quantifiers perform even more subtle, yet influential, functions by conveying information about the expectations of the interlocutors.

TABLE 19. 1. Classification of Quantifiers and Percentage Expressions into Strong and Weak COMPSET Focusing and REFSET Focusing

Description	Quantifier/Adverb	% COMPSET[a]
Strong COMPSET	Hardly any	>90
" "	Very few	~73
" "	Few	~60
" "	Not many	~79
" "	Rarely	_[b]
" "	Seldom	_[b]
Weak COMPSET	Only a few	~5
" "	Only occasionally	_[b]
REFSET (no COMPSET)	Some	0
" "	A few	~2
" "	0.5%, 2%, 5%, 10%	0
" "	Only 0.5%	0
" "	Occasionally	_[b]

[a]The percentages refer to typical proportions of compset continuations in the experiments described in the text. Data from Moxey and Sanford (1987), Moxey et al. (1990), and Moxey, Sanford, and McGinley (unpublished data).

[b]No figures are provided for adverbs, since a different method had to be used to assess focus patterns. For a full discussion, see Moxey et al. (1990).

Quantifiers and the Beliefs of Their Producers

It was argued earlier that one's interpretation of a quantifier (i.e., the proportion that it denotes) can be influenced by the prior expectation that we have of the proportion that the quantifier is intended to describe. That is, if a large-denoting quantifier such as "many" is used to describe a proportion that we expect to be quite small (say, 25%), then one will interpret the quantifier as denoting a smaller proportion than if we had expected, say, 75%. Given that interpretation is affected by expectation, it is likely not only that the production of quantifiers is affected but also that when we produce quantifiers, our audience takes account of the fact that we are producing them in a context that carries with it a set of expectations. In other words, when a writer uses a quantifier in a context, the quantifier may provide the reader with information about what the writer expected.

Figure 19.2 illustrates different ways in which the use of a quantifier can provide information about speaker/listener expectations. In the figure, Sheena uses the quantifier "a lot" to denote the proportion of boys who kissed her on her birthday. One of Donald's interpretations of Sheena's statement is that X% of the boys kissed her. X might be a unique number, a range of numbers, or a distribution, but the point is that he interprets the statement as a statement about the proportion of boys who kissed her. Another interpretation illustrated in the figure, which may or may not be in addition to the first interpretation, is that whatever proportion kissed Sheena, she must have expected Y% to kiss her. In this example, Y is likely to be less than X, since Sheena is conveying her surprise about the largeness of the proportion who kissed her, but this need not always be the case. In our view, quantity expressions often appear to be used as a way of indicating the extent and direction of deviation from what was expected at this level.

Yet another level of interpretation for Sheena's statement is illustrated by the final thought bubble (the top one) in Figure 19.2. Donald may interpret her statement to mean that Sheena must have thought that he had expected Z% of the boys to kiss her. Again Z in this example is likely to be less than X, the force of the statement being that more kissed her than Donald thinks. Yet again it is our belief that some expressions (such as "a lot") can convey information at this level.

The levels of interpretation illustrated in Figure 19.2 have a complicated relationship with linguistic expressions in the context of attitude or opinion surveys. The reason for this complication is simply that the purpose of such surveys is generally to find out what *are* the expectations of respondents. Suppose, for example, that a survey respondent says that "a lot" of his or her friends drank alcohol before the age of 16. Although level 1 of Figure 19.2 (the proportion conveyed by "a lot") and level 3 (assumptions made by the respondent about what the researcher expects) are relevant, level 2 (the researcher's perception of the respondent's expectations) is not relevant, since the respondent's answer is itself an expression of his or her expectations. Perhaps then, level 2 of the diagram should be left out of discussions about the use of quantifiers in survey

FIGURE 19.2. An Illustration of the Levels at Which a Quantifier Might Be Interpreted

questionnaires. Not at all. Suppose now that "a lot" appears in a survey item rather than in the response category, that is, produced by the researcher rather than by the respondent. In this case, level 2 (the respondent's perception of the researcher's expectations) is relevant to the respondent's understanding of the quantity. However, level 3 (the respondent's perception of the assumptions made by the researcher about the respondent's expectations) is less relevant because the researcher is asking the respondent directly for his or her expectations.

Thus, each of the three levels of Figure 19.2 is relevant to the use of quantifiers in surveys. We did not illustrate the levels of interpretation with a survey example because the purpose of the survey would make our illustration more complicated than is necessary to understand what the levels of interpretation are.

It should be noted that just as X in Figure 19.2 can be influenced by Donald's prior baseline expectations about the proportion of boys who might kiss Sheena, so too are the implications that can be drawn from Y and Z. If Donald thinks Sheena is popular and likely to be kissed by a large proportion of the boys, but he interprets her statement to mean that Y is small, then he is likely to infer not only that her expectations were low but that they were abnormally low (she is pleasantly unaware of her popularity). On the other hand, if Sheena is not the sort of girl to be kissed and Y is small, then the force of the statement is really to indicate that the number was much larger than anyone would expect.

Similarly, if Sheena is a popular kisser and Z is interpreted as a small proportion, then Donald would be justified in thinking that Sheena is being a little defensive, since she is letting him know that his expectations are *abnormally* low. If Sheena is not so popular while Z is interpreted as a small proportion, then the force of Sheena's statement is again that the proportion of boys who kissed her was abnormally high.

The above discussion of Figure 19.2 reveals the various ways in which the use of a particular quantifier can influence our beliefs about the user and therefore the inferences that we make about the user's perceptions of himself or herself. Such factors are undoubtedly of great importance in language understanding, especially when we know little of the communicator apart from what he or she is now saying. If we believe, for example, that the speaker or writer believes A, we will temper our statement for someone who believes A. Rather than answering with our true opinions, we may, for example, give some sort of compromise.

The large-scale study of quantifiers mentioned earlier shows that quantifiers do, in fact, influence interpretations at all three of the levels illustrated in Figure 19.2. Subjects in the experiment were presented with what they were told was a snippet from a local newspaper. Each subject saw 1 of 10 quantifiers in one of three different contexts (the proportion of people who had enjoyed a Christmas party, the proportion of an audience who were influenced by a speech, and the proportion of local doctors who are female). One-third of the subjects in each condition were asked a question corresponding to the bottommost of Donald's thought bubbles in Figure 19.2; that is, they were asked to indicate what proportion was being conveyed by the writer's statement. In the Christmas party context, for example, subjects were asked to indicate what percentage of the guests had enjoyed the party. Another third of the subjects in each of the quantifier/context conditions were asked to indicate what percentage they thought that the writer had expected before attending the event or knowing the "facts." For example, in the Christmas party context, subjects were asked what percentage of the guests they thought that the writer had expected to enjoy the party before he found out. This question corresponds to the middle thought that Donald has in Figure 19.2. The final third of the subjects were asked a question corresponding to the topmost thought bubble. For example, in the party condition, they were asked to indicate what percentage of the guests the writer had believed his readers to have expected to enjoy the party before he wrote the article.

A detailed description of the above experiment is provided in Moxey (1990), as are the data and analyses. The following is a brief summary. The denotational interpretation of quantifiers (corresponding to the value of X in Figure 19.2) was found to depend on the context as well as on the quantifier. These data are shown in Figure 19.1. However, this dependency was only apparent for quantifiers that normally denote large proportions. The context made little difference to the denotations of small-denoting quantifiers such as "few" and "a few." This finding is consistent with research, mentioned earlier, using different types of quantity expressions.

A summary of the data relating to levels 2 and 3 of Figure 19.2 (questions about the expectations of reader and writer) is presented in Table 19.2. Subjects' responses to the question about the writer's prior expectations (corresponding to Y in Figure 19.2) depended on an interaction between context and quantifier. When subjects' own prior expectations were high or low (the Christmas party and doctor contexts, respectively) subjects' estimates of what the writer expected were not influenced by the quantifier used in the writer's description, except possibly by "a few" and "quite a few," which always led subjects to indicate that

TABLE 19.2. A Summary of the Relationship between Subject's Prior Expectations, Quantifier Used, and Perceived Expectations/Assumptions of the Writer

Subject's Prior Expectation	Effect of Quantifier on Perception of the Writer's Prior Expectation (Level 2 of Fig. 2)	Effect of Quanitifer on Perception of the Writer's Assumption about the Reader's Prior Expectation (Level 3 of Fig. 2)
Low	None	"A few," "few," "quite a few," and "very few" reduce expectation
Medium	"A few," "quite a few," "many," and "not many" reduce expectation	Same as above
High	None	Same as above

the writer had had low expectations before knowing "the facts." A pretest that had been carried out before the main experiment had determined that the three contexts used in the main study carried with them different expectations about the proportions expected. On average, independent groups of subjects indicated that 66% of the guests were likely to enjoy the Christmas party, 50% of the audience were likely to be influenced by the speech, and 27% of the local doctors were likely to be female. When subjects' own prior expectations are likely to be neither high nor low (in the speech context), the quantifier used by the writer in his description did influence subjects' judgments about what the writer had previously expected. Specifically, "a few," "quite a few," "not many," and" many" all led subjects to believe that the writer's prior expectations had been *low*.

Subjects' estimates of what the writer believed his readers to have expected are influenced both by the context of the quantifier and by the quantifier itself, although there is no interaction between them. "A few," "few," "quite a few," and "very few" all indicate that the writer believes his readers to have expected a small proportion.

In this experiment, subjects were all presented with a newspaper snippet that contained two sentences. The first introduced a topic, for example, "A recent survey has been carried out to find out whether or not female students prefer to be examined by female doctors"; the second was a quantified statement about the proportion in question, for example, "Quite a few of the local doctors are female." A second major experiment reversed the order in which these sentences were presented to subjects, so that they read the quantified statement before the topic sentence—indeed, the quantifier was always the first word. The aim of this second study was to discover whether the contextual effects of the first study would be weakened when the quantifier had no *prior* context. The main findings of the first study were found to be unchanged in the second, however. The effects reported above are robust.

Nevertheless, it is difficult to draw strong conclusions about the interaction between specific quantifiers and their contexts. Our study examined only three possible contexts, and it is easy to imagine that using further contexts would provide further uses of the quantifiers placed in them. Suffice it to say that the evidence indicates the power of quantifiers to provide us with information about the mutual expectations of writers and readers and hence with the tools to make inferences based on what the writer says versus what we believe to be normal expectations.

Some Conditions of Use of Quantifying Expressions

Our arguments to this point are to the effect that if we wish to understand what is meant when a quantifier is used or selected, then there is considerably more to be taken into account than the proportion that it denotes. Preferences regarding which quantifiers to use should be a function of their rhetorical functions; and, of course, since the use of numbers carries a very narrow range of rhetorical possibility, this may also be an argument for why people prefer to use words (quantifiers) rather than numbers. In this main section, we present three demonstrations of how these rhetorical functions impinge on the selection of a quantifier. The object is simply to show how preferences for the use of one quantifier rather than another in various contexts bear a sensible relationship to the properties discussed earlier. On the basis that they do, in the final main section of this chapter we discuss how the properties might play a role in data elicited through questionnaires and other methods of eliciting information and opinions.

Quantification and the Control of Attribution

Typical laboratory experiments on variables controlling overt attribution have frequently used vignettes in which an event is described (e.g., "John kicks a dog"). Other information is then typically provided, signaling the status of the event in terms of consistency, distinctiveness, and consensus. Such information is usually offered in the form of "normative" information, such as "Other people kick the dog." Of course, since such information is implicitly quantified, this statement means something like "Most/Almost all/other people kick the dog." Barton and Sanford (1990) investigated how attributional patterns depend on the use of quantifiers signaling exceptions. Consider the following example:

(4) John listens to the local jazz band when they play in town.
    Few others listen to the local jazz band when they play in town.

The term "few others" indicates that such behavior is exceptional, and therefore for John it is exceptional. Thus, this pair suggests that there is "something special about John," to use Hilton and Slugoski's (1986) terminology. In contrast, the following example suggests that there is something special about the band:

(5) John seldom listens to the local band.
    Few other people listen to the local band.

Barton and Sanford (1990) tested the role that the quantifiers "few," "a few," and "only a few" and the quantifying adverbs "occasionally," "seldom," and "only occasionally" play in signaling attributional patterns. They found that only those serving to *comment* on small proportions or low frequencies directly trigger attributional patterns. Thus, "a few" and "occasionally" do not do this. To get a feel for this, compare (6) with (4):

(6) John listens to the local jazz band when they play in town.
    A few other people listen to the local jazz band when they play in town.

There is no attributional bias at all here, despite the fact that "a few" nearly always signals a low percentage and almost invariably less than 50%. Barton and Sanford (1990) conclude that it is quantifiers carrying a comment on the low frequency that they denote that are critical in inducing attribution. It is not sufficient just to indicate a low frequency of an event. However, a strong

COMPSET emphasis is not necessary: "Only a few" and "only occasionally," both of which are only weak COMPSET inducers (Table 19.1), are as good as strong COMPSET inducers at bringing about the attributional patterns observed.

The Salesman Problem

Attribution depends on the comment function, but the salesman problem depends on much more subtle factors. Consider a car salesman who is asked of a particular kind of car, "How reliable is this car?" The following options are not equally acceptable as responses:

> Few/not many/hardly any/only a few/a few of our cars break down within the first three years of purchase.

In a study of preferences, "hardly any" and "few" were the most preferred, followed by "not many" and "only a few," with "a few" firmly at the bottom of the list. Thus, these preferences are much more finely tuned than is necessary to generate the attributional data. First, the salesman must focus the listener on the COMPSET and not on the REFSET, as the data indicate, which is why only "a few" has a relatively low rating: Recall that "only a few" is a relatively weak producer of COMPSET focus. Although this was unimportant for the attribution effect described above, it is critical in the salesman case. Beyond this, there is a preference for "few" and "hardly any" over "not many," although these are roughly equivalent in focus potential. We believe that this may be explained by the expectation function discussed earlier (and in Moxey, 1990): In the context of the salesman problem, subjects' beliefs about the writer's prior expectations are not relevant, since the salesman's beliefs about the percentage of cars likely to break down *before he knew the facts* are of no use to the customer. The assumptions made by the salesman about his customer's prior beliefs are, however, important, since he clearly wants them to be as low as possible. Since, at this level (the topmost bubble of Figure 19.2), the speaker who uses "few" is assuming that the expectations of his listeners are low, this is clearly a good expression for the salesman to use. "Not many," on the other hand, does not lead subjects to believe that the speaker is assuming his listener's expectations to be low. It is interesting to note that the use of a very low percentage, such as 0.5%, instead of a quantifier has a preference level as low as the quantifier "a few" (Sanford, Moxey, & McGinley, unpublished data). This is because very low percentages do not produce the required COMPSET bias of focus.

Relaxing a Hedge

Our third example also concerns the impact of focus and expectation. Imagine that there is a local village football team and that Harry has been trying to build it up over a period of years, but attendance of fans is very patchy and, on occasion, nonexistent. He falls ill and cannot attend a match. His friend goes to the match and then comes to visit Harry. Harry asks how many fans were at the match (in fact, none were there). Not wishing to upset Harry, the question is, which is it best for his friend to say?

Few   }
A few   }
Only a few   }   of the fans were there. (pause) In fact, none were/nobody was.
Not many   }

Sanford, Moxey, and McGinley (unpublished data) found that the preferred ordering put "not many" before "few" and that the other two were very low down the scale of acceptability. Thus, once more COMPSET focus seems to correlate well with acceptability. However, once more there is a clear difference between the preferences for "few" and "not many," only the order is reversed over the salesman problem. Again, the answer might be found in expectation. Since Harry's friend is assuming that Harry expected more than none to have been there, his choice of quantifier takes this into account. If he had used "few," this not only would convey the fact that he himself (Harry's friend) had high expectations about the number of fans turning up but would indicate that Harry's own expectations were (perhaps abnormally) low. This hardly prepares Harry for the second half of the message! Using "not many" indicates that a only small percentage was expected (by Harry's friend). This takes Harry one step down, preparing him for the fact that an even smaller percentage (none) turned out to be the case.

These three examples serve to show how functions besides denotation of proportion serve to control the preference for one quantifier over another. We are currently constructing a fuller decision tree for the conditions of application of quantifiers (Moxey & Sanford, 1990). However, even at this stage it is possible to see how the broader spectrum of meaning will influence the interpretation and use of quantifiers in questionnaires and freer description settings.

Quantification and the Elicitation of Attitude Data

There are two views of how quantification relates to attitude and opinion data: (a) the mapping of an expression onto the amounts or proportions that it denotes and (b) the relation of quantifiers to attentional focus—the rhetorical and pragmatic aspects of their meaning. The former has been treated in some detail by Wallsten, Budescu, Rapoport, Zwick, and Forsyth (1986) in terms of membership functions, but the latter is the main point of the present review.

The aim of most attitude questionnaires and large-scale surveys is to assess the opinions held by members of the public about (a) particular issue(s). This rests on the assumption that we can discover the "true" opinion of a population by asking its members for their opinions. The problem is that opinions and attitudes are not always expressible in so many words, and the way in which they are elicited can influence how they are expressed and therefore how they are interpreted. A respondent's answer to any questionnaire item not only will depend on his or her opinion on the matter at hand but is also possibly influenced by the phrasing of the question, by preceding questions, or, indeed, by previous answers.

Research shows that our interpretation of quantifiers can depend on our prior expectations regarding the proportion being described. This is especially true for quantifiers that generally denote large proportions. Hence, if the survey researcher wishes to assume that subjects give consistent interpretations to his or her quantifiers, it is probably better to use quantifiers that normally denote small proportions and to phrase questions such that the smaller subset is described. At any rate, items should contain quantifiers whose interpretation does not vary dramatically between contexts. Alternatively, the researcher should be aware of the respondents' prior expectations before asking the question. The latter may be difficult, whereas the former requires care over the choice of quantifier, since it is quantifiers denoting low proportions that have interesting effects on focus. For example, the COMPSET-focusing items in Table 19.1 will tend to be chosen by respondents who think that the proportion in a question is low and that the low proportion is worthy of comment (being either abnormal with respect to some view that they hold or being as low as they hold to be desirable). In contrast, the REFSET-focusing items will be chosen by people who accept a low frequency but do not believe it to be worthy of comment for some reason (see Barton & Sanford, 1990).

Questionnaire items containing quantifiers that influence focus might also alter the perspective taken by the respondent both for the item at hand and for subsequent items. Suppose that one of the following appears in a questionnaire about the AIDS virus:

(7) Few drug abusers protect themselves adequately against the AIDS virus.

or

(8) Only a few drug abusers protect themselves adequately against the AIDS virus.

or

(9) A few drug abusers protect themselves adequately against the AIDS virus.

Suppose that respondents are asked to indicate "true," "false," or "don't know" to one of (7), (8), or (9), and suppose that all three are answered "true." So what is the difference? The respondent who answered (7) is now focusing on the large number of drug abusers who do not protect themselves; the respondent who answered (8) is focusing on the smallness of the number of drug abusers who do protect themselves; and the respondent who answered (9) is focusing on the drug abusers who do protect themselves.

The respondent's perspective will differ after (7), (8), and (9) and is likely to influence interpretation of subsequent items. For example:

(10) People who use drugs are practically asking to get AIDS.

Those previously presented with (7) who are now thinking of the many irresponsible drug users are most likely—out of those presented with (7), (8), or (9)—to answer "true" to (10); those presented with (9) are most likely to answer "false" to (10); and those presented with (8) may go either way. Although this example does not come from an actual survey, it is sufficient to illustrate what we believe to be a real effect of using quantifiers that focus on the complement set in questionnaire items.

Another problem with natural language quantifiers in survey research comes from the way in which the use of a quantifier might influence beliefs about the expectations of the questioner, and assumptions being made about the expectations of the respondent. Respondents who wish to please the question asker, or who do not wish to look foolish, for example, may answer questions differently depending on their perception of these "mutual knowledge of expectation" factors, especially when the respondent has neither high nor low expectations about the proportion being described in the question. Suppose, for example, that a survey on the student population in the United States contains one of the following items:

(11) Few of the students in U.S. universities are over 21 years old.

or

(12) Not many of the students in U.S. universities are over 21 years old.

Respondents who wish to please the researcher, and who previously believed or expected that about half of the students in the U.S. were over 21 years old, might interpret both (11) and (12) to mean that, say, 20% of the students are over 21. With this information alone, it seems likely that the answer will be "false" in both cases. This type of respondent, however, is likely to be influenced by any information about the prior expectations of the questioner. The respondent is less likely to be concerned about what the questioner is assuming about the respondent. "Few" in (11) suggests that the questioner expected a high proportion, so that the respondent feels perfectly at ease answering "false." "Not many" indicates that the questioner had lower expectations. If the respondent's view is at all uncertain, he or she might decide that his or her previous beliefs were wrong and feel greater pressure to say "true" to (12). This last example is speculative, and the idea remains to be tested in the context of a survey. Nevertheless, the underlying notion that perception of the questioner's beliefs and assumptions might (a) be influenced by the use of particular quantifiers and (b) influence responses is one worthy of attention.

Needless to say, all of the above effects of quantifier use occur when respondents use quantifiers in their responses, just as much as when they express an opinion about a questionnaire item. It seems almost impossible to escape the possibility that questionnaire items influence the responses given by respondents. We can use our knowledge of quantifier function to do two things: First, we can include our knowledge of their function in our interpretation of responses; second, we can attempt to explore further the interaction between linguistic expression and the vague and seemingly transient information that we wish to quantify.

Acknowledgments. This research was partially supported by a British Academy Fellowship award to the first author.

20
Cognitive Representation of Bipolar Survey Items

Thomas M. Ostrom, Andrew L. Betz, and John J. Skowronski

Cognitive psychology is concerned with how people mentally represent the objects and information that they encounter in their world. Survey instruments are one such class of objects. People do not just passively respond to survey questions as if they were looking up answers in a dictionary, but they actively form cognitive representations of the survey and its items. These representations, in turn, guide the respondent's answers.

This chapter examines the nature of the cognitive representations that people access and utilize when making evaluative judgments. The chapter has two objectives: (a) it questions whether it is theoretically appropriate to view the underlying latent variable as being a unidimensional continuum, and (b) it shows that the order of items affects both the cognitive representation of the test and the factor structure of the judgments.

If cognitive representations do indeed play the central role assigned to them in models of information processing, it follows that such representations should directly influence an individual's responses to attitude survey items. In particular, two hypotheses concerning the impact of representations on responses to survey items should be true. First, responses to attitude survey items should reflect the structures used to generate those responses. Second, responses to attitude survey items should change if the structures involved in response generation are changed. The remainder of this chapter will present the results of research pertaining to both hypotheses.

Relations between Cognitive Representations and Attitude Survey Responses

Researchers investigating the nature of social attitudes have relied heavily on the idea that attitudes (as latent variables) can be adequately measured on a bipolar response scale. The use of these scales is consistent with the assumptions of classic psychophysical judgment models. These models assume that the cognitive structures underlying responses to bipolar survey scales are both *unidimensional* and *continuous*. The term "unidimensional" refers to the notion that there is a single dimension of variability for the class of stimuli being judged. The term "continuous" refers to the fact that there are no breaks in the dimension, that is, that there is a seamless gradient from one end of the latent variable to the other.

A cognitive structure that has the properties of unidimensionality and continuity should produce judgments that are reciprocally antagonistic; that is, as one moves away from one pole of the response continuum, one will inevitably move toward the opposite pole. For example, in judgments of the psychophysical qualities of light, a stimulus that increases in brightness must, by definition, become proportionally less dim.

As noted elsewhere (Ostrom, 1987), contemporary cognitive theory moves the field away from the psychophysical model of attitude representation. The attitude construct, traditionally viewed as a bipolar continuum, can be reconceptualized in terms of two discrete categories that are separately stored in a semantic network. For example, consider a bipolar variable ranging from "kind" to "mean." A person may have a set of beliefs that is organized around a cognitive category corresponding to the concept "mean," while having another set of beliefs that is organized around a cognitive category corresponding to the concept "kind." Instead of a single continuum, the representation consists of two independent categories.

Because of this possibility, attitude theorists should begin to examine the assumption that the latent cognitive structures are *dualistic* and *discrete*. By discrete we mean that the categories corresponding to each end of the bipolar scale have properties that are independent of one another. Each is not merely the negation or inverse of the categorical properties defining the end other. By dualistic we mean that the continuum is not unidimensional but is instead a concatenation of two independent categorical gradients. Dualistic categories are not reciprocally antagonistic. In terms of our "kind" versus "mean" example, it is possible for a person to show a lack of kindness without behaving in a mean fashion, and vice versa.

The idea of duality in latent cognitive structures has arisen periodically in the past. For example, early work on job satisfaction (Herzberg, Mausner, & Snyderman, 1959) attacked the supposedly unidimensional, bipolar nature of that latent variable, claiming instead that satisfaction and dissatisfaction were regulated by different variables (essentially a dualistic approach). Although Herzberg's ideas were not well received (e.g., Locke, 1976), recent research focusing on job-related affect (e.g., Burke, Brief, George, Roberson, & Webster, 1989) suggests that Herzberg's intuition about a basic negative/positive dualistic dichotomy has considerable merit. Similarly, research on the construct of well-being/optimism is supportive of a dualistic dichotomy in affect (for examples, see Diener & Emmons, 1985; Watson & Pennebaker, 1989). Other examples of dualistic ideas can be found in the areas of management (Bobko, 1985), cooperation/competition (D. W. Johnson & Ahlgren, 1976), personality (Marsh & Richards, 1989; Sande, Goethals, & Radloff, 1988), interpersonal attraction (Rodin, 1978), and person perception (Skowronski & Carlston, 1989).

The most concentrated body of evidence supporting duality in the attitudinal domain comes from Kerlinger's research on his Criterial Referents Theory of attitudes (Kerlinger, 1967, 1984). Kerlinger (who coined the term "duality") argued that factor analysis is a powerful tool for discriminating between bipolar/continuous and dual/discontinuous latent cognitive structures. He hypothesized that if attitudes are bipolar, then attitudinal items related to opposing poles of the attitude continuum should all load on the same factor. By contrast, if attitudes are dualistic, then one should obtain separate factors for each pole of the supposed continuum. Research by Kerlinger (1984) and others indeed found dualistic factor structures across a variety of attitudinal domains, including educational attitudes, political attitudes, and attitudes toward the self.

Other evidence supporting attitudinal duality comes from work on ambivalence. Kaplan (1972) noted that unidimensional approaches to attitudes cannot easily distinguish between "neutrality" (i.e., no feelings on the issue) and "ambivalence" (i.e., mixed feelings). The duality approach easily accommodates this distinction. Work by Kaplan (1972) and Moore (1973, 1980) provided data consistent with the dualistic view, demonstrating that separate measurement of the positive and negative poles yields both an index of overall attitude and an index of ambivalence.

Present Research

Past tests of attitudinal duality have dealt only with well-developed attitudes. However, many surveys are interested in newly formed attitudes. For example, consumer surveys elicit reactions to new products, campaign surveys ask impressions of new candidates for political office, and political surveys ask questions about new legislative initiatives or policy options.

The present studies examine the duality issue in the context of impressions of an unfamiliar person. The impressions are based on a brief description of a day in that person's life. This approach has the special benefit of holding the information base constant: All respondents have exactly the same information about the attitude object. Consequently, any resulting evidence for duality would be determined exclusively by the nature of the latent cognitive structures used by the respondents and not by differential exposure (in amount or bias) to information about the attitude object.

The research reported here uses Kerlinger's reasoning (also see Green & Goldfried, 1965) to make inferences about the latent cognitive structures underlying attitudinal judgments. In our studies, subjects made a number of trait ratings about the target person. Three of those trait scales were related to hostility (hostile, dislikable, unfriendly) and three were related to hostility's antonym, kindness (kind, considerate, thoughtful).

Measures of Cognitive Structure

These trait ratings were entered into a factor analysis. If the responses to all of these items are reflective of a single bipolar and continuous latent cognitive structure, then the factor analysis should yield a one-factor solution. All of the items should load highly on this factor, but positive and negative items should have oppositely signed loadings. However, if these ratings are reflective of two separate cognitive categories, then one would expect the factor analysis to yield a two-factor solution. Positive items should load strongly on one factor, and negative items should load strongly on the other.

Because the interpretation of the results of factor analyses is sometimes disputable, confidence in the duality concept would be substantially enhanced if supportive data from converging operations were available. This chapter reports such supportive data from three tasks: recall of test items, semantic-label generation, and item recognition.

The rationale for using recall measures is straightforward. The results of past research suggest that cognitive structures influence recall. This influence can be detected in either of two ways. Some research suggests that people tend to have better recall for items relevant to an activated cognitive structure than for structure-irrelevant (i.e., distractor) items (e.g., Ostrom, Lingle, Pryor, & Geva, 1980). Other research suggests that an activated cognitive structure will sometimes cause people to erroneously recall items that are consistent with the structure (Graesser, Woll, Kowalski, & Smith, 1980; Spiro, 1977). Hence, the patterns of recall obtained after the test can be diagnostic of the structures used during the test.

The rationales for using the semantic-label generation task and the item-recognition task are similarly straightforward. If people do explicitly form a cognitive representation of the test, they should be able to verbalize that construct. Even when irrelevant distractor items are included (as is the case in our research), the respondents should be able to generate a semantic label that correctly identifies the latent construct being measured. Further, if people develop an accurate conception of the test, then they should be able to identify which items are related (versus unrelated) to the construct.

Order Effects

If cognitive structures regulate information processing on survey items, then changing the structures should change the responses. Some researchers have used this idea to explain order effects and context effects in survey research. For example, Tourangeau and Rasinski (1988) suggested that a number of cognitive changes can be induced by varying item-order effects on a survey. These changes occur passively as a result of accessibility and anchoring processes.

However, several researchers (Knowles, 1988; Rogers, 1974a, 1974b) have argued that order effects may not always be the result of these passive processes. Rogers noted that personality tests often ask many questions designed to measure the same latent personality variable and that one of the effects of this repeated questioning may be to "educate" the test taker about the purpose of the test. In short, repeatedly accessing the same latent memory structures may eventually cause people to develop ideas about what the test is measuring, ideas that, in turn, might influence subsequent item responses.

A recent example of how order-induced latent memory structures may influence processing was provided by Budd (1987), who varied the order in which subjects were asked questions about several attitude objects. One version of Budd's questionnaire grouped items together such that all items in a block related to the same attitude object. A second version of the questionnaire contained a randomized item presentation that intermixed items about a variety of attitude objects. Budd found that the internal consistency of items relating to the same attitude object was much stronger when the items were blocked than when they were randomly presented. These heightened correlations suggest that subjects abstracted a construct for each item block and then used that construct to answer the remaining questions in the block.

We used a related manipulation to explore the nature of the cognitive representation that people form of a multi-item test and how that representation is affected by item sequence. Three different item sequences were examined in the present studies. All three sequences contained 12 items (i.e., rating scales) on which respondents reported their impressions of the target person. Six of the scales were relevant to the latent dimension of kind/hostile. The other six were construct-irrelevant distractor scales, three positive (intelligent, dependable, interesting) and three negative (boring, selfish, narrow minded). Each rating scale ranged from 0 (not at all) to 10 (extremely). The scales were presented on two pages with six scales per page.

The three item-order conditions differed in terms of how the relevant items were interspersed among the irrelevant distractor items. In the *random* condition, all 12 items were randomly ordered with 3 relevant and 3 irrelevant items on each of the two pages. In the *3-6-3* condition, the first 3 items of the first page were all either relevant to kind or to hostile. The last 3 items of the second page consisted of the opposite relevant item set. The middle 6 items in this condition were all distractors. In the *6-6* condition, all of the relevant items were on one page and all of the irrelevant distractor items were on the other page. In all three conditions, item order was counterbalanced.

The three sequence conditions were selected for two reasons. First, the two blocked conditions (3-6-3 and 6-6) were expected to activate the test construct more strongly than was the random condition. Blocking the relevant items should increase the likelihood that a latent category structure is activated by the items (Budd, 1987). Second, the two blocked conditions may differ in terms of whether they make kind and hostile salient as two separate latent cognitive structures (3-6-3) or as a single bipolar dimension (6-6). It was argued earlier that duality seemed to be a more plausible latent representation than bipolarity, but it is possible that both forms of representation exist and can be activated. If this is the case, then the 3-6-3 condition should favor duality (i.e., be more likely to activate the separate structures of kind and hostile) and the 6-6 condition should favor bipolarity (i.e., be more likely to activate a unidimensional bipolar representation).

This analysis leads to several predictions. It suggests that the order in which questions are asked might influence the factor structure that emerges from a factor analysis of those items. Specifically, item blocking in the 3-6-3 condition should yield clearer evidence for duality (i.e., a two-dimensional factor structure) than the random condition. The question of whether bipolar structures can be activated is answered by the 6-6 condition. If only dualistic structures exist, then the 6-6 factor structure should look similar to the 3-6-3 factor structure. If, on the other hand, the 6-6 condition activates a bipolar structure, then its factor structure should show that unidimensionality. Other predictions pertain to the cognitive measures. They should show that persons do acquire a cognitive representation of the test (despite the presence of distractor items) and that this representation is dualistic. In addition, the effects of item order on the structure displayed by the cognitive measures should parallel those obtained for the factor analyses.

Research Procedure

Two studies were conducted. Both provided respondents with the following sequence of tasks: a brief description of the target person (Donald), 12 impression rating scales, a 2 1/2 minute distractor task, and a memory task. Both studies randomly assigned respondents to one of the three item-sequence conditions: random, 3-6-3, or 6-6. The two studies were identical, except for the nature of the memory task. The first survey was administered to introductory psychology students in the classroom, and the second survey was administered to small groups in a laboratory setting. Study 1 involved 102 respondents, and Study 2 involved 106 respondents.

The description of the target person portrayed a day in the life of Donald, who periodically engaged in ambiguously hostile activities. This Donald paragraph and the 12-item impression test have been used by a number of investigators in social psychology (e.g., Srull & Wyer, 1979). The test has been used (with randomized item order) to assess hostile/kind as a unidimensional construct.

The memory measures were collected after a distractor task, which was used to eliminate recency effects. Different memory measures were collected in the two studies. In Study 1, respondents were reminded that they had previously rated Donald on 12 trait scales. They were then asked to write down as many of the 12 traits as they could, using the exact word if possible. This provided our *recall* index. Study 2 informed respondents that 6 of the 12 scales measured the same trait and asked them to guess which trait it was. Their answer to this question provided our *semantic-label* index. These respondents were then given the 12 original trait words (in alphabetical order) and were asked to indicate which 6 words provided the basis of the semantic label that they had given on the previous page. These data were used to calculate the index of *construct-relevant item recognition*.

The Cognitive Representation of the Test:
Factor Analytic Data

To provide a stable estimate of the factor structure for each of the three conditions, the impression rating data from the two studies were combined. The total sample sizes for the random, 3-6-3, and 6-6 conditions were 70, 70, and 68, respectively. A principal-components factor analysis with varimax rotation was conducted for each condition. Only the 6 scales relevant to the hostile/kind construct were entered into these analyses.

Scree plots of the factor eigenvalues were similar for all three conditions, but some important differences were apparent. Using 1 as the cutoff for a significant eigenvalue, the random condition yielded a one-factor solution and the two blocked conditions each yielded a two-factor solution. This difference in number of factors is supported by the percentage of variance explained by the first two factors in each condition. The two factors explained more variance in the 3-6-3 (70.7%) and 6-6 (64.8%) conditions than in the random condition (61.4%).

The pattern of factor loadings also provides support for the prediction of greater duality in the two blocked conditions. Rotated factor loadings were obtained for the two-factor solution for all three conditions. In all conditions, the three hostile traits loaded most strongly on one factor (labeled the "hostile" factor) and the three kind items loaded most strongly on the other factor (labeled the "kind" factor).

Figure 20.1 shows how the hostile traits loaded on the two factors, and Figure 20.2 shows how the kind traits loaded on the two factors. The mean and range of the factor loadings are given for all item-sequence conditions. Both figures tell essentially the same story: Duality was stronger in the blocked conditions than in the random condition.

Three features of these figures support this conclusion. First, items load higher on their own factor in the blocked conditions than in the random condition. This suggests that dual constructs were more important to respondents in the blocked conditions than to those in the random condition. Second, loadings on the opposite factor are nearer 0 in the blocked conditions than in the random condition. This demonstrates that blocking reduced the tendency of items to contribute negatively to the opposite factor (which is a feature of bipolarity). Third, the range of factor loadings is over twice as large in the random condition ($M = .54$) than in the 3-6-3 ($M = .25$) or 6-6 ($M = .24$) conditions. This indicates that the factor structure was more coherent in the blocked conditions than in the random condition.

There was no substantial difference between the two blocked conditions: Both yielded strong support for duality over bipolarity. Even in the 6-6 condition, where the item sequence should have activated a bipolar structure (had such been cognitively available), there was little support for bipolarity. The strongest evidence for bipolarity appeared in the random condition, which yielded only one factor. In addition, Figures 20.1 and 20.2 show that the strongest negative loadings (indicating that the two factors are negatively correlated) occur for the

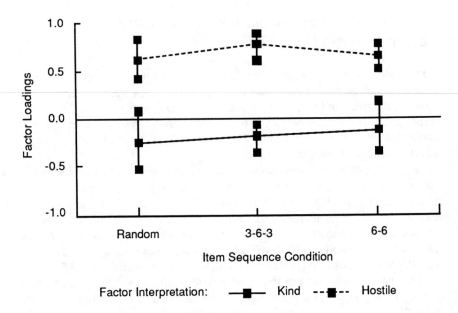

FIGURE 20.1. Mean and Range of Factor Loadings for the Hostile Items as a Function of Item Sequence Condition (Studies 1 and 2)

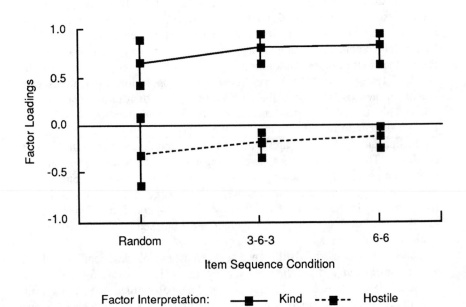

FIGURE 20.2. Mean and Range of Factor Loadings for the Kind Items as a Function of Item Sequence Condition (Studies 1 and 2)

random condition. Perhaps this bipolarity was a byproduct of forming a general evaluative (i.e., positive/negative) factor involving all 12 items.

The Cognitive Representation of the Test: Cognitive Measures

Item Recall

Study 1 provided evidence about respondents' memory for the traits used to rate Donald. It was predicted that respondents should (a) recall more traits relevant to hostile and kind than traits that were irrelevant and (b) show more trait-relevant memory intrusions than trait-irrelevant intrusions.

To test these hypotheses, the recalled traits were scored as being either accurate (involving the same root word as the test items) or guesses (denotatively related to the test items). Figure 20.3 shows that there was an interaction between the accuracy of recall and the relevance of the traits recalled, $F(1,90) = 77.26$, $p < .001$. Our hypothesis that subjects formed a concept of the test is strongly supported by the guesses data: Relevant guesses emerged more often than irrelevant guesses. However, for accurately recalled traits, the recall of relevant terms was somewhat lower than the recall of irrelevant terms. This reversal is not a critical violation of our hypotheses. The reversal could be due to different levels of memorability for the two kinds of traits; such reversals have been observed in other research (Graesser et al., 1980; D. A. Smith & Graesser, 1981).

It was expected that of the three item-sequence conditions, respondents in the two blocked conditions would show clearest evidence of the latent construct. The test of this interaction (between item relevance, item accuracy, and item sequence) was only marginally significant, $F(2,90) = 2.41$, $p < .10$. The pattern shown in Figure 20.3 was strongest for the 6-6 condition, and the remaining two conditions were indistinguishable. Hence, our expectations regarding the effects of item order on recall were only partially supported by these data.

Semantic Labeling

One consequence of the view that people acquire a representation of a test is that they may be able to provide an accurate semantic label for the inferred construct. We tested this possibility in Study 2 by asking subjects to generate a semantic label for the construct assessed by the test. These labels were coded as being either relevant or irrelevant to the hostile/kind construct. Overall, respondents accurately identified the construct 64.8% of the time (chi-square(1) = 7.10, $p < .01$). It is clear that the construct was detectable to a majority of the respondents in this study.

We also assessed the possibility that item sequence affected subjects' labeling accuracy. Item sequence could affect accuracy of the semantic label in either of two ways. First, grouping the relevant items together may enhance the salience

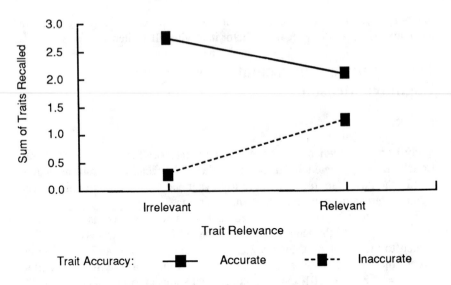

FIGURE 20.3. Recall of Traits as a Function of Trait Relevance and Trait Accuracy (Study 1)

of the latent construct. Increased salience should lead to an increased ability to detect the construct. Second, the conditions differ in the opportunities that they provide to use items late in the test to validate hypotheses formed early in the test. Both the random and 3-6-3 conditions present relevant items both early and late in the test. On the other hand, the 6-6 condition presents all of the relevant items together on one page (either on the first or second page). Respondents receiving the relevant items on the first page might form accurate hypotheses but would not find confirmation on the second page. Respondents receiving the relevant items on the second page would not have even considered the correct hypothesis by the time that they had ended the first page.

Our results indicate that item sequence did affect construct accuracy. Respondents correctly provided a semantic label 68.8% of the time in the random condition, 70.0% of the time in the 3-6-3 condition, but only 55.2% of the time in the 6-6 condition (chi-square(2) $= 9.77$, $p < .01$). This pattern of differences goes against the salience prediction but directly supports the hypothesis validation prediction. The data are completely consistent with a dynamic view of the respondent as one who is actively searching for a valid way to represent the test instrument cognitively.

Item Recognition

In Study 2, respondents were asked to indicate the 6 trait scales that most closely reflected the construct that they felt the test was designed to measure. Because duality assumes independence between hostility (evaluatively negative) and kindness (evaluatively positive), the traits that subjects circled should reflect only one of the relevant traits; that is, respondents who gave a negative semantic label should tend to circle negative traits and those who gave a positive label should tend to circle positive traits. On the other hand, bipolarity demands reciprocity of the positive and negative poles. Kind scales are as relevant to the measurement of hostility as they are to the measurement of kindness. The proportion of positive and negative traits circled should remain the same regardless of whether the respondent indicated a positive or negative construct.

The data clearly support the duality prediction of congruence between valence of items and valence of generated construct, interaction $F(1,76) = 44.87$, $p < .001$. When the generated construct was positive, people circled more positive than negative constructs; when the generated trait was negative, people circled more negative than positive constructs. To simplify subsequent discussions of these data, we shall refer to this interaction as a "congruence main effect" in which the two congruent values are combined into one mean and the two incongruent values are combined into the other mean.

A possible problem with interpreting this congruence main effect as support for duality is that not all respondents provided a semantic label that related to the hostile/kind construct. Respondents who gave other constructs faced a dilemma in that there could be no more than one scale that was semantically related to their label and there was no scale that had the opposite valence. For example, there was only one trait relevant to intelligent and no corresponding negative traits (such as stupid). When forced to select 6 scales, respondents may have simply circled traits that were evaluatively congruent with their generated construct. This would imply that if bipolarity is correct, the congruence effect should disappear for respondents who correctly identified the hostile/kind construct.

This did not happen. The congruence effect was not significantly different for respondents who generated the correct construct and for those who gave an incorrect construct, interaction $F(1,76) = 1.99$, $p < .17$. In fact, the congruence effect was actually stronger for accurate than for inaccurate respondents. This finding further bolsters the duality interpretation of the congruence main effect.

The trait-circling data provide an additional basis for determining whether the hostile/kind construct formed the basis of the respondents' representation of the test. The primary issue is whether respondents circled more construct-relevant than construct-irrelevant traits. As predicted, more relevant ($M = 3.35$) than irrelevant ($M = 2.60$) traits were circled, $F(1,76) = 6.28$, $p < .02$.

This overall relevance effect should emerge most strongly under two conditions. First, the relevance effect should be strongest for those giving the correct semantic label. As Figure 20.4 shows, this effect was obtained, $F(1,76) = 8.96$, $p < .004$. Second, the relevance effect should be influenced by whether the traits are congruent or incongruent with the evaluative nature of the generated construct. Duality suggests that the hostility cluster is independent of the kindness cluster. If this is true, then relevance effects should occur only for congruent traits. Bipolarity, on the other hand, suggests that the relevance effect should be observed for both congruent and incongruent traits. The analysis revealed that

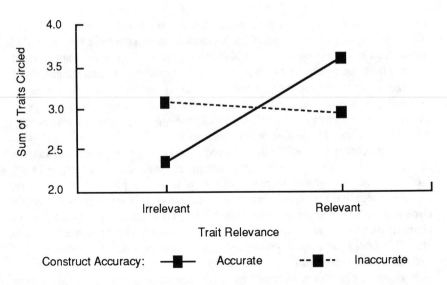

FIGURE 20.4. Number of Traits Circled as a Function of Trait Relevance and Accuracy of Respondents' Construct (Study 2)

there was no relevance effect for the incongruent traits. The relevance effect appeared only for the congruent traits, interaction $F(1,76) = 11.61$, $p < .001$. Once again, duality is supported over bipolarity.

These data establish that the effect of relevance is localized in (a) the respondents who correctly identified the construct and (b) the subset of traits that were congruent with the semantic label generated by those respondents (regardless of whether it related to hostility or kindness). The effects of item sequence should also be localized in the same way.

These considerations imply that the effects of item sequence should emerge as a 5-way interaction, and this occurred, $F(2,76) = 4.56$, $p < .02$. The exact character of this interaction is difficult to convey. However, the two blocked conditions (3-6-3 and 6-6) produced a much stronger joint effect of trait relevance and trait congruence than did the random condition. These data, then, are consistent with the factor analyses and the labeling data, indicating that question sequence did have an impact on the cognitive representations that were derived from the test.

Conclusions

The cognitive measures and the factor analysis data converge to support several conclusions. First, people do form a latent representation of psychometric instruments, and they do so very quickly—quickly enough, in fact, that it guides their responses to the remaining items in the test. Our data on this point converge nicely with those of Knowles (1988; Knowles et al., chap. 15, this volume), who shows increases in item-test correlations even across the earliest items in a test.

The second conclusion pertains to the psychological properties of the latent construct. Most psychometric instruments are based on the assumption that latent variables are continuous. This assumption has been accepted by most who use the kinds of bipolar scales that were the focus of the present chapter (e.g., semantic differential scales). This traditional view is contradicted by the studies reported in this chapter. The item-recognition data from the second study, along with the results of the factor analyses, argue persuasively for duality over bipolarity.

One other point deserves emphasis. This is the first research to examine the duality question using newly developed attitudes. This approach has the special advantage of not confounding informational content with attitudinal reactions. Duality could be obtained in well-developed attitudes merely from the respondent learning hostile facts about the person in one context and kind facts in another context. The present data, in contrast, directly suggest that people have independent semantic structures that are accessed when making separate judgments of bipolar trait constructs.

The third conclusion pertains to item order. Item order moderates several of the effects obtained in these studies. Accuracy in labeling the intended construct was poorest in the 6-6 condition. This supported a hypothesis validation process over a salience process. People naturally assume that relevant items will be distributed across the entire test. If they are unable to generate the correct hypothesis early in the test or are unable to validate a correct hypothesis late in the test, they are less likely to draw a correct conclusion. The findings also indicate that randomly interspersing relevant items among distractors was not successful in concealing the purpose of the test. Accuracy in the random condition was much higher than in the 6-6 condition and was equivalent to that found in the 3-6-3 condition.

Accuracy in labeling does not tell the whole story. The item-recognition data established that the label had different meanings in the random condition than in the two blocked conditions; that is, the localized relevancy effect showed that duality better described the latent representation in the blocked conditions than in the random condition. This was true despite the fact that the localized relevancy effect in all three conditions was restricted to respondents who gave an accurate semantic label.

Support for duality was equally strong for the two blocked conditions. This finding is relevant to the question of whether people may possess both dual and bipolar structures instead of just one. The 3-6-3 condition was designed to encourage duality. Placing the hostile and kind items into separate blocks should encourage independent cognitive representations. In contrast, the 6-6 condition, by commingling the hostile and kind item sets, was designed to facilitate the emergence of bipolarity. The domination of duality across both conditions, as evidenced by the trait-recognition data, suggests that bipolar dimensional cognitive structures may not even exist as possibilities for representing test constructs.

The factor analysis results suggest that the construct acquired by respondents in the random condition was less clearly focused on the dual hostile/kind construct. This raises the question of what representation of the test actually emerged in the random condition. Perhaps those respondents formed a more globally evaluative construct, or perhaps they formed a dual structure that was diluted by the heterogeneous distractor traits.

It is important to add a cautionary note to our interpretation of the factor analysis findings. The observed item-sequence differences require replication. They were based on a relatively small sample size, and no analytic technique was available to assess their stability statistically. However, our confidence in the factor analysis results is bolstered by their close fit with the clearly reliable item-recognition data.

Implications for Survey Research

The results of these studies are relevant to several issues that arise in many surveys. Surveys sometimes include multi-item inventories that have been previously developed and validated by psychologists and sociologists for other purposes. Often the original tests will include distractor items. When used in surveys, these distractor items are often omitted in the interests of reducing the time and expense involved in survey preparation and administration. Since the inventories are normally validated with the distractor items included, questions of validity arise when those items are removed.

The present studies suggest that when it is desirable for respondents to acquire a test construct, omitting distractor items should help more than it hurts. Responses that derive from a correctly inferred test construct should more consistently reflect the latent variable intended by the survey designer than do responses that derive from an incorrectly activated cognitive representation. Of course, the ultimate criterion is whether respondents using a correctly activated latent construct produce answers that have higher construct and predictive validity. Research by Hewstone and Young (1988) suggests that this may be the case. They found that unipolar attitude measures were better predictors of behavior than were bipolar measures. It is clear that more work is needed on this point.

A second implication for survey research concerns the use of bipolar rating scales in surveys. For example, candidates for political office may be rated on a scale of trustworthy to untrustworthy. Our conclusions regarding duality suggest that it would be better to provide two unipolar scales than one bipolar scale. Each of the separate scales coincides with existing cognitive structures, thereby yielding responses that are more valid indicators of the latent structures.

The duality conception provides theoretical support for an interesting finding by Krosnick and Berent (in press). They report superior test–retest reliability when using branching over nonbranching attitude measures. Branching measures first ask persons to select the pole (e.g., Republican vs. Democrat) that they endorse. Then the respondents indicate how strongly or weakly they support the chosen position. Nonbranching questions present respondents with the usual bipolar rating format. The branching technique has the advantage of framing the question in terms of the dual structures that people actually have and use for issues such as party identification (Republican/Democrat), ideological orientation (liberal/conservative), and defense spending (more/less).

The use of separate unipolar scales has an additional advantage. For example, research might show that a particular group of political candidates were perceived as differing on ratings of untrustworthiness but not on ratings of trustworthiness. This would suggest that trustworthiness, as a representational structure, is not relevant to the respondents when appraising these candidates. One possible implication of this outcome would be that campaign advertising should not focus on the positive (making one's own candidate a better exemplar of trustworthiness) because this is not a source of differentiation between candidates for the voters. On the other hand, negative campaigns (moving one's opponent to become a better exemplar of the untrustworthy category) should be highly effective.

In conclusion, we propose that item-order effects are driven by the construct that respondents develop as they move through a test or survey. In the case of many psychological tests (such as the one used in the present studies), only one construct is being measured. Respondents are often aware of that fact. However, in the typical survey, a heterogeneous array of constructs are assessed, including demographic, attitudinal, and informational constructs. Survey researchers must be cognizant of the fact that while transitions from one construct to another may be obvious to them, those transitions may not be evident to the respondents. Respondents may carry a hypothesis about the purpose of the survey from one section to another, with the consequence of using a completely inappropriate latent construct as the basis of their later responses. To the extent that this happens, the resulting answers will certainly have poor construct and predictive validity.

The present chapter is consistent with many others in this volume that advocate a need to understand the cognitive activity of respondents as they generate responses to survey items. The unique contributions of this chapter are to show that bipolar constructs appear to have a dualistic cognitive representation, that the cognitive properties of latent psychometric constructs can actually be measured, and that the cognitive representation of a test or survey item can be affected by item sequence. Undoubtedly, new issues will arise as we move from multi-item trait-rating tasks to other test structures. Nonetheless, emerging principles from cognitive psychology are certain to prove helpful regardless of the latent construct under investigation.

Acknowledgments. We are indebted to helpful suggestions from Brooke Leaton. Support for statistical analyses was provided by the Ohio State University Computer and Information Sciences computer facilities.

Part VI
Summary

21
What Have We Learned?

Norman N. Bradburn

I approach the consideration of order effects in surveys with the opposite bias from Howard Schuman (cf. chap. 2). It seems to me quite likely that the order in which questions are asked will have effects on the answers that respondents give. Indeed, there have been many examples in the literature almost from the beginning of surveys (American Marketing Association, 1937; Cantril, 1944). The results from research on order effects, however, have been so confusing and contradictory that it is tempting to conclude that the positive cases demonstrating order effects are really artifacts of some sort or build on chance findings. Why, then, do I persist in the belief that there are probably significant order effects and that it is important for us to understand them?

The answer lies in my conception of the survey interview and what we know about ordinary behavior. I view the survey interview as a special case of conversations between individuals. It is a special case, a "conversation with a purpose," as Bingham and Moore (1934) described it long ago, because it has a definite structure and some rules of its own that make it different from casual conversations between friends or instrumental conversations between colleagues, to take examples of two other types of conversations. The structure consists of a social situation in which one person (the interviewer) has the role of asking the questions and the other person (the respondent) has the role of answering the questions, with the task defined by another person (the researcher), who has a particular purpose in mind—for example, to obtain information to answer some general scientific or practical questions. It is like all conversations in some ways, like many conversations in some ways, and like no other conversation in other ways. Methodological research on the survey process tends to focus on those aspects of the survey that are unique to a particular survey, thus like some or no other conversations, but to ignore those aspects of the survey process that it shares with most or all other types of conversations (see Suchman & Jordan, 1990, for a fuller discussion).

Everything that occurs during an interview has the potential to influence the answers given by respondents to the questions asked by the interviewer. The order in which questions are asked is only one part of the process and is unlikely to be the most important part. The most important part is surely the wording of the question itself, for the wording of the question is what the respondent must process in order to know what information is being sought, or, for that matter, to know that it is information that is being sought rather than, say, an expression of intentions or affect or some other type of communication that might be part of a conversation. This point is so fundamental that its importance is often overlooked. To take a vivid, but perhaps trivial, example, the difference between estimates of age based on the questions "How old are you?" and "When were you born?" will be much less than the difference between estimates based on the questions "How old are you?" and "When was your father born?" We know that there is a small difference in estimates made on the basis of the two questions about age; but these differences, although they may be extremely important in some cases, are trivial when compared with asking a question about the topic that you are interested in and asking about something else. Bradburn's rule for question asking is, "Ask about what you want to know, not something else"—a deceptively simple and obvious rule but one that is all too often violated.

Compared with the effects of differences in question wording, even for questions on the same topic, order effects are apt to be rather small. In addition, they are likely to interact with other things that are going on, such as the topic under consideration, question wording, and characteristics of the respondent, hence causing some of the difficulty in finding them consistently or finding them where you might think that they are most likely to occur.

In oral interviews, whether in person or on the telephone, questions have to be asked in some order, although, of course, they need not be asked in the same order for everyone; but they must be in some order, usually predetermined, nonetheless. Unless there are some special arrangements, the predetermined order is (usually) known to the interviewer but not to the respondent. On mail questionnaires, the respondent can see the entire set of questions before answering any of them, although I do not know of any research that has investigated whether respondents typically do read or even leaf through the entire questionnaire before answering it. If order effects are due to the sequencing of information extracted from the questions, as is commonly assumed, then either we should find no order effects in self-administered questionnaires or at least the order effects should be considerably attenuated (Bishop, Hippler, Schwarz, & Strack, 1988; Schwarz, Strack, Hippler, & Bishop, in press).

There are, of course, many other things that go on in interviews besides asking questions, things that include nonsemantic information. For example, there is the social context within which the interview takes place—is it in the home with the respondent as a member of a sample of the population, is it in the workplace with the respondent as an employee of the sponsor of the research, is it in a researcher's office or laboratory with the respondent as a "subject" in an experiment or study whose purpose is perceived to contribute to scientific or practical knowledge? What are the social characteristics of the interviewer and the respondent? Many of these types of variables will have different effects depending on the interaction between the characteristics and the content of the questionnaire. And, of course, there will be individual differences in the degree to which respondents are influenced by any of these factors.

We must view order effects, then, as just one part of a complicated process of obtaining information through survey methods and not expect them to dominate all others. Instead, we must study them as a part of this whole process and understand the particular contribution that they may make to our goal of obtaining the most valid and reliable information possible.

Framework for Investigating Order Effects

One of the factors that has inhibited our progress in understanding order effects has been the lack of a theoretical structure within which to investigate the mechanisms by which they might occur. The recent attempts to view the question/answer interchange within the more general framework of information processing are, I believe, an important step in moving us forward. Two such frameworks, that of Strack and Martin (1987) and Tourangeau (1984), formed the basis of much of the discussion at the conference at Nags Head on which this volume is based. These models conceptualize the process as one of components that require different types of cognitive processing and thus might be susceptible to different types of context effects. I believe that viewing information processing as composed of different components is useful in directing us toward thinking about how information from preceding questions can affect responses. For convenience, I shall organize this discussion around Tourangeau's model of four components: interpretation, retrieval, judgment, and response.

Interpretation

One theme in studying order effects has been the way in which preceding questions affect the interpretation that respondents give to questions. Jaak Billiet (in a discussion at the conference) gave a good example of how preceding questions can radically influence the interpretation of what appears on the surface to be a fairly unambiguous question. Consider the question, "How many children do you have?" When this question was asked of teachers in the context of questions about their own families, it was interpreted as referring to their own biological children. When it was asked in the context of questions about their classroom, it was interpreted as referring to the number of children in their class. In their chapter in this volume, Moxey and Sanford (chap. 19) discuss many instances in which the context in which quantifiers are used affects the interpretations that respondents give the quantifier.

The degree to which the order of questions may influence their interpretation may depend on the relation of the content between questions. In order to study this problem more precisely, we need a better measure of the relatedness of consecutive questions. We need to be more sensitive, that is, have better ways to classify the ambiguity in language and contexts, in order to be able to predict better the types of influences that will occur. Some of the effects demonstrated in the work presented by Tourangeau (chap. 4) appear to be a function of the degree of relatedness between context and target items. These results, however, are based on the degree of correlation between earlier responses to context and target items, a measure that is not really adequate to measure relatedness of questions, since the measure should be focused on the relatedness of meaning, not of attitude.

Knowles et al. (chap. 15) indicate that order of questions also affects the interpretation given to items in a personality test. They argue that as respondents go through a multi-item personality test, they become more efficient in answering items and are able to neglect irrelevant meanings of an item. Answering early items teaches respondents about the abstract test construct and thereby concentrates their attention on the commonality of meanings that underlie the test items. For those who work primarily in the world of attitudinal surveys, it is heartening to see phenomena showing up in psychological measurement that are not usually thought to be subject to such order effects.

One of the more well established findings of research on order effects is that when a general question and a more specific related question are asked together, the general question may be affected by its position, whereas the more specific question is not. Such effects, particularly the elusive question-order effects on abortion questions, were discussed by Schuman (chap. 2) and Smith (chap. 12). Although we still have much to learn before we can reliably produce the phenomenon, it seems likely that the effects that do occur come at the interpretation component; that is, the interpretation of the general questions under some circumstances that are still poorly known can be altered by the preceding questions. We are still far from understanding exactly how or even when this happens.

Interpretive order effects can also involve response categories. The response categories read or shown to respondents may give them information about the meaning of questions. Schuman and Presser (1981) suggest something like this when they discuss the differences in responses to questions such as "What are the most important problems facing the nation today?" when they are given in open- and closed-ended form. Additional examples are given by Schwarz, Hippler, and Noelle-Neumann (chap. 13).

A particularly elegant demonstration of serial context effects is given by Daamen and de Bie (chap. 8). They show that ratings about the probabilities of events happening are affected by the characteristics of series of preceding questions that share the same response scale. The characteristics of the series that are most important appear to be the range of stimulus values and the frequency with which respondents have to deal with the response categories.

Tarnai and Dillman (chap. 9) and Schwarz et al. (chap. 13) remind us, however, that some effects may be limited by the mode of administration. In particular, telephone and face-to-face interviewing limit the amount of information that respondents have at any one time and emphasize the serial nature of questions. In contrast, mail or self-administered questionnaires allow the respondents to see all of the questions at more or less the same time and reduce the serial way in which questions and information are presented. Respondents can easily go back to earlier questions, answer questions out of the order in which they are in the questionnaire, and usually have more time in which to reflect on their answers. Thus it is not surprising that many of the context effects that are dependent on the order of presentation are eliminated or much reduced in mail questionnaires.

Retrieval

Priming, that is, previous stimuli making information differentially available in memory, is an important phenomenon studied by cognitive psychologists. The effect of priming is seen in the faster retrieval of the primed information from memory. Under standard survey conditions in which respondents are asked to answer questions on a number of topics under fairly rapid time pressure, particularly in telephone interviews, we might expect that questions (or introductions to groups of questions) will have a priming effect on memories related to the topic under discussion. Thus, questions later in a section of related questions might be influenced by those earlier in the questionnaire through their priming effect on related information. Such effects may be particularly important for questions about behavior that require retrieval of behavioral episodes from memory. Indeed, as Bradburn, Sudman, and Associates (1979) and Cannell, Marquis, and Laurent (1977) have shown, longer introductions to behavioral questions result in fuller reporting of behavior, an effect that is interpreted as due to priming of related memories. Salancik and Brand (chap. 16) show that priming of certain contexts can alter the way in which teaching assistants describe their jobs.

The priming of memories through activation of semantic networks is thought to be an automatic process. Individuals, however, will have somewhat different networks or hierarchies, so that the effect of activation will not be simple. If we think of attitudes as organized semantic structures in memory, priming may cause some respondents to retrieve new information, or it may just make some information more available than other information, so that it comes to the fore more readily than the nonprimed information.

Both Tourangeau (chap. 4) and a previously published article by Tourangeau, Rasinski, Bradburn, and D'Andrade (1989b) report studies suggesting that preceding context questions can prime schemata—sets of closely related arguments—that lead to different responses. Of particular interest is the finding that some attitudes (e.g., those about welfare) consist of schemata that are organized along a pro/con dimension, so that once one knows the schema activated, one knows the direction of support, whereas other attitudes (e.g., about abortion) consist of schemata that are not so organized and knowing which schema is activated does not give you any clear picture of what the resulting judgment would be. This difference in the underlying organization of schemata for different attitudes may be a clue to help us unravel the often-conflicting findings in the literature about order effects.

One of the mysteries still to be solved in the study of order effects is their differing direction. Sometimes the effect is one of assimilation, that is, subsequent responses are in the same direction as the preceding ones; sometimes the effect is one of contrast, that is, subsequent responses are in the opposite direction from the preceding ones. Both assimilation and contrast effects have been reported in the literature. Strack (chap. 3) argues that priming may have two functions: an activation and an information function. When activation of relevant information occurs automatically without respondent awareness, there may be an assimilation effect at the judgmental phase. When the priming results in awareness by the respondent of the relation between the context-setting question and the target question, then a contrast effect may occur as the primed information is consciously disregarded by the respondent.

The contrast effect is hypothesized to result from the Gricean Maxim of Quantity (Grice, 1975); that is, the respondent should be informative and avoid redundancy. The analysis of the survey questioning process in terms of ordinary conversational analysis is an interesting and potentially fruitful way to look at what is going on in a survey. As noted above, the survey interview shares some of the attributes of ordinary conversations and would not be expected to be exempt from the principles that govern any meaningful linguistic interchange. Insofar as there are general principles that structure expectations about such interchanges, they will be influential in the survey interview and we must understand them (see also Suchman & Jordan, 1990). Although priming is thought to be automatic, it is also clear that retrieval is partially a function of the amount of cognitive work that respondents are willing to do. If respondents are motivated to put a lot of effort into recall, they can report many more events than if they are not willing to put the effort into it (Williams & Hollan, 1981). Chapter 7 by Martin and Harlow is particularly intriguing because it suggests that filter questions may play a role in motivating respondents to engage in more or less cognitive effort depending on their reaction to their performance on a filter question. Further, the authors suggest a possible mechanism to account for why one sometimes gets assimilation and sometimes contrast effects, since contrast demands more cognitive effort than does assimilation. The effects of different forms of question order in motivating respondents to do more intensive cognitive work is definitely a line of research that should be pursued further.

Judgment

After questions are interpreted and the relevant information is retrieved from memory, respondents must still make a judgment about how the retrieved information can be used to answer the question; that is, they must still map their answers onto the response categories offered by the interviewer. Schwarz et al. (chap. 13) discuss ways in which the length and form of response alternatives can affect responses. Although some observed effects of position on long lists may be due to primacy and recency effects, which may work in the retrieval component, some of the effects of response alternatives appear to come about because of the implicit information in the response alternatives that allows respondents to fit their own attitudes or behavior onto a comparative scale and make a judgment about where they belong. Questions often explicitly, but sometimes implicitly, ask respondents to rate themselves in relation to an average value or along a dimension that has implicit distributional properties—for example, the response categories may require that respondents rate themselves as high or low or very high or very low, etc., on some dimension such as agreement, satisfaction, or support.

Bickart (chap. 6) notes that viewing brand evaluations as a judgment computed in response to questions in a marketing survey may be an informative way to understand how prior knowledge as well as question order may affect consumers' evaluations of products. Computed judgments in response to advertising or other information may be more prevalent for brand evaluations than for evaluations in other domains, such as social values, because consumers most often have comparative brand information available to them at the time that they are making the judgment. Such effects, however, might be mediated by the amount of expertise that a consumer had in the particular area of consumer products being investigated. The more knowledgeable the consumers are about the product class, the less they should depend on the questions in the survey for information about the product and, thus, the less susceptible they should be to order effects.

Krosnick (chap. 14) also reminds us that some order effects are conditional on the characteristics of the respondent, such as their cognitive sophistication (perhaps similar to Bickart's experts) and the importance to them of their attitudes. Smith (chap. 12) also shows the importance of conditional effects.

Evoking norms explicitly or implicitly may affect responses at the judgment component. Question order may evoke a norm of reciprocity that, I would argue, affects responses at the judgment component. Billiet, Waterplas, and Loosveldt (chap. 10) also report an experiment that suggests that question order can evoke different norms, which, in turn, affect the responses given to questions.

The general point here is that both preceding questions and response categories may evoke some sort of norms or standards of reference that respondents use to match the ideas and thoughts retrieved with the answer alternatives being offered by the interviewer. We would expect that the effect is somewhat more pronounced in closed-ended questions, where the response categories are fixed and respondents are forced to pick among a limited array of possibilities, than in open-ended questions, where respondents can answer in their own terms. Even here, however, contextual information about norms and standards of reference will be used by respondents.

Bodenhausen (chap. 18) takes the general point further by discussing ways in which generic knowledge structures perform different information-processing functions and how they might influence responses if evoked prior to the asking of particular target questions. He points out the importance of the order of questions that evoke generic knowledge structures because "pre-information effects" are different from "post-information effects." Ostrom, Betz, and Skowronski (chap. 20) approach the same general question from the point of view of the cognitive representation of latent variables but use the order effects to infer something about the underlying structure of response scales. In effect, they turn the questions that most of the other authors address inside out. They use order effects to show that a test will have a specific cognitive representation and that this latent structure can be measured by manipulating the order of items.

Responses

After respondents make their judgments about the answers that fit the questions, they must actually produce the answers so that the interviewers can record them. It is at this component that issues such as self-presentation and consistency may come into play, which might alter the answers that are reported. The chapters in this volume do not deal with this component of the response process, possibly because question order is less likely to influence perceptions of social desirability, although order can certainly provide opportunities for inconsistency. This is a topic that could be profitably pursued at a future conference.

What Progress Have We Made?

At conferences such as the one at Nags Head, we often lament the lack of progress in our understanding of some phenomena. This conference was no exception, but I think that we may be overreacting. I believe that we have made some progress over the years since scientific surveys have been on the scene. I would distinguish three stages in our understanding. The first stage, which began almost with the birth of survey research in the 1930s, consisted of research that demonstrated that question-order effects did in fact exist and could alter results. We might call this a "demonstration period." Sometime in the 1950s, concern began to move toward classifying the types of effects that might result from question order. In an early paper of mine (Bradburn & Mason, 1964), I distinguished four types of order effects: redundancy, salience, consistency, and fatigue. It now looks to me as if the first three might map fairly easily onto the effects in the components discussed here; that is, redundancy effects look like what we discussed here as occurring in the interpretation component, salience is similar to priming, and consistency looks as if it may be either at the judgment or response component. Smith (chap. 12) has done an excellent job in reviewing some of the major types of order effects and comparing our taxonomy with that of Schuman and Presser (1981) and testing it against the Tourangeau and Rasinski (1988) framework. It is too much to ask that there should be an easy correspondence, but it is encouraging that the discussions of types of effects in the 1960s and early 1970s can be interpreted in the new framework.

With the advent of the information-processing approach to studying response errors in surveys, we are moving from classification to explanation. We now have the beginning of a theoretical framework within which we can investigate order effects and expect that our work will be cumulative and that we will begin to make greater headway in understanding the mechanisms by which different types of order effects are produced. We also are using some new methods, such as think-aloud protocols, to understand better the actual cognitive processes that respondents go through when they are answering questions (see Bishop, chap. 11) and are experiencing an exciting growth in experiments testing the new theoretical frameworks. The chapters in this volume demonstrate the vigor of the current work and move us a good way in the direction of explanation. I look forward to further progress.

References

Abelson, R. P. (1981). The psychological status of the script concept. *American Psychologist, 36*, 715–729.

Abelson, R. P. (1984.) Contextual influences within sets of survey questions. In C. F. Turner & E. Martin (Eds.), *Surveying subjective phenomena* (Vol. 1, pp. 287–295). New York: Russell Sage Foundation.

Alba, J. W., & Hasher, L. (1983). Is memory schematic? *Psychological Bulletin, 93*, 203–231.

Alba, J. W., & Hutchinson, J. W. (1987). Dimensions of consumer expertise. *Journal of Consumer Research, 13*, 411–454.

Alba, J. W., Hutchinson, J. W., & Lynch, J. G., Jr. (1991). Memory and decision making. In T. S. Robertson & H. H. Kassarjian (Eds.), *Handbook of consumer behavior* (pp. 1–49). Englewood Cliffs, NJ: Prentice-Hall.

Allport, G. (1943). The ego in contemporary psychology. *Psychological Review, 50*, 451–478.

American Marketing Association. (1937). *The technique of marketing research.* New York: McGraw-Hill.

Anastasi, A. (1988). *Psychological testing* (6th ed.). New York: Macmillan.

Anderson, J. R. (1983). *The architecture of cognition.* Cambridge: Harvard University Press.

Anderson, N. H. (1981). *Foundations of information integration theory.* New York: Academic Press.

Anderson, N. H., & Hubert, S. (1963). Effects of concomitant verbal recall on order effects in personality impression formation. *Journal of Verbal Learning and Verbal Behavior, 2*, 379–391.

Anderson, R. C., & Pichert, J. W. (1978). Recall of previously unrecallable information following a shift in perspective. *Journal of Verbal Learning and Verbal Behavior, 17*, 1–12.

Aronson, E. (1969). The theory of cognitive dissonance: A current perspective. In L. Berkowitz (Ed.), *Advances in experimental social psychology* (Vol. 4, pp. 1–34). New York: Academic Press.

Aronson, E., Ellsworth, P. C., Carlsmith, J. M., & Gonzales, M. (1990). *Methods in research in social psychology* (2nd ed.). New York: McGraw-Hill.

Astin, A. W., Green, K. C., Korn, W. S., Schalit, M., & Berz, E. R. (1988). *The American freshman: National norms for fall 1988.* Los Angeles: Higher Education Research Institute.

Baillet, S. D., & Keenan, J. M. (1986). The role of encoding and retrieval processes in the recall of text. *Discourse Processes, 9,* 247–268.

Bargh, J. A. (1984). Automatic and conscious processing of social information. In R. S. Wyer, Jr., & T. K. Srull (Eds.), *Handbook of social cognition* (Vol. 3, pp. 1–43). Hillsdale, NJ: Erlbaum.

Bargh, J. A. (1988). Conditional automaticity: Varieties of automatic influence in social perception and cognition. In J. S. Uleman & J. A. Bargh (Eds.), *Unintended thought* (pp. 3–51). New York: Guilford Press.

Bargh, J. A., & Pratto, F. (1986). Individual construct accessibility and perceptual selection. *Journal of Experimental Social Psychology, 22,* 293–311.

Baron, R. S., & Roper, G. (1976). Reaffirmation of social comparison views of choice shifts: Averaging and extremity effects in an autokenetic situation. *Journal of Personality and Social Psychology, 33,* 521–530.

Barsalou, L. W. (1987). The instability of graded structure: Implications for the nature of concepts. In U. Neisser (Ed.), *Concepts and conceptual development: Ecological and intellectual factors in categorization* (pp. 101–140). Cambridge, England: Cambridge University Press.

Barton, S. B., & Sanford, A. J. (1990). The control of attributional patterns by the focussing properties of quantifying expressions. *Journal of Semantics, 7.*

Bass, B. M., Cascio, W. F., & O'Connor, E. J. (1974). Magnitude estimations of expressions of frequency and amount. *Journal of Applied Psychology, 59,* 313–320.

Beck, A. T., Rush, A. J., Shaw, B. F., & Emmery, G. (1979). *Cognitive therapy of depression: A treatment manual.* New York: Guilford Press.

Becker, S. L. (1954). Why an order effect? *Public Opinion Quarterly, 18,* 271–278.

Bellezza, F. S., & Bower, G. H. (1981). Person stereotypes and memory for people. *Journal of Personality and Social Psychology, 41,* 856–865.

Belson, W. A. (1966). The effects of reversing the presentation order of verbal rating scales. *Journal of Advertising Research, 6,* 30–37.

Bem, D. J. (1972). Self-perception theory. In L. Berkowitz (Ed.), *Advances in experimental social psychology* (Vol. 6, pp. 2–62). New York: Academic Press.

Berscheid, E., & Walster, E. H. (1978). *Interpersonal attraction.* Reading, MA: Addison-Wesley.

Bettman, J. R. (1979). *An information processing theory of consumer choice.* Reading, MA: Addison-Wesley.

Bettman, J. R., & Sujan, M. (1987). Effects of framing on evaluation of comparable and noncomparable alternatives by expert and novice consumers. *Journal of Consumer Research, 14,* 141–154.

Biehal, G., & Chakravarti, D. (1983). Information accessibility as a moderator of consumer choice. *Journal of Consumer Research, 10,* 1–14.

Billiet, J. (1989, August). *Question-wording and context effects in survey questions about religion.* Paper presented at the 20th International Conference for the Sociology of Religion, Helsinki.

Billiet, J., & Dobbelaere, K. (1985). Vers une désinstitutionalisation du pilier chrétien? In L. Voyé, J. Billiet, & J. Remy, *La Belgique et ses dieux.* Louvain-La-Neuve, Belgium: Cabay.

Billiet, J., Waterplas, L., & Loosveldt, G. (1988). *Response-effecten bij survey-vragen in het Nederlands taalgebied.* Leuven, Belgium: Sociologisch Onder-zoeksinstuut.

Bingham,W. V. D., & Moore, B. V. (1934). *How to interview.* New York: Harper & Row.

Bishop, G. F. (1985, November). *Think-aloud responses to survey questions: Some first impressions from a pilot project.* Paper presented at the annual meeting of the Midwest Association for Public Opinion Research, Chicago.

Bishop, G. F. (1986, July) Think-aloud responses to survey questions: Some evidence on context effects. Paper presented at the NORC Conference on Context Effects in Surveys, University of Chicago, Chicago.

Bishop, G. F. (1987). Context effects on self-perceptions of interest in government and public affairs. In H.-J. Hippler, N. Schwarz, & S. Sudman (Eds.), *Social information processing and survey methodology* (pp. 179–199). New York: Springer-Verlag.

Bishop, G. F., Hippler, H.-J., Schwarz, N. & Strack F. (1988). A comparison of response effects in self-administered and telephone surveys. In R. M. Groves, P. P. Biemer, L. E. Lyberg, J. T. Massey, W. L. Nicholls II, & J. Waksberg (Eds.), *Telephone survey methodology* (pp. 321–340). New York: Wiley.

Bishop, G. F., Oldendick, R. W., & Tuchfarber, A. J. (1982). Political information processing: Question order and context effects. *Political Behavior, 4,* 177–200.

Bishop, G. F., Oldendick, R. W., & Tuchfarber, A. J. (1984a). Interest in political campaigns: The influence of question order and electoral context. *Political Behavior, 6,* 159–169.

Bishop, G. F., Oldendick, R. W., & Tuchfarber, A. (1984b). What must my interest in politics be if I just told you "I don't know"? *Public Opinion Quarterly, 48,* 510–519.

Bishop, G. F., Oldendick, R. W., & Tuchfarber, A. J. (1985). The importance of replicating a failure to replicate: Order effects on abortion items. *Public Opinion Quarterly 49,* 105–114.

Bishop, G. F., Oldendick, R. W., Tuchfarber, A. J., & Bennett, S. E. (1980). Pseudo-opinions on public affairs. *Public Opinion Quarterly, 44,* 198–209.

Bishop, G. F., Tuchfarber, A. J., & Oldendick, R. W. (1986). Opinions on fictitious issues: The pressure to answer survey questions. *Public Opinion Quarterly, 50,* 240–250.

Bless, H., Bohner, G., Schwarz, N., & Strack, F. (1990). Mood persuasion: A cognitive response analysis. *Personality and Social Psychology Bulletin, 16,* 331–345.

Bobko, P. (1985). Removing assumptions of bipolarity: Towards variation and circularity. *Academy of Management Review, 10,* 99–108.

Bock, R. D., & Aitken, M. (1981). Marginal maximum likelihood estimation of item parameters: An application of the EM algorithm. *Psychometrika, 46,* 443–445.

Bock, R. D., & Lieberman, M. (1970). Fitting a response model for n dichotomously scored items. *Psychometrika, 35,* 179–197.

Bodenhausen, G. V. (1988). Stereotypic biases in social decision making and memory: Testing process models of stereotype use. *Journal of Personality and Social Psychology, 55,* 726–737.

Bodenhausen, G. V., & Wyer, R. S., Jr. (1987). Social cognition and social reality: Information acquisition and use in the laboratory and the real world. In H.-J.

Hippler, N. Schwarz, & S. Sudman (Eds.), *Social information processing and survey methodology* (pp. 6–41). New York: Springer-Verlag.

Bower, G., Black, J., & Turner, T. (1979). Scripts in comprehension and memory. *Cognitive Psychology, 11*, 177–220.

Bradburn, N. M. (1982). Question-wording effects in surveys. In R. M. Hogarth (Ed.), *Question framing and response consistency* (pp. 65–76). San Francisco: Jossey-Bass.

Bradburn, N. M. (1983). Response effects. In P. H. Rossi, J. D. Wright, & A. B. Anderson (Eds.), *Handbook of survey research* (pp. 289–328). New York: Academic Press.

Bradburn, N. M., & Mason, W. M. (1964). The effect of question order on responses. *Journal of Marketing Research, 1*, 57–61.

Bradburn, N. M., Rips, L. J., & Shevell, S. K. (1987). Answering autobiographical questions: The impact of memory and inference on surveys. *Science, 236*, 157–161.

Bradburn, N. M., Sudman, S., & Associates. (1979). *Improving interview method and questionnaire design: Response effects to threatening questions in survey research.* San Francisco: Jossey-Bass.

Brennan, R. L. (1983). *Elements of generalizability theory.* Iowa City, IA: American College Testing.

Brewer, M. B. (1988). A dual process model of impression formation. In T. K. Srull & R. S. Wyer, Jr. (Eds.), *Advances in social cognition* (Vol. 1, pp. 1–36). Hillsdale, NJ: Erlbaum.

Brewer, W. F., & Nakamura, G. V. (1984). The nature and functions of schemas. In R. S. Wyer, Jr., & T. K. Srull (Eds.), *Handbook of social cognition* (Vol. 1, pp. 119–160). Hillsdale, NJ: Erlbaum.

Brook, D., & Upton, G. J. G. (1974). Biases in local government elections due to position on the ballot paper. *Applied Statistics, 23*, 414–419.

Brown, D. R. (1953). Stimulus-similarity and the anchoring of subjective scales. *American Journal of Psychology, 66*, 199–214.

Bruce, D., & Papay, J. P. (1970). Primacy effects in free recall. *Journal of Verbal Learning and Verbal Behavior, 9*, 473–486.

Budd, R. J. (1987). Response bias and the theory of reasoned action. *Social Cognition, 5*, 95–107.

Budescu, D. V., Weinberg, S., & Wallsten, T. S. (1988). Decisions based on numerically and verbally expressed uncertainties. *Journal of Experimental Psychology: Human Perception and Performance, 14*, 281–294.

Burke, M. J., Brief, A. P., George, J. M., Roberson, L., & Webster, J. (1989). Measuring affect at work: Confirmatory analyses of competing mood structures with conceptual linkage to cortical regulatory systems. *Journal of Personality and Social Psychology, 57*, 1091–1102.

Burnkrant, R. E., & Unnava, H. R. (1989). Self-referencing: A strategy for increasing processing of message content. *Personality and Social Psychology Bulletin, 15*, 628–638.

Cacioppo, J. T., & Petty, R. E. (1982). The need for cognition. *Journal of Personality and Social Psychology, 42*, 116–131.

Campbell, J. D. (1986). Similarity and uniqueness: The effects of attribute type, relevance, and individual differences in self-esteem and depression. *Journal of Personality and Social Psychology, 50*, 281–294.

Cannell, C., Marquis, K. H., & Laurent, A. (1977). *A summary of studies of interviewing methodology* (Vital and Health Statistics, Series 2, No. 69). Washington, DC: U.S. Public Health Service.

Cantor, N., & Mischel, W. (1977). Traits as prototypes: Effects on recognition memory. *Journal of Personality and Social Psychology, 35,* 38–48.

Cantril, H. (1944). *Gauging public opinion.* Princeton, NJ: Princeton University Press.

Carlston, D. E. (1980). The recall and use of traits and events in social inference processes. *Journal of Experimental Social Psychology, 16,* 303–328.

Carp, F. M. (1974). Position effects on interview responses. *Journal of Gerontology, 29,* 581–587.

Carpenter, E. H., & Blackwood, L. G. (1979). The effect of question position on responses to attitudinal questions. *Rural Sociology, 44,* 56–72.

Chance, J. E. (1955). Prediction of changes in a personality inventory on retesting. *Psychological Reports, 1,* 383–387.

Chattopadhyay, A. (1986). *The relationship between message recall, cognitive responses and advertising effectiveness: The moderating effects of delay, context, and prior knowledge.* Doctoral dissertation, University of Florida.

Cialdini, R. B. (1984). *Influence: The new psychology of modern persuasion.* New York: Morrow.

Cialdini, R. B., Levy, A., Herman, C. P., & Evenback, S. (1973). Attitudinal politics: The strategy of moderation. *Journal of Personality and Social Psychology, 25,* 100–108.

Clark, H. H. (1985). Language use and language users. In G. Lindzey & E. Aronson (Eds.), *The handbook of social psychology: Vol 2. Special fields and applications* (3rd ed., pp. 179–231). New York: Random House.

Cliff, N. (1983). Some cautions concerning the application of causal modeling methods. *Multivariate Behavioral Research, 18,* 115–126.

Cochrane, R., & Rokeach, M. (1970). Rokeach's value survey: A methodological note. *Journal of Experimental Research in Personality, 4,* 159–161.

Cohen, C. E. (1981). Person categories and social perception: Testing some boundaries of the processing effects of prior knowledge. *Journal of Personality and Social Psychology, 40,* 441–452.

Coker, M. C., & Knowles, E. S. (1987, May). *Testing alters the test score: Test–retest improvements in anxiety also occur within the test.* Paper presented at the meeting of the Midwestern Psychological Association, Chicago.

Comrey, A. L. (1973). *A first course in factor analysis.* New York: Academic Press.

Converse, P. E. (1964). The nature of belief systems in mass publics. In D. E. Apter (Ed.), *Ideology and discontent* (pp. 75–169). New York: Free Press.

Converse, P. E. (1970). Attitudes and non-attitudes: Continuation of a dialogue. In E. R. Tufte (Ed.), *The quantitative analysis of social problems* (pp. 168–189). Reading, MA: Addison-Wesley.

Converse, P. E. (1980). Rejoinder to Judd and Milburn. *American Sociological Review, 45,* 644–646.

Cowan, C. D., Murphy, L. R., & Wiener, J. (1978). Effects of supplemental questions on victimization estimates from the National Crime Survey. *Proceedings of the American Statistical Association Section on Survey Research Methods* (pp. 277–285). Washington, DC: American Statistical Association.

Crano, W. D. (1983). Assumed consensus of attitudes: The effect of vested interest. *Personality and Social Psychology Bulletin, 9,* 597–608.

Crespi, I., & Morris, D . (1984). Question order effect and the measurement of candidate preference in the 1982 Connecticut elections. *Public Opinion Quarterly, 48,* 578–591.

Crowder, R. G. (1969). Behavioral strategies in immediate memory. *Journal of Verbal Learning and Verbal Behavior, 8,* 524–528.

Crowne, D. P., & Marlowe, D. (1964). *The approval motive: Studies in evaluative dependence.* New York: Wiley.

Daamen, D. D. L., & de Bie, S. E. (1989). *Context effects in face to face and telephone surveys: Effects of range and skewness of series of preceding questions on subjective probability judgments.* Unpublished manuscript, Association of Social Research Institutes, Amsterdam.

Daamen, D. D. L., & de Bie, S. E. (1990). *The relational nature of probability ratings in telephone surveys.* Manuscript submitted for publication.

Daemen, L. (1988). Een nieuwe blik op loglineaire modelselectie. Centrum voor Dataverzameling en-Analyze. Bulletin nr. 20. Leuven, Dept. Sociologie.

Davis, J. A., & Smith, T. W. (1989). *General Social Surveys, 1972–1989: Cumulative Codebook.* Chicago: NORC.

Dawes, R., & Smith, T. L. (1985). Attitude and opinion measurement. In G. Lindzey & E. Aronson (Eds.), *The handbook of social psychology: Vol. 1* (3rd ed., pp. 509–566). New York: Random House.

Devine, P. G. (1989). Stereotypes and prejudice: Their automatic and controlled components. *Journal of Personality and Social Psychology, 56,* 5–18.

Diener, E. (1984). Subjective well-being. *Psychological Bulletin, 95,* 542–575.

Diener, E., & Emmons, R. A. (1985). The independence of positive and negative affect. *Journal of Personality and Social Psychology, 47,* 1105–1117.

Dijkstra, W., & van der Zouwen, J. (1977). Testing auxiliary hypotheses behind the interview. *Annals of System Research, 6,* 49–63.

Dillehay, R., & Jernigan, L. R. (1970). The biased questionnaire as an instrument of opinion change. *Journal of Personality and Social Psychology, 15,* 144–150.

Dillman, D. A. (1978). *Mail and telephone surveys: The total design method.* New York: Wiley.

Dillman, D. A., & Mason, R. G. (1984, May). *The influence of survey method on question response.* Paper presented at the annual meeting of the American Association for Public Opinion Research, Delavan, WI.

Dillman, D. A., & Tarnai, J. (1988). Administrative issues in mixed mode surveys. In R. M. Groves, P. P. Biemer, L.E. Lyberg, J. T. Massey, W. L. Nicholls II, & J. Waksberg (Eds.), *Telephone survey methodology* (pp. 509–528). New York: Wiley.

Dobbelaere, K. (1985). La dominante Catholique. In L. Voyé, J. Billiet, & J. Remy, *La Belgique et ses dieux.* Louvain-La-Neuve, Belgium: Cabay.

Dobbelaere, K. (1988). Secularization, pillarization, religious involvement, and religious change in the low countries. In T. M. Gannon (Ed.), *World catholicism in transition* (pp. 80–115). New York: MacMillan.

Dreben, E. K., Fiske, S. T., & Hastie, R. (1979). The independence of evaluative and item information: Impression and recall order effects in behavior-based impression formation. *Journal of Personality and Social Psychology, 37,* 1758–1768.

Duncan, O. D. (1984). *Notes on social measurement: Historical and critical.* New York: Russell Sage.

Duverger, M. (1964). *Introduction to the social sciences*. London: George Allen & Unwin.

Ericsson, K. A., & Simon, H. A. (1984). *Protocol analysis: Verbal reports as data*. Cambridge: MIT Press.

Fazio, R. H. (1989). On the power and functionality of attitudes: The role of attitude accessibility. In A. R. Pratkanis, S. J. Breckler, and A. G. Greenwald (Eds.), *Attitude structure and function* (pp. 153–179). Hillsdale, NJ: Erlbaum.

Fazio, R. H., Chen, J., McDonel, E. C., & Sherman, S. J. (1982). Attitude accessibility, attitude–behavior consistency, and the strength of the object–evaluation association. *Journal of Experimental Social Psychology, 18*, 339–357.

Fazio, R. H., Lenn, T. M., & Effrein, E. A. (1983–1984). Spontaneous attitude formation. *Social Cognition, 2*, 217–234.

Fazio, R. H., Powell, M. C., & Herr, P. M. (1983). Toward a process model of the attitude-behavior relation: Accessing one's attitude upon mere observation of the attitude object. *Journal of Personality and Social Psychology, 44*, 723–735.

Fazio, R. H., Sanbonmatsu, D. M., Powell, M. C., & Kardes, F. R. (1986). On the automatic activation of attitudes. *Journal of Personality and Social Psychology, 50*, 229–238.

Fazio, R. H., & Zanna, M. P. (1981). Direct experience and attitude-behavior consistency. In L. Berkowitz (Ed.), *Advances in experimental social psychology* (Vol. 14, pp. 162–203). New York: Academic Press.

Fee, J. (1979). *Symbols and attitudes: How people think about politics*. Doctoral dissertation, University of Chicago.

Fehrer, E. (1952). Shifts in scale values of attitude statements as a function of the composition of the scale. *Journal of Experimental Psychology 44*, 179–188.

Feldman, J. M. (1981). Beyond attribution theory: Cognitive processes in performance appraisal. *Journal of Applied Psychology, 66*, 127–148.

Feldman, J. M. (1986). Instrumentation and training for performance appraisal: A perceptual-cognitive viewpoint. In K. M. Rowland and G. R. Ferris (Eds.), *Research in personnel and human resources management* (Vol. 4, pp. 45–100). Greenwich, CT: JAI Press.

Feldman, J. M. (1988, April). *Social cognition, reality, and job perception*. Paper presented at the annual meeting of the Society for Industrial and Organizational Psychology, Dallas, TX.

Feldman, J. M., & Lindell, M. K. (1990). On rationality. In I. Horowitz (Ed.), *Organization and decision theory* (pp. 83–164). Boston: Kluwer Academic.

Feldman, J. M., & Lynch, J. G., Jr. (1988). Self-generated validity and other effects of measurement on belief, attitude, intention, and behavior. *Journal of Applied Psychology, 73*, 421–435.

Feldman, J. M., Wesley, S. Hein, M., & Gilmore, A. (1989, October). *The influence of survey format on judgment processes: The case of ideals and perceived similarity*. Paper presented at the annual meeting of the Association for Consumer Research, New Orleans.

Fenigstein, A., Scheier, M. F., & Buss, A. H. (1975). Public and private self-consciousness: Assessment and theory. *Journal of Consulting and Clinical Psychology, 43*, 522–527.

Ferguson, G. A. (1941). The factorial interpretation of test difficulty. *Psychometrika, 6*, 323–329.

Fienberg, S. E., & Tanur, J. M. (1989). Combining cognitive and statistical approaches to survey design. *Science, 243*, 1017–1022.

Fischhoff, B., Slovic, P., & Lichtenstein, S. (1978). Fault trees: Sensitivity of estimated failure probabilities to problem representation. *Journal of Experimental Psychology: Human Perception and Performance, 4*, 330–344.

Fischhoff, B., Slovic, P., & Lichtenstein, S. (1980). Knowing what you want: Measuring labile values. In T. S. Wallsten (Ed.), *Cognitive processes in choice and decision behavior* (pp. 117–141). Hillsdale, NJ: Erlbaum.

Fishbein, M., & Ajzen, I. (1975). *Belief, attitude, intention and behavior: An introduction to theory and research.* Reading, MA: Addison-Wesley.

Fiske, D. W. (1957). An intensive study of variability scores. *Educational and Psychological Measurement, 17*, 453–465.

Fiske, D. W. (1967). The subject reacts to tests. *American Psychologist, 22*, 287–296.

Fiske, S. T., & Kinder, D. R. (1981). Involvement, expertise, and schema use: Evidence from political cognition. In N. Cantor and J. F. Kihlstrom (Eds.), *Personality, cognition, and social interaction* (pp. 171–190). Hillsdale, NJ: Erlbaum.

Fiske, S. T., & Linville, P. W. (1980). What does the schema construct buy us? *Personality and Social Psychology Bulletin, 6*, 543–557.

Fiske, S. T., & Pavelchak, M. A. (1986). Category-based versus piecemeal-based affective responses: Developments in schema-triggered affect. In R. M. Sorrentino & E. T. Higgins (Eds.), *The handbook of motivation and cognition: Foundations of social behavior* (pp. 167–203). New York: Guilford Press.

Fiske, S. T., & Taylor, S. E. (1990). *Social cognition* (2nd ed.). New York: Random House.

Gallup, G. (1947). The quintamensional plan of question design. *Public Opinion Quarterly, 11*, 385–393.

Getzels, J. W. (1982). The problem of the problem. In R. M. Hogarth (Ed.), *Question framing and response consistency* (pp. 37–49). San Francisco: Jossey-Bass.

Gibson, C. O., Shapiro, G. M., Murphy, L. R., & Stanko, G. J. (1978). Interaction of survey questions as it relates to interview-respondent bias. *Proceedings of the American Statistical Association Section on Survey Research Methods* (pp. 251–256). Washington, DC: American Statistical Association.

Glazner, M. (1972). Storage mechanisms in recall. In G. H. Bower (Ed.), *The psychology of learning and motivation* (Vol. 5, pp. 129–193). New York: Academic Press.

Glick, W. H., Jenkins, G. D., & Gupta, N. (1986). Method versus substance: How strong are underlying relationships between job characteristics and attitudinal outcomes? *Academy of Management Journal, 29*, 441–464.

Goldberg, L. R. (1978). The reliability of reliability: The generality and correlates of intra-individual consistency in responses to structured personality inventories. *Applied Psychological Measurement, 2*, 269–291.

Goocher, B. E. (1965). Effect of attitude and experience on the selection of frequency adverbs. *Journal of Verbal Learning and Verbal Behavior, 4*, 193–195.

Goocher, B. E. (1969). More about often. *American Psychologist, 24*, 608–609.

Graesser, A. C., & Black, J. B. (Eds.). (1985). *The psychology of questions.* Hillsdale, NJ: Erlbaum.

Graesser, A. C., Woll, S. B., Kowalski, D. J., & Smith, D. A. (1980). Memory for typical and atypical actions in scripted activities. *Journal of Experimental Psychology: Human Learning and Memory, 6,* 503–515.

Gravetter, F., & Lockhead, G. R. (1973). Critical range as frame of reference for stimulus judgment. *Psychological Review, 80,* 203–216.

Green, R. F., & Goldfried, M. R. (1965). On the bipolarity of semantic space. *Psychological Monographs: General and Applied, 79,* No. 6.

Greenwald, A. G., Pratkanis, A. R., Leippe, M. R., & Baumgardner, M. H. (1986). Under what conditions does theory obstruct research progress? *Psychological Review, 93,* 216–229.

Grice, H. P. (1975). Logic and conservation. In P. Cole & J. L. Morgan (Eds.), *Syntax and semantics 3: Speech acts* (pp. 41–58). New York: Academic Press.

Griffin, R. W. (1983). Objective and social sources of information in task redesign: A field experiment. *Administrative Science Quarterly, 28,* 184–200.

Groves, R. M. (1989). *Survey error and survey costs.* New York: Wiley.

Hackman, J. R., & Oldham, G. (1980). *Work redesign.* Reading, MA.: Addison-Wesley.

Hambleton, R. K., & Swaminathan, H. (1985). *Item response theory: Principles and applications.* Boston: Kluwer-Nijhoff.

Hambleton, R. K., & Traub, R. S. (1974). The effects of item order on test performance and stress. *Journal of Experimental Education, 43,* 40–46.

Hamilton, D. L., & Trolier, T. K. (1986). Stereotypes and stereotyping: An overview of the cognitive approach. In J. Dovidio & S. Gaertner (Eds.), *Prejudice, discrimination, and racism* (pp. 127–163). Orlando, FL: Academic Press.

Harkins, S. G., & Petty, R. E. (1981). The multiple source effect in persuasion: The effects of distraction. *Personality and Social Psychology Bulletin, 7,* 627–635.

Harman, H. H. (1976). *Modern factor analysis* (3rd ed.). Chicago: University of Chicago Press.

Harris, R. J. (1975). *A primer of multivariate statistics.* New York: Academic Press.

Hastie, R., & Park, B. (1986). The relationship between memory and judgment depends on whether the judgment task is memory-based or on-line. *Psychological Review, 93,* 258–268.

Haubensak, G. (1981). Eine erweiterung der range-frequency-theorie des absoluten urteils (An extension of range-frequency theory on absolute judgments). *Psychologische Beiträge, 23,* 46–64.

Haviland, S. E., & Clark, H. H. (1974). What's new? Acquiring new information as a process in comprehension. *Journal of Verbal Learning and Verbal Behavior, 13,* 512–521.

Hayes, D. P. (1964). Item order and Guttman scales. *American Journal of Sociology, 70,* 51–58.

Heisenberg, W. (1958). *The physicist's conception of nature* (A. J. Pomerans, Trans.). New York: Harcourt, Brace. (Original work published 1955).

Helson, H. (1964). *Adaptation-level theory: An experimental and systematic approach to behavior.* New York: Harper & Row.

Herr, P. M. (1989). Priming price: Prior knowledge and context effects. *Journal of Consumer Research, 16,* 67–75.

Herr, P. M., Sherman, S. J., & Fazio, R. H. (1983). On the consequences of priming: Assimilation and contrast effects. *Journal of Experimental Social Psychology, 19,* 323–340.

Herzberg, F., Mausner, B., & Snyderman, B. (1959). *The motivation to work.* New York: Wiley.

Hewstone, M., & Young, L. (1988). Expectancy-value models of attitude: measurement and combination of evaluations and beliefs. *Journal of Applied Social Psychology, 18*, 958–971.

Higgins, E. T. (1989a). Knowledge accessibility and activation: Subjectivity and suffering from unconscious sources. In J. S. Uleman & J. A. Bargh (Eds.), *Unintended thought* (pp. 75–123). New York: Guilford Press.

Higgins, E. T. (1989b). Self-discrepancy theory: What patterns of self-beliefs cause people to suffer? In L. Berkowitz (Ed.), *Advances in experimental social psychology* (Vol. 22, pp. 93–136). San Diego: Academic Press.

Higgins, E. T., Bargh, J. A., & Lombardi, W. J. (1985). Nature of priming effects on categorization. *Journal of Experimental Psychology: Learning, Memory, and Cognition, 11*, 59–69.

Higgins, E. T., & King, G. (1981). Accessibility of social constructs: Information-processing consequences of individual and contextual variability. In N. Cantor and J. F. Kihlstrom (Eds.), *Personality, cognition, and social interaction* (pp. 69–121). Hillsdale, NJ: Erlbaum.

Higgins, E. T., King, G. A., & Mavin, G. H. (1982). Individual construct accessibility and subjective impressions and recall. *Journal of Personality and Social Psychology, 43*, 35–47.

Higgins, E. T., & Lurie, L. (1983). Context, categorization, and recall: The "change-of-standard" effect. *Cognitive Psychology, 15*, 525–547.

Higgins, E. T., & Rholes, W. S. (1978). "Saying is believing": Effects of message modification on memory and liking for the person described. *Journal of Experimental Social Psychology, 14*, 363–378.

Higgins, E. T., Rholes, W. S., & Jones, C. R. (1977). Category accessibility and impression formation. *Journal of Experimental Social Psychology, 13*, 141–154.

Hilton, D. J., & Slugoski, B. R. (1986). Knowledge-based causal attribution: The abnormal conditions focus model. *Psychological Review, 93*, 75–88.

Hippler, H.-J., & Schwarz, N. (1986). Not forbidding isn't allowing: The cognitive basis of the forbid-allow asymmetry. *Public Opinion Quarterly, 50*, 87–96.

Hippler, H.-J., & Schwarz, N. (1987). Response effects in surveys. In H.-J. Hippler, N. Schwarz, & S. Sudman (Eds.), *Social information processing and survey methodology* (pp. 102–112). New York: Springer-Verlag.

Hippler, H.-J., Schwarz, N., & Noelle-Neumann, E. (1989, May). *Response order effects: The impact of administration mode* (ZUMA-Arbeitsbericht No. 17/89). Paper presented at the annual meeting of American Association for Public Opinion Research, St. Petersburg Beach, FL.

Hippler, H.-J., Schwarz, N., & Sudman, S. (Eds.). (1987). *Social information processing and survey methodology*. New York: Springer-Verlag.

Hoch, S. J. (1984). Availability and interference in predictive judgment. *Journal of Experimental Psychology: Learning, Memory, and Cognition, 10*, 649–662.

Hochstim, J. R. (1967). A critical comparison of three strategies of collecting data from households. *American Statistical Association Journal, 62*, 976–989.

Hogarth, R. M. (Ed.). (1982). *Question framing and response consistency*. San Francisco: Jossey-Bass.

Hogarth, R. M. (1987). *Judgment and choice* (2nd ed.) New York: Wiley.

Holyoak, K. J., & Koh, K. (1987). Surface and structural similarity in analogical transfer. *Memory & Cognition, 15*, 332–340.

Hörmann, H. (1983). The calculating listener or how many are *einige, mehrere,* and *ein paar* (some, several, and a few)? In R. Bauerle, C. Schwarze, & A. von Stechow (Eds.), *Meaning, use, and interpretation of language* (pp. 221–234). Berlin: de Gruyter.

Hovland, C., Harvey, O., & Sherif, M. (1957). Assimilation and contrast effects in communication and attitude change. *Journal of Abnormal and Social Psychology, 55*, 242–252.

Howard, K. I. (1964). Differentiation of individuals as a function of repeated testing. *Educational and Psychological Measurement, 24*, 875–894.

Howard, K. I., & Diesenhaus, H. (1965). 16 PF item response patterns as a function of repeated testing. *Educational and Psychological Measurement, 25*, 365–379.

Howell, W. C., & Burnett, S. A. (1978). Uncertainty measurement: A cognitive taxonomy. *Organizational Behavior and Human Performance, 22*, 45–68.

Hulin, C. L., Drasgow, F., & Parsons, C. K. (1983). *Item response theory: Application to psychological measurement*. Homewood, IL: Dorsey.

Hutchinson, J. W. (1983). On the locus of range effects in judgment and choice. In R. P. Bagozzi and A. M. Tybout (Eds.), *Advances in consumer research* (Vol. 10, pp. 305–308). Ann Arbor, MI: Association for Consumer Research.

Hyman, H. H., & Sheatsley, P. B. (1950). The current status of American public opinion. In J. C. Payne (Ed.), *The teaching of contemporary affairs: Twenty-first yearbook of the National Council for the Social Studies* (pp. 11–34). New York: National Education Association.

Idazak, J., & Drasgow, F. (1987). A revision of the Job Diagnostic Survey: Elimination of a measurement artifact. *Journal of Applied Psychology, 72*, 69–74.

Isen, A. M. (1989). Some ways in which affect influences cognitive processes: Implications for advertising and consumer behavior. In P. Caffereta & A. Tybout (Eds.), *Cognitive and affective responses to advertising* (pp. 90–117). New York: Lexington.

Israelski, E. W., & Lenoble, J. S. (1982). Rater fatigue in job analysis surveys. *Proceedings of the Human Factors Society* (pp. 35–39). Santa Monica, CA: Human Factors Society.

Iyengar, S., Kinder, D.R., Peters, M. D., & Krosnick, J. A. (1984). The evening news and presidential evaluations. *Journal of Personality and Social Psychology, 46*, 778–787.

Jackson, D. N. (1971). The dynamics of structured personality tests. *Psychological Review, 78*, 229–248.

Jacoby, L. L. (1984). Incidental vs. intentional retrieval: Remembering and awareness as separate issues. In L. R. Squire & N. Butters (Eds.), *Neuropsychology of memory*. New York: Guilford Press.

Jacoby, L. L., & Kelley, C. M. (1987). Unconscious influences of memory for a prior event. *Personality and Social Psychology Bulletin, 13*, 314–336.

Jacoby, L. L., Kelley, C., Brown, J., & Jasechko, J. (1989). Becoming famous overnight: Limits on the ability to avoid unconscious influences of the past. *Journal of Personality and Social Psychology, 56*, 326–338.

Jacoby, L. L., Woloshyn, V., & Kelley, C. (1989). Becoming famous without being recognized: Unconscious influences of memory produced by dividing attention. *Journal of Experimental Psychology: General, 118*, 115–125.

James, L. R., & Tetrick, L. E. (1986). Confirmatory analytic tests of three causal models relating job perceptions to job satisfaction: An examination of reciprocal causation. *Journal of Applied Psychology, 71*, 77–82.

James, W. H. (1957). *Internal versus external control of reinforcement as a basic variable in learning theory.* Doctoral dissertation, Ohio State University.

Johnson, D. W., & Ahlgren, A. (1976). Relationship between student attitudes about cooperation and competition and attitudes toward schooling. *Journal of Educational Psychology, 68,* 92–102.

Johnson, R. M. (1971). Market segmentation: A strategic management tool. *Journal of Marketing Research, 13,* 13–18.

Jones, E. E., & Harris, V. A. (1967). The attribution of attitudes. *Journal of Experimental Social Psychology, 3,* 1–24.

Jones, E. E., & Nisbett, R. E. (1972). The actor and the observer: Divergent perceptions of the causes of behavior. In E. E. Jones, D. AE Kanouse, H. H. Kelley, R. E. Nisbett, S. Valins, & B. Weiner (Eds.), *Attribution: Perceiving the causes of behavior* (pp. 79–94). Morristown, NJ: General Learning Press.

Jöreskog, K. G. (1974). Analyzing psychological data by structural analysis of covariance matrices. In D. H. Krantz, R. C. Atkinson, R. D. Luce, & P. Suppes (Eds.), *Contemporary developments in mathematical psychology: Vol. II. Measurement, psychophysics, and neural information processing* (pp. 1–56). San Francisco: Freeman.

Jöreskog, K. G., & Sörbom, D. (1989). *LISREL 7: A guide to the program and application.* Chicago: SPSS.

Judd, C. M., & Krosnick, J. A. (1989). The structural bases of consistency among political attitudes: Effects of political expertise and attitude importance. In A. R. Pratkanis, S. J. Breckler, and A. G. Greenwald (Eds.), *Attitude structure and function* (pp. 99–128). Hillsdale, NJ: Erlbaum.

Judd, C. M., & Lusk, C. M. (1984). Knowledge structures and evaluative judgments: Effects of structural variables on judgmental extremity. *Journal of Personality and Social Psychology, 46,* 1193–1207.

Judd, C. M., & Milburn, M. A. (1980). The structure of attitude systems in the general public: Comparisons of a structural equation model. *American Sociological Review, 45,* 627–643.

Kahn, R. L., & Cannell, C. F. (1957). *The dynamics of interviewing.* New York: Wiley.

Kahneman, D., & Miller, D. T. (1986). Norm theory: Comparing reality to its alternatives. *Psychological Review, 93,* 136–153.

Kahneman, D., Slovic, P., & Tversky, A. (Eds.). (1982). *Judgment under uncertainty: Heuristics and biases.* New York: Cambridge University Press.

Kalton, G., Collins, M., & Brook, L. (1978). Experiments in wording opinion questions. *Applied Statistics, 27,* 149–161.

Kalton, G., Collins, M., & Brook, L. (1978). Experiments in wording opinion questions. *Journal of the Royal Statistical Society (Series C), 27,* 149–161.

Kaplan, K. (1972). On the ambivalence-indifference problem in attitude theory and measurement. *Psychological Bulletin, 77,* 361–372.

Kardes, F. R. (1986a). Effects of initial product judgments on subsequent memory-based judgments. *Journal of Consumer Research, 13,* 1–11.

Kardes, F. R. (1986b) *Spontaneous inference processes in advertising: The effects of conclusion omission and salience of consequences on attitudes and memory* (MIT Working Paper No. 1832–87). Cambridge: Massachusetts Institute of Technology, Sloan School of Management.

Katz, D. (1960). The functional approach to the study of attitudes. *Public Opinion Quarterly, 24,* 163–204.

Keller, K. L. (1987). Memory factors in advertising: The effect of advertising retrieval cues on brand evaluations. *Journal of Consumer Research, 14,* 316–333.

Keller, K. L. (1991). Memory and evaluation effects in competitive advertising environments. *Journal of Consumer Research, 17,* 463–476.

Kerlinger, F. N. (1967). Social attitudes and their criterial referents. *Psychological Review, 74,* 110–122.

Kerlinger, F. N. (1984). *Liberalism and conservatism: The nature and structure of social attitudes.* Hillsdale, NJ: Erlbaum.

Kiesler, C. A. (1971). *The psychology of commitment: Experiments linking behavior to belief.* New York: Academic Press.

Kimble, G. A., & Perlmuter, L. C. (1970). The problem of volition. *Psychological Review, 77,* 361–384.

Kinder, D. R., & Sanders, L. M. (1990). Mimicking political debate with survey questions: The case of white opinion on affirmative action for blacks. *Social Cognition, 8,* 73–103.

Klayman, J., & Ha, Y. (1984). *Confirmation, disconfirmation, and information in hypothesis-testing.* Unpublished manuscript, University of Chicago, Graduate School of Business, Center for Decision Research.

Knowles, E. S. (1988). Item context effects on personality scales: Measuring changes the measure. *Journal of Personality and Social Psychology, 55,* 312–320.

Knowles, E. S., Coker, M. C., & Diercks, S. R. (1988). [Failure to find reliability shifts with the Beck Depression Inventory]. Unpublished data, University of Arkansas, Department of Psychology.

Knowles, E. S., Cook, D. A., & Neville, J. W. (1989a, June). *Modifiers of context effects on personality tests: Verbal ability and need for cognition.* Paper presented at the meeting of the American Psychological Society, Alexandria, VA.

Knowles, E. S., Cook, D. A., & Neville, J. W. (1989b, August). *Assessing adjustment improves subsequent adjustment scores.* Paper presented at the meeting of the American Psychological Association, New Orleans.

Knowles, E. S., & Diercks, S. R. (1988, April). *Experience with personality test items augments a subject's understanding of what is being measured.* Paper presented at the meeting of the Midwestern Psychological Association, Chicago.

Knowles, E. S., Lundeen, E. J., & Irwin, M. E. (1988, May). *Experience with the personality test changes factor loadings on externality but not self-monitoring.* Paper presented at the meeting of the Midwestern Psychological Association, Chicago.

Koriat, A., Lichtenstein, S., & Fischhoff, B. (1980). Reasons for confidence. *Journal of Experimental Psychology: Human Learning and Memory, 6,* 107–118.

Krosnick, J. A. (1986). *Policy voting in American presidential elections: An application of psychological theory to American politics.* Doctoral dissertation, University of Michigan.

Krosnick, J. A. (1988). The role of attitude importance in social evaluation: A study of policy preferences, presidential candidate evaluations, and voting behavior. *Journal of Personality and Social Psychology, 55,* 196–210.

Krosnick, J. A. (1989). Attitude importance and attitude accessibility. *Personality and Social Psychology Bulletin, 15,* 297–308.

Krosnick, J. A. (in press). Response strategies for coping with the cognitive demands of attitude measures in surveys. *Applied Cognitive Psychology*.

Krosnick, J. A., & Alwin, D. F. (1987). An evaluation of a cognitive theory of response-order effects in survey measurement. *Public Opinion Quarterly, 51*, 201–219.

Krosnick, J. A., & Alwin, D. F. (1988). A test of the form-resistant correlation hypothesis: Ratings, rankings, and the measurement of values. *Public Opinion Quarterly, 52*, 526–538.

Krosnick, J. A., & Berent, M. K. (in press). The impact of verbal labeling of response alternatives and branching on attitude measurement reliability in surveys. *Public Opinion Quarterly*.

Krosnick, J. A., & Schuman, H. (1988). Attitude intensity, importance, and certainty and susceptibility to response effects. *Journal of Personality and Social Psychology, 54*, 6, 940–952.

Kubovy, M. (1977). Response availability and the apparent spontaneity of numerical choices. *Journal of Experimental Psychology: Human Perception and Performance, 3*, 359–364.

Lachman, R., Lachman, J. J., & Butterfield, E. C. (1979). *Cognitive psychology and information processing: An introduction*. Hillsdale, NJ: Erlbaum.

Landy, F. J., & Farr, J. L. (1980). Performance rating. *Psychological Bulletin, 87*, 72–107.

Langer, E. J. (1989). Minding matters: The consequences of mindlessness-mindfulness. In L. Berkowitz (Ed.), *Advances in experimental social psychology* (Vol. 22, pp. 137–174). San Diego: Academic Press.

Langer, E. J., & Abelson, R. P. (1972). The semantics of asking a favor: How to succeed in getting help without really dying. *Journal of Personality and Social Psychology, 24*, 26–32.

La Rue, A., & Olejnik, A. B. (1980). Cognitive "priming" of principled moral thought. *Personality and Social Psychology Bulletin, 6*, 413–416.

Leary, L. F. & Dorans, N. J. (1985). Implications for altering the context in which test items appear: A historical perspective on an immediate concern. *Review of Educational Research, 55*, 387–413.

Lehnert, W. G. (1978). *The process of question answering: A computer simulation of cognition*. Hillsdale, NJ: Erlbaum.

Leone, C., & Ensley, E. (1986). Self-generated attitude change: A person by situation analysis of attitude polarization and attenuation. *Journal of Research in Personality, 20*, 434–446.

Levinson, S. C. (1983). *Pragmatics*. Cambridge, England: Cambridge University Press.

Lichtenstein, M., & Srull, T. K. (1985). Conceptual and methodological issues in examining the relationship between consumer memory and judgment. In L. F. Alwitt & A. A. Mitchell (Eds.), *Psychological processes and advertising effects: Theory, research, application* (pp. 113–128). Hillsdale, NJ: Erlbaum.

Lichtenstein, M., & Srull, T. K. (1987). Processing objectives as a determinant of the relationship between judgment and recall. *Journal of Experimental Social Psychology, 23*, 93–118.

Lingle, J. H., Altom, M. W., & Medin, D. L. (1984). Of cabbages and kings: Assessing the extendability of natural object concept models to social things. In

R. S. Wyer, Jr., & T. K. Srull (Eds.), *Handbook of social cognition* (Vol. 1, pp. 71–117). Hillsdale, NJ: Erlbaum.

Locander, W., Sudman, S., & Bradburn, N. (1976). An investigation of interview method, threat, and response distortion. *Journal of the American Statistical Association, 71,* 269–275.

Locke, E. A. (1976). The nature and causes of job satisfaction. In M. D. Dunnette (Ed.), *Handbook of industrial and organizational psychology* (pp. 1297–1349). Chicago: Rand McNally.

Loftus, E. (1984). Protocol analysis of responses to survey recall questions. In T. B. Jabine, M. L. Straf, J. M. Tanur, & R. Tourangeau (Eds.), *Cognitive aspects of survey methodology: Building a bridge between disciplines* (pp. 61–64). Washington, DC: National Academy Press.

Loftus, E. F., Fienberg, S. E., & Tanur, J. M. (1985). Cognitive psychology meets the national survey. *American Psychologist, 40,* 175–180.

Loken, B., & Hoverstadt, R. (1985). Relationships between information recall and subsequent attitudes: Some exploratory findings. *Journal of Consumer Research, 12,* 155–168.

Lombardi, W. J., Higgins, E. T., & Bargh, J. A. (1987). The role of consciousness in priming effects on categorization: Assimilation versus contrast as a function of awareness of the priming task. *Personality and Social Psychology Bulletin, 13,* 411–429.

Lord, C. G., Lepper, M. R., & Preston, E. (1984). Considering the opposite: A corrective strategy for social judgment. *Journal of Personality and Social Psychology, 47,* 1231–1243.

Lord, F. M. (1980). *Applications of item response theory to practical testing problems.* Hillsdale, NJ: Erlbaum.

Lord, F. M., & Novick, M. R. (1968). *Statistical theories of mental test scores.* Reading, MA: Addison-Wesley.

Luker, K. (1984). *Abortion and the politics of motherhood.* Berkeley: University of California Press.

Lumsden, J. (1976). Test theory. *Annual Review of Psychology, 27,* 251–280.

Lynch, J. E., Jr., Chakravarti, D., & Mitra, A. (1989). Contrast effects: Changes in mental representations or in anchoring of rating scales? Manuscript submitted for publication, Department of Marketing, University of Florida.

Lynch, J. G., Jr., Mamorstein, H., & Weigold, M. F. (1988). Choice from sets including remembered brands: Use of recalled attributes and prior overall evaluations. *Journal of Consumer Research, 15,* 169–184.

Lynch, J. G., Jr. & Srull, T. K. (1982). Memory and attentional factors in consumer choice: Concepts and research methods. *Journal of Consumer Research, 9,* 18–37.

MacNicol, K. (1956). *Effects of varying order of item difficulty in an unspeeded verbal test.* Unpublished manuscript, Educational Testing Service, Princeton, NJ.

Mangione, T. W., Hingson, R., & Barrett, J. (1982). Collecting sensitive data: A comparison of three survey strategies. *Sociological Methods & Research, 10,* 337–346.

Marks, G., & Miller, N. (1987). Ten years of research on the false-consensus effect: An empirical and theoretical review. *Psychological Bulletin, 102,* 72–90.

Markus, H., & Wurf, E. (1987). The dynamic self-concept: A social psychological perspective. *Annual Review of Psychology, 38,* 299–337.

Marsh, H. W., & Richards, G. E. (1989). A test of bipolar and androgyny perspectives of masculinity and femininity: The effect of participation in an outward bound program. *Journal of Personality, 57,* 115–138.

Martin, L. L. (1985). *Categorization and differentiation: A set, re-set, comparison analysis of the effects of context on person perception.* New York: Springer-Verlag.

Martin, L. L. (1986). Set/reset: Use and disuse of concepts in impression formation. *Journal of Personality and Social Psychology, 51,* 493–504.

Martin, L. L., Seta, J.J., & Crelia, R. A. (1990). Assimilation and contrast as a function of people's willingness and ability to expend effort in forming an impression. *Journal of Personality and Social Psychology, 59,* 27–37.

Martin, L. L., & Tesser, A. (1989). Toward a motivational and structural theory of ruminative thought. In J. S. Uleman & J. A. Bargh (Eds.), *Unintended thought* (pp. 306–326). New York: Guilford Press.

Massad, C. M., Hubbard, M., & Newtson, D. (1979). Selective perception of events. *Journal of Experimental Social Psychology, 15,* 513–532.

McCauley, C., Kogan, N., & Teger, A. I. (1971). Order effects in answering risk dilemmas for self and others. *Journal of Personality and Social Psychology, 20,* 423–424.

McClendon, M. J. (1986). Response-order effects for dichotomous questions. *Social Science Quarterly, 67,* 205–211.

McClendon, M. J., & O'Brien, D. J. (1988). Question-order effects on the determinants of subjective well-being. *Public Opinion Quarterly, 52,* 351–364.

McFarland, S. G. (1981). Effects of question order on survey responses. *Public Opinion Quarterly, 45,* 208–215.

McGuire, W. J. (1960). A syllogistic analysis of cognitive relationships. In M. J. Rosenberg, C. I. Hovland, W. J. McGuire, R. P. Abelson, & J. W. Brehm (Eds.), *Attitude organization and change: An analysis of consistency among attitude components* (pp. 65–111). New Haven, CT: Yale University Press.

McKoon, G., & Keenan, J. M. (1974). Response latencies to explicit and implicit statements as a function of the delay between reading and test. In W. Kintsch, *The representation of meaning in memory* (pp. 166–176). Hillsdale, NJ: Erlbaum.

McReynolds, P., & Ludwig, K. (1984). Christian Thomasius and the origin of psychological rating scales. *Isis, 75,* 546–553.

Mellers, B. A. (1986). "Fair" allocations of salaries and taxes. *Journal of Experimental Psychology: Human Perception and Performance, 12,* 80–91.

Mellers, B. A., & Birnbaum, M. H. (1982) Loci of contextual effects. *Journal of Experimental Psychology: Human Perception and Performance, 8,* 582–601.

Mellers, B. A., & Birnbaum, M. H. (1983) Contextual effects in social judgment. *Journal of Experimental and Social Psychology, 19,* 157–171.

Millar, M. G., & Tesser, A. (1986). Thought induced attitude change: The effects of schema structure and commitment. *Journal of Personality and Social Psychology, 51,* 259–269.

Mingay, D. J., & Greenwell, M. T. (1989). Memory bias and response-order effects. *Journal of Official Statistics, 5,* 253–263.

Mislevy, R. (1986). Recent developments in the factor analysis of categorical variables. *Journal of Educational Psychology, 11,* 3–31.

Mollenkopf, W. G. (1950). An experimental study of the effects of item-analysis data of changing item placement and test time limit. *Psychometrika, 15,* 291–315.

Moore, M. (1973). Ambivalence in attitude measurement. *Educational and Psychological Measurement, 33*, 481–483.

Moore, M. (1980). Validation of the attitude toward any practice scale through the use of ambivalence as a moderator variable. *Educational and Psychological Measurement, 40*, 205–208.

Moorthy, K. S. (1989). *Measuring overall judgments and attribute evaluations: An application of information-processing theory.* Working paper, Yale University.

Moxey, L. M. (1986). *A psychological investigation of the use and interpretation of English quantifiers.* Doctoral dissertation, University of Glasgow, Department of Psychology.

Moxey, L. M. (1990). *Expectations and the interpretation of quantifiers.* Manuscript in preparation.

Moxey, L. M., & Sanford, A. J. (1987). Quantifiers and focus. *Journal of Semantics, 5*, 189–206.

Moxey, L. M., & Sanford, A. J. (1990). *Communicating under uncertainty: The use and selection of English language quantifiers.* Manuscript in preparation.

Moxey, L. M., Sanford, A. J., & Barton, S. B. (1990). Control of attentional focus by quantifiers. In K. J. Gilhooly, M. T. G. Keane, R. H. Logie, & G. Erdos (Eds.), *Lines of thinking: Reflections on the psychology of thought* (Vol. 1, pp. 109–124). Chichester: Wiley.

Mueller, J. E. (1970). Choosing among 133 candidates. *Public Opinion Quarterly, 34*, 395–402.

Mullen, B., Atkins, J. L., Champion, D. S., Edwards, C., Hardy, D., Story, J. E., & Vanderklok, M. (1985). The false consensus effect: A meta-analysis of 115 hypothesis tests. *Journal of Experimental Social Psychology, 21*, 262–283.

Mullen, B., Driskell, J. E., & Smith, C. (1989). Availability and social projection: The effects of sequence of measurement and wording of question on estimates of consensus. *Personality and Social Psychology Bulletin, 15*, 84–90.

Mullen, B., & Hu, L. (1988). Social projection as a function of cognitive mechanisms: Two meta-analytic integrations. *British Journal of Social Psychology, 27*, 333–356.

Murdock, B. B. (1962). The serial position effect in free recall. *Journal of Experimental Psychology, 64*, 482–488.

Murdock, B. B., & Walker, K. D. (1969). Modality effects in free recall. *Journal of Verbal Learning and Verbal Behavior, 8*, 665–676.

Murphy, K. R., Balzer, W. K., Lockhart, M. C., & Eisenman, E. J. (1985). Effects of previous performance on evaluations of present performance. *Journal of Applied Psychology, 70*, 72–84.

Muthén, B. O. (1978). A general structural equation model with dichotomous variables. *Psychometrika, 43*, 551–560.

Muthén, B. O. (1981). Factor analysis of dichotomous variables: American attitudes towards abortion. In D. J. Jackson & E. F. Borgatta (Eds.), *Factor analysis and measurement in sociological research* (pp. 201–214). Beverly Hills, CA: Sage.

Muthén, B. O. (1984). A general structural equation model with dichotomous, ordered categorical, and continuous latent variable indicators. *Psychometrika, 49*, 115–132.

Muthén, B. O. (1987). *LISCOMP user's manual.* Mooresville, IN: Scientific Software.

Muthén, B. O., & Christoffersson, A. (1981). Simultaneous factor analysis of dichotomous variables in several groups. *Psychometrika, 46*, 407–419.

Nathan, B. R., & Lord, R. G. (1983). Cognitive categorization and dimensional schemata: A process approach to the study of halo in performance rating. *Journal of Applied Psychology, 68,* 102–114.

Neville, J. W., Coker, M. C., & Knowles, E. S. (1988, April). *Anxiety measurement reduces anxiety on retest regardless of anxiety level.* Paper presented at the meeting of the Southwestern Psychological Association, Tulsa, OK.

Neville, J. W., & Knowles, E. S. (1990). *Context effects on extracted MMPI Scales.* Unpublished paper, University of Arkansas, Fayetteville.

Newcomb, T. M. (1961). *The acquaintance process.* New York: Holt, Rinehart, & Winston.

Newman, L. S. & Uleman, J. S. (1990). Assimilation and contrast effects in spontaneous trait inferences. *Personality and Social Psychology Bulletin, 16,* 224–240.

Newstead, S. E., & Pollard, P. (1984). *Quantifiers and context* (Tech. Rep.). Plymouth, England: Plymouth Polytechnic, Department of Psychology. (Paper presented at the NATO Advanced Study Institute on Human Assessment, Athens, December 1984)

Nisbett, R. E., & Wilson, T. D. (1977). Telling more than we can know: Verbal reports on mental processes. *Psychological Review, 84,* 231–259.

Noelle-Neumann, E. (1970). Wanted: Rules for wording questions. *Public Opinion Quarterly, 34,* 191–201.

Noelle-Neumann, E. (1974, May). Empirical studies of question wording. Paper presented at the annual meeting of the American Association for Public Opinion Research, Bolton Landing, NY.

Nolen-Hoecksema, S. (1987). Sex differences in unipolar depression: Evidence and theory. *Psychological Bulletin, 101,* 259–282.

O'Reilly, C. A., III, & Caldwell, D. (1979). Informational influence as a determinant of perceived task characteristics and job satisfaction. *Journal of Applied Psychology, 64,* 157–165.

Oliver, R. L. (1980). A cognitive model of antecedents and consequences of satisfaction decisions. *Journal of Marketing Research, 17,* 460–469.

Osberg, T. M. (1985). Order effects in the administration of personality measures: The case of the Self-Consciousness Scale. *Journal of Personality Assessment, 49,* 536–540.

Ostrom, T. M. (1966). Perspective as an intervening construct in the judgment of attitude statements. *Journal of Personality and Social Psychology, 5,* 135–144.

Ostrom, T. M. (1987). Bipolar survey items: an information-processing perspective. In H.-J. Hippler, N. Schwarz, & S. Sudman (Eds.), *Social information processing and survey methodology* (pp. 71–85). New York: Springer-Verlag.

Ostrom, T. M., Isaac, P. D., & McCann, C. D. (1983). *"Pairwise balanced" latin squares should always be used for within-subjects designs.* Unpublished manuscript, Ohio State University, Columbus.

Ostrom, T. M., Lingle, J. H., Pryor, J. B., & Geva, N. (1980). Cognitive organization of person impressions. In R. Hastie, T. M. Ostrom, E. B. Ebbesen, R. S. Wyer, Jr., D. Hamilton, & D. E. Carlston (Eds.), *Person memory: The cognitive basis of social perception* (pp. 55–88). Hillsdale, NJ: Erlbaum.

Ostrom, T . M., & Upshaw, H. S. (1968). Psychological perspective and attitude change. In A. C. Greenwald, T. C. Brock, & T. M. Ostrom (Eds.), *Psychological foundations of attitudes* (pp. 217–242). New York: Academic Press.

Ottati, V. C., Riggle, E. J., Wyer, R. S., Jr., Schwarz, N., & Kuklinski, J. (1989). Cognitive and affective bases of opinion survey responses. *Journal of Personality and Social Psychology, 57*, 404–415.

Panter, A. T. (1989). *A person by item model of responding to personality inventories.* Doctoral dissertation, New York University.

Parducci, A. (1982). Category ratings: Still more contextual effects! In B. Wegener (Ed.), *Social attitudes and psychological measurement* (pp. 89–105). Hillsdale, NJ: Erlbaum.

Parducci, A. (1983). Category ratings and the relational character of judgment. In H. G. Geissler, H. F. J. M. Bulfart, E. L. H. Leeuwenberg, & V. Sarris (Eds.), *Modern issues in perception* (pp. 262–282). Berlin: VEB Deutsche Verlag der Wissenschaften.

Parducci, A., Calfee, R. C., Marshall, L. M, & Davidson, L. P. (1960). Context effects in judgment: Adaptation level as a function of the mean, midpoint, and median of the stimuli. *Journal of Experimental Psychology, 60*, 65–77.

Parducci, A., Knobel, S., & Thomas, C. (1976). Independent contexts for category ratings: A range-frequency analysis. *Perception and Psychophysics, 20*, 360–366.

Parducci, A., & Marshall, L. M. (1961). Supplementary report: The effects of mean, midpoint, and median upon adaptation level in judgment. *Journal of Experimental Psychology, 61*, 261–262.

Parducci, A., & Perrett, L. F. (1971). Category rating scales: Effects of relative spacing and frequency of stimulus values. *Journal of Experimental Psychology Monograph, 89*, 427–452.

Parducci, A., & Wedell, D. H. (1986). The category effect with rating scales: Number of categories, number of stimuli, and method of presentation. *Journal of Experimental Psychology: Human Perception and Performance, 12*, 496–516.

Payne, F. D. (1974). Relationships between response stability and item endorsement, social desirability, and ambiguity in the MMPI and the CPI. *Multivariate Behavior Research, 9*, 127–148.

Payne, J. D. (1972). The effects of reversing the order of verbal rating scales in a postal survey. *Journal of the Market Research Society, 14*, 30–44.

Payne, J. W. (1982). Contingent decision behavior. *Psychological Bulletin, 92*, 382–402.

Payne, S. L. (1951). *The art of asking questions.* Princeton: Princeton University Press.

Pepper, S. (1981). Problems in the quantification of frequency expressions. In D. W. Fiske (Ed.), *Problems with language imprecision.* San Francisco: Jossey-Bass.

Pepper, S., & Prytulak, L. S. (1974). Sometimes frequently means seldom: Context effects in the interpretation of quantitative expressions. *Journal of Research in Personality, 8*, 95–101.

Perkins, J. E., & Goldberg, L. R. (1964). Contextual effects on the MMPI. *Journal of Counseling Psychology, 28*, 133–140.

Perreault, W. D., Jr. (1975). Controlling order effect bias. *Public Opinion Quarterly, 39*, 544–551.

Petty, R. E., & Brock, T. C. (1981). Thought disruption and persuasion: Assessing the validity of attitude change experiments. In R. E. Petty, T. M. Ostrom, & T. C. Brock (Eds.), *Cognitive responses in persuasion* (pp. 55–79). Hillsdale, NJ: Erlbaum.

Petty, R. E., & Cacioppo, J. T. (1986a). *Communication and persuasion: Central and peripheral routes to attitude change.* New York: Springer-Verlag.

Petty, R. E., & Cacioppo, J. T. (1986b). The elaboration likelihood model of persuasion. In L. Berkowitz (Ed.), *Advances in experimental social psychology* (Vol. 19, pp. 123–205). Orlando, FL: Academic Press.

Petty, R. E., Harkins, S. G., & WIlliams, K. D. (1980). The effects of group diffusion of cognitive effort on attitudes: An information-processing view. *Journal of Personality and Social Psychology, 38,* 81–92.

Petty, R. E., Ostrom, T. M., & Brock T. C. (Eds.). (1981). *Cognitive responses in persuasion.* Hillsdale, NJ: Erlbaum.

Petty, R. E., Rennier, G. A., & Cacioppo, J. T. (1987). Assertion versus interrogation format in opinion surveys: Questions enhance thoughtful responding. *Public Opinion Quarterly, 51,* 481–494.

Pindyck, R., & Rubinfeld, L. (1981). *Econometric models and economic forecasts.* New York: McGraw-Hill.

Pintner, R., & Forlano, G. (1938). Four retests of a personality inventory. *Journal of Educational Psychology, 29,* 93–100.

Porter, L. W. (1962). Job attitudes in management: Perceived deficiencies in need fulfillment as a function of job level. *Journal of Applied Psychology, 46,* 375–384.

Posner, M. I. (1978). *Chronometric explorations of mind.* Hillsdale, NJ: Erlbaum.

Posner, M. I. (1982). Cumulative development of attentional theory. *American Psychologist, 37,* 168–180.

Poulton, E. C. (1973). Unwanted range effects from using within-subject experimental designs. *Psychological Bulletin, 80,* 113–121.

Poulton, E. C. (1979). Models for biases in judging sensory magnitude. *Psychological Bulletin, 86,* 777–803.

Poulton, E. C. (1989). *Bias in quantifying judgments.* Hove: Erlbaum.

Powell, M. C., & Fazio, R. H. (1984). Attitude accessibility as a function of repeated attitudinal expression. *Personality and Social Psychology Bulletin, 10,* 139–148.

Quinn, S. B., & Belson, W. A. (1969). *The effects of reversing the order of presentation of verbal rating scales in survey interviews.* London: Survey Research Centre.

Rao, A. R. & Monroe, K. B. (1988). The moderating effect of prior knowledge on cue utilization in product evaluations. *Journal of Consumer Research, 15,* 253–264.

Rapoport, A., Wallsten, T. S., Erev, I., & Cohen, B. L. (in press). Revision of opinion with verbally and numerically expressed uncertainties. *Acta Psychologica.*

Rasch, G. (1980). *Probabilistic models for some intelligence and attainment tests.* Chicago: University of Chicago Press.

Ray, M. L. (1982). *Advertising and communication management.* Englewood Cliffs, NJ: Prentice-Hall.

Reckase, M. D. (1979). Unifactor latent trait models applied to multifactor tests. *Journal of Educational Statistics, 4,* 207–230.

Reckase, M. D. (1985). The difficulty of test items that measure more than one ability. *Applied Psychological Measurement, 9,* 401–412.

Reise, S. P., & Waller, N. G. (1990). Fitting the two-parameter model to personality data. *Applied Psychological Measurement, 14,* 45–58.

Reiser, M. (1980). Latent trait modeling of attitude items. In G. W. Bohrnstedt & E. F. Borgatta (Eds.), *Social measurement: Current issues* (pp. 117–144). Beverly Hills, CA: Sage.

Reyes, R. M., Thompson, C. C., & Bower, G. H. (1980). Judgmental biases resulting from differing availabilities of arguments. *Journal of Personality and Social Psychology, 39,* 2–12.

Ring, E. (1974). Wie man bei listenfragen einflüsse der reihenfolge ausschalten kann. *Psychologie und Praxis, 17,* 105–113.

Ring, E. (1975). Asymmetrical rotation. *European Research, 3,* 111–119.

Riskey, D. R., Parducci, A., & Beauchamp, G. K. (1979). Effects of context in judgments of sweetness and pleasantness. *Perception and Psychophysics, 26,* 171–176.

Rodin, M. J. (1978). Liking and disliking: Sketch of an alternative view. *Personality and Social Psychology Bulletin, 4,* 473–478.

Rogers, T. B. (1974a). An analysis of the stages underlying the process of responding to personality items. *Acta Psychologica, 38,* 205–213.

Rogers, T. B. (1974b). An analysis of the two central stages underlying the process of responding to personality items. *Journal of Research in Personality, 8,* 128–138.

Rokeach, M. (1956). Political and religious dogmatism: An alternative to the authoritarian personality. *Psychological Monograph, No. 425, 43* (Whole No. 18).

Rosen, N., and Wyer, R. S., Jr. (1972). Some evidence for the "Socratic effect" using a subjective probability model of cognitive organization. *Journal of Personality and Social Psychology, 24,* 420–424.

Ross, L., Greene, D., & House, P. (1977). The "false consensus effect": An egocentric bias in social perception and attribution processes. *Journal of Experimental Social Psychology, 13,* 279–301.

Ross, L., Lepper, M. R., Strack, F., & Steinmetz, J. L. (1977). Social explanation and social expectation: The effects of real and hypothetical explanations upon subjective likelihood. *Journal of Personality and Social Psychology, 45,* 817–829.

Rothbart, M., Evans, M., & Fulero, S. (1979). Recall for confirming events: Memory processes and the maintenance of social stereotypes. *Journal of Experimental Social Psychology, 15,* 343–355.

Rugg, D., & Cantril, H. (1944). The wording of questions. In H. Cantril, *Gauging public opinion* (pp. 23–50). Princeton, NJ: Princeton University Press.

Rumelhart, D. E. (1980). Schemata: The building blocks of cognition. In R. J. Spiro, B. C. Bruce, & W. F. Brewer (Eds.), *Theoretical issues in reading comprehension: Perspectives from cognitive psychology, linguistics, artificial intelligence, and education* (pp. 33–58). Hillsdale, NJ: Erlbaum.

Rundus, D. (1971). Analysis of rehearsal processes in free recall. *Journal of Experimental Psychology, 89,* 63–77.

Sadler, O., & Tesser, A. (1973). Some effects of salience and time upon interpersonal hostility and attraction during social interaction. *Sociometry, 36,* 99–112.

Sagar, H. A., & Schofield, J. W. (1980). Racial and behavioral cues in black and white children's perceptions of ambiguously aggressive acts. *Journal of Personality and Social Psychology, 39,* 590–598.

Sakamoto, Y. (1982). Efficient use of Akaike's information criterion for model selection in high dimensional contingency tables analysis. *Metron, 40,* 257–275.

Sakamoto, Y., Ishiguro, M., & Kitagawa, G. (1986). *Akaike information criterion statistics.* Dordrecht, Holland: D. Reidel.

Salancik, G. R. (1982). Attitude-behavior consistencies as social logics. In M. P.

Zanna, E. T. Higgins, & C. P. Herman (Eds.), *Consistency in social behavior: The Ontario Symposium* (Vol. 2, pp. 51–73). Hilldale, NJ.: Erlbaum.

Salancik, G. R., & Conway, M. (1975). Attitude inferences from salient and relevant cognitive content about behavior. *Journal of Personality and Social Psychology, 32*, 829–840.

Sande, G. N., Goethals, G., & Radloff, C. E. (1988). Perceiving one's own traits and others': the multifaceted self. *Journal of Personality and Social Psychology, 54*, 13–20.

Sandelands, L. E., & Larson, J. R., Jr. (1985). When measurement causes task attitudes: A note from the laboratory. *Journal of Applied Psychology, 70*, 116–121.

Schönemann, P. H., & Steiger, J. H. (1976). Regression component analysis. *British Journal of Mathematical and Statistical Psychology, 29*, 175–189.

Schubert, D. S. P., & Fiske, D. W. (1973). Increase of item response consistency by prior item response. *Educational and Psychological Measurement, 33*, 113–121.

Schuman, H. (1974). *Old wine in new bottles: Some sources of response error in the use of attitude surveys to study social change.* Paper presented to the Research Seminar Group in Quantitative Social Science, University of Surrey, England.

Schuman, H. (1982). Artifacts are in the mind of the beholder. *American Sociologist, 17*, 21–28.

Schuman, H., Kalton, G., & Ludwig, J. (1983). Context and contiguity in survey questionnaires. *Public Opinion Quarterly, 47*, 112–115.

Schuman, H., & Ludwig, J. (1983). The norm of even-handedness in surveys as in life. *American Sociological Review, 48*, 112–120.

Schuman, H., & Presser, S. (1981). *Questions and answers in attitude surveys: Experiments in question form, wording, and context.* New York: Academic Press.

Schuman, H., Presser, S., & Ludwig, J. (1981). Context effects on survey responses to questions about abortion. *Public Opinion Quarterly, 45*, 216–223.

Schuman, H., Steeh, C., & Bobo L. (1985). *Racial attitudes in America: Trends and interpretations.* Cambridge: Harvard University Press.

Schwarz, N. (1990). Feelings as information: Informational and motivational functions of affective states. In E. T. Higgins & R. Sorrentino (Eds.), *Handbook of motivation and cognition: Foundations of social behavior* (Vol. 2, pp. 527–561). New York: Guilford Press.

Schwarz, N., Bless, H., Bohner, G., Harlacher, U., & Kellenbenz, M. (1991). Response scales as frames of reference: The impact of frequency range on diagnostic judgment. *Applied Cognitive Psychology, 5*, 37–50.

Schwarz, N., & Clore, G. L. (1983). Mood, misattribution, and judgments of well-being: Informative and directive functions of affective states. *Journal of Personality and Social Psychology, 45*, 513–523.

Schwarz, N., & Hippler, H.-J. (1987). What response scales may tell your respondents: Informative functions of response alternatives. In H.-J. Hippler, N. Schwarz, & S. Sudman (Eds.), *Social information processing and survey methodology* (pp. 163–178). New York: Springer-Verlag.

Schwarz, N., Hippler, H.-J., Deutsch, B., & Strack, F. (1985). Response categories: Effects on behavioral reports. *Public Opinion Quarterly, 49*, 388–395.

Schwarz, N., Hippler, H.-J., Noelle-Neumann, E., Ring, E., & Münkel, T. (1989, May). *Response order effects in long lists: Primacy, recency, and asymmetric contrast effects* (ZUMA-Arbeitsbericht No. 18/89). Paper presented at the annual meeting of American Association for Public Opinion Research, St. Petersburg Beach, FL.

Schwarz, N., & Münkel, T. (1988). *Asymmetric contrast effects: A perspective theory account*. Unpublished manuscript.

Schwarz, N., Münkel, T., & Hippler, H.-J. (1990). What determines a "perspective"? Contrast effects as a function of the dimension tapped by preceding questions. *European Journal of Social Psychology, 20,* 357–361.

Schwarz, N., Strack, F., Hippler, H.-J., & Bishop, G. (in press). The impact of administration mode on response effects in survey measurement. *Applied Cognitive Psychology.*

Schwarz, N., Strack, F., & Mai, H. P. (1991). Assimilation and contrast effects in part–whole question sequences: A conversational logic analysis. *Public Opinion Quarterly, 55,* 3–23.

Schwarz, N., Strack, F., Müller, G., & Chassein, B. (1988). The range of response alternatives may determine the meaning of the question: Further evidence on informative functions of response alternatives. *Social Cognition, 6,* 107–117.

Scott, J. L. (1987a). *Conflicting values and compromise beliefs about abortion.* Doctoral dissertation, University of Michigan.

Scott, J. L. (1987b). *Explaining the abortion context effect.* Paper presented at the annual meeting of the American Association for Public Opinion Research, Hershey, PA.

Shavitt, S. (1989). Operationalizing functional theories of attitude. In A. R. Pratkanis, S. J. Breckler, & A. G. Greenwald (Eds.), *Attitude structure and function* (pp. 311–337). Hillsdale, NJ: Erlbaum.

Shavitt, S. & Fazio, R. H. (1987, May). *Attitude functions in the attitude-behavior relation.* Paper presented at the meeting of the Midwestern Psychological Association, Chicago.

Sherif, C., Sherif, M., & Nebergall, R. E. (1965). *Attitude and attitude change: The social judgment-involvement approach.* Philadelphia: Saunders.

Sherman, S. J. (1980). On the self-erasing nature of errors of prediction. *Journal of Personality and Social Psychology, 39,* 211–221.

Siegel, S. (1956). *Nonparametric statistics for the behavioral sciences.* New York: McGraw-Hill.

Siemiatycki, J. (1979). A comparison of mail, telephone, and home interview strategies for household health surveys. *American Journal of Public Health, 69,* 238–245.

Sigelman, L. (1981). Question-order effects in presidential popularity. *Public Opinion Quarterly, 45,* 199–207.

Singer, E., & Presser, S. (1989). *Survey research methods: A reader.* Chicago: University of Chicago Press.

Skowronski, J. J., & Carlston, D. E. (1989). Negativity and extremity biases in impression formation: A review of explanations. *Psychological Bulletin, 105,* 131–142.

Smith, D. A., & Graesser, A. C. (1981). Memory for actions in scripted activities as a function of typicality, retention interval, and retrieval task. *Memory and Cognition, 9,* 550–559.

Smith, E. E. (1988). Concepts and thought. In R. J. Sternberg & E. E. Smith (Eds.), *The psychology of human thought* (pp. 19–49). New York: Cambridge University Press.

Smith, R. H., Diener, E., & Wedell, D. H. (1989). Intrapersonal and social comparison determinants of happiness: A range-frequency analysis. *Journal of Personality and Social Psychology, 56,* 317–325.

Smith, T. W. (1978). In search of house effects: A comparison of responses to various questions by different survey organizations. *Public Opinion Quarterly, 42,* 443–463.

Smith, T. W. (1979). Happiness: Time trends, seasonal variations, inter-survey differences, and other mysteries. *Social Psychology Quarterly, 42,* 18–30.

Smith, T. W. (1981a). Can we have confidence in confidence? Revisited. In D. F. Johnston (Ed.), *Measurement of subjective phenomena* (U.S. Bureau of the Census, Special Demographic Analyses, CDS-80-3; pp. 119–189). Washington, DC: U.S. Government Printing Office.

Smith, T. W. (1981b). *Contradictions on the abortion scale* (GSS Methodological Rep. No.19). Chicago: NORC.

Smith, T. W. (1981c). Qualifications to generalized absolutes: "Approval of hitting" questions on the GSS. *Public Opinion Quarterly, 45,* 224–230.

Smith, T. W. (1982). House effects: A comparison of the 1980 General Social Survey and the 1980 American National Election Study. *Public Opinion Quarterly, 46,* 54–68.

Smith, T. W. (1983a). *Children and abortions: An experiment in question order* (GSS Methodological Rep. No. 27). Chicago: NORC.

Smith, T. W. (1983b). An experimental comparison of clustered and scattered scale items. *Social Psychology Quarterly, 46,* 163–168.

Smith, T. W. (1984). *A preliminary analysis of methodological experiments on the 1984 GSS* (GSS Methodological Rep. No. 30). Chicago: NORC.

Smith, T. W. (1986a). *Conditional order effects* (GSS Methodological Rep. No. 20). Chicago: NORC. (Updated from 1982)

Smith, T. W. (1986b). *Unhappiness on the 1985 GSS: Confounding change and context* (GSS Methodological Rep. No. 34). Chicago: NORC.

Smith, T. W. (1988a). *Ballot position: An analysis of context effects related to rotation design* (GSS Methodological Rep. No. 55). Chicago: NORC.

Smith, T. W. (1988b). *Rotation designs of the GSS* (GSS Methodological Rep. No. 52). Chicago: NORC.

Smith, T. W. (1988c). *Timely artifacts: A review of measurement variation in the 1972–1988 GSS* (GSS Methodological Rep. No. 56). Chicago: NORC.

Smith, T. W., & Stephenson, C. B. (1979). *An analysis of test/retest experiments on the 1972, 1973, 1974, and 1978 General Social Surveys* (GSS Methodological Rep. No. 8). Chicago: NORC.

Smouse, A. D., & Munz, D. C. (1968). The effects of anxiety and item difficulty sequence on achievement testing scores. *Journal of Psychology, 68,* 181–184.

Smyth, M. M., Morris, P. E., Levy, P., & Ellis, A. W. (1987). *Cognition in action.* Hillsdale, NJ: Erlbaum.

Snyder, M. (1974). Self-monitoring of expressive behavior. *Journal of Personality and Social Psychology, 30,* 526–537.

Snyder, M., & Uranowitz, S. W. (1978). Reconstructing the past: Some cognitive consequences of person perception. *Journal of Personality and Social Psychology, 36,* 941–950.

Solso, R. L. (1989). Prototypes, schemata, and the form of human knowledge: The cognition of abstraction. In C. Izawa (Ed.), *Current issues in cognitive processes* (pp. 345–368). Hillsdale, NJ: Erlbaum.

Spiro, R. J. (1977). Remembering information from text: The state of the schema approach. In R. Anderson, R. Spiro, & W. Montague (Eds.), *Schooling and the acquisition of knowledge* (pp. 137–166). Hillsdale, NJ: Erlbaum.

Srull, T. K. (1983). The role of prior knowledge in the acquisition, retention, and use of new information. In R. Bagozzi & A. Tybout (Eds.), *Advances in Consumer Research* (Vol. 10, pp. 572–576). Ann Arbor, MI: Association for Consumer Research.

Srull, T. K., & Wyer, R. S., Jr. (1979). The role of category accessibility in the interpretation of information about persons: Some determinants and implications. *Journal of Personality and Social Psychology, 37,* 1660–1672.

Srull, T. K., & Wyer, R. S., Jr. (1980). Category accessibility and social perception: Some implications for the study of person memory and interpersonal judgments. *Journal of Personality and Social Psychology, 38,* 841–856.

Srull, T. K., & Wyer, R. S., Jr. (1989). Person memory and judgment. *Psychological Review, 96,* 58–83.

Steele, C. M. (1988). The psychology of self-affirmation: Sustaining the integrity of the self. In L. Berkowitz (Ed.), *Advances in experimental social psychology* (Vol. 21, pp. 261–302). San Diego: Academic Press.

Strack, F., & Martin, L. L. (1987). Thinking, judging, and communicating: A process account of context effects in attitude surveys. In H.-J. Hippler, N. Schwarz, & S. Sudman (Eds.), *Social information processing and survey methodology* (pp. 123–148). New York: Springer-Verlag.

Strack, F., Martin, L. L., & Schwarz, N. (1987). *The context paradox in attitude surveys: Assimilation or contrast?* ZUMA-Arbeitsbericht, No. 87/07.

Strack, F., Martin, L. L., & Schwarz, N. (1988). Priming and communication: Social determinants of information use in judgments of life satisfaction. *European Journal of Social Psychology, 18,* 429–442.

Strack, F., Schwarz, N., Bless, H., Kübler, A., & Wänke, M. (1990). *Remember the priming events! A test of Jacoby's bifunctional model of memory.* Unpublished manuscript.

Strack, F., Schwarz, N., & Gschneidinger, E. (1985). Happiness and reminiscing: The role of time perspective, affect, and mode of thinking. *Journal of Personality and Social Psychology, 49,* 1460–1469.

Suchman, L., & Jordan, B. (1990). Interactional troubles in face-to-face survey interviews. *Journal of the American Statistical Association, 85,* 232–241.

Sudman, S., & Bradburn, N. M. (1974). *Response effects in surveys: A review and synthesis.* Chicago: Aldine.

Sudman, S., & Bradburn, N. M. (1982). *Asking questions: A practical guide to questionnaire design.* San Francisco: Jossey-Bass.

Sudman, S., & Schwarz, N. (1989). Contributions of cognitive psychology to advertising research. *Journal of Advertising Research, 29,* 43–53.

Sudman, S., & Swenson, K. (1985). *Measuring the effects of attitude crystallization on response effects.* Paper presented at the annual meeting of the American Association for Public Opinion Research, McAfee, NJ.

Swyngedouw, M. (1988). *Explorative log-linear factor-response analysis of high dimensional tables by a restricted table analysis procedure.* Paper presented at the International Conference on Social Science Methodology, Dubrovnic.

Tanaka, J. S., Panter, A. T., Winborne, W. C., & Huba, G. J. (1990). Theory testing in personality and social psychology with latent variable models: A primer in 20 questions. In C. Hendrick & M. S. Clark (Eds.), *Research methods in personality and social psychology* (pp. 217–242). Newbury Park, CA: Sage.

Taylor, J. A. (1953). A personality scale of manifest anxiety. *Journal of Abnormal and Social Psychology, 48,* 285–290.

Tedin, K. L. (1980). Assessing peer and parental influence on adolescent political attitudes. *American Journal of Political Science, 24,* 136–154.

Tesser, A. (1978). Self-generated attitude change. In L. Berkowitz (Ed.), *Advances in experimental social psychology* (Vol. 11, pp. 289–338). New York: Academic Press.

Tesser, A. (1988). Toward a self-evaluation maintenance model of social behavior. In L. Berkowitz (Ed.), *Advances in experimental social psychology* (Vol. 21, pp. 181–227). New York: Academic Press.

Tesser, A., & Conlee, M. C. (1975). Some effects of time and thought on attitude polarization. *Journal of Personality and Social Psychology, 31,* 262–270.

Tesser, A., & Cowan, C. L. (1977). Some attitudinal and cognitive consequences of thought. *Journal of Research in Personality, 11,* 216–226.

Thorngate, W. (1976). Must we always think before we act? *Personality and Social Psychology Bulletin, 2,* 31–35.

Tourangeau, R. (1984). Cognitive sciences and survey methods. In T. B. Jabine, M. L. Straf, J. M. Tanur, & R. Tourangeau (Eds.), *Cognitive aspects of survey methodology: Building a bridge between disciplines* (pp. 73–100). Washington, DC: National Academy Press.

Tourangeau, R. (1987). Attitude measurement: A cognitive perspective. In H.-J. Hippler, N. Schwarz, & S. Sudman (Eds.), *Social information processing and survey methodology* (pp. 149–162). New York: Springer-Verlag.

Tourangeau, R., & Rasinski, K. A. (1986). *Context effects in attitude surveys* (NORC Report). Chicago: NORC.

Tourangeau, R., & Rasinski, K. A. (1988). Cognitive processes underlying context effects in attitude measurement. *Psychological Bulletin, 103,* 299–314.

Tourangeau, R., Rasinski, K. A., Bradburn, N., & D'Andrade, R. (1988, May). It's not just what you ask but when you ask it: Context effects in attitude surveys. Paper presented at the annual meeting of the American Association for Public Opinion Research, Toronto.

Tourangeau, R., Rasinski, K. A, Bradburn, N., & D'Andrade, R. (1989a). Belief accessibility and context effects in attitude measurement. *Journal of Experimental Social Psychology, 25,* 401–421.

Tourangeau, R., Rasinski, K. A., Bradburn, N., & D'Andrade, R. (1989b). Carryover effects in attitude surveys. *Public Opinion Quarterly, 53,* 495–524.

Tourangeau, R., Rasinski, K., & D'Andrade, R. (1991). Attitude structure and belief accessibility. *Journal of Experimental Social Psychology, 27,* 48–75.

Tschirgi, J. E. (1980). Sensible reasoning: A hypothesis about children. *Child Development, 51,* 1–10.

Tulving, E. (1983). *Elements of episodic memory.* New York: Oxford University Press.

Tulving, E., Schacter, D. L, & Stark, H. A. (1982). Priming effects in word-fragment completion are independent of recognition memory. *Learning, Memory, and Cognition, 8,* 336–342.

Tulving, E., & Thompson, D. M. (1973). Encoding specificity and retrieval processes in episodic memory. *Psychological Review, 80,* 352–373.

Turner, C. F., & Krauss, E. (1978). Fallible indicators of the subjective state of the nation. *American Psychologist, 33,* 456–470.

Turner, C. F., & Martin, E. (Eds.) (1984). *Surveying subjective phenomena.* New York: Russell Sage Foundation.

Tverksy, A. (1977). Features of similarity. *Psychological Review, 84,* 327–352.

U.S. Office of Management and Budget. (1984). *The role of telephone data collection in federal statistics* (Statistical Policy Working Paper 12).

Upshaw, H. S. (1962). Own attitude as an anchor in equal appearing intervals. *Journal of Abnormal and Social Psychology, 64,* 85–96.

Upshaw, H. S. (1984). Output processes in judgment. In R. S. Wyer, Jr., & T. K. Srull (Eds)., *Handbook of social cognition* (Vol. 3, pp. 237–256). Hillsdale, NJ: Erlbaum.

Upton, G. J. G. (1978). *The analysis of cross-tabulated data.* Chichester: Wiley.

Urban, G. L., & Hauser, J. R. (1980). *Design and marketing of new products.* Englewood Cliffs, NJ: Prentice-Hall.

van den Broek, P. (1988). The effects of causal relations and hierarchical position on the importance of story statements. *Journal of Memory and Language, 27,* 1–22.

van Eys, P. P., & McKeever, W. F. (1988). Subject knowledge of the experimenter's interest in handedness and familial sinistrality variables and laterality test outcomes. *Brain and Cognition, 7,* 324–334.

Volkmann, J. (1951). Scales of judgment and their implications for social psychology. In J. H. Rohrer & M. Sherif (Eds.), *Social psychology at the crossroads* (pp. 273–294). New York: Harper.

Wainer, H., & Braun, H. I. (Eds.) (1988). *Test validity.* Hillsdale, NJ: Erlbaum.

Wainer, H., & Kiely, G. L. (1987). Item clusters and computerized adaptive testing: A case for testlets. *Journal of Educational Measurement, 24,* 185–201.

Wainer, H., & Lewis, C. (1990). Towards a psychometrics for testlets. *Journal of Educational Measurement, 27,* 1–14.

Wallsten, T. S. (1990). The costs and benefits of vague information. In R. M. Hogarth & M. W. Reder (Eds.), *Insights in decision making: A Tribute to Hillel J. Einhorn.* Chicago: University of Chicago Press.

Wallsten, T. S., Budescu, D. V., Rapoport, A., Zwick, R., & Forsyth, B. (1986). Measuring the vague meanings of probability terms. *Journal of Experimental Psychology: General, 115,* 348–365.

Wallsten, T. S., Fillenbaum, S., & Cox, J. A. (1986) Base rate effects on the interpretations of probability and frequency expressions. *Journal of Memory and Language, 25,* 571–587.

Wason, P. C., & Johnson-Laird, P. N. (1972). *Psychology of reasoning: Structure and content.* Cambridge: Harvard University Press.

Watson, D., & Pennebaker, J. W. (1989). Health complaints, stress and distress: Exploring the central role of negative affectivity. *Psychological Review, 96,* 234–254.

Waugh, N. C., & Norman, D. A. (1965). Primary memory. *Psychological Review, 72,* 89–104.

Webb, E. S., Campbell, D. T., Schwartz, R. D., & Sechrest, L. (1966). *Unobtrusive measures: Nonreactive research in the social sciences.* Chicago: Rand McNally.

Webb, E. S., Campbell, D. T., Schwartz, R. D., Sechrest, L., & Grove, J. (1981). *Nonreactive measures in the social sciences.* Boston: Houghton Mifflin.

Wedell, D. H., & Parducci, A. (1988). The category effect in social judgment: Experimental ratings of happiness. *Journal of Personality and Social Psychology, 55,* 341–356.

Wedell, D. H., Parducci, A., & Geiselman, R. E. (1987). A formal analysis of ratings of physical attractiveness: Successive contrast and simultaneous assimilation. *Journal of Experimental Social Psychology, 23,* 230–249.

Wegner, D. M., Schneider, D. J., Carter, S. R., & White, T. L. (1987). Paradoxical effects of thought suppression. *Journal of Personality and Social Psychology, 53,* 5–13.

Wegner, D. M., Vallacher, R. R., Kiersted, G. W., & Dizadji, D. (1986). Action identification in the emergence of social behavior. *Social Cognition, 4,* 18–38.

Weinstein, N. D. (1984). Why it won't happen to me: Perceptions of risk factors and susceptibility. *Health Psychology, 3,* 431–457.

Wexley, K. N., Yukl, G. A., Kovacs, S. Z., & Sanders, R. E. (1972). Importance of contrast effects in employment interviews. *Journal of Applied Psychology, 56,* 45–48.

Whitely, S. E., & Dawis, R. V. (1976). The influence of test context on item difficulty. *Educational and Psychological Measurement, 36,* 329–337.

Williams, M. D., & Hollan, J. D. (1981). The process of retrieval from very long-term memory *Cognitive Science, 5,* 87–119.

Willick, D. H., & Ashley, R. K. (1971). Survey question order and the political party preference of college students and their parents. *Public Opinion Quarterly, 35,* 189–199.

Wilson, D., Wood, R. L., & Gibbons, R. (1984). *TESTFACT: User's guide.* Mooresville, IN: Scientific Software.

Wilson, T. D., Dunn, D. S., Kraft, D., & Lisle, D. J. (1989). Introspection, attitude change, and attitude-behavior consistency: The disruptive effects of explaining why we feel the way we do. In L. Berkowitz (Ed.), *Advances in experimental social psychology* (Vol. 22, pp. 287–344). San Diego: Academic Press.

Wilson, T. D., Kraft, D., & Dunn, D.S. (1989). The disruptive effects of explaining attitudes: The moderating effect of knowledge about the attitude object. *Journal of Experimental Social Psychology, 25,* 379–400.

Windle, C. (1954). Test–retest effect on personality questionnaires. *Educational and Psychological Measurement, 14,* 617–633.

Windle, C. (1955). Further studies of test–retest effect on personality questionnaires. *Educational and Psychological Measurement, 15,* 246–253.

Woehr, D. J., & Feldman, J. M. (1989). *Processing objective and question order effects on the causal relationships among memory, judgment and appraisal accuracy: The tip of the iceberg.* Unpublished manuscript, Texas A & M University, Department of Psychology.

Wyer, R. S., Jr., & Hartwick, J. (1980). The role of information retrieval and conditional inference processes in belief formation and change. In L. Berkowitz (Ed.), *Advances in experimental social psychology* (Vol. 13, pp. 241–284). New York: Academic Press.

Wyer, R. S., Jr., & Hartwick, J. (1984). The recall and use of belief statements as bases for judgments: Some determinants and implications. *Journal of Experimental Social Psychology, 20,* 65–85.

Wyer, R. S., Jr., & Srull, T. K. (1986). Human cognition in its social context. *Psychological Review, 93*, 322–359.

Wyer, R. S., Jr., & Srull, T. K. (1989). *Memory and cognition in its social context.* Hillsdale, NJ: Erlbaum.

Yen, W. M. (1980). The extent, causes, and importance of context effects on item parameters for two latent trait models. *Journal of Educational Measurement, 17*, 297–311.

Zachary, R. A. (1986). *Shipley Institute of Living Scale, Revised Manual.* Los Angeles: Western Psychological Services.

Zaller, J. (1984). *Toward a theory of the survey response.* Paper presented at the annual meeting of the American Political Science Association, Washington, DC.

Zaller, J. (1988). *Vague minds vs. vague questions: An experimental attempt to reduce measurement error.* Unpublished manuscript.

Zoeke, B., & Sarris, V. (1983). A comparison of "frame of reference" paradigms in human and animal psychophysics. In H. G. Geissler, H. F. J. M. Bulfart, E. L. J. Leeuwenberg, & V. Sarris (Eds.), *Modern issues in perception* (pp. 283–317). Berlin: VEB Deutsche Verlag der Wissenschaften.